FROM
NEW FEDERALISM
TO
DEVOLUTION

FROM
NEW FEDERALISM
TO
DEVOLUTION

*Twenty-Five Years of
Intergovernmental Reform*

Timothy Conlan

BROOKINGS INSTITUTION PRESS
Washington, D.C.

Copyright © 1998 by
THE BROOKINGS INSTITUTION
1775 Massachusetts Avenue, N.W., Washington, D.C. 20036

All rights reserved

Library of Congress Cataloging-in-Publication Data:
Conlan, Timothy J.
    From new federalism to devolution : twenty-five years of
intergovernmental reform / Timothy Conlan. — Rev. ed.
    p. cm.
Includes bibliographical references and index.

    ISBN 0-8157-1532-3 (cloth : alk. paper)
    ISBN 0-8157-1531-5 (pbk. : alk. paper)
    1. Federal government—United States. 2. Intergovernmental fiscal
relations—United States. 3. United States—Politics and
government—1969–1974. 4. United States—Politics and
government—1981–1989. I. Title.
    JK325 .C617   1998
    321.02'0973—ddc21
                                                        98-19780
                                                           CIP

9 8 7 6 5 4 3 2 1

The paper used in this publication meets the minimum requirements of the American National Standard for Information Sciences—Permanence of Paper for Printed Library Materials, ANSI Z39.48-1984.

Typeset in Sabon

Composition by Cynthia Stock
Silver Spring, Maryland

Printed by R. R. Donnelley & Sons
Harrisonburg, Virginia

Preface

THIS BOOK was completed while I was a Fulbright program fellow at Erasmus Universiteit in the Netherlands. Although Holland is far from the political debates and events described in this book, it provided a surprisingly good vantage point from which to assess the process of reforming American federalism. In the United States, the forest of federalism is often obscured by the dense underbrush of intergovernmental relations. From Europe, however, the degree to which federalism shapes and colors American politics and policymaking stands out in sharp relief. The sweeping federalism reform initiatives that repeatedly captured center stage in the United States during the 1970s, 1980s, and 1990s were but one expression of this tendency.

The dynamic forces that are shaping and reshaping federal systems around the world were also evident from the Netherlands. My office overlooked the busy harbor of Rotterdam. The dense traffic of ships moving through the port to the industrial heartland of Europe provides tangible evidence of European economic integration. Just to the south, the slow disintegration of Belgium provides equally graphic evidence of the powerful forces of regionalism and ethnicity that are reemerging across Europe. Together, these developments are redefining the role of the nation state and reshaping its political environment.

The movement for federalism reform and devolution in the United States has been influenced by this pattern of global change, which is weakening central governments and strengthening regions in many countries around the world. Indeed, so much has happened since the first edition of this book, *New Federalism: Intergovernmental Reform from Nixon to Reagan*, appeared in 1988 that a new edition was clearly needed. The changes made in this edition have been so substantial that they generated a quite different book with a new title to highlight that fact. About one-third of this book is completely new or substantially revised, covering the most important developments in federalism reform over the past ten years. Three new chapters have been added. Chapter 11 examines developments in federalism and intergovernmental reform in the Bush and early Clinton administrations. Chapter 12 analyzes the federalism dimensions of the "Republican revolution" in 1995 and 1996. And chapter 13 focuses on the major intergovernmental reforms, affecting federal mandates and welfare programs, that were adopted during the 104th Congress. Other chapters, particularly the introduction and conclusion, were also substantially revised and rewritten to accommodate new developments.

All authors are indebted to people who helped them along the way, and I owe more debts than most. Intellectually, three people in particular have assisted me with this project over the years. Samuel H. Beer first excited my interest in federalism while I was a graduate student at Harvard University. He wrote a marvelous introduction to the first edition of this book, and although this edition is longer than the first, it is shorter on wisdom and insight without Sam's contribution. I would also like to thank David B. Walker, whose encyclopedic knowledge of intergovernmental relations has been of great help to me on many occasions. His ability to meld first-rate scholarship with government service established a standard that few others can hope to attain. Last, I would like to give special thanks to David R. Beam, whose intense curiosity and breadth of knowledge never cease to amaze me. His ability to distill patterns out of the cacaphony of contemporary politics is remarkable, and I have benefited enormously from my opportunities to discuss and share ideas with him.

I am also grateful to Martha Derthick, Thomas E. Mann, Paul E. Peterson, James P. Pfiffner, A. James Reichley, and two anonymous reviewers, who read parts of this book in either the first or second edition. I would also like to thank Barbara de Boinville, Venka Macintyre, and Caroline Lalire, each of whom helped edit portions of the manuscript. Carlotta Ribar proofread the pages, and Julia Petrakis prepared the index. Above all, I would like to thank Nancy Davidson, the acquisitions editor for the Brookings Press, for her patience during this project. She never lost her cool or her confidence that the book would be completed, even when most other editors would have lost both.

I would also like to acknowledge the support of George Mason University, which assisted me with a faculty study leave during part of the time while I was working on this manuscript, and the faculty in public administration at Erasmus Universiteit, which provided generous support to me during the final editing process. I am also grateful to the Fulbright pro-gram of the United States Information Agency and the Netherlands America Commission for Educational Exchange for support during this period as well.

Finally, I would like to give special thanks to my wife, Margaret L. Wieners, and my two daughters, Elizabeth and Catherine, for putting up with me during the long process of writing and revising this book. To them I make a solemn promise: no third editions!

Earlier versions of parts of this book appeared in "The Politics of Fed-eral Block Grants: From Nixon to Reagan," *Political Science Quarterly* (Summer 1984), pp. 247–70; "Federalism and Competing Values in the Reagan Administration," *Publius* (Winter 1986), pp. 29–47; and Timothy J. Conlan, James D. Riggle, and Donna E. Schwartz, "Deregulating Feder-alism? The Politics of Mandate Reform in the 104th Congress," *Publius* (Summer 1995), pp. 23–39.

Contents

Tables

Figures

Boxes

FROM
NEW FEDERALISM
TO
DEVOLUTION

CHAPTER 1

Federalism Reform
and the Modern State

Since taking office, one of my first priorities has been to repair the machinery of government and . . . to make government more effective as well as more efficient.

President Richard Nixon, 1969 Television Address on Federalism

Government is not the solution to our problem. Government is the problem.

President Ronald Reagan, First Inaugural Address, 1981

We are going to rethink the entire structure of American society, and the entire structure of American government. . . . This is a real revolution.

Speaker of the House Newt Gingrich, 1995

W ITH THESE WORDS three Republican leaders summarized their philosophies of governance as a prelude to launching major reforms of the federal system. Nixon sought more effective and efficient government; Reagan and Gingrich, a reduction of governmental initiative at every level. All three prescribed intergovernmental changes to cure ills involving government's role in society.

At a minimum their reform initiatives have underscored the importance of federalism and intergovernmental relations within the American system of government. From welfare to health care to environmental protection, intergovernmental programs have grown dramatically in the postwar era. Today the design, operation, and performance of most federal domestic programs cannot be understood without an intergovernmental perspective. Thus it is no accident that political leaders since the 1950s have launched federalism initiatives of one kind or another.

These prescriptions for federalism reform have varied greatly. The centralizing Creative Federalism of President Lyndon Johnson in the 1960s and the devolutionary initiatives of Reagan and Gingrich anchor the opposing poles of contemporary intergovernmental policy. Contrasts between such liberal and conservative reforms are frequently drawn. Less commonly recognized are the more subtle but substantial differences between the intergovernmental reform initiatives of the 1970s, 1980s, and 1990s. Analysis of these Republican agendas for federalism reform is particularly informative because it controls for many factors that complicate comparisons with the 1960s.

All three federalism reform efforts were responses to perceived policy failures of the past; all advanced decentralization as a goal for responding to these failures; all shared certain common instruments, such as block grants; and all were launched in an era of divided party government. Yet the initiatives differed remarkably in their policy objectives, philosophical assumptions, patterns of politics, and policy outcomes.

These differences in the policy programs of Nixon, Reagan, and the Republican Congress reflect not only the changing domestic priorities of recent Republican leaders but also important developments in the evolution of modern conservative thought. From 1970 to the early 1990s, the goals of conservative policymakers became more ambitious as their rhetoric grew more strident. As the preceding quotations illustrate, the stated objectives of Republican reformers changed markedly—from rationalizing and decentralizing an activist government, to rolling back the welfare state, to replacing it altogether.

Equally important were the changes that occurred in the dynamics of national policymaking during this period. The Nixon years were characterized by a degree of political fragmentation unusual even by American standards. The traditional pluralism of American government was magnified by an extraordinary proliferation of new interests, new decisionmaking centers, and new opportunities and incentives for independent political behavior. In contrast, the Reagan administration and the 104th Congress (1995–97) generated a far more interdependent policymaking process, marked by heightened partisanship and budgetary stringency. Decisions affecting one part of the agenda could no longer be made in isolation from the others.

Underlying these political developments are broader changes in the interaction between government and society. Under conservative and liberal administrations alike, government has ceased to be the receptive instrument of external social and political pressures and has become an active and autonomous agent for change. In short, this book does more than simply document an important chapter in the history of American federalism. It argues that intergovernmental reform initiatives address important questions about conservative ideology and the nature of contemporary politics and government.

Federalism Reform from Nixon to Gingrich

Nixon's New Federalism sought to rationalize the intergovernmental system and restructure the roles and responsibilities of governments at all levels. The strategy devised for this purpose was composed of four important elements. The first was a broad array of management reforms designed to improve program coordination, efficiency, and planning. The second was a series of block grants that were to consolidate individual federal aid programs into comprehensive grants. In part, block grants were intended to further the administrative goals of improved coordination, planning, and funding reliability, but they were also expected to simplify program operations, increase state and local policymaking flexibility and accountability, and reduce bureaucratic influence in favor of elected officials. Third, Nixon proposed to expand upon the block grant principle of flexibility with general revenue sharing, which would provide "no strings" federal aid to state and local governments. Revenue sharing sought to use the progressive federal income tax system to increase overall levels of public sector spending by providing larger grants to the most active states and localities and to those with the greatest needs. Fourth, the Nixon administration endeavored to nationalize public sector responsibilities in those areas where the federal government was deemed to be more efficient or effective, such as welfare, direct entitlements, and many areas of social regulation.

Although Reagan's New Federalism employed some of the same instruments and strategies as Nixon's, it did so in different combinations and to pursue different ends. For example, the primary focus of management reforms in the Reagan administration was to reduce the power, influence, and morale of the national bureaucracy, rather than to improve intergovernmental management and effectiveness. Block grants, also a popular mechanism in the arsenal of Reagan federalism, were proposed as a stepping-stone to the ultimate elimination of federal involvement in the affected program areas, rather than a means of rationalizing an accepted federal role in a given field. The Reagan administration opposed the very idea of revenue sharing and terminated the program.

Devolution initiatives in the 104th Congress extended the logic of the Reagan era even farther. The first Republican-controlled House of Representatives in forty years led a concerted effort to shrink the size and influence of the federal government. Federal spending was to be cut and capped by a stringent balanced budget amendment. Block grants and regulatory reform were again advanced to reduce federal policy control. Unlike Nixon and Reagan, however, the new Congress showed little interest in management reforms of federal programs and agencies. Rather, reform advocates favored wholesale elimination of federal programs, departments, and agencies, and concomitant reductions of federal spending and taxes.

The Significance and Origins of New Federalism

Why have conservatives placed so much emphasis on federalism reform in their domestic agendas? The answer has three related dimensions: administrative, partisan, and philosophical.

The reformist thrust of this renewed federalism was in part a managerial response to the administrative dysfunctions and implementation failures stemming from the Great Society. Although not confined to any single party or ideology, the criticisms of federal program structures and their management were reinforced by long-held party differences over the proper size and role of the federal government. Disputes involving governmental centralization and decentralization have been among the most powerful and consistent issues dividing political parties in the United States since the 1930s.[1] In turn, this dispute resonates with philosophical chords that date back to the founding of the Republic. New Federalism, in this sense, is the contemporary expression of debates that began before the Constitution was ratified and that formed the basis of the first political party system. Since Ronald Reagan, issues of federalism reform have broadened as they have merged with a related but larger debate over the legitimate scope and definition of the public sector itself.

Administrative Roots

The administrative problems to which Richard Nixon and, to a lesser extent, his successors responded were the product of a more nationally integrated form of government that had evolved during the twentieth century. This occurred in two basic stages.

Before the 1930s, the responsibility for most public services and spending rested with state and local governments. Although the federal role had gradually increased after the Civil War, particularly as a result of regulatory expansions of the Progressive Era, it was not until the 1930s and 1940s that the scope of federal activities was dramatically expanded in response to the twin crises of depression and global war. By midcentury the federal government had acquired major new responsibilities for economic planning and regulation, social insurance, unemployment and family assistance, and military defense on a continuing and historic scale. The tenor of the change was captured by V. O. Key:

> The federal government underwent a radical transformation after . . . 1932. It had been a remote authority with a limited range of activity. It operated the postal system, improved rivers and harbors, maintained armed forces on a scale fearsome only to banana republics, and performed other functions of which the average citizen was hardly aware. Within a brief time, it became an institution that affected intimately the lives and fortunes of most, if not all, citizens.[2]

Initially, these developments helped produce an unusual degree of political parity between the federal government and the states. Whereas domestic federal spending had equaled only 20 percent of state and local spending from own-source funds in 1929, by 1949 it totaled 108 percent of state and local own-source spending. Throughout the 1950s, the two remained approximately equal.[3]

Then in the 1960s the intergovernmental system began to evolve at an accelerated pace. The ensuing changes in the scope, content, and structure of federal assistance programs not only made the system far more complex, but also upset the temporary balance of intergovernmental power that had been achieved. Sweeping changes were ushered in by the Great Society:

—The federal government became more involved in virtually all existing fields of governmental activity—including many that had been highly local in character (for example, elementary and secondary education, local law enforcement, libraries, and fire protection). In addition, new public functions were established, such as adult employment training, air pollution control, health planning, and community antipoverty programs.

—The locus of policy initiation and leadership shifted toward the national level.

—The numbers of new federal grant programs—especially narrow and often unpredictable project grants—nearly tripled between 1960 and 1968, from 132 to 379.

—Federal aid dollars more than tripled, from $7 billion in 1960 to $24 billion in 1970.

—State and local governments' financial dependence on federal funding increased by 35 percent. Federal aid increased from 17 percent of state and local own-source revenues in 1960 to 23 percent in 1970.

—More and more federal grants bypassed states and went directly to a multiplicity of local governments. Within states, as well, the percentage of state agencies receiving federal aid grew substantially.

—New, more coercive and expensive types of federal regulations affecting states and localities proliferated.

—Federal programs relied more on the "service strategy," which fostered the use of professionals to deliver services to targeted clients at the local level rather than the less bureaucratized approach of cash assistance prevalent in the 1930s.[4]

This transformation to federal preeminence produced numerous positive outcomes. It forced many backward state and local governments to modernize, while it increased fiscal reliance on the relatively more progressive federal income tax. It reduced levels of poverty and infant mortality and brought increased public services to many who had never known them. Most important, it provided a fiscal and administrative structure for turning the hitherto empty promises of equal protection and civil rights for many African Americans into meaningful constitutional protections and greater opportunities.

At the same time the transformation of intergovernmental relationships in the 1960s was also plagued by serious administrative problems. These generated seemingly unnecessary conflicts and prevented the attainment of many other policy objectives. Paralleling the growth in federal programs, functions, and policy activism was a rising chorus of complaints from citizens, scholars, and elected officials about governmental fragmentation, inadequate coordination, growing intergovernmental conflict, and federal intrusiveness. In a comprehensive evaluation of the federal aid system in the late 1960s, the U.S. Advisory Commission on Intergovernmental Relations (ACIR) concluded that many of these difficulties were the result of "excessive categorization of grants," the "increasing variety and inconsistency in matching ratios," the "multiplication and inconsistency of planning requirements," and the "trend toward bypassing the States."[5]

Similar opinions were reiterated by other management-oriented organizations, from the General Accounting Office to the Bureau of the Budget.

The Budget Bureau voiced particular concern that administrative overload was undermining the federal government's own program goals: "The complexity and fragmentation of federal grant programs . . . creates major problems of administration for both the federal government and local governments and inhibits the development of a unified approach to the solution of community problems."[6] Such difficulties led Lyndon Johnson's own budget director to question the limits of federal activism. Shortly after leaving office, Charles Schultze wrote: "The ability of a central staff in Washington to judge the quality and practicality of the thousands of local plans submitted under federal program requirements and to control their performance is severely limited. . . . I believe that greater decentralization in the government's social programs should and will be made."[7]

Objections at the state and local levels were more vociferous. The ACIR's landmark report on the state of federalism in 1967 took thirteen pages just to summarize state and local government complaints. Holding hearings to investigate such problems in 1966, Senator Edmund S. Muskie (Democrat of Maine) concluded that "the picture . . . is one of too much tension and conflict rather than coordination all along the line of administration."[8]

These administrative dysfunctions were a major target of Richard Nixon's New Federalism agenda. As the first quotation in this chapter makes clear, both Nixon's rhetoric and thinking about federalism contained a powerful current of managerialism. Many of his administration's initiatives were designed to improve intergovernmental administration, from new procedures to standardize federal aid requirements across programs to proposed agency and program reorganizations designed to streamline coordination and planning.

Nonetheless, many administrative problems in federal assistance persisted and in some ways grew worse as the 1970s progressed. The number of narrowly defined categorical grants continued to increase; state and local fiscal dependency on federal aid grew an additional 50 percent; and new, more intrusive, regulations proliferated. Thus by 1980 the ACIR concluded that intergovernmental relations had become even "more unmanageable" than in the 1960s.[9] As a result, management issues remained a legitimate concern and motivating factor in the design of Reagan's New Federalism, although, in contrast to the Nixon years, they were clearly of secondary concern. As President Reagan remarked in a 1981 speech to state legislators, "the Federal Government is overloaded . . . having assumed more responsibilities than it can properly manage."[10]

Partisan Dimensions

The New Federalism initiatives of Nixon and Reagan involved far more than arcane features of program administration. They tapped one of the central divisions of American party politics since the New Deal, when Franklin Roosevelt—with his vigorous use of federal authority and his expansion of the fiscal, personnel, and administrative apparatus of the national government—refashioned party alignments and established a new foundation for partisan competition in America. Put simply, Roosevelt's platform—and certainly his rhetoric—boiled down to two elements: that government can help solve society's economic problems and that the federal government should take the lead in doing so. The success of this formula transformed the Democratic party from the party of parochialism, suspicious of any new exertion of national power, into the party of national vigor.[11] This was a profound reversal of historic partisan roles. The Republican party had favored more energetic national policies since its founding before the Civil War. During the 1930s, however, it fell back on a program of laissez-faire and opposed further federal intervention in the economy. In the process the Republicans gradually attracted many of the more provincial elements of society that rejected the newly acquired nationalism of the Democrats.

For more than thirty years public opinion analysts argued that fundamental party lines were drawn around issues involving the proper size and scope of the government's role in society and the economy.[12] These issues not only shaped party loyalties among the general public; they elicited strong differences among partisan elites that continued even after most citizens had accepted an activist role for the federal government.[13]

Though persistent, this partisan cleavage over the federal role acquired renewed salience during the late 1960s. The Great Society programs gave the federal government a new and powerful role extending far beyond that accepted in the 1930s. The Great Society supplemented the New Deal's legacy of social insurance and economic regulation with a large dose of what opponents called social engineering, the melding and application of professional services and social science technology to solve society's problems. As Samuel Beer has demonstrated, the strongest elements of this "service strategy" were concentrated in federal education, training, and social service programs that constituted the core of the Great Society. All used trained professionals to diagnose problems and prescribe their solutions.[14] In these years activist federal policies came to touch on some of the most emotional of social and regional issues: racial integration in housing and education, migrant labor in agriculture, affirmative action, sex discrimination, local education reform, community and neighborhood development, and urban and rural poverty.

Amidst the prosperity of the 1960s, these policies created deep cultural cleavages that overshadowed issues that had favored the Democratic party. Not only was popular support for federal activism far less secure in these areas, but the Democratic coalition was splintered by these issues.[15] Even traditional Democratic constituencies were disaffected by many federal policies: big-city mayors by federally sponsored community organizations; southern Democrats by racial integration; and blue-collar workers by the cultural liberalism of professional elites.[16]

Hence, beginning under Nixon, the decentralization long celebrated by Republican party platforms and now the central goal of New Federalism touched a responsive chord among broader segments of American society. This was something Republicans could and did exploit. New Federalism complemented vigorous efforts in both the Nixon and Reagan administrations to court blue-collar and white southern voters by promising to curb the power and energy of decisionmakers in Washington. After his reelection in 1972, Nixon blamed the nation's problems on a "breakdown in . . . the leadership class in this country . . . the Georgetown cocktail set." He repeated his determination to "diffuse the power throughout the country."[17] Likewise, Ronald Reagan swept into office denouncing the "puzzle palaces on the Potomac" and reiterating his twenty-year crusade against "disciples of 'big government knows best' [who] don't think private citizens should be messing around with their government."[18] By the 104th Congress, this strategy's success was obvious. For the first time since Reconstruction, Republicans captured a majority of southern seats in the House, and the Republican leadership in Congress had a distinctly southern cast.

Philosophical Roots

The contemporary disagreements about intergovernmental roles in the United States have their roots in a debate over the virtues and limitations of localistic democracy that is as old as the Republic itself. In fact, the central question here has concerned philosophers and statesmen for centuries.

It has been argued since Aristotle that genuine democracy can flourish only in small political entities. This notion arises ultimately from the physical constraints on a direct democracy, which must be able to accommodate an assembly of its citizens. Even allowing for representation, many have maintained that the association between democratic vigor and small size is a strong one. It is thought that, in a small community, citizens are apt to be more familiar with the issues and will perceive that they have a greater stake and more influence in public affairs.

Thus Montesquieu argued in the mid-eighteenth century that "it is natural for a republic to have only a small territory." His arguments were well known to leading American colonists at the time of the revolution, and antifederalist opponents of the federal Constitution utilized his arguments to justify their own passionate views. Men like Patrick Henry, Luther Martin, and Richard Henry Lee were against the creation of a stronger national government because they thought it would threaten individual liberty and the survival of the states.

These arguments were ultimately rejected by those attending the Constitutional Convention and by the states that ratified the Constitution. Yet the practical and philosophical merits of small versus large governments and the proper balance of power and authority between the federal government and the states have remained concerns throughout American history. In one form or another, they have contributed to the philosophical differences between political parties—not only since the New Deal, but in every party system since Thomas Jefferson and Alexander Hamilton organized the Federalist and Jeffersonian-Republican protoparties in the 1790s.[19] As a policy matter, these issues seem to receive the greatest attention after periods of extraordinary federal activism or policy failures, often as a provincial response to threats of sweeping social or economic change and a movement toward mass democracy.

With their federalism initiatives, Nixon, Reagan, and Gingrich sought to revive these old questions. All have extolled the merits of the local democratic process and its policy decisions and contrasted these with the failures of national policies and the national policymaking process. As Nixon argued in his 1971 State of the Union address:

The time has come in America to reverse the flow of power and resources from the states and communities to Washington. . . . The

further away government is from the people, the stronger government becomes and the weaker people become. . . . Local government
is the government closest to the people and it is most responsive to
the individual person; it is people's government in a far more intimate
way than the government in Washington can ever be.[20]

Likewise, Reagan argued that "by centralizing responsibility for social
programs in Washington, liberal experimenters destroyed the sense of community that sustains local institutions." His stated alternative was to restore America as "an archipelago of prospering communities."[21] This would
"return the citizen to his rightful place in the scheme of our democracy,
and that place is close to his government."[22] Similarly, in a televised address to the nation in 1995, Newt Gingrich declared that

the [federal] government is out of touch and out of control. . . . This
country is too big and too diverse for Washington to have the knowledge to make the right decision on local matters; we've got to return
power back to you—to your families, your neighborhoods, your local and state governments.[23]

New Federalism and the Evolution of Conservative Thought

There are, in short, at least three answers to the question, "Why New
Federalism?" A coherent program of decentralization represented a plausible policy response to real and contemporary problems of governmental
management and performance. It also provided a solution that reinforced
natural partisan predispositions and was grounded in a long philosophical
tradition.

Yet, as stated in the beginning of this chapter, the federalism reform
programs of Nixon, Reagan, and the 104th Congress, as well as the political reactions to them, were as different as they were alike. Those differences reveal much about contemporary American politics—both about
the framework of ideas that organizes the political agenda and gives rise
to specific policies and about the political interests and institutions that
shape the policymaking system.

At the philosophical level, although Nixon, Reagan, and Gingrich shared
a belief that the federal government had grown too powerful and that
local decisionmaking was generally preferable to national, they differed

markedly in their beliefs about the ends of decentralization and the role of the public sector. Of course, actions do not always follow rhetoric, and every administration's policies—not to mention positions taken by any given Congress—are diverse and evolving. Nevertheless, the policies advanced in all three eras proved consistent, on the whole, with the ideas advanced by the leaders of each period.

Nixon viewed his federalism strategy as a means of improving and strengthening government, especially at the state and local levels. His proposals, unlike those of subsequent Republican reformers, were intended to improve government, not dismantle it. Time and again he argued that "the American people are fed up with government that doesn't deliver" and that New Federalism reforms were needed to "clos[e] the gap between promise and performance."[24] Improved governmental efficiency and management were part of his solution, to "make government run better at less cost."[25] Since the main problem in the system was thought to be an overextended federal government, he also prescribed decentralization. Yet where the nationalization of shared or local functions appeared more likely to enhance the efficiency and rationality of public services—as with welfare or environmental regulation—Nixon recommended that instead.

Nixon was deeply suspicious of the federal bureaucracy and the national policymaking system, which he thought was dominated by "iron triangles" of congressional committees, federal agencies, and interest groups. His New Federalism policies were designed in part to disrupt that system. Nevertheless, at heart, Nixon's reforms were presented as a means for strengthening government and making it more active and creative. As Nixon declared at the start of his second term: "Fat government is weak, weak in handling the problems. . . . The reforms we are instituting . . . will diffuse power throughout the country . . . and will make government leaner but in a sense will make it stronger."[26] Programs like revenue sharing and block grants were designed to reward and promote governmental activism and problem solving at the state and local levels and to give such governments "a new sense of responsibility." As President Nixon put it: "If we put more power in more places, we can make government more creative in more places."[27] At the same time, the federal government's role could be strengthened in its own areas of special competence. For example, its efficient revenue-raising apparatus could be used to help stimulate and fund local creativity and to establish and finance a national minimum benefit level for public assistance.

Reagan, in contrast, viewed his New Federalism proposals as part of a broader strategy to reduce the role of government in society at every level. As president, he focused his retrenchment program on the federal government, and his rhetoric on this score was often extreme. "We need relief from the oppression of big government," he told an assembly of state legislators in 1981. He went on in the speech to lay out his strategy for restoring balance to the federal system. That strategy was not the Nixonian approach of rationalizing roles and responsibilities and encouraging the renaissance of state and local creativity and activism. Instead, balance was to be achieved by purely negative means—by pruning the resources of state and local governments less drastically than resources at the federal level. "We are strengthening federalism by cutting back on the activities of the Federal government," he told the legislators.[28] He argued, in short, that a reduced role for the federal government would by itself mean an enhanced role for state and local governments.

Far from encouraging states and localities to step in to fill the void left by federal tax and budget cuts, the Reagan administration focused many of its most severe budget cuts on programs that subsidized activism at the state and local levels. In one of the most pointed and ironic contrasts with his Republican predecessor, Reagan even urged that general revenue sharing—which had been the programmatic heart of Nixon's New Federalism—be eliminated. Reagan subsequently denounced state efforts to raise the taxes needed to replace these budget cuts and to assume new responsibilities—despite earlier assurances that his revenue policies were designed to create "tax room" for states.[29] Furthermore, as chapter 10 details, his administration vigorously used federal law and federal regulation to challenge state and local initiatives that he considered intrusive in the private marketplace or that conflicted with his social and economic policies. In this way the Reagan administration gave concrete expression to the emerging theory of "competitive federalism" being developed by conservative "public choice" economists—a theory that applauds interjurisdictional competition in a federal system as a means of restraining governmental activism.[30]

Reagan's positive vision, though heavily localistic, lacked a strong role for government of any kind. His quest for community entailed "an end to giantism, . . . a return to the human scale." Yet this was not the scale of local government but "the scale of the local fraternal lodge, the church organization, the block club, the farm bureau"—the scale, in short, of the private association.[31] It was this private communal action that spurred his administration to emphasize "voluntarism, the mobilization of private groupings to deal with our social ills." Ronald Reagan's strategy was precisely what he detailed to Congress in his first economic message: "we leave to private initiative all the functions that individuals can perform privately," and only reluctantly turn to states and localities to address public needs, with federal action as a last resort.

In contrast to both Nixon and Reagan, Speaker Newt Gingrich began with the premise that contemporary American society was deeply flawed. As he argued in a nationwide address in 1995: "No civilization can survive with 12-year-olds having babies, with 15-year-olds killing each other, with 17-year-olds dying of AIDS, with 18-year-olds getting diplomas they can't read." Echoing Reagan's assertion that "government is the problem," Gingrich argued that these "human tragedies have grown out of the current welfare state."[32] Accordingly, the appropriate solution would be to eliminate the national welfare state, root and branch. As Gingrich proclaimed after the Republican landslide in November 1994:

> We have to replace the welfare state with an opportunity society. Let me be very explicit. It is impossible to take the Great Society structure of bureaucracy, the redistributionist model of how wealth is acquired, and the counter-culture value system that now permeates the way we deal with the poor, and have any hope of fixing it. They are a disaster. They ruin the poor, they create a culture of poverty and a culture of violence . . . and they have to be replaced thoroughly, from the ground up.[33]

The Politics of Federalism Reform from the 1970s to the 1990s

Nixon, Reagan, and Gingrich differed also in their political strategies, which in turn elicited different political responses. To gain enactment of his New Federalism policies, Nixon tried various lines of attack, from conciliatory proposals for modest incremental program changes to presentations of sweeping blueprints for comprehensive intergovernmental reform that led to bitter confrontation with the Congress. He had mixed success. Ultimately, the political responses to Nixon's New Federalism were defined by the fragmented character of the policy process in the 1970s. Even seemingly similar or related issues elicited independent political reactions depending on the prevailing interests and attitudes in any given policy arena. Although pluralism and institutional fragmentation had long characterized American politics, they were greatly exacerbated in the late 1960s and the 1970s by the extreme decentralization of authority in Congress, the declining role of political parties, the professionally based autonomy of proliferating governmental agencies and programs, and the growing numbers and influence of interest groups. As a result, unique political coalitions had to be constructed for each issue in Nixon's agenda—a process described by one analyst as "building coalitions in the sand."[34]

Ironically, Nixon had proposed an unusually coherent and balanced program for federalism reform. But he faced a highly fragmented and complicated political system—especially in Congress—that made coherent policymaking unusually difficult. Nixon both encountered and, through the politics of confrontation and the weaknesses of Watergate, helped to create a highly individualistic Congress that was approaching at least a temporary zenith in its influence vis-à-vis the executive. In the wake of the congressional reforms of the 1960s and 1970s, this was the heyday of independent congressional entrepreneurship and "subcommittee government."[35]

Fragmentation in Congress was reinforced by atomization in the broader political environment. By the early 1970s, political parties in the United States were approaching a nadir in their traditional influence. They had lost their near-monopoly role in nominating, financing, and electing candidates; their long-held grip on public loyalties was weakening; and they had barely begun to adapt to the candidate-servicing role that was being successfully developed by independent campaign consultants, the mass media, and other functional competitors. Although the obituary was premature, David Broder's judgment that "the party's over" accurately captured the conventional wisdom and considerable reality at the time.[36]

The increasing fragmentation of the political community was also attributable to the proliferation of new interest groups. By one estimate, approximately one-quarter of all organizations represented in Washington in 1980 were established in just the fifteen-year period from 1960 to 1975; the fastest growing were the citizens' and social welfare groups.[37] Many of these new groups owed their existence directly or indirectly to governmental action, either in the form of direct subsidies or opportunities for organizing new categories of government clients and service providers.[38]

This situation greatly influenced the reform policies of the Nixon administration. That is to say, Nixon's New Federalism agenda was shaped to a remarkable degree by earlier governmental actions. From consolidating and coordinating proliferating categorical grants, to sorting out governmental responsibilities, to controlling escalating health care costs, the

Nixon administration sought to respond to and rationalize the dysfunctions of previous federal policies. So, too, were politics in this period increasingly shaped by the organizational consequences of prior programs and governmental actions. The development of new interest groups often followed rather than inspired the development of new programs in the 1960s. Even the decline of parties had important roots in the New Deal's social insurance policies. Both developments encouraged more independent behavior in Congress as members adapted to the demands of a more fluid electoral environment and made use of the new policymaking opportunities provided by the policy breakthroughs of the 1960s.

In contrast, Ronald Reagan won a series of comprehensive policy victories early in his administration by using strongly confrontational tactics and organizing a stable winning coalition based on partisan and ideological loyalties. Levels of party unity and support on key votes in Congress reached relative and in some cases historic highs during Reagan's tenure, after sinking to postwar lows under Nixon. Although Reagan's record of congressional success fell steadily after his first year in office, and his winning coalition eroded, his administration's early budgetary, tax, and defense victories altered the subsequent policymaking environment.

Above all, Reagan's domestic policies elicited far more interdependent patterns of policymaking than was the case under Richard Nixon. For example, budgetary decisions came to dominate the legislative agenda as never before, symbolized by the evolving and continuing constraints of the Gramm-Rudman-Hollings deficit reduction process. Spending priorities were repeatedly addressed in omnibus budget reconciliation packages and massive continuing resolutions. Opportunities for independent, entrepreneurial program initiatives—particularly if they increased the federal deficit—were severely restricted, and the character of those that succeeded was altered. This restricted and increasingly zero-sum policy agenda was evident in each successive year of the Reagan presidency.

Policymaking in the 104th Congress picked up where Ronald Reagan's conservative coalition left off in 1981. The first Republican-controlled Congress since President Dwight Eisenhower's first term was characterized by extraordinary partisanship and party cohesion. Buoyed by the excitement of being in the majority and supported by an influx of new, ideologically committed members, congressional Republicans in 1995 achieved levels of party voting that were 50 percent higher than in the Nixon era and 25 percent higher than in Reagan's first year in office.[39] In response, many interest groups that once operated in a bipartisan and independent way were driven into closer partnerships with one or the other political party.

Policy interdependence reached new levels in the 104th Congress as well. Thanks to the "Contract with America," the new majority came into office with a remarkably specific and coherent policy agenda and proceeded to act accordingly. Most of the major congressional initiatives of 1995 (including welfare reform, multiple block grants, tax cuts, spending reductions, departmental consolidations, and agency eliminations) were subsumed within the framework of a seven-year balanced budget package. Only when this package was defeated in a budget showdown with President Clinton did the 104th Congress begin to resemble legislative politics as usual—fractious and fragmented. Items like welfare reform were split off from the budget and advanced separately, attractive new pieces like health insurance portability were added to the agenda, and normal intraparty dissension between conservatives and moderates broke out in the open. Yet, in the end, strong levels of partisanship characterized congressional behavior in 1996 as well.[40]

These Republican reform agendas shed considerable light on the way in which political thought and culture are evolving in the United States, as well as on important developments in American politics during this period—from the rise of an activist decentralized Congress to the growth of budgetary constraints and issue entrepreneurship in the modern Congress. Underlying all of these changes is a common dynamic: government now helps to shape its own agenda and political environment.

Chapters 2 through 4 examine the New Federalism program of Richard Nixon, including management reforms, block grants, special revenue sharing, and general revenue sharing. Chapter 5 also takes a close look at the politics of centralization in the Nixon years, including welfare reform, entitlement growth, and regulatory expansion.

Chapters 6 through 10 analyze the politics of federalism reform under President Reagan. This section begins with political developments in the late 1970s that set the stage for the "Reagan revolution." It then examines budget and tax policies in the Reagan administration, reductions and changes in intergovernmental grants in the 1980s, and the ill-fated federalism reform initiative of 1982. Finally, Chapter 10 explores the politics of regulatory reform and expansion during the Reagan years.

Chapters 11 through 14 assess the intergovernmental implications of the "Republican revolution" in the 104th Congress. Chapter 11 begins with an overview of political and federalism developments during George

Bush's presidency and the first two years of Clinton's initial term. It shows how these developments led up to Republican victories at the polls in 1994. Chapter 12 describes the bold congressional policy initiatives of 1995 and their ultimate demise, while Chapter 13 focuses on the two principal intergovernmental achievements of the 104th Congress: reform of federal mandates and welfare reform. Finally, Chapter 14 traces the remarkable evolution of federalism reform politics and ideology during the past twenty-five years and sketches alternative scenarios for the future of American federalism.

CHAPTER 2

The Origins of Nixon's
New Federalism

PUBLIC POLICIES have traditionally been viewed as governmental responses to outside pressures and demands. Such pressures may come in the form of events and crises that require attention by policymakers. Or they may be expressed as external demands for government action generated by public opinion, interest groups, or political parties.

As the public sector has grown larger, more active, and more complex, however, an increasing number of public policy initiatives have originated with actors, forces, and ideas internal to government itself. One increasingly important category of such governmentally inspired policies includes those policies that respond directly to the perceived failures or consequences of prior programs and public actions. Such initiatives have been termed "rationalizing policies" by Lawrence Brown—products of "a government-led search for solutions to government's problems."[1]

Such rationalizing policies formed the heart of President Richard Nixon's domestic policy agenda. Throughout Nixon's six years in office (1969–74), repeated efforts were made to reform and rationalize the plethora of federal assistance programs to states and localities, to improve program efficiency, to decentralize decisionmaking, and to restrain—but not halt—rapid program growth. Many means were employed on behalf of these ends, but chief among them were grant consolidation, general revenue sharing, and an assortment of intergovernmental management initiatives.

Although the Nixon administration's policy objectives remained relatively constant over time, its strategy for achieving them did not. Initially, the administration's support for block grants and revenue sharing was part of a broad agenda of management-oriented reforms in intergovernmental relations. These initiatives grew out of a long and distinguished tradition of incremental administrative reforms that extended back to the Truman and Eisenhower administrations.

In 1971, dissatisfied with this strategy's lack of progress, Nixon adopted a far more ideological and confrontational approach to enacting his program of federalism reforms. After revising and renewing his earlier call for general revenue sharing and a nationally funded income maintenance program, the president proposed consolidating 129 existing categorical programs—comprising nearly one-third of all federal aid expenditures—into six broad and extremely flexible block grants called "special revenue sharing." The substantive boldness of this initiative was matched by an aggressive new political strategy. The administration turned away from fashioning a professional consensus in favor of grant reform to forging a conservative coalition capable of enacting sweeping changes in federal aid structures all at once. When this high-risk strategy fell short, the administration sought to coerce Congress into accepting special revenue sharing by impounding congressional appropriations for categorical programs and attempting to implement consolidation unilaterally through administrative actions. When this strategy also failed, individual officials in the administration—enjoying new autonomy as the Watergate scandal increasingly preoccupied White House attention—returned to a more incremental style of policymaking and helped build consensus for grant reform within specific fields of government policy.

Despite these great swings in political strategy, the basic policy objectives of the Nixon administration remained relatively constant over time: to rationalize, reform, and restructure active governmental intervention across the broad range of public functions and governmental levels. The Nixon administration never sought to reverse the course of governmental activism or to halt the growth of government expenditures in any consistent or comprehensive manner. Rather, it partly shared and partly accommodated itself to the prevailing political culture of liberalism that established the tone and context for political debate in the early 1970s. It sought to channel governmental activity into certain areas and patterns of intervention and to modify and manage the rate of growth of the federal government.

Thus the Nixon administration sought to decentralize federal involvement in some traditional state and local fields—community development, education, and manpower training—and at the same time proposed a complete national assumption of the costs of income maintenance, on the grounds that a more uniform, effective, and equitable welfare system could best be achieved through greater nationalization. Through grant consolidation, the Nixon administration endeavored to streamline intergovernmental program management and, at times, to alter the political dynamics of policymaking and program expansion at both the national and local levels. But it did not seek in any systematic way to substantially diminish or halt government involvement in most of the affected areas.

On the contrary, the Nixon administration proved willing and at times eager to encourage and fund locally determined governmental activism in many of the fields where it opposed more direct national involvement. The objective, in the words of one high administration official, was to establish "a positive Republican alternative to running things out of Washington . . . something to be *for*."[2] Thus it proposed and fought vigorously for a multibillion-dollar program of general revenue sharing, and it acceded to substantial spending increases to obtain congressional approval of its community development and job training block grants. It also presided over the greatest expansion in federal regulatory authority and entitlement spending since the 1930s. In short, it sought to reform, remake, and refashion the increasingly complex intergovernmental relations of the modern welfare state. But it did not attempt to halt federal funding or to undermine such activities when they were consistent with better management or local government priorities. In this respect the Nixon administration differed greatly from its Republican successors and marked the culmination of a long tradition of intergovernmental reform attempts.

Nixon and the Managerial Reform Tradition

When Richard Nixon was inaugurated in 1969, there was growing agreement among government officials and public administrators about the need to simplify and streamline the intergovernmental aid system. Serious efforts to reform the intergovernmental system had begun as early as the Truman and Eisenhower administrations, and the rapid growth in federal programs and administrative complexity since that time had forged a broad consensus for reform among generalist officials with broad functional responsibilities. Backed by growing political demands from beleaguered state and local government officials, such sentiments inspired a stream of intergovernmental reform initiatives by the Johnson administration. Despite such mounting support, however, serious differences existed over how reform might best be accomplished. In particular, three distinct but comple-

mentary approaches were espoused: intergovernmental management reforms, block grants, and general revenue sharing. All were used aggressively by the Nixon administration, which also added a fourth element:
comprehensive welfare reform.

Intergovernmental Management Reforms

The first and most modest reform approach was grant simplification.
This strategy left existing categorical program structures essentially unchanged but attempted to develop new administrative processes and organizational structures to help coordinate them. This approach was extremely
flexible and could be directed at any level of programmatic activity—
federal, state, regional, local, or neighborhood. It was generally favored
by those who sought to effect rapid changes—often purely administrative
in nature—and who viewed more far-reaching program changes as politically and bureaucratically impractical.

The management reform strategy was utilized heavily during the Johnson
administration virtually from the beginning. Even the community action
program, which formed the very core of the "war on poverty" effort, was
viewed initially by high administration officials as a relatively low-cost
administrative mechanism for coordinating existing federal programs at
the local level.[3] Similarly, improved program coordination was the leading goal behind a range of other prominent initiatives of the Johnson administration, including

—multistate regional planning through the Appalachian Regional Commission, the nationwide system of Title V economic development planning commissions, and Budget Bureau efforts to standardize federal
administrative regions;

—the "A-85" process of intergovernmental consultation;

—the Intergovernmental Cooperation Act of 1968, which helped lay
the legislative groundwork for expanded program coordination;

—the cooperative area manpower planning system for coordinating state
and local job training efforts;

—the model cities program for coordinating and targeting community
development and social service resources in poor urban neighborhoods; and

—the concentrated employment program for developing comprehensive
manpower and social service programs in selected poor communities.[4]

The Nixon administration built and expanded upon this framework of
managerial efforts to streamline the administration of intergovernmental

programs. In 1969, as part of its general thrust to decentralize service delivery, the administration cemented and formalized the earlier proposal by the Budget Bureau for standardized administrative regions, providing each with its own Federal Regional Council to improve interdepartmental coordination and intergovernmental liaison. The administration also sought to simplify and standardize federal grant applications and program administration through the Federal Assistance Review process and related management circulars. In 1969 the Office of Management and Budget (OMB) promulgated circular "A-95," which established formal mechanisms for coordinating federal programs at the state and substate regional levels. The administration also helped enact the Joint Funding Simplification Act of 1974, which allowed state and local governments to combine and expedite applications for several related federal assistance programs. Finally, in an attempt to permit greater local government control over the model cities program, the Nixon administration experimented with a program of "planned variations" that formed one of the building blocks for the later block grant in community development.

In general, these rather arcane managerial reforms enjoyed considerable support throughout the public administration and intergovernmental policy communities. By most accounts, however, their impact was modest and even disappointing. Though most of the reforms proved useful in certain circumstances, advocates of more substantial changes in the intergovernmental system advocated two additional strategies of reform: grant consolidation and general aid to state and local governments.

Block Grants in the Professional Stream

Block grants comprised a second approach to intergovernmental reform. This strategy required legislative action to consolidate numerous related or overlapping programs into a few large grants, each covering a broad functional area. Within these broadly defined spheres, state and local governments would have wide latitude to decide precisely how the monies should be spent.

This concept of federal aid reform was first advanced by scholars and public administrators in the 1940s and early 1950s. Examining performance problems in categorical grant programs, they argued that such programs had sprung up in a piecemeal and uncoordinated way, that they neglected some vital services and overstimulated others, that they distorted state and local budgets, and that they ignored or exacerbated differentials in service levels among the states. As Paul Studenski wrote in 1949, "The most immediate need is for the consolidation of the multiple and separately apportioned grant programs into unified grants, on an equalization basis, covering each major grant field."[5] Likewise, the first Hoover Commission identified five significant flaws in categorical assistance programs and concluded: "A system of grants should be established based upon broad categories—such as highways, education, public assistance, and public health—as contrasted with the present system of extensive fragmentation."[6]

Encouraged by the recommendations of the Hoover Commission, the Truman administration advocated block grant legislation in the fields of public health and welfare. Both proposals met defeat in Congress for reasons unrelated to grant consolidation. During the 1950s, the Eisenhower administration advanced an even broader set of grant reform proposals. In 1954 President Dwight D. Eisenhower endorsed grant consolidation legislation covering several public health and social service functions, though nothing was enacted. The president also established the Kestnbaum Commission in 1953 to undertake a comprehensive review of federal aid and intergovernmental relations as a whole. This was followed in 1957 by the Joint Federal-State Action Committee, whose mission was to simplify and sort out federal-state responsibilities. Despite its hopeful title, the committee generated precious little "action." It recommended returning only two modest federal programs to the states, and the recommendations received little congressional attention.

These failures underscored the political obstacles to grant consolidation and reform in the 1950s. Opposition came from many categorical program defenders and beneficiaries who resisted the perceived threat to their existing funding sources. Repeated failures also reflected public administrators' lack of professional consensus on behalf of grant reform. Throughout the 1950s, the categorical grant system remained modest in size and complexity, and many administrative experts were unconvinced that administrative problems necessitated comprehensive grant reform.[7]

Block Grants in the 1960s

Professional dissension lessened during the 1960s, as the growing size and complexity of the federal aid system generated a host of intergovernmental problems. By the late 1960s, prominent students of intergovernmental relations regarded block grants as the leading remedy for problems in the federal aid system.[8] Block grants also were strongly supported by state and local government interest groups, whose members were confronted with a rising tide of political and administrative problems tied to federal grants.

Growing administrative complexity was one such problem. By 1970 there were seventeen separately authorized federal programs for employment and training alone, and they were administered by thirteen different agencies and bureaus.[9] Even program supporters decried the possibility of effectively managing a network of training programs administered through 30,000 separate contracts with 10,000 local governments and community organizations. "The proliferation of programs made the need for administrative rationalization increasingly clear," concluded Sar Levitan and Joyce Zickler. "Each program had different authorizations, guidelines, clienteles, and delivery mechanisms."[10]

As a result, stories of mismanagement were legion. One Labor Department administrator illustrated "the limits of federal control" by recounting her experience at the conclusion of a grant cycle when a group of manpower officials met to allocate remaining program funds:

> One year, when we finished matching requests for funds on the night before the deadline, we discovered we had millions left over. Here it was, three in the morning and we were trading surplus finds for soda and pizza. I got millions in Job Corps money for a piece of pepperoni.[11]

Local officials also grew increasingly concerned about the managerial and political problems stemming from this proliferating array of categorical grants. During congressional testimony, the mayor of Oakland, California, complained that there were twenty-two separate manpower projects operating in his city, yet few needy individuals were receiving job training appropriate for the local labor market. His efforts to remedy the situation had quickly failed because each separately authorized federal program "tended to resist coordination, and unfortunately local government was all but ignored."[12] A community development official in another city painted the problem of inadequate coordination more graphically: "Our city is a battleground among federal Cabinet agencies."[13] The mayor of Omaha even suggested that city employees had become more concerned with the administration of federal programs than with the locally determined needs of their own community. "Are we going to wake up some morning and find that only 25% of city employees are working on city business?" he asked.[14]

As predicted by the model of rationalizing politics, however, some of the most influential voices advocating block grants in the 1960s came from within the federal government itself. Organizations such as the Advisory Commission on Intergovernmental Relations, the General Accounting Office, and the Budget Bureau—whose responsibilities gave them a broad perspective on the growing dysfunctions across the grant system as a whole—all expressed strong support for block grants as a tool for comprehensive reform of the federal aid system.

Even more important were the views of high officials in the Johnson administration. Walter Heller, former chairman of the President's Council of Economic Advisers and a well-known proponent of general revenue sharing, endorsed grant consolidation in 1967, arguing that "we must move toward broader categories [of aid] that will give states and localities more freedom of choice."[15] President Johnson's budget director, Charles Schultze, also endorsed the block grant concept. In testimony before Congress, he called it a means of making "further progress . . . in overcoming the problem of excessive categorization and fractionating of Federal aid."[16]

The Johnson administration did more than preach the merits of grant consolidation, however. In the public health field, President Johnson proposed and obtained enactment of the Partnership for Health Act in 1966. This long-sought-after consolidation, which combined nine public health formula grants into a single block grant program, had been recommended since the days of the first Hoover Commission. By 1966 the concept was supported by most members of the public health community, and the president's proposal faced little opposition in Congress. Although he had recommended a categorical program structure in law enforcement, President Johnson signed into law a congressionally inspired block grant, the Law Enforcement Assistance Act, in 1968. Finally, in the closing weeks of the administration, additional block grants were under active consideration in the Budget Bureau for such broad purposes as "reducing economic dependency," "children and youth" services, and "improving our physical environment."[17] The level of refinement in some of these proposals illustrates the degree of organizational capacity and institutional support for grant consolidation that existed within the federal government before Nixon's inauguration.

Nixon and Block Grants

Originally, President Nixon hewed closely to this managerial tradition in grant consolidation. In one of his first speeches on the subject, he endorsed block grants as a means "to remedy the confusion, arbitrariness and rigidity of the present system."[18] Early in his administration he proposed legislation to establish a streamlined process for congressional consideration of grant consolidation proposals, similar to the one used in executive reorganizations.

The president's first proposal for a job training block grant in 1969 reflected similar managerial concerns and differed sharply from the later "no strings" consolidation approach utilized in "special revenue sharing." Developed by policy professionals in the Labor Department, the proposed "Manpower Training Act" featured a range of management-oriented provisions, including management incentive grants, a regional planning focus, and a phased consolidation of programs to facilitate the gradual enhancement of states' capacities to administer the program. The administration also deferred to policy specialists in community development and elected to retain the model cities program while experimenting with adding block grant features to it. Through the planned variations program, it increased mayoral involvement, expanded program activities, and reduced federal paperwork in sixteen selected cities.

Indeed, the administration nearly won congressional approval of a management-oriented employment training block grant in 1970. A compromise proposal, combining manpower block grant features with a temporary public service jobs program, passed the House of Representatives that year with the president's support. The Senate, however, refused to accept the consolidation of many members' favored categorical programs, and Congress failed to pass a bill that the president would accept. Frustrated with the lack of progress on this bill and other managerial reform attempts, Nixon abruptly altered his grant reform strategy in January 1971 with his sweeping proposal for six highly decentralized "special revenue sharing" block grants.

Revenue Sharing and the Mainstream

The third approach to grant reform—after intergovernmental management reforms and block grants—was general revenue sharing (GRS). Offered as a replacement or supplement to existing categorical grants, a revenue sharing program would provide a source of virtually unrestricted federal assistance to state and local governments, to be spent in almost any manner deemed appropriate. Because of this "no strings" approach, the GRS concept was strongly favored by state and local governments and their organizations in Washington.

The concept also drew favor from many economists. They viewed it as an efficient way to equalize interstate variations in fiscal capacity, reduce the "fiscal drag" expected from projected federal budget surpluses during the 1960s, and harness the relatively progressive federal income tax apparatus to provide needed revenues for fiscally starved state and local governments.[19] Overall, proponents of revenue sharing tended to focus on the problem of inadequate state and local revenues, and they tended to trust such governments to make wise or appropriate spending decisions if only this fiscal inadequacy could be overcome.

As the 1950s and 1960s progressed, the revenue sharing concept received growing political support in both political parties. In 1958 Representative Melvin Laird, a mainstream conservative Republican from Wisconsin, introduced the first major revenue sharing bill. A more important boost came early in the Johnson administration. The chairman of the Council of Economic Advisors, Walter Heller, endorsed revenue sharing along with grant consolidation, and he sought to gain the president's backing for it during the 1964 campaign. A White House task force established to study the idea endorsed it in the fall of 1964, but the president ultimately rejected the concept for a complex of personal and political reasons.[20] When Heller left the White House staff soon thereafter, he escalated his efforts on behalf of revenue sharing. In an influential series of lectures at Harvard and in a subsequent book, he argued vigorously that

> revenue sharing, or similar general-purpose grants, could provide the missing fiscal link . . . a dependable flow of Federal funds in a form that would enlarge, not restrict, the options of state and local decision makers. . . . [Such grants] combine the sound conservative principle of preserving the decentralization of power and intellectual diversity that are essential to a workable federalism with the compassionate liberal principle of promoting equality of opportunity among different income groups and regions of the United States.[21]

By 1968 the revenue sharing concept was supported by both parties' candidates for president, although significant differences existed in program content and emphasis. By this time, too, most state and local government officials in both parties had placed GRS at the top of their legislative agendas and were prepared to fight vigorously for such a program. Scholars also supported the revenue sharing concept in large numbers, and many viewed it as the most attractive strategy for reforming the intergovernmental system.[22]

Revenue Sharing and the New Federalism

Revenue sharing received new momentum with the election of Richard Nixon. In the president's first major address on domestic policy in 1969, he made revenue sharing one of the three main pillars of the New Federalism. Although the president's proposals were billed as "the first major reversal of the trend toward ever more centralization of government in Washington," they had, in the words of one participant, "a quite progressive cast."[23]

Specifically, Nixon's first revenue sharing bill adopted an *entitlement* approach to intergovernmental assistance. It proposed that 1 percent of personal taxable income eventually be allocated to state and local governments, phased in gradually to minimize the immediate impact on the federal budget. Equally significant, the program's formula was designed to reward active and innovative state and local governments rather than simply siphon funds away from Washington. Grants were to be distributed to states partly on the basis of "tax effort," the level of tax burden that states were willing to impose on themselves. In congressional testimony, administration officials explained that one of the "ultimate purposes" of the president's revenue sharing proposal was to "provide both the encouragement and the necessary resources for local and State officials to exercise leadership in solving their own problems" and "to restore strength and vigor to local and State governments."[24]

Despite the high priority given to revenue sharing by President Nixon and growing support for the concept throughout the intergovernmental community, Congress failed even to hold hearings on the legislation during the administration's first two years. This failure partly reflected the president's own focus on foreign policy matters and issues like welfare reform. But it sprang primarily from powerful opposition to the administration's bill itself. Although local governments vigorously endorsed the revenue sharing concept, they were unhappy with the distribution of funds to them under the administration's plan. Supporters of existing categorical programs viewed revenue sharing as a dangerous threat to their own funding, and they were strongly backed by congressional committee chairmen who saw unrestricted federal aid as a challenge to their own prerogatives to establish federal priorities. Finally, many fiscal conservatives were opposed to the program's price tag, and they too viewed unrestricted aid as fiscally irresponsible.

Nationalizing Welfare: The Family Assistance Plan

To those who mistakenly interpreted Nixon's federalism initiatives as disguised attempts to dismantle the federal establishment, no element of the New Federalism was as incongruous as the family assistance plan (FAP). This proposal, which was part of the original New Federalism package unveiled in 1969, would have abolished the aid to families with dependent children (AFDC) program and established a federal minimum income payment of $1,600 annually for a family of four. It would have substantially increased government support for families in many poor states and enlarged the total welfare budget of the federal government. Combined with other elements of the New Federalism, FAP was part of a strategy for "sorting out" intergovernmental functions. It enlarged the federal government's role in income maintenance—a policy area with broad national ramifications—while decentralizing several areas of predominantly state and local interest.

Like block grants and general revenue sharing, the concept of a guaranteed national income had a heritage of bipartisan support. The concept was first seriously proposed by conservative economist Milton Friedman in 1962. Calling his proposal a "negative income tax," Friedman proposed replacing the existing welfare structure with a system of graduated income supplements whose size would vary with earnings. Friedman believed the primary failure of the welfare system lay in its financial disincentives for recipients to accept low-paying jobs and end welfare dependency. For those at the bottom of the employment ladder, welfare payments could be larger than earnings, and they were eliminated on a dollar-for-dollar basis for wages received. Thus he proposed graduated welfare payments that would decline as earned income rose but always provide greater combined income with employment than without it. Such a system, he argued, would preserve incentives for recipients to find and retain jobs.[25]

Despite its conservative origins, the negative income tax found its major political champion inside the Johnson administration—at the vanguard of the Great Society. Sargent Shriver, the first director of the Office of Economic Opportunity, endorsed the concept in 1965. Although President Johnson never agreed to adopt it on a large scale, OEO funded a multiyear project to experiment with such a program in 1967.

Two years later this concept was sold to Nixon by Richard Nathan, the assistant director of the Office of Management and Budget, and White House domestic adviser Daniel Patrick Moynihan. Over strenuous objections from more conservative members of his administration, the president made a multibillion-dollar national income floor one of the three pillars of his original New Federalism plan.

As described in chapter 5, this proposal enjoyed mixed success in Congress. It passed the House in 1970 but was stymied in the Senate. There it was caught in a difficult bind between southern conservatives, who worried about the plan's effects on low-wage workers in the South, and northern liberals and welfare rights proponents, who saw the minimum payment as too low.

Political Dimensions of the New Federalism

By 1971, except for a few modest management initiatives, virtually the entire New Federalism agenda was bogged down in Congress. No block grants had been enacted. Key members of Congress had refused even to hold hearings on general revenue sharing. And the family assistance plan had died an unceremonious death in the Senate.

This congressional inertia spurred a dramatic change in administration strategy that broke ties to the managerial reform tradition and heightened the salience of the political aims of the New Federalism. A bold New Federalism initiative was made the centerpiece of Nixon's 1971 domestic agenda. In his State of the Union address, the president renewed his call for the family assistance plan, raising the federal minimum floor for a family of four by one-third, to $2,400. A revamped, $5 billion general revenue sharing plan was unveiled. Finally and dramatically, President Nixon proposed six highly decentralized block grants that consolidated 129 programs in the fields of urban community development, rural development, job training, law enforcement, education, and transportation. Combined with GRS, the $11.3 billion price tag for these six "special revenue sharing" initiatives totaled 45 percent of all federal aid in 1972 and consolidated more than one quarter of all intergovernmental programs.

This sweeping initiative, and the legislative strategy developed to advance it, focused new attention on the political objectives of New Federalism. Nixon's federalism proposals always were intended to redistribute power in the intergovernmental system, as well as to improve governmental management. In his first address on decentralization in 1969—in which he announced proposals for general revenue sharing, an employment training block grant, and welfare reform—Nixon stated that his purpose was

> to . . . present a new . . . drastically different approach . . . to the way the responsibilities are shared between the State and Federal Governments. . . . These proposals . . . represent the first major reversal of the trend toward ever more centralization of government in Washington. . . . It is time for a New Federalism in which power, funds, and responsibility will flow from Washington to the States and to the people.[26]

The objective was to use grant consolidation to alter the ground rules of federal aid politics, undercutting the influence of Washington-centered interest groups and their congressional and bureaucratic allies who promoted and benefited from individual categorical grants. As Richard Nathan, then assistant OMB director and chief architect of the Nixon administration's New Federalism proposals, observed in a subsequent interview, the administration hoped that individual program clienteles would reduce their lobbying efforts once the payoff was diluted in a consolidated grant: "There were people in the administration who understood that once there was a broad based grant, it would weaken the individual claims for more money." Elsewhere Nathan has added that "the idea was to weaken the federal bureaucracy."[27] Even the historic family assistance plan was partly sold to Nixon as a way to bypass human services bureaucracies and to "get rid of social workers."[28]

Despite these political objectives, the primary motivation for this sweeping new initiative was dissatisfaction with the tactics of the past, not a fundamental change in goals. Management reforms continued. In fact, the federalism thrust shared top billing on the president's agenda with a historic restructuring of cabinet departments, reducing their number from twelve to eight. An expanded national welfare role was retained. The revenue sharing formula retained incentives for state and local activism.

At the same time, top White House officials concluded that emphasizing continuities with past reforms would not succeed. They believed that established power centers in Washington—interest groups, bureaucrats, and members of Congress—had stymied change and had to be challenged more directly and aggressively. As Nathan wrote in early 1971 with regard to block grants:

> It has become increasingly clear that a new strategy is needed. . . .
> [The old] approach is one which emphasized the consolidation of
> individual grants and would have us work within the system to take
> successive incremental steps to streamline Federal aids. The problem,
> simply put, is that this approach doesn't work.[29]

John Ehrlichman, then President Nixon's chief domestic adviser, also
believed that the initial grant consolidation efforts and GRS had failed in
Congress because they were "too small." Ehrlichman felt the proposals
were not dramatic enough, that "they didn't grab the point."[30] Consequently, a search was launched in 1970 for an alternative approach to the
reform of federal grant programs.

A Megagrant Rejected

As early as July 1970, the president decided to focus this search on some
sort of tax sharing or expanded revenue sharing approach to federal aid.[31]
The real work, however, did not begin until November. The first alternative explored at that time was a gigantic general revenue sharing program,
with funds derived from terminating a wide variety of federal grant and
nongrant programs. At one point, reports Paul Dommel, the White House
considered eliminating "*all* categorical grants," although this idea "did
not last long."[32] Nonetheless, work on selecting a group of programs to be
merged into a giant revenue sharing package continued into December.

As the details of this revenue sharing proposal were elaborated, its differences with the subsequent special revenue sharing approach became
sharply defined. OMB and Treasury officials developed economic criteria
for selecting candidate programs for merger and termination. Programs,
like contagious disease control, whose effects were deemed to "spill over"
into a number of different states or other jurisdictions, were deemed inappropriate for merger into an unrestricted grant program. Many direct income transfers and grants for human and social services were also excluded
as "long term investments in human capital."[33] On the other hand, a broad
range of grant and nongrant expenditures with "primarily local benefits"
were selected for inclusion in the GRS initiative.

Accordingly, forty-one diverse federal programs were identified as candidates for revenue sharing, including the Army Corps of Engineers, the
Agricultural Extension Service, the Tennessee Valley Authority (TVA),
urban renewal, model cities, and the tax subsidy for state and local gov-

Table 2-1. *Programs Proposed for Inclusion in Revenue Sharing by the Office of Management and Budget, 1970*
Millions of dollars

Program	Outlays
Appalachian Regional Commission	288
Economic Development Administration	240
Regional Action Planning Commissions	9
Highway beauty	30
Forest highways	23
Public lands highways	8
State and community highway safety	70
Cooperative State Research Service	60
Extension Service	156
Farmers Cooperative Service	2
Rural electrification	292
FHA sewer and water grants	58
Forest Service grants	22
Forest Service permanent	120
Bureau of Land Management permanent	93
Sport fish permanent	57
Land and water conservation fund	90
Anadromous fish	3
Bureau of Reclamation	358
Bonneville Power Administration	129
Southwest Power Administration	8
Southeast Power Administration	1
Alaska Power Administration	1
Corps of Engineers—civil works	1,350
Tennessee Valley Authority	685
Waste treatment facility grants	702
Minor categoricals (books and libraries)	287
Medical facilities construction grants	218
Regional medical program grants	70
Community mental health staffing grants	50
Partnership for health grant	125
Maternal and child health formula grants	117
Air pollution abatement control grants	25
Social services (excludes administrative costs for public assistance)	760
Model cities	210
OEO direct operations (excludes R&D, Indian, and migrant programs)	575
Urban renewal	1,300
Water and sewer	170
Open space	70
Planning	50
Tax subsidy	400
Total	9,282

Source: Office of Management and Budget, Revenue Sharing Working Group, "Initial Report," Washington, December 1, 1970.

ernment bonds. Altogether, these programs had 1972 outlays of approximately $9.25 billion (see table 2-1). In contrast, many programs that would later be marked for consolidation into special revenue sharing plans were excluded by these criteria, including Title I of the Elementary and Secondary Education Act, manpower training programs, and vocational education. In all, more than $15 billion in federal grant programs was excluded from the GRS package.

Just one month before the State of the Union address, this massive revenue sharing plan was suddenly abandoned as too impractical and impolitic. "We shot that down," said Nathan of OMB, "that plan was Ehrlichman's and Harper's. They didn't have much idea of what they were doing, or an understanding of the politics of it."[34] Nevertheless, the White House continued to insist on a dramatic proposal, and OMB director George P. Shultz agreed. "I favor a bold approach," he told the president in mid-December, "cutting into the categorical programs to the maximum extent possible." But Shultz successfully pushed for a series of virtually unrestricted block grants instead of the gigantic revenue sharing plan because block grants will "offend the interest group less."[35] These arguments carried the day, and in the few remaining weeks before January 22, 1971, the broad outlines of the president's proposal were quickly thrown together.

Despite the high visibility and new strategy given the revised proposals, they met with mixed success. The specific politics of each component of Nixon's New Federalism—block grants, revenue sharing, and welfare reform—are reviewed in subsequent chapters. But the overriding factor shaping the political fortunes of Nixon's New Federalism was simply this: neither Congress nor the broader political system of the 1970s was prepared to deal coherently with the complex, comprehensive reform strategy the president proposed. Nixon's early efforts to encourage and persuade and his later efforts to cajole and compel congressional acceptance of his plans faltered in the fragmented politics of the era. The dynamics of that process and the policy consequences are described in the following three chapters.

CHAPTER 3

The Fragmented Politics
of Block Grants

IF ONE WERE to choose a single term to characterize the national policymaking process in the 1970s, that term would probably be "fragmentation." From the rise of "subcommittee government" in Congress, to the proliferation of interest groups and political action committees in Washington, to the decline of party loyalties in the electorate and party voting in Congress, the splintering of power was a pervasive theme throughout the decade. Nowhere was such fragmentation more apparent than in the politics of federalism reform.

By 1971 the Nixon administration had raised an ambitious New Federalism program to the top of its domestic policy agenda. With its mix of block grants, revenue sharing, and welfare reform, it was an unusually coherent policy response to an integrated set of public sector problems. Even in the best of circumstances, no president could expect an independent and pluralistic Congress to accept such a framework in toto. Given the Democrats' control of Congress and the ideological overtones of decentralization, a vigorous partisan conflict appeared likely. Yet the conceptual unity of the New Federalism agenda, once in the congressional arena, confronted a multitude of idiosyncratic coalitions rather than a disciplined legion of steadfast opponents. Each of the administration's reform initiatives elicited a unique political reception that was shaped by the predominant forces and political sentiments internal to each specific policy arena.

This politics of fragmentation was especially clear in the case of Nixon's block grant proposals. Old-fashioned grant consolidation was at the core of his proposal to meld one-third of all federal programs into six loosely defined megagrants called "special" revenue sharing. Even though they were part of the primary domestic initiative of an "imperial" presidency, four of these special revenue sharing initiatives were dismissed summarily by Congress. In so doing, legislators were responding to the clearly stated preferences of interest groups and legislative specialists most familiar with the affected programs. Only two block grants were passed in modified form, and even these owed more to the support for grant consolidation among program clients and supporters than to presidential leadership. A careful examination of the fate of Nixon's block grants illuminates not only the fortunes of the New Federalism, but also the predominant patterns of policymaking in the political system of the early 1970s.

Block Grant Failures and Models of the Policy Process

As chapter 2 detailed, President Nixon's New Federalism initiative in 1971 proposed consolidating 129 existing categorical programs into six special revenue sharing programs in the fields of transportation, education, rural development, law enforcement, community development, and employment training (see table 3-1). The first four proposals failed to pass either house of Congress. Across these varied policy arenas, this negative legislative response reflected both commonalities and differences. Some of the failed initiatives were summarily dismissed; others were debated and rejected. In every case, however, one important fact was overriding: interest groups and program specialists in the affected policy area were almost unanimously opposed to the president's proposals.

Transportation revenue sharing was a case in point. The president of the American Trucking Association expressed "revulsion" at portions of the administration's plan, calling it a "large scale raid on the federal Highway Trust Fund."[1] Other affected highway and airport interests were similarly opposed, as were state highway officials who feared losing some of their control over highway programs to the governors. Even some officials within the Nixon administration had reservations about the proposal. Richard Nathan, assistant director of the Office of Management and Budget (OMB), later reported that he "never thought transportation [revenue sharing] made sense." It was one of the "least studied" proposals before its introduction to Congress, he said, and could be considered one of the "throwaways" in the president' package.[2]

Given lukewarm support from the administration and a hostile reception from powerful interest groups, it is hardly surprising that little support was found for the transportation program in Congress. Congressional

Table 3-1. *Proposed Program Consolidations and Spending Authorizations in Special Revenue Sharing Plan, 1971*
Amounts in billions of dollars

Program	Amount in first full year	Number of programs folded in
Education	3.0	33
Transportation	2.6	26
Urban community development	2.1	12
Manpower training	2.0	17
Rural community development	1.1	39
Law enforcement	0.5	2
Total	11.3	129

Source: U.S. Advisory Commission on Intergovernmental Relations, *Special Revenue Sharing: An Analysis of the Administration's Grant Consolidation Proposals*, M-70 (GPO, 1971), p.6.

opposition, however, was ensured by a final consideration: control over pork barrel projects. As the undersecretary of transportation observed: "Our categorical programs are nearer and dearer to Congressmen's hearts than any other. They are the porkiest of the pork, and Congress guards them very jealously."[3] Since even Republicans refused to introduce the administration's transportation bill, hearings were never held on it in either chamber of Congress.

Similarly, the rural development revenue sharing proposal came under vigorous attack from important members of both parties before it was formally sent to Capitol Hill. Leading Republicans, like Senate Minority Leader Hugh Scott of Pennsylvania and Senator John Sherman Cooper of Kentucky, ranking member of the Senate Public Works Committee, opposed consolidation—and what they perceived to be the effective elimination—of the Appalachian Regional Commission into a broadly based rural revenue sharing grant. Supporters of the Agricultural Extension Service mobilized to thwart consolidation of their program as well. Meanwhile, the public interest groups were indifferent or opposed to the president's proposal. The National League of Cities and U. S. Conference of Mayors testified against the proposal at Senate hearings because it placed authority for administering rural development programs in the Agriculture Department rather than in the normally more sympathetic Department of Housing and Urban Development (HUD). They also opposed the plan's distribution of funds to the states rather than directly to municipalities.

Consequently, rural revenue sharing was hardly considered by the House Agriculture Committee, where opposition by outside constituency groups was reinforced by the views of the committee's chairman, Texas Democrat W. R. Poage. On both personal and institutional grounds, Poage staunchly rejected the very concept of block grants as antithetical to the principles of fiscal conservatism and to the interests of Congress. Rather than accept the concept of program consolidation and simplification, the House Agriculture Committee recommended increased funding in existing rural development programs and the establishment of new grant programs for planning, pollution control, and land use.

The Senate Agriculture Committee also rejected the idea of program consolidation, although a coalition of liberal and conservative Democrats did propose that a supplemental rural development "block grant" be appended to existing categoricals as a means of increasing federal spending for rural areas. Even this supplemental block grant was opposed by a combination of liberal opponents of block grants, led by Democratic senator Adlai Stevenson III of Illinois and by Republican fiscal conservatives such as Senators Carl Curtis of Nebraska and Milton Young of North Dakota. Although the Senate adopted the supplemental block grant, it was deleted in the House-Senate conference on the Rural Development Act of 1972.

The Nixon administration's education revenue sharing (ERS) proposals elicited yet another negative response from interest groups and Congress. The liberal chairman of the House Education and Labor Committee complained that special revenue sharing allowed too little federal control over education funds and likened it to "throwing money down ratholes."[4] Others feared that ERS was simply an indirect method of reducing the education budget. "People didn't believe they'd spend the money under ERS," observed one congressional staffer. "They thought it was just a new attempt to subvert the programs." Education interest groups echoed these reactions. The federal relations director of a major education organization remarked frankly in an interview that "our reaction was literally 'screw them.' We weren't going to give it the light of day." So strong were the negative reactions that even many Republicans who had supported education block grants in the 1960s, such as Representative Albert Quie of Minnesota, expressed reservations about the president's revenue sharing approach. "You do not want a flat block grant in education," he stated in an interview.[5]

Given such massive resistance, it is not surprising that ERS was given a dismal reception in Congress. Congressional hearings in 1971 were little more than a lonely soliloquy by the administration on behalf of ERS followed by education interests' chorus of dissent. The administration, however, was unwilling to give up quickly on ERS as it had on transportation and rural development. Following his landslide reelection in 1972, President Nixon sent Congress a proposal similar to ERS, this time labeling it the Better Schools Act.

Despite the presidential victory and administration threats to reject all other options, the congressional response was nearly identical. Only fears of a presidential veto led Congress to enact a "compromise" consolidation of seven minor programs in 1974—at the price of keeping all the major education programs intact. With this small symbolic victory, the president declared success and announced it was "an important first step" toward creation of a genuine education block grant.[6]

Opposition to Block Grants: Theoretical Perspectives

As the negative reactions of influential Republicans like Representative Quie illustrate, many potential supporters of block grants failed to support Nixon's initiatives in the three areas of transportation, rural development, and education. Even staunch conservatives were often ambivalent. Some feared that special revenue sharing lacked adequate financial and programmatic accountability, while others sought to protect their own pet programs from consolidation. Outside of Congress potential allies also failed to support these plans. Members of the intergovernmental lobby—such as National Governors' Conference chairman Arch Moore, a Republican from West Virginia, and spokespersons for the National League of Cities—opposed rural development revenue sharing as a threat to other, more important, interests. Nor did the governors make education revenue sharing a priority; many feared that it might generate dangerous political infighting within their own states.

These patterns of opposition and neglect were consistent with prevailing theories of congressional behavior in the modern decentralized Congress. They suggest that rational, election-seeking members will strongly favor categorical grants over consolidated block grants. Such conclusions are reinforced by the familiar logic of the "iron triangle" model of policymaking, which underscores the difficulties of enacting comprehensive legislation that upsets the policy preferences and established relationships among program specialists within discrete policy subsystems.

The implications of the incentive model of congressional behavior for intergovernmental grants-in-aid were most thoroughly developed by David Mayhew. Members of Congress, writes Mayhew, strive above all for re-election. The means by which they tailor their behavior to this goal are through *advertising*, "any effort to disseminate one's name among constituents in such as fashion as to create a favorable image," and *credit claiming*, "acting so as to generate a belief . . . that one is personally responsible for causing the government . . . to do something." Both advertising and credit claiming rely on "particularized benefits."[7]

Narrow categorical grants permit members of Congress to obtain particularized benefits corresponding to their own constituency needs, and they can do so in such a way that members can be identified with a program for advertising purposes, announcing grant awards and so forth. As Mayhew argues:

> The only benefits intrinsically worth anything . . . are ones that can be packaged. . . . Across policy areas generally, the programmatic mainstay of congressmen is the categorical grant. In fact the categorical grant is for modern Democratic Congresses what rivers and harbors and the tariff were for pre–New Deal Republican Congresses. It supplies goods in small manipulable packets.[8]

Starting from similar premises, Morris Fiorina has identified another factor that tends to reinforce this outcome. An added means by which members of Congress appeal to their constituents, asserts Fiorina, is legislative casework. Members assume an ombudsman role with respect to the bureaucracy, helping voters deal with governmental problems:

> Congressmen . . . earn electoral credits by establishing various programs. . . . At the next stage, aggrieved and/or hopeful constituents petition their congressman to intervene in the complex . . . decision processes of the bureaucracy. The cycle closes when the congressman lends a sympathetic ear, piously denounces the evils of bureaucracy, intervenes in the latter's decisions, and rides a grateful electorate to ever more impressive showings. Congressmen take credit coming and going.[9]

Because of their specificity and complexity, categorical grants are much better designed to enhance bureaucratic accountability to Congress than are block grants, which are more general in nature and administered by means of set formulas. As Fiorina observed:

> We have heard talk about more flexible, less centralized policies [but]
> . . . we should expect . . . little action. . . . To lessen federal control
> over the daily operation of the country is to lessen incumbent
> congressmen's chances of reelection.[10]

In short, block grants pose a threat to congressional behavior, as it is understood through such incentive theories, because they diminish opportunities for advertising, credit claiming, and casework. They do this not only by consolidating many separate pieces of what some have labeled "social pork barrel," but also by decentralizing significant decision-making authority to state and local governments, which, in turn, take credit for their own projects more or less beyond the reach of congressional oversight.

Influential models of the public policy process are equally pessimistic about the politics of block grants. One commonly accepted model emphasizes the role of specialized subunits of government in the formation of public policy. These policy "subsystems" consist of congressional subcommittees, executive bureaus, and affiliated interest groups, arranged in interlocking "triangles" of influence and expertise. They are said to shape the bulk of federal policy, to which Congress as a whole and the president largely defer. Former White House aide Douglass Cater described them this way:

> In one important area of policy after another, substantial efforts to
> exercise power are waged by alliances cutting across the two branches
> of government and including key operatives from the outside. In ef-
> fect, they constitute subgovernments of Washington comprising the
> expert, the interested, and the engaged. The subgovernment's ten-
> dency is to strive to become self-sustaining in control of power in its
> own sphere.[11]

Categorical grants are generally consistent with the dynamics of policy subsystems because their narrow design can be contained with a single policy community. The interests of each partner within the subsystem can be served in the process. Benefits can be targeted to specific clienteles. Members of Congress can tailor programs to their particular constituencies or to the interests of particular groups associated with a subcommittee. And each agency's penchant for a stable and predictable program environment can be satisfied.

Block grants, in contrast, challenge the "iron triangles" on all three sides. By consolidating individually funded programs into a single authorization spanning a broad functional area, block grants eliminate the guarantee of benefits to specific clienteles. Similarly, members of Congress lose control over programs as more players are brought into decisions, and as authority to allocate resources is decentralized to subnational governments. Executive agencies experience a similar loss of program control, along with the specter of elimination or reduced budgets and authority as functions are reorganized and devolved.

Hugh Heclo and others have rightly criticized this subsystem model as exaggerated and simplistic. Heclo argues that most policy arenas are much more porous and open to interested and informed external opinion than the enclosed and autonomous "subgovernment" model suggests.[12] Even with this important modification, however, the implications for grant consolidation remain relatively unchanged. Genuine and sustained policy influence continues to be shaped by unevenly distributed incentives for participation in policy debates—incentives that favor concentrated attention by the interest groups, agencies, and members of Congress most deeply affected by a given policy decision. Such incentives are not deterministic; they may be overcome by the power of new ideas, new participants, and new circumstances. But they do establish certain predispositions toward particular outcomes and the views of particular actors.

The response to education revenue sharing underscored the workings of an active subsystem in education. Major education groups met two or three times a week to compare notes on administration activities, funding, politics, and other common interests. In the process, groups received considerable assistance from allies within the Office of Education. As one lobbyist recalled: "I never knew what my mail would bring. I would receive something from the HEW mail and see the schedule of a secret meeting. . . . These people [in the agency] were unsung heroes. They were providing us with all sorts of inside information. When a meeting took place, it was almost as if we were present." Congressional staff members also reported seeing "those [reform] proposals before the Commissioner [of Education] did." Such staffers considered themselves allied with the bureaucrats who were hostile toward ERS. "Most of the career people considered it as a means to abolish their jobs," said one.[13]

Block Grant Enactments and Their Implications for Policymaking

Despite the sharply negative response to most of Nixon's block grant proposals and the pessimistic implications of the policy models discussed earlier, not all the special revenue sharing proposals met with failure. Although significantly modified from what the president proposed, two major block grants were enacted by Congress during the 93d Congress: the Comprehensive Employment and Training Act of 1973 (CETA) and the community development block grant (CDBG) program, established in 1974.

On the surface, the success of these enactments appears to be inconsistent with the policy models described above. Indeed, a careful examination of the politics of these block grants suggests that such models underestimate the importance of ideas and a normative commitment to making "good policy" within the legislative process.[14] Equally important, however, the politics of these programs underscores the fragmented character of the policy process during the 1970s—a fragmentation that is largely consistent with the rational choice and subsystem models. In particular, the enactment process reflected the peculiar political composition and programmatic experiences of these two political arenas.

Factors Promoting Block Grant Enactments

Both CDBG and CETA enjoyed considerable support from members of Congress, relevant professionals, and powerful interest groups. This support was consistent with but independent of President Nixon's federalism initiatives. Influential members of key congressional committees from both sides of the aisle actively supported, rather than opposed, grant consolidation for political and policy reasons. In part, they were responding to active lobbying by local government officials, who were among the chief clients of programs in these areas. Moreover, they shared in an emerging consensus among policy professionals that existing programs had been unsuccessful and that block grants could achieve the relevant policy objectives more effectively. Because some important members of Congress—especially Senate liberals—remained protective of the individual grants that they had sponsored, the ultimate block grant legislation was modified to retain greater federal oversight and control. But given the level of support for the block grant concept within these two policy arenas, the most interesting question was why it took so long to enact them rather than why they were passed at all.

A TROUBLED CATEGORICAL HERITAGE. By 1970 disenchantment with categorical programs had led many individuals familiar with community development and job training programs to support the concept of grant consolidation and decentralization. These sentiments were shared not only by officials in the Nixon administration but also by many program administrators, grant recipients, academic experts, and members of Congress. Over time, this dissatisfaction became increasingly evident in both trade and scholarly writings about these programs, in conversations with administrators and participants in the programs, and in the actions of relevant interest groups and public officials. More important, it was expressed in a series of gradual policy initiatives that moved in the direction of block grants even before the Nixon administration launched its own proposals.

The evolution toward grant reform was particularly evident in manpower training. Apart from venerable programs for vocational education and unemployment compensation, employment and training programs were mostly very recent products of the 1960s. In that brief decade a rapid-fire series of concerns with "structural unemployment," automation, and persistent poverty produced a sudden proliferation of new employment and training programs. By 1969 fourteen different federal agencies were involved in operating seventeen separate job training programs administered through thousands of contracts with local governments and nonprofit agencies. Although goals and clients frequently overlapped, each program had its own administrative structure, funded different sponsors at the local level, and utilized a range of different job enhancement techniques.[15]

Nationally, this complex of programs meant that Congress and federal agencies often had little clear understanding of how individual programs were being implemented locally or related to each other, despite sometimes strenuous and even intrusive efforts to find out. Locally, the situation created problems for both program administration and service delivery. As Garth Mangum summarized the situation:

> The different sources of funds posed serious, if not insurmountable, obstacles to development of integrated local manpower programs. . . .
> The eligibility rules, application procedures, allocation formulas, expiration dates, and contracting arrangements varied as widely as funding sources.[16]

Political problems added to administrative ones. Many mayors became embroiled in bitter disputes over what they perceived as politicization of job training and other new social programs administered by local community groups. They began demanding more control over these programs.[17] Other mayors were frustrated by their inability to coordinate conflicting federal programs or to focus them on local priority needs.

The emerging science of program evaluation exacerbated the political problems. Newly refined and developed evaluation techniques like cost-benefit analysis produced little concrete evidence of positive program results—results that might have increased tolerance for administrative difficulties. On the contrary, some programs could demonstrate no lasting benefits at all, much less cost-effective results.[18]

Beginning in 1967 the Johnson administration sought to redress these concerns through administrative reforms. It launched two separate efforts to improve the coordination and performance of job training programs within the framework of existing categorical structures. The cooperative area manpower planning system (CAMPS) and the concentrated employment program (CEP) both endeavored to overlay existing programs with new planning and administrative bodies intended to bring together disparate program administrators and services. Unfortunately, these processes had little authority to influence categorical funding decisions and were often little more than "makework projects."[19] Politically, however, the planning and consultation processes were helpful in drawing more elected officials directly into manpower policy issues and helping to mobilize a constituency for reform.

Thus, when President Nixon was inaugurated in 1969, growing numbers of job training professionals both inside and outside of government had embraced a structural reform approach. They had concluded that legislative consolidation of narrowly specified training programs and decentralization of program control offered the best hope for improving program performance and enhancing the adaptation of manpower services to local labor market conditions. One prominent group of employment professionals on the National Manpower Policy Task Force declared:

> There is a pressing need to overhaul these categorical and disjointed efforts. . . . Consolidation . . . is an important first step in improving [their] effectiveness. . . . Government roles must take into account the inherent limits of the federal government . . . and steps taken by state and local governments to improve their capabilities.[20]

Through the National League of Cities and U.S. Conference of Mayors, local elected officials also expressed their support for a job training block grant and emphasized the "urgent need for the coordination of local manpower programs."[21] Even some members of Congress began to enunciate support for grant reform in this area. Although they differed in the programs included and their degree of decentralization, two bills consolidating job training programs were introduced in Congress in 1969 by members of the House Education and Labor Committee.

As indicated earlier, this emerging policy consensus was evident in the Nixon administration's initial block grant proposal in 1969. The Manpower Training Act of 1969 was developed primarily by specialists at the Labor Department, and its features reflected that fact. Not only did it consolidate almost all of the principal training programs of the 1960s into a single block grant to state governments, but it contained "good management" features shaped by careerists rather than political officials. These features included incentives for effective state administration and for regional cooperation, innovations like a computerized job bank and countercyclical funding during economic downturns, and a multiyear phase-in of decentralization to promote state and local "capacity building" and a smooth administrative transition.

A similar consensus for reform was building in community development, growing largely out of dissatisfaction with the two most prominent programs in this area, urban renewal and model cities. Urban renewal was the oldest and largest federal program for community development and it was the first to turn sour. First established in 1949, the urban renewal program was intended to enhance urban housing and economic development by eliminating "slums and blight." Although the program was initially popular with civic leaders and businesspeople, opposition to it grew rapidly in disrupted communities during the 1950s and 1960s, until the program often became a political liability to political leaders associated with it. Liberals at the grass-roots level condemned the program for destroying low-income housing on behalf of downtown businesses, and some derisively dubbed the program "Negro removal." Conservatives, on the other hand, condemned the urban renewal program for waste and inefficiency. One conservative critic called it a "thundering failure . . . a regressive program." Its results were "negligible," wrote Martin Anderson, while its costs were "high."[22] For their part, local officials condemned the program's complexity and sought to obtain the desired federal funds under less convoluted and politically risky conditions.

In part, the model cities program was developed in 1966 to address some of the problems apparent in urban renewal and other rigid (though less controversial) categorical programs. Model cities was originally intended to enhance program coordination at the national and local levels and to provide a source of flexible funding to cities under the auspices of the mayor. As Bernard Frieden and Marshall Kaplan observed, some early supporters of the program "saw it as a step in the direction of block grants."[23] Although model cities became popular with many mayors as a source of new funds, the hoped-for breadth and flexibility were diminished during the enactment process as Congress "redefined the program to make it another grant-in-aid to the cities, not the unifier of all other federal aid programs."[24]

Once in operation, the program soon became immersed in bitter conflicts between mayors and local neighborhood groups. Partly to deal with these conflicts, planning and citizen participation requirements mounted, and the program drifted even farther from the goal of flexible funding. The federal paperwork requirements of the model cities program, like the urban renewal program, soon became a major source of local complaints.

By the late 1960s, there was broad agreement on the need to restructure community development programs in favor of more flexible federal assistance. As a lobbyist for local urban renewal agencies commented in an interview, "The old programs were done, discredited. Something had to take their place."[25]

Initial reform attempts centered on the model cities program. After briefly considering phasing it out as a symbol of the Great Society's failings, the Nixon administration concluded that the original goals of the model cities program were consistent with the Republican party's philosophy. Efforts were made to enlarge local discretion and coordination under the program in 1969 and 1970. Most important were the experiments, called "planned variations," which were carried out in twenty "model cities" and were designed to grant additional authority to local chief executives, reduce federal regulations, and expand the program beyond model neighborhoods to include entire cities. Such changes, announced Housing Secretary George Romney, would "go a long way" toward testing the feasibility of block grants.[26]

Local government officials supported these developments and urged even stronger action. By 1970 organizations representing the nation's mayors were "aggressively pushing for block grant authority."[27] These sentiments for reform stimulated considerable interest on Capitol Hill, and before the president's special revenue sharing initiative, congressional efforts were proceeding so rapidly that the Nixon administration was reported to be "in danger of losing legislative initiative in housing and urban programs."[28] Staff members of the Senate Housing Subcommittee had begun earnest consultations with mayoral and community development groups on legislation to consolidate and streamline community development programs. In the House, members of the Subcommittee on Housing released a report in late 1970 denouncing the "piecemeal" scope, "delay," and "excessive red tape" of existing programs.[29] The subcommittee report recommended altering community development programs to provide "maximum flexibility for local elected officials . . . within broad national guidelines," and members began work on block grant legislation.

SUBSYSTEM INFLUENCE. The growing consensus for reform in community development and job training was reinforced by a second important factor promoting the enactment of block grants in these two fields: support from major interests within the respective policy systems. This was particularly true in community development, where the principal clients and beneficiaries of existing programs were the nation's mayors. In contrast to block grants in education and rural development, which would have transferred authority from influential clienteles to generalist elected officials, the community development block grant gave mayors additional power to pursue their principal goals for urban policy.

Although housing agency officials and local community groups were active in the community development subsystem, the mayors had the most influence in the policy community during the late 1960s, especially among members of the House Banking and Urban Affairs Committee. Some of the mayors had been active in urban renewal programs from the beginning, but others became increasingly involved during the 1960s as community development programs grew more controversial. This trend was consciously accelerated by federal policies like model cities and planned variations, which were intended to increase direct mayoral involvement in community development programs so as to promote greater coordination and policy commitment at the local level. Finally, mayoral influence in Washington was heightened during this period by what proved to be a temporary merger of the two major urban interest groups: the National League of Cities and the U.S. Conference of Mayors. The resulting impact on policy was such that the staff director of the House Housing Subcommittee traced his committee's block grant proposal not to the Nixon administration, but to "a series of dinners I had with [the deputy mayor of

New York]. As we sat and talked about what mayors needed most . . . we arrived at the concept of a block grant."[30]

The legislative subsystem in employment and training was more complex, and partly as a result the final legislation was somewhat less responsive to the preferences of state and local governments. As their name implies, the House and Senate Labor committees had jurisdiction over a range of labor-management issues and, particularly on the Democratic side, had developed close ties with organized labor. In addition, especially in the Senate, many members had close political relationships with minority and community groups representing clients of specialized job training programs. Thus state and local government officials shared influence and access in the policy community with the beneficiaries and protectors of specific categorical programs.

State and especially local government involvement in training programs, as in community development programs, was deliberately stimulated by federal policies. Indeed, some came to view the CAMPS process as primarily an exercise in constituency building by the Nixon administration for a manpower block grant, a "part of the legislative strategy," according to one county official.[31] Moreover, Labor Department grants funded seminars for mayors on manpower planning and the creation of permanent manpower planning staffs reporting to elected officials. One ranking Labor Department official likened the process to creating an uncontrolled political monster:

> Probably the strongest interest groups have been the PIGs [Public Interest Groups], and that was sort of creating our own Frankenstein. We had used them in the voluntary CAMPS program. We'd give them funds to hire planning staffs and this built up a strong infrastructure. We also had policy assistance contracts with the various PIGs to provide a mechanism for educating and sensitizing officials on the new initiative. But yes, we were creating a constituency and an adversary group prior to CETA.[32]

Factors Inhibiting Enactment

Given the important forces propelling creation of these two block grants, it is not surprising that CETA and CDBG were ultimately enacted. They were major legislative priorities of the Nixon administration, and they enjoyed considerable support in Congress and from the principal interest groups affected. Moreover, the block grant concept in these two fields was endorsed by many policy professionals as an appropriate remedy for implementation problems and perceived policy failures in existing programs. In short, unlike in education or transportation, block grant proposals in community development and job training were not dismissed by the established policy community as an inappropriate or threatening policy transformation imposed by a hostile or untrustworthy administration.

In light of this, the interesting analytical question is not "how were these block grants enacted?" but "why did it take so long?" It took more than four years to enact a job training block grant, from the time it was first proposed in 1969 to the final signing of CETA in late 1973. The community development block grant program was actually signed into law by President Gerald Ford in August 1974, a few days after Nixon resigned from office.

These delays were not the inevitable result of intractable opposition to block grants. In fact, major grant reform legislation was almost passed in both areas much sooner (see legislative chronologies in tables 3-2 and 3-3). A manpower training block grant could have been signed into law in 1970 if President Nixon had then been willing (as eventually he was) to accept the creation of a federally funded public service employment program and the retention of more categorical grants than the administration preferred. Similarly, a community development block grant was almost enacted in 1972 as part of an omnibus housing and community development bill. Although it was kept from final consideration by the full House in the waning days of the 92d Congress, this failure was mainly attributable to other elements of this large and complex bill.

These two near-misses underscore the difficulties of enacting comprehensive reform legislation in Congress. As a rule, it is easier to obstruct legislation than to pass it, even when such measures enjoy support from key sources. It is not enough to build a supportive coalition for a policy concept. Majority support must be garnered for each important legislative provision, even though supporters themselves may differ strongly over key details in the structure, funding, and operation of the program.

The conflicts over block grants among major political actors were extensive, and many were common to both programs. They can be classified into two main types: policy differences and contests for power. Policy differences arose over which programs should be consolidated, what residual level of federal control should be retained, which recipients should be au-

Table 3-2. *Events Leading to Enactment of the Community Development Block Grant Program, 1966–74*

Date	Event
1966	Model cities program established to coordinate urban programs
1970	Planned variations program instituted by Nixon administration to improve model cities
	Mayors urge reform of urban program in national municipal policy
	House Subcommittee on Housing creates study panels to explore block grants and other program reforms
	Outlines of HUD proposal for an urban block grant developed
1971	Community development revenue sharing legislation formulated by Nixon administration
1972	Senate passes a community development block grant in omnibus housing bill
	Omnibus housing and urban development bill, including a community development block grant, is blocked by House Rules Committee
1973	President Nixon proposes the better communities act, special revenue sharing bill
	President impounds housing and community development funds
1974	Senate passes housing and community development bill, including block grant title opposed by administration
	House passes compromise community development block grant in omnibus housing and community development bill
	President Ford signs community development block grant legislation

tomatically eligible for funding, and how much funding should be provided. Power contests included partisan differences between the Democratic Congress and Republican administration, personality disputes within the Congress, and turf battles within the administration, among congressional committees, and between state and local governments. These two conflict types are analytically distinct and are treated independently below, but in practice they often overlapped: policy disputes do not occur in a political vacuum. This was evident in the often bitter disputes among state and local jurisdictions over program formulas and operating authority.

POLICY DIFFERENCES. Despite considerable agreement about the general merits of grant reform in these two fields, there were limits to the degree of consensus. Indeed, block grant advocates often differed strenuously

Table 3-3. *Events Leading to Enactment of the Comprehensive Employment and Training Act, 1962–73*

Date	Event
1962	Enactment of the Manpower Development and Training Act (MDTA)
1964	Enactment of the Economic Opportunity Act (EOA)
1967	Incremental efforts begin to reform categorical job training programs: concentrated employment program (CEP) and coordinated area manpower planning system (CAMPS)
1969	Academic specialists on National Manpower Policy Task Force endorse reform
	Representative William Steiger introduces a state-oriented block grant: Comprehensive Manpower Act (H.R. 10908)
	Representative James O'Hara introduces a nationally oriented consolidation bill: Manpower Act (H.R. 11620)
	Nixon administration proposes a job training block grant bill: Manpower Training Act (S. 2838)
1970	Senate passes omnibus manpower bill with public employment, categorical, and block grant provisions: Employment and Training Opportunities Act (S. 2867)
	House passes compromise manpower reform bill with modest public employment title: Comprehensive Manpower Act (H.R. 19519)
	President Nixon vetoes conference bill patterned after Senate legislation
1971	President Nixon proposes manpower revenue sharing legislation (H.R. 6181)
	Each amendment to substitute a revenue sharing–like block grant for temporary public employment program fails on the House floor
	Emergency Employment Act signed by President Nixon
1973	Nixon administration attempts to implement manpower revenue sharing through administrative means
	Senate passes separate block grant and public employment programs in a conciliatory gesture
	House passes compromise proposal linking public employment and block grant programs
	President Nixon signs the Comprehensive Employment and Training Act

over a proposed program's basic features: the funding, the specific categorical grants to be consolidated, the amount of residual control by the federal government over recipients' use of funds, and the level of government that should be eligible for automatic formula grants. Reaching majority agreement on each and every one of these basic issues proved to be a difficult task.

In community development, vigorous battles were fought to keep certain programs out of the community development block grant. Representative William Widnall of New Jersey, the ranking Republican on the House Banking Committee, refused to sponsor the administration's special revenue sharing plan until the large water and sewer program was removed. Widnall originally had sponsored the program in 1965 to address the needs of rapidly expanding suburban communities. He was appalled that a Republican administration would propose to fold it in with larger programs aimed at distressed urban areas, effectively distributing most of the funds to big-city Democratic mayors.

Similar problems emerged over the inclusion of appropriations for model cities, which up to then were distributed through discretionary grants to a select number of cities. Communities with large model cities grants would lose funds under any conceivable block grant formula, and for three years they fought a rearguard action against including model cities. After threatening to take all actions to save the program "short of kidnapping Patty Hearst," they settled for a special "hold harmless" formula provision that gave them extra funds.[33]

Significant as they were, these disputes over which programs to consolidate in community development were modest compared with the battles fought over this issue in employment and training. The differences are obvious in the results. Both the model cities program and the water and sewer program were eventually included in the final community development block grant. By contrast, CETA was enacted as a "hybrid" block grant. One portion of the program was a genuine consolidated grant, but it was surrounded by other legislative titles that created or preserved separate authorizations for public service employment, the Job Corps, and special programs for Native Americans, migrant workers, and certain categories of young people.

As with the water and sewer program, much of the opposition stemmed from particular legislators' close identification with programs slated for consolidation. The chairman of the Senate Labor and Human Resources Committee, Democratic senator Gaylord Nelson of Wisconsin, was a former governor who supported the block grant concept. Yet he was fiercely protective of the "green thumb" program he had sponsored in 1965 to provide employment opportunities to older workers. Similarly, Senator Jacob Javits of New York, the ranking Republican on the committee, worked to preserve the "special impact" program for jobless inner-city youths. Other members wanted to protect other favored programs or clienteles. Outside groups like labor unions fought strenuously to preserve apprenticeship training programs operated by union locals. All were motivated by a common fear: that guaranteed funding for their particular program would evaporate once program decisions were turned over to state and local governments.

Thus job training was not exempt from the categorical incentives that dominated politics in policy fields like education. But preserving old or established priorities was not the only hurdle confronting a manpower block grant. Equally important was congressional interest in establishing a new responsibility for the federal government: providing public service jobs. By 1970 many leading Democrats in Congress made public service jobs their number one priority, even as manpower reformers and the Nixon administration focused on consolidating existing grants. Because the president strongly opposed such public employment, a stalemate developed that took four years to break. A compromise was almost reached in 1970, when the House passed a bill—with the administration's backing—to consolidate most manpower programs into a single block grant and to establish a modest public jobs program for training participants. This compromise fell apart, however, when the House-Senate conference committee overreached and adopted Senate provisions that limited the block grant's scope, preserved many categorical programs, and expanded the public employment program. The president vetoed this bill in the waning hours of 1970.

Bitter feelings and hardened positions produced a three-year hiatus in serious block grant negotiations. In response to rapidly climbing unemployment, the president reluctantly agreed to a temporary public jobs bill in 1971, but he opposed renewing it when it came up for renewal in 1973. Then, after months of compromise and wrangling, Congress and the president agreed to final legislation that was not unlike the basic outlines of the bill passed three years before. It was a hybrid block grant with "something for everybody." The president got his block grant; categorical sponsors preserved a range of special programs outside of the consolidated grant; and public jobs supporters got renewal of public service jobs. It was the ultimate form of compromise.

FEDERAL CONTROL. Disputes over which programs to consolidate into proposed block grants indicate that legislators in the fields of community development and job training were not immune to the political attractions of categorical grants that Mayhew identified. Suspicions in Congress about proposals limiting its authority were equally evident in the arguments involving how much federal control should be retained over recipients' use of block grant funds. In fact, the mechanisms of legislative oversight and the degree of residual federal authority proved to be the most salient topics of debate in congressional deliberations over CDBG.

The issue of federal control was raised immediately upon introduction of the president's plan for urban revenue sharing. The revenue sharing concept was premised on providing "automatic" grants to eligible communities, with few federal planning or reporting requirements or standards governing the use of funds. So long as federal aid was expended on eligible projects, funds could be used in virtually any manner a community desired.

Such lax controls struck even many block grant advocates in Congress as unacceptable. While granting further flexibility, most congressional adherents sought to ensure that depressed neighborhoods would receive some if not most of the benefits of the program, that certain traditional activities like slum clearance would be continued, and that communities would report their activities and remain accountable to Congress for their use of federal funds. As George Gross, chief counsel of the House Housing Subcommittee and a leading advocate of block grants, exclaimed, "Revenue sharing was never seriously considered. The *idea* of just sending out money and saying, 'just use it for whatever you want so long as it's legal!'"[34]

Senator Robert Taft Jr. of Ohio and other Republicans dismissed the president's approach, believing that "strong federal directives" were a "necessity for fulfillment of the federal responsibility to the taxpayers." Indeed, Taft argued that "community development is one of the least suitable . . . programs . . . for a totally 'hands off' revenue sharing approach" because it deals with "problems of economic and racial integration that have proved so difficult for localities to handle."[35]

Even local government officials supported stronger federal program restrictions than those contained in community development revenue sharing (CDRS). This position sprang from the mayors' recognition that certain kinds of federal requirements offered them political protection when making unpopular decisions. According to one League of Cities aide, "some mayors feared [CDRS] would be a political nightmare."

Retaining adequate federal control was also a prevalent concern in job training. Much of this came from intractable opponents of the block grant concept, who saw no way to reconcile national policy objectives (and their own control over categorical programs) with the decentralized block grant structure. As one community activist declared in hearings over manpower reform: "Block grants to state and local governmental entities [are] an open invitation to socially irresponsible political leaders to act even more irresponsibly."[36]

These concerns distressed senior members of the Senate Manpower Subcommittee, who sought to reconcile the conflicting desires for greater decentralization within a framework of federal control. As Senator Javits remarked during the first Senate hearing on manpower reform:

> The thing that bedevils us here is the fundamental question of government relations. . . . Suppose we get crossed up? . . . We know that for all practical purposes a State or locality could ruin a program. . . . [We must] retain the ability to go in and do what needs to be done.[37]

In both fields these basic concerns were finally addressed through carefully crafted compromises and artful ambiguity. Complex planning and application procedures—hundreds of pages long in the case of the urban renewal and model cities programs—were streamlined and simplified. Instead, a brief application outlining each city's needs, objectives, planned activities, and expected costs was required. The major emphasis, however, was placed on an audit of actual activities undertaken. To give flexibility to recipient jurisdictions, the legislation included a broad list of eligible activities. In addition, three potentially contradictory national goals for the program were specified: to assist poor and moderate income residents, to eliminate slums and blight, and to address emergency situations. Federal authorities would not be able to second-guess the local use of funds to address these objectives unless the use was "plainly inconsistent" with one of these goals.

Such provisions maximized local discretion. Senate liberals had wanted 80 percent of block grant funds to be spent on low-income areas in each community, but this requirement was deleted in the final bill. Instead, the bill's language was ambiguous: localities should place "maximum feasible priority" on serving low- and moderate-income residents. This compromise promoted final passage of the bill because each side could read it as a victory for greater or lesser discretion. Subsequent regulations and program reauthorizations, however, were plagued by renewed battles over the meaning of this vague language and whether recipients had complied with its provisions.

In employment and training this issue was resolved through a different sort of compromise. As discussed above, CETA was enacted as a "hybrid" block grant, with numerous categorical programs retained. Although the block grant title resembled CDBG in its broad discretion and use of streamlined application, reporting, and auditing requirements, the specialized programs retained a federal emphasis on particular activities and target populations that Congress was unwilling to abandon to the local political fray.

FUNDING ISSUES. A final set of policy disputes centered on program funding. The White House and Congress disagreed about overall funding levels. In addition, state and local governments fought bitterly—among themselves and through members of Congress—over funding formulas and the types of jurisdictions that would be eligible for automatic entitlements under the formulas.

Throughout the debates over grant reform proposals, the Nixon administration consistently sought to restrict levels of funding for both community development and job training programs. The most important dispute grew out of the administration's aggressive use of program impoundments during 1973. In order to force congressional action on CDRS, the administration requested no new funds for community development in the fiscal 1974 budget. Similarly, several controversial housing programs were suspended, including public housing and low-income subsidy programs. All together, more than $1 billion was involved. As the president's budget message explained, the intention was "to accelerate major reforms"; once Congress accepted the administration's proposals for housing vouchers and CD revenue sharing, "new funds [could] begin to flow."[38]

Rather than forcing Congress to adopt the administration's proposals quickly, the controversial impoundment strategy delayed progress for months. In Congress even many Republicans were angered by the president's approach, which "almost smacks of blackmail." Among the mayors, many felt the tactic gave credence to suspicions that New Federalism was a ruse for spending cuts—a "Trojan horse," filled with "broken promises."[39]

Equally disruptive were disputes among states, municipalities, and counties over which units of government would qualify for automatic grants under a block grant formula. A critical issue in CDBG was how cities that had received large amounts of categorical aid would be treated under the programs slated for consolidation. Many such cities would inevitably lose funds under any kind of formula allocation, even if funds were given only to other equally deserving communities. Although this situation led some cities to oppose any kind of formula distribution of block grant funds, most of the losers accepted the need for a formula and were placated by inclusion of a "hold harmless" provision that temporarily provided larger payments to former grant recipients and eased the pain of transition.

Community development and job training programs were also beset by disputes among different levels of government over formula entitlements. States generally argued that all block grant funds should be sent to them, leaving them with the decision of which localities should receive various amounts of funding. This position had strong support in constitutional theory but little support in the political arena. The administration originally favored such an approach in its initial manpower block grant proposal, but it soon abandoned it as politically unrealistic when the states proved politically incapable of muscling this position through Congress. Local governments successfully argued that they had had the most experience in administering the programs slated for consolidation and contained the highest concentrations of jobless workers most in need of training programs. They also proved to have the strongest political relationships to members of the Democratically controlled Congress.

Governors, in contrast, were often slow to organize, take positions, and advocate them in Congress until legislation was complete. Thus it came as no surprise that, even with administration backing, an amendment to increase the role of states in the 1970 manpower training reform bill failed badly on the Senate floor by a vote of 28 to 46.[40] In future legislation the administration refused to champion a stronger state role. According to the states' lobbyist on manpower programs, when CETA was finally enacted in 1973, the states were consigned largely to "the jackrabbits and the sage"—controlling funding, planning, and administration only in the least densely populated areas of most states.[41]

In CDBG, the most bitter disputes over funding allocations occurred among local governments themselves—especially between cities and counties. During the course of three years, counties waged an often bitter but eventually successful battle for inclusion into the CDBG formula. "The mayors saw us as ripping off the cities," observed the counties' lobbyist.[42] In fact, some urban lobbyists alleged that including counties in the formula was just part of the Nixon administration's political strategy to "get the money to the suburbs where its political strength was."[43]

The counties countered such objections with a sound case and excellent political tactics. Certain "urban counties," they pointed out, had many of the developmental problems of cities and performed many of the same functions and responsibilities. In certain states, in fact, counties were more significant units of government than cities. Politically, while the cities carried the ball on enacting the block grant, the counties focused exclusively on gaining inclusion for qualified members into the formula. This they did brilliantly. For example, in the House Banking Committee they devised a successful formula amendment under which counties with a population of 200,000 or above became eligible for automatic formula entitlements, while cities qualified at the 50,000 level. As the counties' lobbyist explained:

> There's nothing magic about the 200,000 eligibility level. We looked at the districts of the members and calculated how high we'd have to go to get a majority. That's how we did it. We needed 21, I think. It was Henry Reuss. 200,000 was just enough to include him.[44]

POWER CONTESTS. Policy disputes were not the only obstacles to the enactment of block grants. In the ego-driven world of congressional politics, ruffled feathers had to be smoothed and turf fights waged. The most notable example was the literal scuttling of a community development block grant in 1972 because of jealous opposition from House Banking Committee chairman Wright Patman, a Democrat from Texas. Like many other senior committee chairmen, Patman believed the very concept of a block grant infringed on his congressional prerogatives. More important, he used the legislation to carry on a "vendetta" against the chairman and members of the Housing Subcommittee. For years he had resented this subcommittee's unique autonomy, resources, and activism. The community development legislation gave him an opportunity to strike back. Using his powers as chairman of the full committee, he delayed considering the housing bill for months, then proceeded to consider its hundreds of pages line by line. Despite appeals from the administration and other members of the House, he did not report the bill from committee until the end of the 92d Congress, when the leadership refused to bring it to floor in the hectic final days before adjournment.

In a more widely recognized conflict, both community development and CETA were sidetracked for much of 1971, 1972, and 1973 by the bitter battles between Congress and the president over funding, vetoes, and impoundments. In the case of CETA, congressional Democrats "badly misjudged the President's mind in 1970," provoking a veto by giving the president too much public employment and too little reform. Two years of legislative work were wasted. "After that, tempers had to cool down" on both sides—a process that took almost two years.[45]

Impoundments of housing community development funds provoked similar distrust on the congressional side, and personality disputes between leading actors in the White House, the Department of Housing and Urban Affairs (HUD), and Capitol Hill aggravated tensions. When the administration suspended or froze over a billion dollars' worth of urban renewal and housing grants, Congress reacted strongly and negatively. Far from hastening the enactment of a community development block grant, as the administration had hoped, the impoundments encouraged Congress to hold the urban block grant hostage in return for resumed funding of the housing programs.[46] Before initiating hearings on new development legislation, the Senate held "oversight" hearings in which members blasted the housing moratorium. By the end of 1973, Senate Democrats were receding from the compromises they had made in the 1972 bill.

This situation finally eased when the Watergate crisis forced Nixon to replace White House aides John Ehrlichman and H. R. Haldeman with Melvin Laird, a respected former member of Congress; the prickly secretary of HUD, George Romney, was replaced by James Lynn. Because of the housing moratorium, Lynn encountered significant resistance from Senate Democrats at his confirmation hearing. Once approved, however, he overcame congressional distrust by working closely and directly with important members of the House. "Lynn was extremely popular in the House," said one key congressional staffer, "and he spent literally ninetenths of 1974 on the Hill negotiating in members' offices." His efforts were aided by the constructive and professional attitude of Democratic representative Thomas Ashley of Ohio, who led the fight to forge community development and housing legislation in both 1972 and 1974 and who "genuinely believed in the block grant concept."[47]

Block Grants and Political Fragmentation in the 1970s

No sequence of specific policy initiatives better illustrates the pervasive fragmentation of the national policymaking process in the 1970s than Richard Nixon's diverse proposals on special revenue sharing. The president proposed block grants in six functional areas, yet he obtained only two. Both of these enactments were passed only after being significantly modified. In the end, despite presidential backing, each case of failure or success was ultimately determined by the peculiar alignment of interests, actors, and program experiences within each policy arena.

This was not for want of presidential effort and resources. Nixon did all he could to raise the salience of these proposals—to elevate them from arcane matters of interest to a few specialists to integral, visible elements of his domestic agenda. During his "imperial presidency," as it was later called, he also brought considerable resources to bear on behalf of his objectives. He enjoyed popular support for most of his presidency, and he benefited from public dissatisfaction with existing programs. He took unprecedented steps to manipulate the federal budget on behalf of his policy objectives, and he enjoyed strong support from the increasingly influential intergovernmental lobby.

Yet in the fields of education, rural development, law enforcement, and transportation, all of these resources proved inadequate to overcome the forces of fragmentation represented by the subsystem and rational choice models of the policy process. In fact, the legislative histories of education and transportation revenue sharing came very close to what the analysts of subsystem politics would predict. These were close-knit policy communities dominated by program specialists, both in and out of government. These specialists viewed the president's special revenue sharing proposals as threats to their policy concerns and interests, and they rallied to defend the categorical programs. Interest group and agency defenders of categorical programs found a ready audience in Congress in all of these areas, where the electorally motivated "categorical imperative" was alive and well. As the ranking House Republican on the Education Subcommittee observed: "Categorization is inherent in the system, really. Members like to make announcements of programs and projects. With a block grant, someone else makes the announcement."[48]

On the surface, the enactment of CETA and CDBG would appear inconsistent with these models of the policy process and would seem to challenge the depth of fragmentation in the system. But a closer examination of the politics of the programs reveals that these outcomes were surprisingly consistent with sophisticated models of congressional and subsystem behavior.

The community development and employment and training communities were not tightly closed subsystems, operating in a policy vacuum impervious to presidential and public influence. Both were open to outside influences and novel ideas. The supporters of grant consolidation, however, were not dependent on outsiders calling for rationality in a wilderness of opposition. Support for block grants reflected the consensus of opinion among insiders—professionals in both fields whose views provided cues for key policymakers. Job training and especially community development were fields where major groups within the subsystem strongly advocated block grants. Apart from these two fields, one would be hard pressed to find another policy arena where elected state and local officials, as opposed to functional bureaucracies, were viewed by Congress as the key program beneficiaries and where relevant committees considered them the major reference group.

As for the categorical imperative, these successes demonstrate that it is not the sole determinant of policy outcomes. Members of Congress respond to public policy concerns as well as electoral incentives. Their strong dissatisfaction with the past performance of community development and employment and training programs had eroded incentives for retaining them in their existing form. Many members seemed more interested in *avoiding blame* for prior failures than in *claiming credit* for often questionable program benefits. Such distancing opened the door for members who wanted to reform existing programs to promote better performance.

Nonetheless, categorical incentives were not entirely absent. They were evident at various stages throughout the process. The Senate's manpower reform bill of 1970 was so heavily categorized that President Nixon vetoed it. Even the final CETA bill was a "hybrid" block grant; only 42 percent of the funds appropriated to CETA in its first full year in operation were allocated to the block grant portion of the bill, and this proportion declined steadily over time.[49] In community development, the ranking Banking Committee Republican rebelled at sponsoring the administration's block grant legislation until his favorite program—water and sewer grants—was removed from the bill. Likewise, many supporters of the model cities program vigorously fought its inclusion in the block grant until the very end, when the program's authority was scheduled to terminate.

Thus even the successful enactment of block grants had much to do with the distinctive characteristics of the two policy arenas. Because of these internal forces, some participants claimed that these block grants would have passed even without the president's support. As the League of Cities lobbyist said in the case of CDBG:

It almost passed without the administration. There was never any concerted opposition to the block grant, if you stripped away the politics of Nixon's New Federalism. Most of the opposition came from the stinko placed on it by Nixon.[50]

This was strictly a minority view. Most participants gave the president considerable credit for placing the block grant concept squarely on the agenda and keeping it there once obstacles were encountered. But there is no question that in community development and job training serious work was under way on developing block grant legislation in both Congress and the bureaucracy before the president's initiative was announced. Once the president became involved in the process, the limits of his influence were also made abundantly clear: his inability to obtain legislation on his own terms led to conflict, stalemate, delay, and eventually, substantial compromises.

In short, during the 1970s the policy system was sufficiently fragmented to prevent a president at the height of his powers from obtaining block grants quickly and on his own terms, even within the most favorable issue arenas. Additional views of this segmented system are provided in the following two chapters, which trace the political fates of Nixon's proposals for general revenue sharing and welfare reform.

CHAPTER 4

The Unique Politics of General Revenue Sharing

$B_{\text{LOCK GRANTS}}$ were not the only decentralizing element of Nixon's New Federalism. In many ways general revenue sharing (GRS) was the principal legacy of Nixon's federalism agenda. Enacted in 1972, GRS annually provided more than $6.1 billion in "no strings" grants to virtually all general-purpose governments in the United States.

The goal of revenue sharing was to combine the advantages of raising revenues at the national level with the advantages of local discretion over spending. With its emphasis on maximizing state and local flexibility in the use of federal funds—while minimizing federal regulations, paperwork, and discretion over the allocation of such funds—revenue sharing carried the principles behind block grants to their logical conclusion. Despite this similarity of purpose, the politics of revenue sharing differed surprisingly from the politics of block grants described in chapter 3. As discussed, each of Nixon's block grant proposals aroused a policy-specific response. Depending on the makeup of each issue area, reactions to the president's proposals ranged from universal opposition to conceptual support.

The coalitions supporting and opposing general revenue sharing were equally distinctive. Opposing GRS was a coalition of fiscally conservative Republicans and southern Democrats who believed that revenue should be raised by the level of government that spends it. They were joined by an unusually united group of committee and subcommittee chairmen—some of whom were very liberal—who opposed GRS as an attack on their prerogatives as committee leaders. On the other side was an equally odd coalition of liberal northern Democrats and mainstream Republicans. The first group supported GRS in response to active lobbying by Democratic mayors and governors. The second responded to the president, local politics, and the ideological appeal of decentralization.

These unique coalitions epitomized the segmented patterns of politics prevalent in the 1970s. The declining influence of political parties, the proliferation of interest groups, and the increasingly independent behavior of voters and politicians encouraged an idiosyncratic approach to policymaking. Issues were addressed on a case-by-case basis, and political coalitions were constructed accordingly.

In addition, GRS marked the apogee of policy influence by a new form of interest group internal to government itself: the "intergovernmental lobby." Composed of increasingly active and sophisticated associations representing mayors, governors, and other state and local officials, the intergovernmental lobby played a critical role in the enactment of general revenue sharing. Although such "public interest groups" were also important in the politics of block grants, they succeeded only in those policy fields where they were a dominant member of the policy community. They failed to advance block grant legislation in fields like education that were dominated by functional specialists. The intergovernmental lobby, however, worked aggressively to pass general revenue sharing legislation over the objections of most senior members of the Congress. In the process GRS epitomized an advanced form of rationalizing politics. Governmental actors not only formulated policies designed to counter prior program outcomes, but they also formed the core of the political coalitions both for and against the issue.

Faltering First Steps

The congressional response to Nixon's first revenue sharing proposal in 1969 and 1970 was decidedly cool, especially among Democrats. Representative Wilbur Mills of Arkansas, the powerful chairman of the House Ways and Means Committee with jurisdiction over GRS, refused to hold hearings on the proposal. Like many fiscal conservatives, he viewed revenue sharing as a recipe for fiscal irresponsibility because it separated the authority for spending public monies from the responsibility for raising taxes. In addition, Mills believed the president's revenue sharing proposal posed a threat to congressional authority. By giving "no strings" grants by automatic formula to state and local governments, Congress sacrificed its power to allocate funds and determine their specific uses. Mills was supported in his opposition by conservative John Byrnes of Wisconsin, the ranking Republican on the committee, and by most of the Democratic leadership in Congress.

The president's strong support and congressional Democrats' widespread opposition gave a highly partisan cast to the revenue sharing debate that state and local program advocates were unable to overcome. Eighty-nine Republicans sponsored the president's first revenue sharing bill in the House, with no Democratic cosponsors. In the Senate thirty-two Republicans supported the president's bill, joined by only two Democrats. Although there was Democratic support for some alternative proposals, few questioned that revenue sharing had become "an increasingly partisan controversy" during Richard Nixon's first term.[1]

The support of Democratic mayors and governors was unable to overcome this partisan cleavage, in part because the intergovernmental coalition on behalf of GRS was still shaky during this period. Initial spending on revenue sharing in the president's first bill was modest (about $1 billion in the first year), and governors and mayors were joined in an uneasy alliance, marked by lingering suspicions and bitterness after their 1968 dispute over state and local roles under the Law Enforcement Assistance Administration (LEAA) block grant.[2] The wounds of this battle were not well healed when the first revenue sharing coalition was constructed in 1969. The administration helped the major intergovernmental groups reach a compromise over GRS by dividing revenues in each state in rough proportion to each government's share of state and local spending, but the alliance remained fragile. Accordingly, the administration's attempts in 1970 to overcome partisan divisions in Congress with active lobbying by state and local elected officials did not succeed.

The Enactment of GRS

This strategy did succeed in the 92d Congress, and an active and united intergovernmental lobby was the key. The president made revenue sharing the centerpiece of his domestic agenda, increased initial expenditures under his proposal from $1 billion to $5 billion annually, and raised the local governmental share of funds from approximately 30 percent to 50 percent.

The increased authorization and formula changes were designed to reward local government officials for their earlier lobbying on behalf of GRS and to generate renewed enthusiasm for the program.[3] This strategy succeeded. State and especially local governments launched a massive lobbying campaign on behalf of GRS, seeking first to secure hearings on the president's proposal in the Ways and Means Committee and then to secure its passage. The signs of intergovernmental activism were everywhere. The mayors made revenue sharing their "most immediate priority issue" in the 92d Congress, and they published articles in municipal publications on how to lobby Congress.[4] The counties put ads in newspapers on behalf of revenue sharing, staged membership "fly-ins" to lobby for the program, and began a membership newsletter focused on general revenue sharing. Summarizing the impact of these activities, Donald Haider wrote:

> The passage of general revenue sharing is the most successful grass roots lobbying effort undertaken thus far. . . . In spring, 1971, delegations of mayors, governors, and county officials swarmed over Capitol Hill demanding congressional passage of this program. . . . The Democratic leadership and Chairman Mills eventually capitulated to this outpouring of favorable support.[5]

Congressional leaders capitulated, but slowly. The intense pressure by local Democrats convinced congressional leaders that they must at least grant the issue a hearing. Mills was persuaded to do so, but he announced that his hearing was strictly for the purpose of killing GRS.[6] Democratic mayors and governors pressed for a more positive response, and they made inroads among junior members of Congress. This intraparty split convinced top party leaders—Democratic National Committee chairman Lawrence O'Brien, House Speaker Carl Albert, Majority Leader Hale Boggs, and Chief Whip Tip O'Neill—that the Democrats had to advance an alternative proposal. In O'Neill's words:

> The tide of so much pressure from the mayors more than anybody else was influential. . . . Nixon kept on pressing . . . and we began to feel pressure from the newer members of Congress who were more likely to succumb to pressure than the old hands. Finally Wilbur was called in and the leaders decided that they would have to go along and do something about revenue sharing.[7]

During the first week of hearings on GRS in May 1971, Chairman Mills personally met with O'Brien and several mayors and governors and expressed support for a need-based program of revenue sharing directed strictly to urban areas, with no state involvement. This change of heart was widely attributed not only to leadership pressure but to Mills's own decision to seek the party's presidential nomination and his corresponding need to build a base of support among local political leaders.

Although many in Congress still opposed the very idea of revenue sharing, Mills's reversal greatly enhanced the prospects for enacting some form of revenue sharing program and thus focused lobbying activity on specific provisions of alternative GRS legislation. As Mills developed his own proposal over the summer and fall of 1971, the president and city officials, eager to keep the intergovernmental coalition together, urged Mills to include in it a state role. He did so, but reversed the relative shares of states and cities from the first Nixon bill, giving local governments two-thirds of the funding and states one-third. Even this state share was tied to incentives for states with income taxes, in order to encourage the broadening of state revenue sources. Mills also enhanced the program's liberal reformist cast by placing greater emphasis on need and by restricting use to several priority activities.

Through the remaining stages of the legislative process, the provisions of the GRS program continued to change—a classic case of legislative compromise and adjustment to competing pressures, according to Samuel Beer.[8] For example, the Ways and Means bill retained its relatively liberal cast, with its formula focus on need and its encouragement of state fiscal reforms, but it was modified further before being reported by the committee and approved on the floor. In another bow to his presidential ambitions, Mills agreed to downplay the bill's promotion of state income taxes since this aroused highly negative emotions in the key primary state of New Hampshire. The restriction that funds be spent only for functions listed as "priority activities" was also negated by eliminating the "maintenance of effort" requirement for these activities. With these changes, despite considerable opposition in the House Rules Committee and on the House floor, the bill was passed by the full House on June 22, 1972.

The politics of adjustment continued in the Senate, where the chief source of controversy was the program's formula. Senators from rural southern and western states altered the program's formula to increase allocations to thirty-four principally rural states.

As passed by the House, the revenue sharing formula distributed funds to the states according to five factors: population, urbanized population, per capita income, general state and local tax effort, and state income tax collections. This formula weighted funds toward populous, urbanized states with high individual income taxes (including New York and California), while penalizing the ten states that did not have an income tax. The formula was also extremely complex, prescribing essentially one allocation system for states and one for local governments. The relative mix of funds between state and local governments varied widely from state to state.

The Senate Finance Committee replaced this complex allocation with a simple three-part formula based on population, relative income, and combined state-local tax effort. This change aided low-income, mostly southern states and, with its greater emphasis on overall tax effort, the central cities within many states.[9] To help compensate for this reallocation of funds and to control the exploding costs of federal aid to state supplemental social service programs, the Senate Finance Committee attached to revenue sharing a new authorization of federal social service grants that capped federal expenditures but weighted funds more heavily to urbanized states. When this provision was combined with the allocation of funds in GRS, only four states lost funding under the Senate legislation.[10]

The Finance Committee bill passed the full Senate with relatively few changes. Attempts to increase formula allocations to more populous states were turned back. Leaders of the Senate Appropriations Committee, like their House counterparts, registered stiff but unsuccessful opposition; they viewed the multiyear commitment of funds under the program as an assault on the integrity of the appropriations process and on the prerogatives of their committee.

The House and Senate conference committee organized to iron out differences between the two bills continued the Senate's process of legislative adjustment and designed the grandest compromise of all. Unable to resolve the differences between the two sharply divergent program formulas, the conference committee incorporated both into the final program and allowed each state to choose the one most advantageous to it. In addition, the Senate program of social service grants was retained, but the funding allocation was based on simple population.

Eager to adjourn as the 1972 elections approached, both houses quickly took up the conference bill and easily passed it. It was signed by President Nixon on October 20, 1972, who hailed it as the start of his "New American Revolution."

The Segmented Politics of Block Grants and Revenue Sharing

As Nixon's rhetoric in signing GRS suggests, he viewed revenue sharing as part of a broad, coherent agenda for reforming American federalism. Whatever its merits as an integrated policy response, however, Nixon's New Federalism aroused surprisingly little coherent response from the political arena. In contrast to the politics of block grants, which ran the gamut from consensual support in some policy areas to nearly universal opposition in others, general revenue sharing produced unique coalitions of its own.

Key roll-call votes in the House on revenue sharing and block grants demonstrate this difference. In the House the crucial test vote on GRS occurred on the rule that allowed consideration of revenue sharing on the floor. Because of its large size, the House establishes a rule for each major bill that sets time limits on debate and defines permissible amendments. The Ways and Means Committee requested and received a "closed" rule, which prohibited amendments to the carefully constructed legislation and allowed only a single up or down vote. Because of its procedural nature and the political cover it provides, a vote on a rule often represents a truer test of members' sentiment on an issue than does a vote on final passage. Indeed, in this case the rules vote constituted the key test of revenue sharing in the House.

Given strong partisan divisions between the White House and Congress, a presidential election year, and the president's placement of revenue sharing high on his agenda, one might have expected the vote on GRS to be decided principally by partisan attachments. Beer's analysis of the key rules vote shows that it did meet the standard definition of a "party vote," but only weakly. A majority of Republicans supported GRS; a small majority of Democrats opposed it.

Much more important in determining the fate of GRS, Beer found, were divisions among the majority Democrats based on committee status and seniority. House committee and subcommittee chairmen opposed GRS almost two to one, while a majority of rank-and-file Democrats voted for it.[11] Region and ideology were not important factors, as they are on many issues that divide Democrats. Southern and northern Democrats were split in their support and opposition to GRS by similar margins, and ideology was found to correlate only modestly with the vote on GRS. Thus, Beer concluded, the key forces influencing Democrats on revenue sharing were forces internal to government—most notably their attachments to categorical programming and the activities of the intergovernmental lobby. Senior Democratic leaders formed a "categorical phalanx" against GRS because it would erode their prerogatives as committee chairs. In contrast, less electorally secure junior Democrats had less attachment to existing program structures and felt more vulnerable to the high-pressure lobbying by mayors and governors.

Block Grants and the Categorical Phalanx

The case studies of block grant politics reviewed in chapter 3 reveal few systematic differences between junior and senior legislators in their attitudes toward block grants. Those grants that passed garnered support from most committee and subcommittee leaders as well as junior members. The opposition of House Banking Committee chairman Wright Patman to the CDBG was an exception that proves the rule, since all of the ranking Democrats on the Housing Subcommittee worked actively for its adoption. On the other hand, block grant failures were universally opposed by junior and senior Democrats alike.

Thus at the committee level block grants elicited a policy-specific response rather than systematic opposition from committee chairmen. It is possible, however, that the pattern found in the revenue sharing vote emerges only on the floor, not in committee. (Especially in the House the dynamics of the floor are distinctive, and many other actors are engaged. As in the case of GRS, winning the support of Wilbur Mills and the Democratic party leadership did not ensure that other committee chairmen would be brought along.)

Though plausible, support for such a thesis is not readily apparent, in part because there were few meaningful floor votes testing block grant sentiment. The failures never made it to the floor, and successful block grants tended to be passed almost unanimously.

Two test votes did occur during this period that allow us to examine this hypothesis, however. The first occurred in 1968 on the so-called Cahill amendment, which proposed to replace a Johnson administration program of categorical aid for urban crime control efforts with a law enforcement block grant. The second vote occurred in 1971 on the Esch amendment, which sought to substitute a job training block grant for a categorical employment program.

In both cases, when we look, as Beer did, at voting behavior by Democratic members of Congress, the categorical phalanx fails to materialize. Table 4-1 shows that committee chairmen were actually more likely to support the Esch amendment than were rank-and-file Democrats; in sharp contrast, committee and subcommittee chairmen were substantially less likely to support GRS than were the Democratic rank and file.

The reverse relationship found in table 4-1, with chairmen somewhat more supportive of the manpower block grant than the party rank and file, reflects sectional and ideological influences. Northern Democratic

Table 4-1. *Comparison of House Voting Behavior on Block Grant and Revenue Sharing Legislation, by Seniority*
Percent

Vote	Chairmen	Rank and file
Esch amendment on a job training block grant[a]		
Yes	18	8
No	82	92
General revenue sharing[b]		
Yes	36	55
No	64	45

a. $N = 236$.
b. $N = 237$.

chairmen (98 percent) and junior Democrats (95 percent) were almost unanimous in opposing the Esch amendment. Only southern Democratic chairmen proved more supportive of the Esch amendment than were the rank and file, with 40 percent of them voting for the block grant. All of these chairmen were extremely conservative, having Americans for Democratic Action (ADA) scores in 1971 of 25 or less. In contrast, southern Democratic chairmen were the group most strongly opposed to general revenue sharing.[12]

The categorical phalanx was similarly absent from the vote on the Law Enforcement Assistance Act. The simple correlation between committee status and the vote on LEAA disappears completely when party and region are controlled. As in the case of manpower, southern Democratic chairmen actually prove somewhat more supportive of the block grant concept than their rank-and-file counterparts.

Comparisons with GRS

The absence of a categorical phalanx on two crucial block grant votes suggests that Congress responded differently to these proposals than to GRS. In fact, House members' votes on the Esch and Cahill amendments hardly correlate at all with their votes on GRS. The gamma correlation between the GRS and Cahill amendment votes was 0.05 (out of a possible 1.00 if all members voted identically on each), while the GRS correlation with the Esch amendment was 0.17.

It appears, then, that GRS and these two block grant proposals tapped different attitudes on Capitol Hill and significantly different sources of

Table 4-2. *Comparison of House Voting Behavior on Two Block Grant Proposals, by Ideology*
Percent

Vote	Conservatives	Liberals	Total
Esch amendment on a job training block grant[a]			
Yes	28	1	12
No	72	99	88
Cahill amendment on a law enforcement block grant[b]			
Yes	70	7	39
No	30	93	61

a. N = 235.
b. N = 185.

political support. The votes on the Esch and Cahill amendments were above all party-line votes. Practically all Republicans supported the block grant position on these amendments (95 percent and 98 percent respectively), while the preponderance of Democrats opposed it.

Within the Democratic ranks, ideology proved to be a determining factor in distinguishing supporters and opponents of the two block grant proposals. All but one of the Democratic supporters of the Esch amendment were conservative (defined here as having a 1971 ADA rating of less than 50), although most conservative Democrats opposed the amendment (see table 4-2). An actual majority of conservative Democrats supported the Cahill amendment, while more liberal Democrats overwhelmingly opposed it.

When it comes to ideology, the contrast between block grants and revenue sharing is marked. Conservative Democrats (and Republicans) proved to be most opposed to GRS, rather than favorable to it. And while the vote on GRS was technically a party-line vote, the strength of the relationship was far weaker than was the case with both the Esch and Cahill amendments. The gamma correlation between party and the vote on GRS equaled 0.40 compared with 0.99 on the Esch amendment and 0.98 on the Cahill amendment.

These differences can be attributed to the public interest groups. They did not march in lockstep on every policy that promised more decentralized control. The intergovernmental lobby, a coalition of different governments with different interests, achieved unity on some issues and divided bitterly on others, depending on the policy specifics.

The mayors, for example, supported GRS vigorously but were opposed to both the Esch and Cahill amendments. Although they had worked to enact a manpower block grant in 1970, the mayors chose to endorse a public jobs program in 1971 when they were forced to choose between this and the Esch block grant proposal. On the Cahill amendment mayors and governors were badly divided, with the former supporting the president's proposal for direct law enforcement grants to cities and the latter leading the support for block grants to the states.

In the absence of pressure from mayors to support these two block grant proposals, northern Democrats freely followed their partisan and ideological proclivities and opposed them. Indeed, these members of Congress were also expressing the views of their urban constituents and, in the case of LEAA, their party's president. In GRS, however, the competing drives of party and constituency worked in opposition to each other. Forced to choose between their partisan and institutional suspicion of GRS and mayoral pressure to support it, a majority of rank-and-file northern Democrats voted in accordance with the mayors' position. Thus the intergovernmental lobby tended to reinforce partisan and ideological differences in the two block grant votes but to dampen them in general revenue sharing.

In summary, the politics of block grants and general revenue sharing were distinctive. Although the different elements of the New Federalism shared certain features in common, they were not treated identically by Congress and the public interest groups. General revenue sharing elicited one political response and block grants yet another. In fact, the case studies of block grant politics suggest that each block grant proposal aroused its own unique response. Although a partisan-conservative coalition in support of certain block grant proposals, like the Esch and Cahill amendments, was constructed, it resulted in the enactment of only one block grant: LEAA. In all other cases it failed to gain a solid majority.

More significant were the policy-specific coalitions that developed around block grant proposals in each functional area. Where substantial support for consolidation and decentralization existed in the policy subsystem, compromise proposals were eventually developed that won almost unanimous support on the floors of both chambers of Congress. Crucial test votes on the block grant concept were anomalies in these fields. Where, on the other hand, little consensus existed in the policy arena on behalf of block grants, even partisan-conservative coalitions were never constructed on their behalf. What began in the Nixon White House as a broad, coherent policy initiative on behalf of program decentralization became in Congress a functionally discrete set of policy issues, each with its own political characteristics.

CHAPTER 5

The National Dimensions
of Nixon's New Federalism

Nixon's New Federalism cannot be fully understood without some consideration of the centralizing elements of his domestic policy agenda. The best example was the family assistance plan (FAP): a sweeping proposal to replace the existing state-centered welfare system with a nationally financed system of uniform minimum support payments to needy families. But other, less obvious examples abound as well. During the Nixon presidency, the federal government dramatically increased entitlement expenditures, enacted new regulatory statutes, created a federalized program of income assistance payments to the elderly poor, established the first major public employment program since the New Deal, and launched an aggressive program of wage and price controls to regulate the entire national economy.

It would be misleading to portray each of these actions as independent decisions of the president. Richard Nixon was not a liberal Democrat in disguise, bent on expanding the power of the national government. A simple listing of enactments and expenditures in the early 1970s obscures the administration's ambivalence toward many of these activities. Much of the apparent activism reflected presidential efforts to accommodate the liberal Democratic Congress, which in the early 1970s was beginning a period of institutional ascendancy as rewards and opportunities for legislative activism proliferated. As the earlier discussion of job training, community development, and housing impoundments makes clear, the president fought significant battles with Congress over spending levels and new programs.

Many of these disagreements, however, were over questions of degree, not direction—that is to say, over the specific character of new programs or the size of budget increases, not about the need to create programs or enlarge them. President Nixon did not object to increased domestic spending, but he tried to moderate its rate of growth. He did not oppose using a training and employment block grant to fund public service jobs, but he fought the creation of a separate program. When his objections were overruled by Congress, he twice signed into law public employment programs unlike any since the 1930s.

Nor was Nixon always the reluctant pragmatist. The family assistance plan was his initiative; he was under no obligation to propose it. Nor was he forced by Congress to propose wage and price controls or stricter environmental and occupational health programs. Beneath his mantle of conservatism, Nixon was a presidential activist in keeping with the temper of his times. Just as he was willing to concentrate power in the White House and launch historic foreign policy initiatives, Richard Nixon was perfectly comfortable with expanding the domestic role of the national government whenever that fit within his broader political and policy agenda.

A National Welfare Policy

In 1969 President Nixon proposed a sweeping change in American welfare policy as an integral component of his federalism reform initiative. Dubbed the family assistance plan, this proposal would have greatly expanded the federal government's financial and administrative role in welfare policy and established for the first time a national income floor for all poor families. Combined with the decentralizing thrust of general revenue sharing and the president's block grant proposals, the plan would have completed the most significant restructuring of federal, state, and local government responsibilities since the New Deal.

The family assistance plan had begun to take shape even before the president's inauguration. A transition task force on welfare policy, chaired by revenue sharing advocate Richard Nathan, recommended a major overhaul of the principal federal-state welfare program, aid to families with dependent children (AFDC). The task force urged that AFDC's system of state-determined benefit levels be replaced with minimum national standards for dependent children, in order to raise extremely low welfare payments in the South, and that the federal share of overall welfare costs be increased to aid northern states with higher welfare payments. When the president endorsed the thrust of these proposals as a means of redressing the "welfare mess," aides began drafting a specific legislative proposal for introduction in Congress.[1]

At this stage the plan was converted into a more radical reform of the welfare system by "holdover Democrats" at the Department of Health, Education, and Welfare (HEW).[2] Analysts at the department objected that truly significant welfare reform could not be accomplished within the constraints of the AFDC program, which offered no benefits to most families with a father present or to working parents, no matter how poor. They argued that raising benefits without structural program changes would contribute to the further breakup of poor families and would create economic disincentives for low-wage work. Instead, they sold the new Republican administration on a broader, negative income tax proposal that guaranteed every poor family, including the working poor, a minimum national income. To provide an incentive for work, they recommended that benefits be phased out gradually as employment income grew, thus eliminating AFDC's penalty for work.

The new Republican appointees at HEW enthusiastically embraced this concept. Ironically, the secretary of the department and long-time Nixon confidant Robert Finch accepted a proposal that Great Society architects like Wilbur Cohen had categorically rejected as too radical.[3] The plan found strong support in the White House as well, not only from Nathan but also from another holdover Democrat, Daniel Patrick Moynihan, who had become Nixon's urban policy adviser. Moynihan had long advocated adopting a European-style program that would make child allowances available to all families in America, and in the Johnson administration he had emerged as a forceful critic of AFDC's negative impact on black families.

Needless to say, a proposal as important and sweeping as the family assistance plan was not accepted uncritically by the Nixon administration or by the president himself. Strong objections came from several members of the Nixon cabinet and from Arthur Burns, the president's chief economic adviser. Burns argued strongly that the proposal would greatly increase dependency on welfare by bringing millions of new working families into the welfare system. Others complained about the program's cost. Less extreme alternatives were proposed during the next several months, while the policy battle was waged within the Nixon White House.

The impasse was broken by the president himself, who became unusually involved in the issue and finally decided to proceed with a modified proposal.[4] The administration was under increasing pressure to launch some kind of domestic policy initiative, and in the end Nixon "wanted a major social program, not a 'me too' Great Society" proposal, in the words of one administration official.[5] Nixon had been swayed by Moynihan's arguments that FAP was an "income strategy" that would alleviate poverty by placing more income directly in the hands of poor individuals, giving them the choice of how to improve their situation. It was viewed as counter to the "service strategy" employed by programs of the Great Society, which relied heavily on middle-class professionals and community organizations to deliver education, training, family assistance, and other social services to the poor. When assured by Moynihan that the plan would be a far more successful assault on poverty and would "get rid of social workers," the president overrode objections and signed on.[6]

In his 1969 television address on the New Federalism, President Nixon launched his drive for revenue sharing, proposed a manpower block grant, and urged "reversal of the trend toward ever more centralization of government in Washington." The first half of his message, however, was devoted, not to decentralization, but to a proposal that "the Federal Government build a foundation under the income of every American family . . . that cannot care for itself. . . . The present welfare system is a colossal failure. . . . It is bringing States and cities to the brink of financial disaster. . . . It breaks up homes. . . . Benefit levels are grossly unequal."[7] Specifically, the president said that every family of four should be guaranteed a minimum national payment of $1,600 per year, plus food stamps. With added day care, job training, and higher federal matching rates, the bill would have raised existing costs of federal welfare spending by $4 billion annually, while expanding coverage to 7 million new working poor recipients. It also required states with higher existing benefits to supplement the minimum federal payment, and it provided for federal administration of welfare payments in the remaining states. Finally, to answer critics' charges that it would increase dependency on welfare, the final version included stronger work incentives and penalties than were originally proposed, allowing the president to claim that he supported "workfare," not welfare.[8]

Thus did Nixon send to Congress what was later termed "the most important piece of domestic legislation proposed in the past 50 years."[9] There it began a frustrating legislative journey where it twice brushed with success before meeting failure. Caught between liberal and conservative notions of welfare reform, the family assistance plan fell prey to political contradictions that would doom many subsequent attempts to fundamentally change welfare in the United States.

Nixon assumed that a liberal and Democratic Congress would be forced to accept his proposal, and twice the House of Representatives did so. Although the chairman of the House Ways and Means Committee, Democrat Wilbur Mills of Arkansas, had misgivings about the proposal, he agreed to support it, as did Representative John Byrnes of Wisconsin, the conservative ranking Republican on the committee. On the House floor the bill passed easily with only slight modifications by a vote of 243 to 155. Although it won the support of a majority of both parties, warning signals about its Senate reception were apparent in the response of southern Democrats, who opposed the measure 85 to 17.[10] Southern states were big winners financially under the proposal, but many southerners opposed the "high" benefits provided under the plan. Despite the program's benefit structure and "workfare" requirements, they argued it would undermine work incentives in the low-wage areas in the South and charged that there would be "no one left to press shirts" if the program passed.[11]

Such arguments found strong support in the Senate. The plan met vigorous opposition in the Finance Committee, which was dominated by conservatives and southerners. Opponents there were led by Senators Russell Long and John Williams, the chairman and the ranking Republican member of the powerful committee. They produced charts showing that some recipients in communities with relatively high welfare benefits could suffer slight income losses under the proposal if they went to work, once the loss of in-kind housing, food, and medical benefits was factored in. Although the plan was modified, additional opposition came from liberals and the National Welfare Rights Organization. They charged that benefits were set too low and work requirements were too onerous. The full committee finally voted down FAP and agreed instead to a temporary demonstration program. Even that proposal was eliminated on the Senate floor, and the session ended before advocates could attempt its restoration in a House-Senate conference committee.

The president tried again in 1971, calling the family assistance plan his "first priority" in the 92d Congress. The plan was introduced as H.R. 1 with several changes. For example, it ended the requirement for state supplemental payments and raised the $1,600 floor to $2,400, but it eliminated food stamps. Again the bill passed the House with a majority from both parties, but southerners still opposed the plan, and the margin of victory on the key procedural vote fell by more than half, down to 234 to 187.[12]

Prospects also turned bleaker in the Senate. The Senate put aside consideration of the plan in 1971 after the president asked for a delay when he announced his wage and price control program in midyear. In 1972 the

Senate Finance Committee again refused to report out the program, replacing it with a workfare program advocated by Chairman Long. That, too, was replaced on the Senate floor by a demonstration program. Efforts to replace this modest provision with the House version of FAP or a more liberal Senate proposal were defeated. Because the two chambers could not see eye to eye on these measures, both the test program and the House version of FAP were deleted from the final bill in conference. Only a relatively noncontroversial program of national income assistance for the elderly and disabled was enacted into law as the supplemental security income (SSI) program.

A Rising Tide of Entitlements

Richard Nixon may not have won an explicit national income floor, but during his tenure the federal government implemented an implicit national welfare program through a vast and complex web of in-kind entitlement programs. Between 1969 and 1974, expenditures for federal programs providing food, housing assistance, and medical care to the needy increased more than 250 percent. In addition, as mentioned above, the 1930s system of providing for the elderly poor was explicitly nationalized in 1972 through enactment of the SSI program.

This active domestic spending contrasts sharply with the Nixon administration's general reputation for budgetary penury. In many ways this reputation was undeserved. It was earned almost entirely from the administration's efforts to slow—not reverse—the growth of annually appropriated programs. Elsewhere Nixon's record of fiscal activism bears surprising similarity to that of his Democratic predecessors. Moreover, as a later section of this chapter demonstrates, this was true with respect to regulation as well as spending.

There was nothing new about the rising tide of entitlements in the early 1970s. Federal spending on such programs grew significantly during the Johnson administration with the establishment of new programs like medicaid and medicare and the expansion of existing programs. Direct payments to individuals—including food stamps, federal retirement, and veterans' payments but not social security—increased 56 percent between 1964 and 1969. Entitlements channeled through state and local governments, such as medicaid and AFDC, grew by more than one-third.

By most relative measures, however, spending increases during the 1960s

Table 5-1. *Federal Spending on Entitlement Programs,*
Fiscal Years 1964, 1969, 1974

Billions of dollars unless otherwise specified

Item	1964	1969	1974
Direct payments to individuals			
(minus social security and medicare)	13.0	20.3	40.7
Grants for individuals	2.8	3.8	13.6
Total	15.7	24.1	54.3
As a percent of federal budget outlays	13.3	13.1	20.2
As a percent of GNP	2.6	2.7	3.9
In constant 1972 dollars	20.5	27.4	48.3

Source: *Budget of the United States Government, Historical Tables, Fiscal Year 1986,* tables 6.1, 6.2, 11.2. Figures are rounded.

were less impressive. Payments to individuals increased substantially in constant dollars, from $20.5 billion in 1964 to $27.4 billion in 1969 (see table 5-1), but such spending remained virtually unchanged as a percentage of GNP or of total federal outlays. Larger increases occurred in programs earmarked specifically for the poor, but these programs were still small even by 1969 (see table 5-2).

By nearly every measure, real and relative, the greatest increases in spending for individuals occurred during the Nixon administration. Entitlement spending—including both direct payments to individuals and grants for individuals—more than doubled during this period (see table 5-1). Even in constant dollars, spending for such programs rose 76 percent

Table 5-2. *Federal Spending on Selected Means-Tested Programs,*
Fiscal Years 1964, 1969, 1974

Millions of dollars

Program	1964	1969	1974
Food stamps	30	248	2,845
Child nutrition	181	237	751
Medicaid	196	2,191	5,549
Housing assistance	193	342	1,794
Total	600	3,018	10,939

Source: *Budget of the United States Government, Historical Tables, Fiscal Year 1986,* table 11.3.

between 1969 and 1974. Still larger increases occurred in programs targeted at the poor. Food stamp outlays multiplied tenfold during this period. Housing assistance to the poor was up five times. The medicaid budget more than doubled. In contrast to the 1960s, entitlement spending relative to other federal outlays and the national economy as a whole also increased sharply.

Two programs, food stamps and SSI, underscore the depth of these changes. The food stamp program was transformed under Nixon. It began as a commodity distribution program for excess agricultural production. Changes during the Johnson administration allowed localities to choose between operating food distribution centers and offering food coupons that allowed impoverished recipients to purchase approved foods at a substantial discount. Nonetheless, when President Lyndon Baines Johnson left office, the program still was not offered in six states, only about one-third of all U.S. counties participated, and only about 22 percent of eligible individuals were enrolled in the program.[13]

Six years later, when Richard Nixon left the White House, food stamps represented a form of surrogate welfare reform: all states participated in the program; every county was obliged to distribute stamps instead of surplus commodities; the number of poor recipients had more than quadrupled; and spending had mushroomed (see table 5-3). These changes reflected amendments to the program that substantially altered its character. Unlike AFDC, food stamps came to have uniform federal standards for eligibility and benefit levels. Food stamp benefits were put on a sliding scale with AFDC to compensate for low welfare payments in the South. Thus by 1974 food stamps constituted a form of minimum national income, albeit at a very low level. Moreover, all counties were required to participate, the program was indexed to inflation, and the federal share of administrative costs was increased.

The SSI program, enacted in 1972, established an explicit national income floor for the aged, blind, and disabled. It was one component of FAP that finally won approval from Congress. Partly as a result, poverty among the elderly declined dramatically in subsequent years. In the federal antipoverty effort, SSI stands as the major success story.[14]

The program began as a relatively overlooked element of the family assistance plan that dealt with the non-AFDC portion of the social security–dependent population. Although these adult groups comprised over one-fourth of the total welfare population, the provisions for them were not as controversial as those for AFDC recipients. In general, the elderly

Table 5-3. *Growth of the Food Stamp Program, Fiscal Years 1964–74*

Year	Number of states	Number of program areas	Participants (thousands)	Federal cost (millions of dollars)
1964	22	43	360	28.6
1965	29	110	632	32.5
1966	41	324	1,218	64.8
1967	42	838	1,831	105.5
1968	44	1,027	2,419	173.1
1969	44	1,489	3,222	228.8
1970	46	1,747	6,457	549.7
1971	47	2,027	10,584	1,522.7
1972	47	2,126	10,594	1,797.3
1973	48	2,228	12,106	2,131.4
1974	50	3,062	13,524	2,714.1

Source: U.S. Advisory Commission on Intergovernmental Relations, *Public Assistance: The Growth of Federal Function*, A-79 (GPO, 1980), p. 82.

poor, blind, and permanently disabled were viewed as the most deserving of the "deserving poor," and questions regarding work disincentives and the morality of AFDC recipients did not pertain to most of these participants.

Nonetheless, SSI was not enacted until 1972 because of Senate opposition to the rest of the welfare reform proposal. When the AFDC provisions were finally separated in 1972, however, SSI was passed with little fanfare as part of a broader package of social security tax and benefit increases and changes in the medical provisions. As enacted, the program established uniform federal eligibility standards for participation, minimum benefit levels that increased payments in a majority of states, largely federal administration of the program, and incentives for state supplements.[15]

Regulatory Federalism

The Nixon administration also presided over and contributed to the greatest expansion of federal regulation of state and local governments up until that point in American history. Equally important, this expansion was not accomplished merely through new accretions of traditional grant-in-aid requirements. It was the result of new forms of federal regulation that were more intrusive, more coercive, and more extensive than any before. These new forms of regulation marked such a departure from prior practice that some authorities believe they ushered in a new era of federal-state relationships:

> State and local governments . . . have been greatly affected by the massive extension of federal controls and standards over the past two decades. These extensions have altered the terms of longstanding intergovernmental partnership. Where the federal government once encouraged state and local actions with fiscal incentives, it now also wields sanctions or simply issues commands. The development of new techniques of intergovernmental regulation presents a challenge to the balance of authority in, and the effective operation of, American federalism.[16]

Most people think of regulation as a form of policy that is directed at private industry or individual citizens. Minimum wage and hour requirements, antitrust statutes, and rules governing rates and entry in transportation all fit that common conception. In the 1960s and 1970s, however, there was a dramatic increase in federal regulations aimed at state and local governments. This included regulations targeted at these jurisdictions as separate entities—affecting everything from their employment practices to the operation of municipal sewage systems—as well as those that sought to enlist states as agents in regulating the private sector on behalf of federal policies.

To accomplish these new aims, new forms of regulation were developed that were very different from anything that had affected state and local governments before. Traditional intergovernmental regulations were attached to specific federal grant programs and were designed to ensure that federal funds were used as intended. They required audits and reports on the use of federal aid and often required the submission in advance of detailed plans and applications. Although such requirements were often annoying and burdensome, the principles behind them were almost as old as federal aid itself, and the burdens could be avoided by simply refusing to apply for a specific program.

The newer intergovernmental regulations can be divided into four types, all of which were more intrusive and difficult to avoid than ordinary grant

Table 5-4. *Original Enactment of Major Intergovernmental Regulations, by Years and Administration*

Item	Pre-Johnson (1931–63)	Johnson (1963–68)	Nixon-Ford (1969–76)	Carter (1977–80)
Number enacted	2	8	21	5
Percent of all intergovernmental regulations enacted	6	22	58	14
Predominant regulatory objectives	Labor rights	Civil rights; consumer protection	Environment; health and safety; civil rights	Energy conservation; environment

Source: Calculated from ACIR, *Regulatory Federalism: Policy, Process, Impact, and Reform,* A-95 (Government Printing Office, 1984), pp. 19–21.

requirements. At the most extreme end were direct order mandates, which simply instructed state and local governments to comply with a given federal policy. Also highly coercive were crossover sanctions: failure to comply with one program's grant requirements led to the reduction or elimination of funds under other, entirely separate programs. More common were partial preemptions: the federal government preempted a field of policy and set minimum national standards, encouraging states to administer and apply these standards. The most common new form was crosscutting requirements, which applied across the board to all or most federal aid programs.[17]

Most of these new forms of regulation were first developed during the 1960s. None was invented by the Nixon administration. However, during that period, particularly between 1969 and 1974, they gained a firm foothold. Fully half of the thirty-six most intrusive intergovernmental regulations identified in 1982 by the U.S. Advisory Commission on Intergovernmental Relations (ACIR) were created in this period (see table 5-4). Ironically, an administration committed to greater decentralization contributed to one of the most centralizing movements in the history of American federalism. In fact, because block grants and general revenue sharing brought federal aid to many communities for the first time, the New Federalism actually became the vehicle for carrying federal influence more deeply into American society than ever before.[18]

Nixon's attitude toward this regulatory buildup ranged from reluctant to forcefully enthusiastic. Some of the major regulations enacted in this period, like the Safe Drinking Water Act of 1974, were opposed by the Nixon administration as unwarranted intrusions on state prerogatives. Others, like landmark provisions outlawing discrimination against women and the handicapped, were tucked away in large omnibus bills, their effect on federalism unrecognized for the time being.[19] Most of the major regulations of this period, however, enjoyed full or partial backing by the president, as can be seen in the following examples.

Environmental Protection

The Nixon administration's regulatory activism was best seen in its environmental policy. Although the president eventually let Congress take the lead in this area, at first he engaged in a bidding war with Capitol Hill over who could appear tougher on environmental issues. In the process he not only responded to the mood of the early 1970s, but he also helped to elevate environmental issues to a prominent position on the policy agenda. The landmark environmental statutes enacted as a consequence extended the reach of federal regulations to unprecedented lengths. More important, this centralized rulemaking stemmed not only from an analytical conclusion that effective pollution control required greater national standard setting, but also from the political needs of those competing for the presidency in 1972. Beginning on New Year's Day in 1970, Nixon attempted to seize the initiative on environmental issues through a series of highly publicized actions. Calling it his "first official act of the new decade," he signed the National Environmental Policy Act, which established a Council on Environmental Quality in the Executive Office of the President and required that federal agencies and federal grant recipients file detailed environmental impact statements before undertaking construction or other projects with environmental ramifications.

Three weeks later the president devoted one-third of his State of the Union Address to environmental concerns. He subsequently sent Congress a thirty-seven-point program for "total mobilization" on environmental issues.[20] Finally, in late 1970 he established the Environmental Protection Agency and consolidated therein most of the federal government's growing environmental responsibilities.

The most significant environmental action of that year, however, was the enactment of the Clean Air Act Amendments of 1970. This legislation established national air quality standards for various pollutants, required states to develop implementation plans for achieving these standards, and regulated automobile emissions. States were given little choice in assuming primary responsibility for administering the act. Therefore, some analysts have argued the act is a form of "legal conscription" that is inconsistent with the essence of federalism:

> Of all the intergovernmental mechanisms used to nationalize regulatory policy, none is more revolutionary than the approach first applied in the Clean Air Act Amendments of 1970. . . . It is a mechanism which challenges the very essence of federalism as a noncentralized system of separate legal jurisdictions. . . . It is an approach allowing national policymakers and policy implementors to mobilize state and local resources on behalf of a national program.[21]

In a seeming reversal of roles, it was the Nixon administration that first proposed establishing federal emissions standards for air pollution. Democratic senator Edmund Muskie of Maine, the leader on most environmental issues in Congress, initially favored giving state and local governments a larger role in making and administering air pollution policy. But Muskie's leadership in this area was challenged by other members of Congress, and he was embarrassed by a blistering attack on his air pollution record in a major report sponsored by Ralph Nader.[22] When the House responded quickly to the president's proposal for national standards by passing a more forceful bill, Senate activists felt compelled to join a game of environmental escalation, passing a still stronger bill. The toughest bill of all emerged from the House-Senate conference, which merged the strongest provisions of both proposals.[23] Although the administration at this point made a modest attempt to restore language giving it more administrative discretion, there was never any doubt the president would sign it.

At first, President Nixon appeared to take the lead on water pollution as well. In 1970 he proposed strengthening existing legislation with federally approved effluent standards and increased federal funding for municipal sewage treatment facilities. The administration also attempted to exert leadership in this area unilaterally by resuscitating the Refuse Act of 1899, which required permits for dumping wastes in navigable waterways. As with the clean air amendments, however, Congress outdid the president by proposing even stronger legislation. Its Federal Water Pollution Control Act Amendments of 1972 increased federal jurisdiction over intrastate waterways, established a federal permit system for all municipal sewage and industrial discharges, set ambitious goals for zero pollution discharges by 1985, required advanced technology regardless of cost, and authorized $18 billion in federal grants for sewage disposal facilities.[24] In short, it was "the most complex and extensive environmental legislation ever passed."[25] Primarily because of its enormous costs, Nixon withdrew his support and vetoed the legislation, but his veto was easily overridden by Congress.

Other Regulations: From Health to Highways

The growth of intergovernmental regulations in the early 1970s extended far beyond environmental policy, and the Nixon administration's support for a stronger federal role was often greater in these areas. Among the most coercive devices developed in this period were crossover sanctions, which stipulated that federal funds for several programs would be jeopardized should recipients fail to comply with regulations in a different program. Despite the coerciveness of crossover sanctions, the Nixon administration endorsed their use for new regulations in both health care and transportation.

Congress and the Nixon administration were at odds in almost every area of health care in the early 1970s, including spending levels, health care block grants, and national health insurance. Congress, however, strongly supported the administration's efforts to control rising health care costs, and it passed the National Health Planning and Resources Act of 1974. This act directed states to pass legislation establishing complicated certificate-of-need programs to evaluate all proposed construction and development projects undertaken by health care facilities. Failure to comply with the program's intricate national standards and detailed administrative procedures would threaten not only federal planning funds but public health, alcoholism, and mental health grants as well. According to one analyst, this legislation "intrudes upon state and local operations to a greater degree than almost any other grant program."[26]

National health planning legislation was bitterly opposed by medical interests and state and local elected officials. Ironically, states had pioneered the concept of hospital cost control, and a majority of them already had laws on the books when this bill was passed. But both the administration and key members of Congress insisted on having a more uniform national system and argued that it should be placed in the hands of nonprofit organizations.

Few federal regulations did more to annoy sparsely populated western states than the creation of a national speed limit, set at fifty-five miles per hour. Despite this opposition, the Nixon administration championed ever stronger proposals for a national speed limit in response to the Arab oil embargo in 1973. Early that year the administration requested that states voluntarily lower their speed limits to save lives and conserve energy. The president made a personal plea in midsummer, and by year's end a majority of states had complied.[27]

Nevertheless, more direct pressure was soon applied. With the president's strong backing, a national maximum speed limit was enacted on a temporary basis in January 1974, enforced by a provision requiring the cutoff of all federal highway aid to any state refusing to comply. By March all fifty states had reduced their speed limits.[28] Later that year the president signed legislation making permanent what had begun as a temporary measure.[29]

In summary, by the time Nixon left office in 1974, the federal government had firmly institutionalized new patterns of interacting with state and local governments. If the expanded federal role seemed somewhat vulnerable immediately after the Great Society, it was now permanently established. New regulatory techniques had become generally accepted, and they supplemented enormous increases in federal domestic spending. Together these developments left no doubt over which level of government was now senior partner in virtually all areas of intergovernmental collaboration.

The Politics of Nixon's New Federalism

Richard Nixon's federalist legacy was a complex one. In attempting to rationalize the intergovernmental system, he devised a strategy that combined centralizing and decentralizing elements. From a personal standpoint, the president clearly emphasized decentralization in this equation. He sought a net increase in state and local power and responsibility in the intergovernmental system. Ironically, the final outcome was quite the opposite. Despite the failure of the family assistance plan and the notable achievements of revenue sharing, the community development block grant (CDBG), and the Comprehensive Employment and Training Act of 1973 (CETA), Nixon left behind a federal system that was probably more centralized than the one he inherited. Federal expenditures for many domestic functions were increased dramatically, and an unprecedented federal intergovernmental regulatory presence was institutionalized.

This paradoxical state of affairs related to the politics of the 1970s, particularly institutional fragmentation, increasing professional influence, and declining partisanship. Each of these factors influenced the fate of Nixon's block grants. Despite the president's best efforts to elevate this issue on the public agenda, the only block grants to succeed in Congress were those that already had consensual support with individual subsystems. Those that did not failed.

Welfare reform, revenue sharing, and environmental regulations, far more salient issues in the Nixon presidency, also had legislative outcomes that depended on the degree of policy consensus. Where consensus was absent, the administration had to mobilize political allies and other available forms of political support, which it did successfully in the case of revenue sharing but not in the case of the family assistance plan.

Although partisanship did not play a determining role in shaping coalitions or deciding the fate of any of Nixon's major New Federalism policies, it was by no means irrelevant. Party loyalties did influence some of the initial reactions to Nixon's block grant proposals, for example, and partisan coalitions did develop on other issues from time to time. In the end, however, the successful block grants had bipartisan support, and those that failed were rejected on a bipartisan basis.

In fact, party coalitions had little to do with the final legislative responses to Nixon's other initiatives. Most regulatory initiatives enjoyed bipartisan support, and some even generated competition over which party was most committed to the goal. Where sharp conflicts existed, as on welfare reform and revenue sharing, the cleavages cut deeply across party lines. In each case both supporting and opposing coalitions were bipartisan.

The parties' inability to frame issues and shape coalitions during the Nixon presidency was not confined to New Federalism initiatives. Many measures of party unity and cohesion reached modern low points under Nixon. Among the most extreme was the decline in party votes in the House, defined as the percentage of all roll-call votes in which a majority of Republicans opposed a majority of Democrats. Party votes in the House during Nixon's six years in office fell to 32 percent, down from 48 percent under Eisenhower and 46 percent under Kennedy and Johnson. Such data, reinforced by factors like the evidence of subsystem dominance on issues of lesser salience, merely underscore the fragmented character of the policymaking environment confronting Richard Nixon's federalism agenda in the early 1970s.

CHAPTER 6

The Context of Reagan's Federalism

Despite many setbacks, federalism reform appeared to be building political momentum when Richard Nixon left office. Many observers believed that Nixon had launched a powerful intergovernmental movement and predicted it would continue through the remainder of the 1970s. As one prominent intergovernmental analyst wrote in 1974: "We should expect the federal government over the next half decade or so to get out of the categorical grant-in-aid business and to continue to shift toward revenue sharing and other broad-purpose fiscal transfers."[1] The following year the U.S. Advisory Commission on Intergovernmental Relations (ACIR) concurred: "The trend is toward the consolidation of previously fragmented, though functionally related, categorical grants."[2]

In successive administrations, however, comprehensive efforts at federalism reform gradually diminished, although the Ford administration did try to consolidate some intergovernmental programs during its brief tenure. It resurrected the proposed education block grant of the Nixon era and formulated plans for consolidating health and child nutrition grants, but all were stalled in Congress. Only one additional block grant—for social services—was created in early 1975, but it was intended to cap a single runaway federal program rather than consolidate a mix of overlapping federal grants.

During the remainder of the 1970s, no additional block grants were established, and few were proposed. On the contrary, Congress gradually proceeded to recategorize and recentralize existing ones. Between 1975 and 1977, the block grant portion of the Comprehensive Employment and Training Act (CETA) program declined from 42 percent of appropriations to 23 percent.[3] New categorical programs appended to CETA included countercyclical public employment, a series of youth employment and training demonstration programs, and a new private sector job training program. Less recategorization took place in the comprehensive development block grant (CDBG) program, apart from enactment of the urban development action grant (UDAG). However, the Carter administration sustained efforts to increase federal control over CDBG, with the result that local discretion over how and where to spend block grant funds was substantially reduced. As Donald Kettl explained, "Regulation gradually emerged as the key strategy for implementing the new generation of urban aid programs. . . . The creeping growth of new rules . . . gradually shifted power back to Washington."[4] Ironically, revenue sharing and the new block grants in some ways extended the reach of federal influence farther than ever before, sending federal funds (and regulations) for the first time to virtually all local governments regardless of size, and inducing many hard-pressed urban centers to rely more and more on federal aid.

Renewed program fragmentation and regulation were not confined to block grants, however. Between 1975 and 1980, 92 new categorical programs were created, bringing the total to a record 534.[5] And although the pace of intrusive new regulatory enactments slowed from the peak decade between 1965 and 1975, five major new intergovernmental regulations were enacted during the Carter administration, including the Clean Air Act Amendments of 1977, the Surface Mining Control and Reclamation Act of 1977, and the Public Utilities Regulatory Policies Act of 1978.

As these developments suggest, federalism reform was simply not a priority of the Carter administration, despite the president's anti-Washington rhetoric. Carter's major management reform initiatives were directed toward federal agency reorganization, not intergovernmental grants. In fact, the president had come into office promising to reduce the number of federal agencies, boards, and commissions from over 1,200 to just 200. Although this goal was eventually dropped as hopelessly naive, Carter expended enormous amounts of staff resources and political capital on over 100 different reorganization plans.[6]

Carter's principal proposal for intergovernmental reform was the ill-fated national urban policy initiative of 1978. Far from being a coherent strategy of the kind proposed by Nixon, Carter's urban affairs proposal was an $8.3 billion amalgam of disparate agency initiatives, most of which had been proposed and rejected many times in the past. A disappointed David Broder called it "a smorgasbord . . . 10 strategies supported by 38 recommendations, plus 160 suggestions for improving old programs left scattered in five agencies."[7] Even White House staff viewed it as a "laundry list" of Cabinet requests.[8]

A more lasting Carter initiative may have been his enhancement of the White House staff responsible for intergovernmental affairs. Carter institutionalized and enlarged the intergovernmental affairs office, and he appointed one of his trusted aides from Georgia, Jack Watson, to head it. Although this office had some policy responsibilities, it focused on ombudsman-like activities on behalf of mayors and governors—relaying their complaints to federal officials and interceding for them with federal agencies. In this role, however, the office was simply one of many—such as those operated on behalf of women, blacks, Jews, Hispanics, the elderly, consumers, and the business community—established under the broad expansion of political liaison activities in the Carter White House.[9]

Consequently, the U.S. Advisory Commission on Intergovernmental Relations concluded in 1980 that the federal system had not been reformed during the 1970s but had become even more unbalanced and in greater need of comprehensive restructuring than ever before. In summarizing its extensive study of intergovernmental trends in seven functional areas, the bipartisan commission concluded that "contemporary intergovernmental relations . . . have become more pervasive, more intrusive, more unmanageable, more ineffective, more costly, and above all, more unaccountable."[10] Some individual scholars went even further, arguing that the United States no longer had a true federal system but had become a decentralized unitary state.[11]

Federalism Reform under Reagan: Political Preconditions

In the 1980s federalism reform found a new champion in Ronald Reagan. In his first inaugural address the new president placed the blame for intergovernmental imbalance squarely on the federal government:

> It is time to check and reverse the growth of government which shows signs of having grown beyond the consent of the governed. It is my intention to curb the size and influence of the Federal establishment and to demand recognition of the distinction between the powers granted to the Federal government and those reserved to the states or to the people.[12]

To accomplish these goals, the president set forth a sweeping agenda of budget reductions, tax cuts, personnel freezes, block grants, and deregulation initiatives—all intended to dramatically lower the fiscal and administrative profile of the federal government.

Although Reagan pursued more extreme objectives than Nixon did, he enjoyed relatively more success in achieving them. This was especially true in 1981, when the Reagan administration achieved its most impressive legislative victories. Although the administration's record after 1981 was far more mixed, those early victories structured and constrained the subsequent policy agenda.

In fact, it is at this level of agenda setting that the contrast between Nixon and Reagan was the sharpest. Nixon's ultimate objective was to improve the manageability of government, rationalizing functions and modestly decentralizing power. By this standard, his efforts were at best a mixed success: revenue sharing was adopted, as were two block grants in modified form, but the family assistance plan was twice rejected by Congress, and most of the special revenue sharing initiatives were total failures. As already mentioned, Nixon's most significant domestic legacy may well have been to increase federal entitlement spending and to expand federal intergovernmental regulations to an unprecedented degree. These policies reflected Nixon's pragmatic acceptance of governmental activism but hardly constituted the core of a balanced New Federalism.

Indeed, by the late 1970s these outcomes were part of a pattern that led analysts across the political spectrum to ask whether government in the United States was spiraling out of control. In the words of one scholar, it was not just the rapid growth of the public sector that was alarming, but the extreme pluralism of the policy process that generated "growth without purpose."[13] This environment made it difficult for Nixon to advance his goals, despite concerted attempts to do so.

In contrast, Reagan's policies dominated the political agenda, primarily as a result of his victories in 1981. In that year federal income tax rates were cut 25 percent and business taxes were reduced an additional $50 billion; federal spending for domestic programs was reduced by $35.2 billion, with savings over subsequent years totaling over $130 billion; nine new block grants were established, consolidating seventy-seven programs, and sixty-two additional programs were terminated. In addition, new regulatory review procedures were instituted, and various pending regulations were halted or amended, leading the administration to claim that it had reduced the regulatory burden on states and localities by millions of work hours and billions of dollars.[14]

These differences in outcomes underscored important changes in the structure of politics from the 1970s to the 1980s—changes that reached beyond intergovernmental policy. Between 1974, when President Nixon left office in disgrace, and 1981, when a new Republican president was inaugurated, the political environment and operating premises of American government had changed in fundamental ways, from "rationalizing" politics in the 1970s to the "reactive" politics of the 1980s.

Unlike Nixon, who sought to rationalize active government by curbing the excesses of the Great Society and improving the management of federal programs, Reagan tried to restrain domestic government as a whole. Although not always consistent or successful, his efforts represented a reaction against fundamental elements of the welfare state itself.[15] In so doing, intergovernmental reform was only a single instrument. State and local government may have been preferred to federal involvement in many circumstances, but often as a fallback to no governmental involvement whatsoever. In those cases where federal policy appeared more conducive to the free reign of private markets than state and local policies, the Reagan administration consistently endorsed preserving or enhancing the federal role—states' rights rhetoric notwithstanding.

Such distinctions were more than a historical curiosity. They underscored important transformations in the character and structure of American politics, public attitudes, and the roles of political institutions. The operating premises of public policy shifted during this period, as did the roles and influence of the president, Congress, interest groups, and political parties. Before the effect of these changes on specific public policies can be analyzed, however, it is necessary to examine the political, institutional, and economic context in which this transformation took place.

Economic Disarray

The magnitude of the changes that occurred between 1970 and 1980 can be seen most clearly in the area of economic policy. Flushed with the success of the 1964 tax cut and armed with more and more sophisticated economic models, economists spent the remainder of the 1960s convincing themselves and government officials that they so thoroughly understood the operation of the economy that they could "fine-tune" economic performance. Recessions had become a thing of the past. "We are all Keynesians," declared Nixon as he announced a comprehensive program of wage and price controls in 1971.[16]

Ten years later this economic hubris lay buried in stagflation, the seemingly inexplicable and insoluble combination of economic stagnation and high inflation. Buried with it, in the view of political observer Theodore White, were the electoral hopes of the Democratic party in 1980 and its post–New Deal reputation as an effective manager of the economy. During the 1970s, the inflation rate more than doubled, averaging more than 12.5 percent in 1980.[17] Largely as a result, interest rates temporarily reached a high of 21 percent in late 1980. This trend, in White's view, ate away at the very fabric of American society, as well as public confidence in the political and economic system. "Inflation is the cancer of modern civilization, the leukemia of planning and hope. . . . [It] comes when governments make too many promises. . . . Ultimately . . . faith is lost."[18]

To make matters worse, the negative effects of rising inflation were not compensated for by commensurate economic growth. The economy suffered a severe recession in 1974, and employment never fully recovered. By 1980, despite multibillion-dollar public jobs programs, unemployment rates totaled 48 percent higher than the average of the 1960s.[19]

In part, these economic dislocations were attributable to the oil price shocks resulting from the Arab oil embargo in 1973 and the growing influence of the OPEC cartel. Oil prices in real dollars rose sharply between 1974 and 1980, and gas lines and shortages imposed additional burdens on the economy. Yet the oil price rise did not fully account for the growth of inflation in the 1970s. Estimates vary, but it appears that no more than one-third of the rise in inflation stemmed from oil prices alone.[20]

In their search for other causes of chronic economic distress, increasing numbers of observers pointed to the federal government itself. Conservative Republicans, in particular, attributed a growing list of social and economic ills to big government as more and more of them came under the sway of a refurbished and muscular version of free-market economics.[21] Their message was translated and disseminated by growing numbers of well-funded conservative think tanks that sprouted up in Washington and around the country during the late 1970s. It fell on sympathetic ears in the business community as well, which increasingly looked at tax rates and government regulation of business as the chief cause of falling productivity and the erosion of American competitiveness worldwide.[22] Thus by 1980 the conventional economic wisdom of the 1970s was not only failing to produce the expected results, it was under increasing intellectual attack by articulate critics throughout society.

Institutional Erosion

Those who concluded that government policies were the source of economic ills complained not only about "excessive" federal spending and large federal budget deficits but also about the apparent inability of political institutions to limit spending and deficits. It was this frustration that helped ignite the movement for a constitutional amendment to balance the federal budget. Although extreme, such indictments underscored broader concerns about the capacity of American political institutions to govern effectively. A succession of weakened presidents in the 1970s had convinced many that strong executive leadership was no longer possible. Serious consideration was given to amending the Constitution to strengthen the presidency, and even to the suggestion that American governing structures be replaced with some elements of a parliamentary system.[23]

These views received powerful symbolic affirmation when the government seemed unable to resolve the agonizing hostage situation in Iran, but their origins went far beyond any single incident or any single president. Although the numerous political and legislative problems that plagued Jimmy Carter were taken to be signs of a weakened presidency, he was merely the last in a series of presidents who found themselves in a similar predicament, beginning with Richard Nixon in the final, Watergate-dominated years of his second term. As table 6-1 shows, Nixon's support on congressional roll-call votes dropped sharply after 1972, and Ford's congressional support remained at historically low levels throughout his tenure. Although Carter enjoyed greater support in Congress than had his Republican predecessors, his average was well below that of other modern Democrats.

In part, this diminished presidential influence was the product of the decentralization of power in Congress, which reached its apogee during the late 1970s as changes in rules, resources, and political incentives all worked in unison to increase congressional independence. "Subcommittee government" became the order of the day as power, staffing, and independent funds were diffused among 139 subcommittees in the House and 140 in the Senate.[24] Never before had individual members of Congress been as influential and independent. As James Sundquist observed,

The [early 1970s] saw the greatest spurt of congressional reform since the Revolution of 1910 transformed the House. It is not too much to

Table 6-1. *Presidential Victories on Votes in Congress, 1953–83*
Percent

President and term	House and Senate votes supporting president
Eisenhower	
First	79.1
Second	65.3
Kennedy	84.6
Johnson	82.6
Nixon	
First	73.2
Second (1973–74)	55.1
Ford	57.6
Carter	76.4
Reagan	
First	72.6

Source: Calculated from table 8-1 in Norman J. Ornstein and others, *Vital Statistics on Congress, 1984–85 Edition* (Washington: American Enterprise Institute, 1984), pp. 177–78.

say that in the 1970s the Congress was transformed again. . . . The dominant element of the new political order is individualism. . . . Junior members will accept leadership only on their own terms, and subject to their continuous control. They insist on the right to decide day by day and case by case, without coercion, when they will be followers and when they will assert their right of independence.[25]

As a result, effective leadership in Congress increasingly demanded Herculean efforts. When Massachusetts Democrat Tip O'Neill became Speaker, his influence was widely expected to rival that of Speaker Sam Rayburn. O'Neill's long years of experience and substantial personal skills were fortified by a series of compensatory reforms intended to strengthen the power of party leaders in the House and provide some measure of central coordination to overcome the centrifugal effects of decentralized resources. These tightened the Speaker's control over the critical House Rules Committee, gave the party caucus in the House new powers, and through the Congressional Budget and Impoundment Control Act of 1974 established powerful new mechanisms for creating an integrated congressional

budget process. Yet by 1980 the general consensus was that "this optimism
. . . proved premature. . . . Defeats during the Carter years . . . indicated that
even with strong personal leaders, increased substantive leadership powers,
a president of the same party, and a two-to-one majority, the leadership
could not overcome the independence of House members."[26]

Such legislative fragmentation was both mirrored in and reinforced by
the political process outside Congress. The proliferation of interest groups
during the Nixon years (see chapter 5) continued unabated during the
remainder of the 1970s. Indeed, owing largely to changes in electoral laws,
interest group participation in the electoral process expanded dramatically in this period. Between 1974 and 1980, the number of political action committees (PACs) exploded from 608 to 2,551, and PAC
contributions to congressional campaigns increased from $1.6 million in
1974 to $83.1 million in 1982.[27]

As in the 1960s, many groups continued to form or relocate in Washington in response to the enormous growth in federal programs.[28] Higher
education was a case in point. Before the Higher Education Act of 1965
was passed, only two higher education groups were permanently active in
Washington, although many more were involved at the state level. Six
years later four more groups had moved to Washington, and three had
been newly created. By the 1980s, more than twenty groups were active in
the nation's capital, about half of which were founded after the federal
government had implemented its new initiatives.[29] Similar examples abound
in many other policy areas, from the environment to the disabled.

Practically the only group that was not experiencing fragmentation was
the Republican party. Shaken by the deep losses caused by Watergate and
frustrated by the party's decades-long minority status in the electorate,
national leaders made an unprecedented effort to strengthen the party's
organizational structure and financial resources. Between 1967 and 1978,
the Republican National Committee increased its permanent staff by 60
percent, and its resources increased by over 500 percent, to almost $10
million in 1978.[30] By 1980 the Republican party had a direct mail donor
base of well over 1 million individuals, who contributed more than $6
million dollars that year to Republican congressional and gubernatorial
candidates.[31] These "party-building" efforts helped the Republicans capture
the Senate in 1980 and provided a foundation for Reagan's subsequent
legislative victories. In contrast, centrifugal forces in the Democratic party
caused a sitting president to face a major primary challenge that year.

In combination, then, a weakened presidency, a decentralized Congress, and an explosion of interest groups produced a new and difficult environment for concerted political action. Seeking a metaphor to contrast the atomization and volatility of politics in the 1970s with the 1960s, Joseph Califano settled on the term "molecular politics."[32] As mentioned earlier, one British analyst despaired that American policymaking had been reduced to "building coalitions in the sand."[33] Since each issue was taken up separately and required a unique coalition all its own, policy outcomes were often wildly unpredictable and the burdens on leaders seemed almost unbearable. It is little wonder that the fragmentation so evident in the consideration of the Nixon era gave rise to serious doubts about the "governability" of the American polity itself.[34]

Attitudinal Change

The economic stagnation and perceived institutional weaknesses of the 1970s, reinforced by foreign policy conflicts and Watergate, had important consequences for public attitudes toward the federal government. Compared with the 1960s, popular support for federal activism had markedly declined by 1980, public confidence in American political institutions had fallen, and the public's willingness to entertain conservative alternatives to established federal policies had increased.

It would be a mistake to interpret Ronald Reagan's election as a popular referendum in favor of the conservative policy agenda he espoused. Most citizens hold mixed and even somewhat contradictory values and attitudes. This allows skillful politicians (and pollsters) to elicit support for quite different policy platforms. Moreover, American elections tend to be retrospective judgments on past performance rather than prospective promises. Still, the electorate wooed by Reagan in 1980 was looking at a dismal record, which led many people to believe that the government in Washington combined the worst of two worlds: it had become excessively intrusive and overbearing and at the same time unmanageable and inept.

Survey data demonstrate clearly that public dissatisfaction with the size, scope, and performance of the federal government grew consistently through the late 1960s and 1970s. These attitudes toward the federal government were a leading indicator of a much broader decline in public confidence in American institutions of all kinds. Indeed, some analysts argue that the overall decline was the direct result of the decline in government confidence.[35]

These trends are reflected in the responses to three survey questions asked first in 1964—at the inauguration of the Great Society—and then at various points during subsequent years (see table 6-2). When people were asked in 1964, "Can you trust the government in Washington to do what's right?" 74 percent of respondents replied they could "always" or "most of the time," and only 22 percent replied "only some of the time." By 1980 these percentages had nearly been reversed. Only 25 percent believed they could trust Washington most of the time; 69 percent now said "only some of the time."

Similarly, 47 percent of Americans surveyed in 1964 agreed that government wastes "a lot of the money we pay in taxes." Fourteen years later that number had climbed thirty points to 78 percent. Finally, the number of citizens agreeing that "the federal government has too much power" increased by half between 1964 and 1978. In the year Barry Goldwater lost his presidential bid, a plurality of citizens thought the federal government's powers were "just about right." Fourteen years later the public had become far more polarized on this question, with a narrow plurality now taking an anti-Washington stance. By 1982 this plurality had been solidified by two years of Reagan rhetoric.

These negative evaluations did not extend to all levels of government. During this period, Washington's standing suffered relative to state and local governments. By the time Reagan reached office, larger majorities than ever favored local responsibility for government services, the federal income tax had become less popular than other state and local taxes, and people believed 4 to 1 that states had a better understanding of "people's real needs" and that the federal government wasted 50 percent more of every tax dollar.

In short, public opinion was receptive to Reagan's anti-Washington message by 1980 because the general perception of the government had changed drastically since Nixon's time. Although these negative views masked considerable and deep-seated public support for specific federal programs and functions, they became solidified during Reagan's first two years. By 1981 nearly 60 percent of the public agreed with the old Jeffersonian maxim that "the best government is that which governs least." The following year almost two-thirds of the populace expressed agreement with the president that the federal government causes more problems than it solves.[36] The White House, the Congress, and the press undoubtedly exaggerated this conservative shift in the electorate, but in politics, perceptions can outweigh reality. Seeing the measurably weakened support for federal activism, the administration seized the opportunity to advance its domestic policy initiatives.

Table 6-2. *Public Attitudes toward the Federal Government, Selected Years, 1964–82*

	Percent of responses unless otherwise specified				
Question	1964	1972–73	1978	1980	1981–82
"*Can you trust the government in Washington to do what's right?*"					
Always/most of the time	76	61	...	25	...
Only some of the time	22	42	...	69	...
"*People in government waste a lot of the money we pay in taxes.*"					
Agree	47	66	77	78	...
"*The federal government*"					
Has too much power	26	...	38	...	38
Has just about the right amount of power	36	...	18	...	18
Should use its powers more vigorously	31	...	36	...	30
"*Local government is closer to the people, so as many services as possible should be local.*"					
Agree	...	72	...	...	82
"*Which do you think is the worst tax—that is, the least fair?*"					
Federal income tax	...	19	30	36	36
"*How many cents of each tax dollar do you think are wasted?*"					
By states	...	...	...	...	0.29
By federal government	...	...	...	...	0.42
"*The best government is the government that governs least.*"					
Agree	...	32	38	...	59
Disagree	...	56	48	...	35
"*The federal government creates more problems than it solves.*"					
Agree	...	...	...	...	63

Sources: David R. Gergen, "Following the Leaders," *Public Opinion,* June–July 1985, p. 56; Arthur Miller, "Is Confidence Rebounding," *Public Opinion,* June–July 1985, p. 17; ACIR, *Changing Public Attitudes on Governments and Taxes,* S-12 (Government Printing Office, 1983), pp. 1, 16, 52; Lloyd A. Free and Hadley Cantril, *The Political Beliefs of Americans: A Study of Public Opinion* (Rutgers University Press, 1967), p. 218; National Research Corp.–National Journal, "Opinion Outlook Briefing Paper—The New Federalism Outlook," February 12, 1982, pp. 4, 5; "Opinion Roundup—A Qualified 'Yes' to New Federalism," *Public Opinion,* December–January 1982, p. 36; and R. W. Apple Jr., "President Highly Popular in Poll; No Ideological Shift Is Discerned," *New York Times,* January 28, 1986.

Reactive Politics and Reagan Federalism

In many ways the major changes in economic performance, institutional processes, and public attitudes that had taken place by the time Reagan assumed office were the product of earlier governmental policies and performance. Collectively, they laid the groundwork for a new type of government-inspired "reactive politics" that emerged during Reagan's administration. Public policies normally are thought to be shaped by forces and demands external to government. Such forces can include the press of crises and events, as well as the activities of interest groups, parties, and public opinion. Because this view of policymaking resonates so deeply with the underlying normative assumptions of democratic theory, it has often been accepted almost without question. Yet since the 1960s, when the government's share of the gross domestic product first exceeded 30 percent, it has become increasingly clear that this simple demand model of the policy process was not only incomplete but misleading. Three decades of intergovernmental policy and reform have shown that the public sector itself is now inspiring many public policies. It does so in three principal ways.

First, actors and institutions within the government may initiate and shape policies independently of the external actors and forces normally associated with policy formation—such as the general public, interest groups, and economic conditions. The war on poverty and other elements of Lyndon Johnson's "creative federalism" were excellent examples of such an internally driven policy process. Johnson's decision to make the war on poverty the centerpiece of his domestic policy agenda was not inevitable or imposed on the administration by external actors. As James Sundquist notes: "The war on poverty did not arise, as have many great national programs, from the pressure of overwhelming public demand—the poor had no lobby."[37] Indeed, before deciding to proceed with a broad anti-poverty initiative, the Johnson White House seriously considered advancing revenue sharing or a broader agenda aimed at America's booming suburbs.[38]

It would be naive, of course, to think that the war on poverty was an entirely autonomous enterprise of government insiders, although the community action program probably came close to this model. Government decisionmakers were influenced by a variety of outside factors, ranging from intellectual works to John F. Kennedy's campaign experiences in 1960. Moreover, enactment of the program depended on a receptive or at least nonhostile response from the outside world. Yet the decision to pursue an antipoverty agenda was in keeping with the tendency of policymaking in the 1960s to rely heavily on professionals, especially in the social sciences, to find solutions to social problems. In Samuel Beer's words:

> The intellectual history of federal domestic programs since the days of the Great Society is deeply marked by the influence of . . . complexes of professional expertise. . . . How rarely additions to the public sector have been initiated by the demands of voters or the advocacy of pressure groups or the platforms of political parties. On the contrary, in the fields of health, housing, urban renewal, transportation, welfare, education, poverty, and energy, it has been . . . people in government service, or closely associated with it, acting on the basis of their specialized and technical knowledge, who first perceived the problem, conceived the program, initially urged it on the President and Congress, went on to help lobby it through to enactment, and then saw to its administration.[39]

Although developed internally, such policies interact with the government's political environment in multiple and complex ways. Federal programs created in the 1960s and early 1970s spawned new interests and lobbies to represent their clients and service providers. Indeed, in the case of community action and several other Great Society initiatives, the government explicitly set out to organize certain groups of citizens and to alter the existing political landscape. Once formed, such groups often pushed aggressively for still more and larger programs. At the same time new expectations were created among citizens who now saw their own problems as appropriate targets of governmental attention. Legislators learned to convert these expectations into political opportunities by adopting an entrepreneurial role in policy initiation, focused on the invention of new programs and the conferring of new benefits.

Such a system creates problems as well as solutions. As pointed out in earlier chapters, Nixon's New Federalism can be viewed largely as a second form of governmentally inspired politics—one that has been labeled "rationalizing politics" by Lawrence Brown.[40] In this instance, policies are shaped in response to earlier program failures and the interests spawned by previous governmental action. Nixon's management reforms and block grant proposals were an explicit response to the problems of previous intergovernmental programs, as were many regulatory programs like the National Health Planning Act. The politics of revenue sharing, which was dominated by the intergovernmental lobby, raised the process of intragovernmental politics to a new level.

This political dimension of the New Federalism had important implications for the formation of public policy. Nixon's initiatives were aimed in part at disrupting the professional and institutional arrangements that were responsible for creating many of the programs targeted for reform. This was clearly evident in Nixon's efforts to replace the "service strategy" of the 1960s with an income strategy and entitlements in public assistance. It was evident, too, in block grants and revenue sharing, which sought to disrupt the "iron triangles" and to consolidate governmental activism within the domain of generalists at the state and local levels. Indeed, the Nixon administration even launched a concerted campaign to build up an intergovernmental lobby of state and local elected officials as a political counterweight to bureaucratic professionals at all levels of government. As the Labor Department official quoted in chapter 3 remarked in the case of CETA:

Probably the strongest interest groups have been the public interest groups [PIGs], and that was sort of creating our own Frankenstein. We'd give them funds to hire planning staffs and this built up a strong infrastructure. We also had policy assistance contracts . . . to provide a mechanism for educating and sensitizing officials on the new initiative. So we were creating a constituency and an adversary group prior to CETA.

In the end this effort to disrupt the dynamics of professionalized policy generation was largely unsuccessful, in part because important elements of Nixon's agenda were not adopted and in part because government technocrats were often found to be important and necessary allies in the effort to rationalize prior policies. As a result, rationalizing politics was layered over the creative federalist model, and new initiatives continued to emanate from Washington largely as a result of the efforts of policy entrepreneurs in Congress.

The politics of Reagan's New Federalism represents a third form of governmentally inspired policymaking, which can be termed "reactive" politics. In this phase the concern with governmental dysfunctions spreads well beyond government and shapes the broader political environment, including public opinion, reform agendas in party platforms, and mass media attention. As a result, reactive politics at times resembles the demand model of the policy process. It is also somewhat like the "break-through politics" that typified the federal government's initial, often difficult incursions into many new fields of policy.[41] The distinction is that the new public agenda has been formed around issues of past and present governmental performance and can ultimately be considered an outgrowth of those policies.

Reagan's Instrumental Federalism

Thus when Ronald Reagan charged that "the most important cause of our . . . problems has been the government itself," his diagnosis may have been simplistic, but it suggested an important truth.[42] The president sounded a new chord in American politics, and he drew a strong response. From an intergovernmental perspective, it was an opening Reagan filled with "instrumental federalism." Some have argued that federalism lay at the very center of Reagan's philosophy of governance, that it organized his stands on a vast range of specific policies. According to Richard S. Williamson, Reagan's former assistant for intergovernmental affairs, Reagan had "a dream." It was "not to cut the bloated federal budget . . . not about tax cuts . . . not about regulatory relief. Rather, the President's dream [was] to change how America is governed. He [was] seeking a 'quiet revolution,' a new federalism which is a meaningful American partnership."[43]

The president's own words lent credence to this interpretation. He told a gathering of state legislators in 1981 that his administration was "committed—heart and soul—to the broad principles of American federalism."[44]

In contrast, others have argued that, rhetoric aside, federalism reform was merely a Trojan horse for Reagan's plan to slash the federal budget and dismantle social programs. In their view it was not the organizing principle of the president's philosophy. As one of Jimmy Carter's intergovernmental aides put it:

> The driving force behind the [Reagan] Administration's decisions about federalism [was] primarily a concern with the federal deficit. . . . At the bottom of the New Federalism [was] . . . the Administration's belief that the best way to cut spending [was] to eliminate the substantial support that the federal government currently provides for a variety of programs administered by state and local governments.[45]

This was the view of many state and local officials, including Democratic governors who complained that Reagan's 1982 federalism initiative was "a diversionary tactic" to "solve the federal deficit."[46]

In truth, both views are partly right and underscore a basic ambivalence in Reagan's views toward federalism reform. Altering the balance of power between the federal government and the states was an important goal of the president and his administration. Far from being the hidden goal of a secret and contradictory agenda, cuts in federal aid were viewed as an important tool of intergovernmental reform because they lessened the influence and fiscal profile of the federal government. In sharp contrast to Nixon, Reagan consistently defined federalism reform as a one-sided equation that reduced the federal role but did little to encourage states and localities.[47]

But it is also true that federalism reform per se was not among the president's ultimate policy objectives. Rather his commitment was to the sometimes contradictory goals of reducing the influence of the public sector at all levels of government (except for national defense), increasing society's reliance on private markets, and advancing traditional social values. Because decentralization was often consistent with these aims, Reagan frequently employed it to implement his policies. But where the president's federalism goals (which were almost always defined in terms of aggressive decentralization) conflicted with these larger ends, federalism concerns were consistently sacrificed on their behalf. As the following chapters demonstrate, this was true in budgetary, tax, and regulatory policy alike and underscored the president's declaration in his first inaugural address: "government is not the solution to our problem. Government is the problem."

CHAPTER 7

The Implicit Federalism of Reagan's Fiscal Policies

IN DECEMBER 1980 David Stockman mailed a job application to the newly elected president. Entitled "Avoiding an Economic Dunkirk," this lengthy résumé raised the specter of an economic crisis on the nation's horizon and spelled out a detailed program for avoiding it.

The fundamental problem, Stockman wrote, was the modern welfare state itself. Nurtured by unholy alliances of bureaucrats, legislators, subsidized industries, and other client groups, the American welfare state was growing at an uncontrollable rate and strangling the economy. The result, he concluded, would be economic collapse: high federal taxes and high levels of federal borrowing would combine with proliferating regulations to stifle business incentives, hamper productivity, undermine private investment, and drain economic vitality, growth, and competitiveness.

To deal with this complex set of problems, Stockman prescribed a comprehensive set of reforms. Large, immediate reductions in federal income tax rates were required to restore incentives for private investment and risk taking. To accommodate tax cuts and to reduce federal interference in the marketplace, federal domestic spending had to be drastically reduced and large numbers of intrusive and ineffective programs eliminated. Finally, specific federal regulations, and the entire regulatory process, had to be reformed and restructured to reduce excessive interference in social and economic decisionmaking and to ensure that social benefits outweighed economic costs.

Stockman's job application was successful, earning him the post of director of the Office of Management and Budget. From this position he was strategically positioned to fashion President Ronald Reagan's program in domestic policy, and the product hewed closely to his initial recommendations.

Nowhere in Stockman's agenda were issues of federalism mentioned outright. But, implicitly, intergovernmental issues were inescapable. Terminating "ineffective" or "inefficient" programs meant, in many cases, terminating federal grant programs to state and local governments. Reforming and reducing the costs of federal entitlements affected federalism directly, by modifying intergovernmental programs like aid to families with dependent children (AFDC) and medicaid, and indirectly, by scaling down the fiscal profile of the federal government. Tax cuts would make this lower profile permanent by putting a fiscal straitjacket around federal activists in Congress. Relieving regulatory costs and burdens altered joint administrative arrangements in some regulatory programs and reduced state and local costs and burdens in others. In short, the comprehensive economic plans recommended to the president constituted a complex strategy for implementing federalism reform as well as economic reform, and the president and his advisers seized on and embellished this dual character.

An explicit package of federalism initiatives—seven sweeping block grant proposals—was added to the 1981 budget proposals. This was followed in 1982 by a huge plan for restructuring federal, state, and local responsibilities. (These initiatives, along with budgetary decisions affecting intergovernmental aid levels and priorities, are reviewed in the following chapters.) However, it was Reagan's implicit agenda—in the form of federal tax and domestic budget cuts—that had greater long-term philosophical and operational implications for the federal system as a whole. As was argued in chapter 6, Reagan's New Federalism policies were one expression of a broader philosophical attack on the modern welfare state. This was not simply a question of giving a greater role to the states vis-à-vis the federal government; Reagan opposed public sector activism at every level of government. His explicit intergovernmental agenda is best appreciated within this wider context.

From a historical standpoint, the preeminence of Reagan's implicit federalism agenda is not unique. Despite all their specific programmatic accomplishments, Presidents Franklin Delano Roosevelt and Lyndon Baines Johnson did most to reshape the federal system by nationalizing policy innovation, by expanding public expectations of the federal government, and by altering the political incentives of politicians. Reagan attempted to do much the same in reverse. Federal tax cuts and defense increases produced unprecedented deficits that came to dominate the national agenda, reducing federal activism and altering its forms.

The political effect of Reagan's implicit federalism agenda was just as significant. Although ambitious in scope, the president's initial proposals mustered surprising political support in Congress. As a result, anticipated federal spending for domestic programs was reduced by more than $35 billion in fiscal 1982, and grants to state and local governments were cut sharply. Federal income tax rates were reduced 25 percent over a three-year period, and sixty pending regulations were delayed or revised by administrative action.[1] Such striking outcomes were produced by a very different style of politics than was evident during the 1970s. These factors in turn redefined the subsequent policy agenda.

Politically, the Reagan administration shunned the tedious process of building a bipartisan consensus for reform in individual policy areas. It succeeded instead in constructing a partisan-conservative phalanx that rolled major portions of the president's program through Congress in one bold sweep. For the single critical year of 1981, the narrow interest subsystem politics and congressional fragmentation that characterized the Nixon and Carter years gave way to a highly visible, majoritarian style of presidential policy leadership.

This pattern of successful party government did not last, but neither did the federal government return to the highly fragmented system of policymaking that dominated the 1970s. With respect to budgetary policy, for example, the legislative changes enacted in 1981 restructured the policymaking environment, and a new politics of budgetary stalemate emerged on most domestic spending issues. Continuing efforts to reduce or eliminate the federal deficit through the Gramm-Rudman-Hollings process and its successors maintained the pressure for additional domestic budget cuts in the years ahead.

In the area of tax policy, Congress waged an incremental effort over four years to restore some of the revenues lost to the federal treasury by the 1981 income tax reductions. This was done without taking on the president's supply-side tax cuts directly, through excise tax increases and closing of tax loopholes. Although these patterns of fiscal stalemate and incremental tax increases were temporarily broken with the passage of sweeping tax reform legislation in 1986, the "revenue-neutral" character of that legislation did nothing to resolve the fiscal tourniquet squeezing the federal agenda.

Budgetary Blitzkrieg in 1981

On February 18, 1981, President Reagan sent Congress an "economic recovery program" containing eighty-three proposals to reduce federal

Table 7-1. *Comparison of Reagan Budget Requests for Fiscal Year 1982 with Actual Fiscal Year 1981 Expenditures on Comparable Programs*

Billions of dollars unless otherwise specified

Program category	Fiscal 1981 expenditures	Fiscal 1982 request	Percent difference
Total block grants	18.7	14.8	−21
New block grants[a]	12.8	9.7	−24
Existing block grants[b]	5.9	5.1	−14
Total federal aid	105.8	86.2	−19
Major entitlements[c]	311.4	335.3	8
Total domestic spending[d]	511.2	546.1	7
National defense	182.4	226.3	24
Total federal spending	718.4	772.4	8

Source: *Budget Appendix, Special Analyses, Budget of the United States Government,* various years.

a. The fiscal 1981 figure is the combined expenditures for the programs consolidated into the fiscal 1982 block grants.

b. Does not include public service employment programs.

c. Includes social security.

d. Total federal spending minus defense and international affairs.

budget outlays by $34.8 billion in 1982. Three weeks later he sent Congress another package of 200 recommendations for an additional $13.8 billion in savings.[2] From an intergovernmental standpoint, the most noteworthy items in these packages were the proposals to (1) establish seven new block grants, with estimated savings in fiscal 1982 of $3.1 billion; (2) cut $5 billion out of income security programs by tightening eligibility requirements and by changing matching ratios in medicaid, food stamps, AFDC, and child nutrition programs; and (3) terminate the remainder of the public employment program under the Comprehensive Employment and Training Act (CETA), thereby saving approximately $2 billion. Overall, the president proposed reducing federal aid expenditures by $19.6 billion, or 19 percent, below fiscal 1981 levels. By one estimate, two-thirds of the administration's proposed cuts came out of intergovernmental programs, even though federal aid constituted only about 17 percent of the federal budget.[3] In contrast, total domestic spending—including social security—was slated to rise by 7 percent, and defense spending by 24 percent, over 1981 levels (see table 7-1).

Although the president did not obtain everything he asked for, he was surprisingly successful, as already mentioned. The final budget to emerge from Congress in 1981 reduced anticipated federal outlays for domestic programs by $35 billion in fiscal 1982 and $131 billion by 1984. This amounted to a reduction of approximately 6 percent below expected 1982 spending levels.[4] Grants to state and local governments were cut even more sharply, falling $6 billion below actual spending in fiscal 1981 and 13 percent below anticipated or baseline expenditures for fiscal 1982. Especially hard hit were grants supporting the delivery of state and local services in education, job training, and social welfare, as well as nongrant programs like housing assistance, Amtrak, government employee benefits, and postal subsidies. Sixty-two programs were terminated altogether, including CETA public employment, and another seventy-seven programs were consolidated into nine new or restructured block grants.[5] Finally, medicaid spending was slowed, and the AFDC and food stamps budgets were reduced by about $2 billion below baseline expenditures.[6]

Evaluations of the effect of these budgetary changes vary. Although most administration officials were jubilant at what they had achieved, David Stockman argued publicly that the cuts agreed upon constituted only half of the domestic cuts needed to complete the president's agenda. Indeed, some observers questioned whether Reagan's victories even amounted to a change in direction. They argued that—far from ushering in a "Reagan revolution"—they merely accelerated budgetary trends that had begun in the Carter administration.[7]

Press accounts at the time were more generous, calling the reconciliation act a "triumph for conservatism rivaling the liberal triumphs of . . . Roosevelt and . . . Johnson."[8] Many policy analysts agreed. Richard Nathan called the Omnibus Budget Reconciliation Act (OBRA) "the single most important piece of social legislation enacted in the United States since the Social Security Act of 1935."[9] Most important from a political standpoint, members of Congress viewed both the budget and tax initiatives as striking departures from "business as usual." Republicans hailed the "two whopping pieces of legislation." "Part of the Great Society program has been repealed," observed House Republican leader Robert H. Michel of Illinois, and "can't be reinstated."[10] Disheartened Democrats called it "the most monumental and historic turnaround in fiscal policy that has ever occurred."[11]

How Reagan achieved this budgetary victory can be traced to three sets of political factors. Philosophically, the president was aided by a widely perceived crisis in New Deal liberalism and the seeming inability of Democrats to defend convincingly the merits of existing programs or to generate viable policy alternatives. Structurally, the president was assisted by Republican control of the Senate, by the revival of the conservative coalition in the House, and by the relative coherence and technical sophistication of the Republican party. Finally, enactment of the new block grants and budget reductions was achieved through brilliant parliamentary tactics that substantially altered the traditional ground rules of budgetary politics. The budget reconciliation process made it possible to subsume a series of discrete policy decisions under the president's economic program, where the particularistic concerns of individual program advocates were overshadowed by high-visibility budgetary politics.

Reconciliation and the Tactical Transformation of Budgetary Politics

A simple chronology of budget politics in 1981 reveals the role of tactical considerations in the Reagan victory. Early in the year, as the president's proposals were being considered individually by congressional committees, the prospects for enactment were anything but promising. Committees in the Republican-controlled Senate made substantial alterations in sections of the president's proposals, and some committees in the Democratic House threatened to block certain cuts altogether. This pattern was reversed, however, when the reconciliation process was used to shift decisionmaking from committees to the floor and to reframe issues on the president's terms.

The seeds of reconciliation were sown long before Reagan was elected president. Ironically, they lay in Congress's negative reaction to the budget tactics associated with the New Federalism of Richard Nixon. In 1974 Congress passed the Congressional Budget and Impoundment Control Act in response to the Nixon administration's abuses of its power to impound appropriated funds. Moreover, there was a growing sense within Congress that, in order to effectively challenge any president's budget, the legislative branch required an independent mechanism that would enable it to produce a coherent set of alternative spending priorities.

The Congressional Budget and Impoundment Control Act required Congress to adopt two comprehensive budget resolutions each year: a preliminary one in the spring setting forth general spending targets to guide individual committees' spending decisions, and a binding one in the fall adjusted for actual appropriation and authorization bills adopted by Congress and for any modifications in revenue and expenditure estimates caused by changing economic conditions. In order to ensure that automatic entitlements would not exceed the binding budget ceilings, the act included a "reconciliation" provision permitting existing statutes to be amended by the budget resolution, so as to "reconcile" them to overall spending limits. This provision was not used until 1980, however, when serious problems with President Carter's fiscal 1991 budget proposal produced a crash effort by White House and congressional leaders to cut federal spending. They used the reconciliation device to reduce the 1980 and 1981 budgets by approximately $5 billion.[12]

This laid the groundwork for the Republicans' use of reconciliation in 1981. The new administration and Republican leaders in Congress seized on the device as a vehicle for making rapid budget cuts before the president's popularity began to slip away. For obvious reasons, administration strategists did not expect congressional committees to willingly make substantial cuts in federal programs or to sacrifice their own influence over policy through program consolidation. A comprehensive budget reconciliation bill, combining spending reductions with consolidations, could be used to bypass committee specialists and to divert political attention from the fate of separately targeted programs and draw it to the president's economic program.

This proved to be a brilliant political move. At a time when individual committees in both chambers of Congress were resisting the president's budget and block grant proposals, the reconciliation vehicle allowed the administration to construct conservative budget coalitions on the floor of each chamber that adopted overall spending ceilings consistent with the president's economic program. The Republican-controlled Senate passed its initial budget resolution on April 2, 1981, by a vote of 88 to 10.[13] The House, in a major victory for the president, rejected the Democratic leadership's proposed budget resolution and on May 7 adopted a lower, administration-backed budget resolution amendment—the so-called Gramm-Latta I amendment—by a vote of 253 to 176.

These initial resolutions instructed recalcitrant committees to develop specific legislative proposals designed to meet the new spending targets and to report these changes to their respective budget committees by June 12, 1981. The budget targets were not binding, however, and so the reconciliation process was implemented in order to establish fixed spending ceilings and make permanent changes in specific legislation. Once again the Senate led the way, passing its version of the Omnibus Budget Reconciliation Act on June 25, 1981, by a vote of 80 to 15. The House passed its final reconciliation bill, as amended by "Gramm-Latta II," in a dramatic showdown vote of 217 to 21 the following day. A conference version of the reconciliation act was signed into law on August 13, 1981.

As Robert Fulton, former chief counsel for the Senate Budget Committee, observed, the tactical key to the success of the reconciliation act was that it combined a wide variety of program changes and spending cuts in one highly visible package:

> Reconciliation made possible a "critical mass" of spending reductions which members could not afford to oppose, and it enabled the media—and the public—to keep a clear view of the progress Congress was making on the president's proposals. It also provided a few highly visible votes upon which maximum leverage could be mobilized by the president and his supporters.[14]

Recognizing the political implications of the reconciliation device, House Democratic leaders made one last-ditch attempt to disrupt the administration's strategy before the act was adopted. They proposed a rule requiring the administration-backed Gramm-Latta II substitute to be considered in five different components, so that House members could go on record for specific cuts in programs such as student aid, social security, and medicaid. The president's budget coalition in the House, however, defeated this rule in a critical vote on June 25, 1981, and the stage was set for a single yes or no vote on the Gramm-Latta II reconciliation amendment.

Accordingly, the budget for fiscal 1982 was developed not through the traditional painstaking and incremental work of the appropriations subcommittees, but through a massive ad hoc amendment pasted together during frenzied last-minute negotiations among Republicans and conservative Democrats. In fact, House members had almost no information concerning the contents of the far-reaching Gramm-Latta amendment.[15]

As Representative Norman Mineta (Democrat of California) complained after the budget was adopted:

> The haste with which the Administration substitute was thrown together . . . made it impossible for Members to know what they were voting on. Copies of the proposal which was hundreds of pages long were only available to Members just hours before the final vote and after debate had begun on the bill. The legislative document contained handwritten notes scribbled in the margin, dollar amounts of

entries pencilled in, others scratched out. In this . . . manner, Congress was asked to consider the largest single bill ever brought before it, affecting virtually every activity of government.[16]

In the end, then, reconciliation allowed the issue to be framed in the president's terms. "The Reagan administration cast it this way," said one newspaper report. "You were either for the president and economic recovery, or you were against it. Cool deliberation took a back seat. . . . Substance gave way to symbolism."[17]

Philosophical and Institutional Dimensions of the Reconciliation Act

The reconciliation act provided a vehicle for the president's victory, but it was not the ultimate cause. The legislation mustered support largely because of two political factors: the philosophical and structural disarray of the Democratic party, which hampered attempts to challenge the administration's program, and the surprising strength of the Republican party in Congress.

THE EROSION OF NEW DEAL LIBERALISM. Conventional wisdom attributes much of the credit for the Reagan administration's legislative successes to the president's landslide election, which was seen as a "mandate" for change. Politicians and the public alike were impressed by the president's sizable margin of victory. Moreover, the appearance of a conservative tide was reinforced by the defeat of several prominent liberal senators and the surprising election of a Republican majority in the Senate for the first time in a quarter century. There is evidence in retrospect that the 1980 elections were overinterpreted—that there was no mandate from the people for conservative policies.[18] What counted at the time, however, was the widespread perception that such a mandate had been granted.[19]

Equally important was the comparison between the new administration's ideological vigor and the philosophical malaise of the Democrats. The administration exuded confidence, believing that it had found in "supply-side economics" an answer to the seemingly intractable problems of stagnation, lagging investment and productivity, and soaring interest rates. In contrast, the Democrats in 1981 were floundering. Because much of the policy agenda stemming from the New Deal had been adopted—with the notable exception of national health insurance—there was an understandable policy vacuum in the party. Capturing the tenor of the times, columnist Russell Baker described the New Deal as "an idea whose time had passed." He wrote poignantly:

Only a sentimentalist could weep. A 50-year-old political idea is like a 30-year-old dog or 150-year-old man. . . . So it was with the New Deal: old, stricken in years, and, despite the accretions of Truman's Fair Deal and Lyndon Johnson's Great Society, finally it gat no heat. It certainly gat none in the new generation of Democrats. For years now they have formed a party in the sense that a party is a conspiracy to get elected and enjoy the pleasures of the feeding trough.[20]

DEMOCRATIC FRAGMENTATION IN CONGRESS. The Democratic party's seeming loss of philosophical identity in 1981 was exacerbated by the effects of organizational fragmentation in Congress. As had occurred earlier in the Senate, power in the House of Representatives was greatly decentralized through a series of procedural reforms in 1970, 1971, and 1973 that stripped committee chairmen of power, greatly expanded the number and influence of subcommittee chairs, and strengthened the position of individual members of Congress. The most significant of these reforms were developed in the House Democratic caucus and then imposed by the majority on the operations of the House. They produced what some observers have called "subcommittee government," which fostered the "extreme individualism" in congressional behavior during the 1970s.[21]

This general fragmentation contributed to growing Democratic disunity in the late 1970s, especially among newly elected Democrats whose support of the party seemed to be waning. Senior Democrats in Congress began complaining that newer members were becoming ideologically aloof and unpredictable.[22] To make matters worse, there was a powerful revival of the conservative coalition in Congress between conservative Republicans and southern Democrats. Indeed, 1981 witnessed the highest success rate ever scored by the conservative coalition during a single session of Congress since *Congressional Quarterly* began compiling its index in 1957. The conservative coalition won victories in a whopping 92 percent of the cases in which a majority of southern Democrats and Republicans opposed a majority of northern Democrats. This success rate was 20 percentage points higher than in 1980 and 28 points above the average score of the previous decade. It is no wonder that President Reagan achieved the highest presidential support in congressional voting since Lyndon Johnson's triumphs in the 89th Congress.[23]

Among southern Democrats, support for the conservative coalition stemmed largely from the president's popularity in their districts in 1981 and increased competition from Republicans for congressional seats in the no longer "solid South." Republicans gained nine House seats in that region in the 1980 election and were up thirteen seats from 1976. Not one House delegation from a southern state was solidly Democratic by 1981, and only two southern states retained two Democratic senators. As a result, White House budget strategists were determined from the start to focus their lobbying on these potentially vulnerable "boll weevil" Democrats.[24] Partly because of such efforts, one renegade Democrat turned Republican, Representative Phil Gramm of Texas, secretly negotiated with the White House and Republican congressional leaders on bipartisan budget legislation and had his name prominently affixed to the key budget amendments that shaped the reconciliation act.

REPUBLICAN SOLIDARITY. Republicans' unity in Congress was an even more important reason for the president's success in 1981. In contrast to the Democrats' disorganization, Republican voting in Congress was marked by striking solidarity. This was especially true in the Senate, where GOP control for the first time in twenty-five years boosted party unity scores among Republicans 16 percentage points above 1980 levels. On critical votes in the House, the president's economic program evoked similar unity from members of his party. House Republicans voted 190 to 0 in support of the first budget resolution, reducing fiscal 1982 spending by $36.6 billion. Six weeks later they voted 188 to 2 in favor of specific budget cuts and block grants in the reconciliation act. Finally, they voted 190 to 1 in favor of the president's tax cut bill, reducing federal income taxes 25 percent over three years.[25]

This unity did not mean that the so-called gypsy moths—moderate northern Republicans who threatened to abandon the president's position—had no influence in 1981. Before the key vote on Gramm-Latta II, for instance, they were able to exact certain concessions on spending for medicaid, Amtrak, and mass transit grants. But such amendments are part of the normal give and take of legislative politics. In 1981 the most important factor was the lack of defections by moderate Republicans on key votes. "We always had 25 or 30 of the Gypsy Moths . . . who voted with us [in prior years]," complained Speaker O'Neill. "But as you look at the discipline of the party, last year the Republicans voted in lockstep. . . . The President never lost a vote."[26]

This unity, in turn, reflected both short- and long-term trends in the Republican party. In the short term it represented a natural—if temporary—response by a party long out of power, buoyed by the president's popularity and ideological vigor and by the Democrats' disorganization. For example, Republicans in Congress departed sharply in 1981 from their historic levels of support for federal aid spending. In 1982, however, they quickly returned to earlier patterns of support.[27]

At the same time more lasting changes in the structure and composition of the Republican party also contributed to party strength and unity. Students of Congress had observed a trend toward increasing ideological consensus among congressional Republicans in the years before 1981, and they found that surviving members of the Watergate era and their newly elected colleagues in both chambers were becoming more conservative.[28] Further contributing to Republican unity were structural developments in national party organization. In the wake of the Watergate debacle, the Republican party became more active in grooming and assisting new candidates for Congress. The party recruited promising candidates for congressional office, staged national training seminars in campaign techniques, provided candidates with polling and consultant services, and distributed substantial campaign contributions.[29] Indeed, the party's success in direct mail fund-raising enabled the National Republican Congressional Committee and the Republican Senatorial Committee to raise $78.8 million for the 1982 campaign (as of September 1981), ten times more than their Democratic counterparts were able to raise.[30] Along with the coattails of Ronald Reagan, such party-building efforts in the 1980 campaign helped Republicans elect twelve new members to the Senate and thirty-three to the House.

The Republican party's organizational sophistication was evident as well in legislative coalition building. White House and congressional leaders skillfully bound the elements of their electoral coalition together by using sympathetic lobbies to campaign for block grants and budget cuts and to mobilize public pressure on Congress to support the president. The administration helped mobilize such groups into an organized blitzkrieg of fifty-one key congressional districts, generating phone calls, mail, and demands for presidential support from the general public, the local media, and campaign contributors. Spurred by this presidential symphony, constituents flooded Capitol Hill with letters and calls supporting the president in the battle over reconciliation.[31]

Budget Politics since 1981

The budget actions of 1981 were a milestone in contemporary budgeting. Before 1981 the normal pattern in budgetary politics was incremental growth.[32] Although it often obscured major differences and shifts in growth rates among individual programs and budget functions, incremental growth remained the norm until 1980, when the budget reconciliation process was first utilized on a small scale under the Carter administration. The large cuts implemented in 1981 were followed by more modest annual reductions in subsequent years.

The unique character of the 1981 reconciliation act is reflected in the outcomes of congressional budgetary actions from 1980 to 1984 (see table 7-2). Congress continued to make incremental budgetary reductions in subsequent years, but they paled in comparison with the 1981 cuts. Measured as outlays, the total annual cuts enacted for the three years between 1982 and 1984 equaled less than one-third of the reductions enacted in

Table 7-2. Congressional Budget Actions, 1980–84
Billions of dollars

Budget action	First-year effect	Three-year effect
Omnibus Reconciliation Act of 1980		
Budget authority	–2.8	...
Outlays	–4.6	...
Omnibus Reconciliation Act of 1981		
Budget authority	–53.2	–172.3
Outlays	–35.2	–130.9
Omnibus Reconciliation Act of 1982		
Budget authority	–3.4	–14.9
Outlays	–6.9	–29.9
Omnibus Reconciliation Act of 1983[a]		
Budget authority	2.0	2.3
Outlays	–0.4	–1.8
Deficit Reduction Act of 1984		
Budget authority	–0.9	–7.2
Outlays	–3.9	–12.2

Source: John Ellwood, "The Great Exception: The Congressional Budget Process in an Age of Decentralization," in Lawrence C. Dodd and Bruce I. Oppenheimer, eds., Congress Reconsidered, 3d ed. (Washington: CQ Press, 1985), p. 332.
a. Enacted on April 18, 1984.

Table 7-3. *Percentage Change in Real Domestic Outlays,*
Fiscal Years 1981–87

Budget category	1981– 82	1982– 83	1983– 84	1984– 85	1985– 86	1986– 87	Total, 1981–87
Total nondefense	0.9	2.7	0.4	7.1	0.6	–2.1	9.8
Payments to individuals[a]	3.6	6.2	–2.8	2.8	2.8	1.2	14.7
Grants in aid	–12.3	0.6	1.4	3.9	2.9	–6.3	–10.1
All other	–10.8	0.5	–6.7	17.0	–9.3	–7.5	–20.1
Net interest	15.3	1.3	18.6	12.7	2.2	–0.7	59.4

Source: Calculated from *Budget of the United States Government, Historical Tables, Fiscal Year 1989*, table 6-1.

a. Including grants to state and local governments for individuals.

1981 alone, and their magnitude was even less significant when measured in terms of budget authority.

This change in budgetary momentum was not for want of trying on the president's part. The administration continued to propose substantial new domestic spending cuts and structural program changes, but it met with limited success. For each fiscal year from 1982 to 1987, the administration consistently proposed lower levels of spending on federal domestic programs than were actually adopted into law, but instead of achieving additional large reductions in domestic expenditures, the administration ushered in a period of relative stability. Federal domestic spending actually increased 10 percent in constant dollars during Reagan's administration, mainly because of large increases in social security, medicare, and interest on the debt, although this was far short of the 47 percent real increase in domestic spending that occurred in the 1970s (see table 7-3). Real spending for federal grants to states and localities fell 10 percent from fiscal 1981 to fiscal 1987; this reflected primarily the steep cuts made in OBRA in 1981 and the elimination of revenue sharing in 1986. Although some components of federal aid continued to decline, notably for government services, grants-in-aid for individuals grew modestly after fiscal 1982. When measured in relative terms as a percentage of GNP or of total federal outlays, total domestic spending and most of its individual components (except for interest on the debt) remained relatively constant after 1981.

This stability in domestic budget outputs was the result of the political stalemate between the president and Congress over fiscal issues. The president's congressional success rating—the percentage of congressional roll-call votes on which the president took a position and was successful in Congress—dropped sharply in the House after his initial victories in 1981. It dropped sixteen points, or nearly 23 percent, in 1982 alone and continued falling in subsequent years.[33] In terms of presidential support in the House, 1981 was clearly an anomaly.

The Politics of Fiscal Constraint

Although the momentum for additional large cuts in domestic programs did not continue past 1981, President Reagan's first-year victories had lasting effects on the government's agenda. For the duration of his tenure in office, Reagan's agenda remained fixed on issues of retrenchment rather than growth, and few important spending initiatives were seriously proposed, much less implemented, in the 1980s. After 1981 the large, structurally embedded federal deficit focused congressional attention each year on deficit reduction rather than program enhancements.

The restricted nature of the post-1981 policy agenda was evident in both the substantive mix and overall scope of Congress's workload during the 1980s. Virtually all measures of congressional productivity in the House and Senate declined under Reagan. The number of bills introduced in the House averaged 13,890 per session in the three Congresses from 1975 to 1980 (see table 7-4), but declined 46 percent to an average of only 7,566 per session between 1981 and 1986. The number of bills passed in the House declined 9 percent during this period, from an average of 975 per session in the late 1970s to 885 in the 1980s. Recorded votes in the House declined an average of 36 percent during the same period.

Similar trends occurred in the Senate, where, on average, 10 percent fewer bills were introduced in the 97th through 99th Congresses compared with the 94th through 96th Congresses. The number of bills passed dropped by 13 percent, and 32 percent fewer votes were recorded in the Senate during this latter period.

To be sure, such data give only a rough idea of actual congressional outputs and activities. They say nothing about the magnitude or content of the legislation passed.[34] Moreover, averaging the data over six-year periods obscures variations and trends within these time periods. As measured by these indicators, congressional activism actually began declining in the late 1970s, while the number of bills passed increased during the 99th Congress, in both the House and Senate, suggesting that the nadir of

Table 7-4. *Indicators of Congressional Activity, 1975–86*

Congress	Bills introduced	Bills passed	Recorded votes
Senate			
Average, 1975–80	3,798	1,028	1,156
Average, 1981–86	3,413	701	788
House			
Average, 1975–80	13,890	975	1,363
Average, 1981–86	7,566	817	869

Sources: Norman Ornstein and others, *Vital Statistics on Congress, 1984–85* (Washington: American Enterprise Institute, 1985), pp. 144, 146; "Resume of Congressional Activity of the 98th Congress," *Congressional Record,* daily ed., November 14, 1984, p. D1347; and "Resume of Congressional Activity of the 99th Congress," *Congressional Record,* daily ed., January 6, 1987, p. D2.

declining productivity was reached during Reagan's first term. There is no question, however, that important forms of congressional activity reached new and lower thresholds in the 1980s.

This new and more constrained congressional agenda had other manifestations as well, altering the mix of congressional activities and members' subjective evaluations of the process. Most important was the growing prominence of budgetary issues. The percentage of budget-related roll-call votes in Congress increased sharply in the mid-1980s compared with the late 1970s (see table 7-5). This was especially true in the Senate, where the average percentage of budget-related votes increased from 38 percent in the late 1970s to 56 percent in the 1980s.[35] In the more carefully regulated House, the percentage of budget-related votes increased from an average of 48 percent in the 1975–78 period to an average of 55 percent in the 1980s.

Especially during Reagan's first term, normally active members of Congress encountered new limits to their capacity to legislate. "The deficit holds everything hostage" became the new conventional wisdom on Capitol Hill.[36] As one astonished member of the House Energy and Commerce Committee observed in 1983, "Reagan put all the issues in the Budget Act and used that as a vehicle for everything he wanted. Virtually everything stopped as we fought those battles. There wasn't much room for authorizing legislation to come down the pipe."[37]

Lobbyists noted the change and adjusted their strategies accordingly. With fewer bills moving through Congress, budget-related vehicles be-

Table 7-5. Selected Budget-Related Roll-Call Votes in Congress, by Type, Selected Years, 1975–86

Type of vote	1975	1978	1981	1984	1986
Senate					
Authorizations	121	83	64	38	34
Appropriations	88	80	131	76	78
Budget resolutions	8	18	26	1	14
Reconciliation	...	...	62	47	12
Debt ceiling	3	1	5	3	3
Miscellaneous	4	10	6	2	23
Total	224	192	294	167	164
Percent of all votes that are budget related	38	37	60	61	46
House					
Authorizations	167	216	97	123	120
Appropriations	93	132	86	75	88
Budget resolutions	12	30	13	10	7
Reconciliation	...	...	12	8	9
Debt ceiling	10	10	2	6	2
Miscellaneous	10	4	1	1	10
Total	292	392	211	223	236
Percent of all votes that are budget related	48	47	60	54	52

Source: Congressional Research Service, derived from all roll-call votes listed in *Congressional Quarterly*. Miscellaneous votes include proposed changes in budget process and proposed rescissions. Each category includes votes on passage, amendments, and relevant procedures.

came prime targets for legislating extraneous matters. Moreover, the increased importance of the centralized budget process forced many groups to band together to protect their interests. One comprehensive study of interest group behavior in the 1980s found that coalition building among interest groups was the fastest growing form of lobbying strategy.[38] On the other hand, decremental budgeting and annual reconciliation bills introduced into the legislative process a new form of zero-sum politics—or negative-sum politics—as the revenues to finance one initiative had to be sought from the appropriation for some other program. "What's happening is that we're trying to put a size 9 foot into a size 7 boot," observed one farm lobbyist. "The budget rules simply prevent anything from moving. The budget process is more important to lobbying now than getting things through the authorizing process."[39]

Increasingly, members adopted strategies for new initiatives that minimized their impact on the federal deficit. The most difficult technique was to levy a new tax for the problem to be addressed, as was done in the case of the superfund program for cleaning up toxic waste sites and the 1982 highway reauthorization bill, which contained a five-cent increase in the federal gasoline tax. The second technique was to reassign funds from existing programs to pay for a new initiative, as was done with the omnibus drug initiative of 1986. Third, Congress could attempt to pass new regulations and unfunded mandates to deflect program costs from the federal budget to third parties, as was done with the urban nonpoint pollution monitoring standards adopted in the Clean Water Act reauthorization in 1986. As discussed in chapter 10, the number of new mandates passed by Congress rose sharply in the 1980s.

Reagan's Budget Legacy

The tax and budgetary policies enacted in 1981 had important intergovernmental consequences, even though they fell short of David Stockman's revolutionary ambitions. In particular, the activist, entrepreneurial Congress of the 1970s was constrained by the new budgetary politics of the 1980s. Although additional domestic spending reductions were modest after 1981, a new and lower equilibrium was achieved in new spending initiatives. Given the importance of congressional entrepreneurship for shaping the intergovernmental system of the 1960s and 1970s, this was an important consequence of Reagan's implicit federalism.

Equally important, the newly constrained agenda shaped the kinds of new policies emerging from the Congress as well as their total volume. Federal budget politics evolved from distributive to redistributive in nature, meaning that the resources available for domestic programs are now reallocated within a stable or shrinking funding base rather than being funded from an expanding budgetary base.[40] In the process the character of congressional initiatives has shifted to "low cost social justice"—often ad hoc forms of spending, tax, and regulatory policies in which the means of financing may acquire greater priority in program design than the substantive goals of the program itself.[41]

Undermining the Welfare State through Tax Policy

Although budget policy had the most obvious indirect impact on inter-governmental relations during the Reagan administration, tax policy was equally important, particularly with the enactment of comprehensive tax reform legislation in 1986. Federal income tax policy underwent tremendous changes under Reagan. Individual income tax rates were effectively reduced 23 percent over a three-year period under the Economic Recovery Tax Act of 1981. The top marginal tax rate was reduced by three-fifths, from 70 percent to 50 percent in 1981 and then down to 28 percent under the Tax Reform Act of 1986. On the revenue side, the combined effects of the individual tax rate reductions and incentives for personal savings and corporate investment enacted in 1981 reduced federal revenues $282 billion below what they would have been during the period between 1982 and 1984.[42] Although some of these lost revenues were restored through increased excise taxes and "loophole closing" in the Tax Equity and Fiscal Responsibility Act of 1982 and the Deficit Reduction Act of 1984, the comprehensive tax reform legislation passed in 1986 shifted an additional $120 billion in tax liabilities from individuals to corporations over five years.

The significance of these changes for federal revenue collections and the structure of the federal tax code has been widely recognized. Indeed, the tax reform act has been called "one of the most important pieces of tax legislation ever passed."[43] It is less widely recognized that, taken collectively, these changes comprised a frontal assault on the revenue base of the modern welfare state, not only in Washington but also at the state and local levels. This assault had three dimensions.

First, the massive tax reductions adopted in 1981 dwarfed the budget cuts adopted that year. This weakened the fiscal underpinnings of future federal spending. Citing David Stockman's published admission that the tax cuts would "pin the craven politicians to the wall," some have charged that this was part of a deliberate strategy to force additional domestic budget cuts. As Representative Ted Weiss, Democrat of New York, put it, "There is substantial evidence that the huge deficits we are now experiencing are not the result of administration bungling, but have been purposefully created . . . to convince the American people that we can no longer afford programs that serve human needs."[44] Stockman himself denied that the administration's tax and budget policies were so elegantly coordinated in 1981, but he admitted that the tax cuts and budget cuts were conceptually consistent and mutually supportive. He certainly made no secret that his personal policy goal was "a radical anti-welfare state premise [that] . . . implied dismantling vast segments of the Second Republic's budget, slashing all the expenditures that reflected its statist enterprises." Having achieved substantial reductions in tax rates and revenues, Stockman admitted that after 1981 "my aim had always been to force down the size of the domestic welfare state to the point where it could be adequately funded with the revenues available after the tax cut."[45]

Although both the president and Congress demonstrated a willingness to live with far higher federal deficits than anyone anticipated, the preceding section of this chapter makes clear that the dramatic tax reductions had important policy consequences. When combined with sizable defense increases, the resulting deficits had a dampening effect on subsequent domestic policy initiatives and the growth and maintenance of the welfare state. Large deficits also induced members of Congress from both parties to try to reverse some of the 1981 tax cuts and raise additional revenues. Although these attempts were partly successful in 1982 and 1984, the president managed to limit them and also to keep Democrats from using tax reform as a vehicle for raising taxes.

Second, Reagan's tax policies eroded support for the welfare state through their attacks on progressive taxation. The progressive federal income tax was one of the primary factors contributing to the enormous growth of federal activity and spending in the twentieth century.[46] Yet close observers of President Reagan noted that reducing federal income tax rates, and especially reducing the top marginal rates for the highest taxpayers, was the one issue closest to Ronald Reagan's heart. Among all the initiatives, it generated the most enthusiasm from him.[47] The results of the president's early efforts went beyond his wildest dreams: Congress stepped away from the principle of progressivity and adopted a modified flat tax in the Tax Reform Act of 1986.

This move had potentially important implications for the future of the welfare state. Progressivity has allowed higher levels of taxation (and thus spending) at key points in American history by concentrating the tax burdens on a minority of wealthy voters. If taxes are spread more evenly over the whole population, a bigger antitax coalition is likely to form. It is significant, then, that post-Reagan Democratic Congresses chose to raise marginal tax rates on the highest income earners in their major deficit reductions packages.

Finally, Reagan administration tax policies included unprecedented challenges to provisions of the internal revenue code that support state and local governments' capacity to raise their own revenues and provide services. Both key intergovernmental components of the tax code—the exemption for interest earned on municipal bonds and the federal income tax deduction for state and local sales, income, and property taxes—were targeted for elimination or substantial reduction by the Reagan administration, and both were significantly restricted by the Tax Reform Act of 1986. In this sense, Ronald Reagan used tax policy to attack the welfare state at every level of government, not just in Washington, and so clearly set his policies apart from those of activist decentralizers like Richard Nixon.

The 1981 Tax Cuts

On August 13, 1981, Ronald Reagan signed the Economic Recovery Tax Act (ERTA) of 1981, calling it "a turnaround of almost a half a century of ... excessive growth in government bureaucracy, government spending, government taxing."[48] While tax policy was turned around, the tax process was turned upside down by the frenzied way in which the legislation was enacted. The administration's initial tax reform proposal was unveiled on February 18, 1981, as part of the president's omnibus economic recovery package. It proposed $54 billion in tax reductions in 1982, which were to be achieved in two basic ways. Most of the cut was to come from the first of three years of 10 percent across the-board rate reductions for individual taxpayers, with much of the remainder from liberalized provisions for depreciating capital assets. Both were intended to stimulate long-term economic growth and investment, the first by promoting individual savings and the second by allowing faster write-offs of capital investments.

The individual tax rate reductions were the political core of the tax reform plan, as well as its most costly component. Although they enjoyed the weakest support on Capitol Hill, they quickly became the chief priority of the president. Patterned after the Kemp-Roth Tax Relief Act of 1977, massive tax reductions were considered a fringe idea in Congress until they were incorporated into the 1980 Republican platform. They were initially included in the president's bill because of their potential political appeal to working- and middle-class taxpayers. Indeed, Stockman argues that the broad, across-the-board cuts were just a "Trojan horse" for lowering the top tax rates. They were the key to stimulating investment and entrepreneurial risk taking, in his view, but they lacked sufficient appeal on their own. "It's kind of hard to sell 'trickle down,'" he observed.[49] In contrast, flat rate reductions ensured that there was something for everyone in the package. The president and many other supply-side theorists appeared to be less cynical about across-the-board tax cuts, however. They viewed the cuts as a direct means of broadening the appeal of conservative policies to blue-collar and other nontraditional constituencies of the Republican party.

Whatever their appeal to conservatives, these tax cuts lacked sufficient support in Congress to be viable on their own. In its bid to attract additional support, the administration became embroiled in a bidding war with Democrats as each side sought to attract a majority of votes in the Congress. The White House revised its package to include "sweeteners" that appealed to key voting blocs in Congress, like accelerated depreciation for businesses and reductions in the marriage penalty for social conservatives. This approach was sufficient to pass in the still reluctant Senate, but only after the addition of costly amendments to index federal income tax rates for inflation, to promote employee stock ownership plans, and to encourage further savings through tax-preferred "all savers certificates."

In the House, Democrats responded with "a blatant move to attract votes."[50] While scaling back and targeting the individual tax rate cuts, Democrats added provisions already adopted by the Senate, like all savers certificates and a marriage penalty provision, plus additional tax preferences for "almost everyone."[51] Included were new tax credits for child care, research and development, and royalty income; exemptions for overseas income, inheritance taxes, and Keogh plans; and provisions benefiting farmers, truckers, utilities, and mass transit operators .

In Stockman's memorable phrase, "the hogs were really feeding"; tax subsidy provisions offered by one party were matched by the other nearly one for one.[52] In the search for votes, both sides had expanded their packages far beyond what anyone had anticipated in the beginning. The revenue implications were so severe, Stockman reports, that he and White House aide Richard Darman contemplated killing the president's own proposal at the last minute.[53] Nevertheless, because of the political stakes involved, both sides were determined to win a victory on the House floor.

The final vote in the House was expected to be very close until the president made a nationwide television address on July 27. In what was called a "masterpiece of propaganda," he rallied public opinion behind his program and stimulated an unparalleled "telephone blitz" by constituents to members of Congress.[54] This had a "devastating effect" on the

Democrats' efforts to hold their supporters, and the president's plan was easily adopted, 238 to 195.[55] Despite the last-minute Democratic defections, the final vote divided the parties more sharply than any other tax vote in the House since 1921.[56]

The Long-Term Effects: Rationalizing Tax Policy

Thus the president won a "victory" on tax policy that exceeded even his budget success. As with the administration's actions on defense spending, however, the unparalleled costs associated with the victory dictated the policy agenda for years to come. The implications were truly staggering. According to the Congressional Budget Office, the cumulative revenue loss to the federal government by 1987 totaled more than $1 trillion, or almost 6 percent of GNP (see table 7-6). These revenue losses "dwarf [ed] other post-war tax reductions."[57] For example, the revenues forgone in just the first two years of ERTA totaled $128 billion, or $110 billion more than the famous Kennedy-Johnson tax cut of 1964.

Revenue losses of this magnitude dominated the federal government's fiscal agenda until 1985, when comprehensive tax reform became the president's top domestic priority for the 99th Congress. On the spending side, if the intention of the deep Kemp-Roth tax cuts had been to "starve the budget beast," as David Stockman put it, this strategy proved to be only partly effective. Mounting deficits placed continual pressure on the domestic budget and ultimately produced the Gramm-Rudman deficit reduction targets. Yet the stalemate between the president and Congress over severe budget reductions permitted deficits to remain at historic levels. Thus tax increases that would partly restore some of the reductions made in 1981 were driven to the top of the congressional revenue agenda. By enacting ERTA, the tax-writing committees of Congress had put themselves "in the tax raising business for years."[58]

This became immediately evident in 1982 with the enactment of the Tax Equity and Fiscal Responsibility Act (TEFRA). Just one year after the enormous tax cuts of 1981, TEFRA raised $98 billion in new revenues over three years with a combination of excise tax increases, restrictions on tax preferences, and compliance reforms. For consumers, the cigarette tax was doubled, the telephone tax was tripled, and airport taxes were increased; for business, the investment tax credit, industrial development bonds, and accelerated depreciation were restricted and the minimum tax on corporations was raised; and for individuals, the medical

Table 7-6. *Revenue Effects of the Economic Recovery Tax Act of 1981, Fiscal Years 1981–87*
Billions of dollars

Item	Actual, 1981	Projections					
		1982	1983	1984	1985	1986	1987
Total federal receipts under							
Prior law	605	670	747	849	982	1,062	1,176
ERTA	603	631	652	701	763	818	882
Difference	–2	–39	–95	–148	–189	–244	–294
Revenue loss as percent of GNP	...	1.3	2.8	3.9	4.5	5.4	5.9

Source: Charles Hulten and June O'Neill, "Tax Policy," in John L. Palmer and Isabel V. Sawhill, eds., *The Reagan Experiment* (Washington: Urban Institute Press, 1982), p. 113.

deduction was restricted and withholding on interest and dividends was instituted.

These provisions—and the strong motivation to restore revenues—were principally the work of the Senate. Faced with ballooning deficits, even the president acknowledged the need to raise additional revenues in his 1982 State of the Union address. However, he objected to any increase in excise taxes and remained adamantly opposed to any delay or reduction in the individual tax rate cuts enacted in 1981. House Democrats "completely abdicated the House's traditional lead in tax matters" in order to avoid all blame for raising taxes. When the House balked, and the administration refused to offer an alternative plan, the Senate departed from its constitutionally prescribed reactive role in revenue matters and put together a compromise proposal.[59]

Despite passing TEFRA, Congress had only begun the task of rationalizing tax policy to the revenue needs generated by ERTA, by continuing demands for federal services, and by defense and domestic spending policies. Driven by an "overwhelming concern with the deficit," Congress launched a series of tax bills and revenue measures over the next two years, beginning with a five-cent increase in the federal gas tax later in 1982. Donald Susswein, former tax counsel for the Senate Finance Committee, aptly summarized this frantic congressional search for additional revenues:

Soon after the '81 give-away, when I came on board [the Finance Committee staff], we began trying to put together revenue enhancing options which ultimately became the '82 tax bill. After we enacted the '82 tax bill, there was the '82 gas tax bill. 1983 saw the reform of Social Security, which had some tax consequences to it. Then, right after the summer of '83, we started working on what became the '84 bill.[60]

As Susswein suggested, this legislation became the basis for the Deficit Reduction Act of 1984 (DEFRA). Once again, Senate Republicans provided leadership on the issue. After both tax-writing committees reported $50 billion multiyear revenue packages in March, Senate leaders arranged a "Rose Garden" agreement on a compromise package with the House leadership and the White House.[61] Again the package placed restrictions on tax preferences (for industrial development bonds, income averaging, and retirement benefits) along with increased excise taxes on liquor and telephones. Again the president agreed to support modest excise tax increases in exchange for insulating the heart of his economic program from change. This ensured that the entire 25 percent cut in individual tax rates would finally be implemented and protected from erosion by the indexation of tax rates to inflation. Having won a consensus by the major parties in each branch of government, the compromise passed both houses of Congress by large margins.

Institutionalizing the Reagan Tax Revolution

Despite ERTA's sizable reductions in federal revenues, the Tax Reform Act of 1986 (TRA) will be remembered as the most important tax legacy of the Reagan administration. The TRA extended and institutionalized Reagan's 1981 revolution in tax policy. For two years it diverted efforts away from raising additional federal revenues and so maintained the deficit's pressure on domestic spending. Moreover, it enabled the president to lower top marginal tax rates, as he had set out to do. By reducing statutory progressivity in federal tax rates and establishing a modified flat tax structure, the TRA created a new environment for any future expansion of federal income tax revenues.

The substance and complex politics of tax reform go well beyond the scope of this study.[62] However, the TRA had both obvious and hidden consequences for intergovernmental relations that warrant attention here.

Equally important, the act constituted a direct assault on the revenue base of state and local governments. As proposed by President Reagan, tax reform would have eliminated the two largest tax "subsidies" for states and localities. The fiscal implications of this policy dwarfed the intergovernmental aid cuts proposed or implemented by the Reagan administration. Although Congress adopted only parts of this intergovernmental strategy, the president's proposals on tax reform illustrate with unusual clarity that federalism policy in the Reagan administration was actually the means to other political ends.

The Origins of Reagan's Tax Reform

How Reagan's tax reform evolved and why it was placed at the top of his agenda are complex questions. Support for tax reform was widely shared by professional economists, who saw it as a means of improving equity and long-term economic growth by evening out tax-induced distortions in investment.[63] These views carried considerable weight in the Treasury Department. However, the president's endorsement of the concept was also influenced by political considerations and the opportunities it provided for furthering his policy agenda. Republican political strategists believed tax reform was a "realigning" issue that could lay the basis for a permanent Republican majority. As one presidential political adviser put it:

Passage of tax reform, with strong Republican support, will erase the cartoon of our party as defender of the rich and privileged. . . .The dramatic relief for the working poor, and the provisions assuring that every corporation and every individual bears a fair share of our national tax burden, would reflect very well on . . . all Republican candidates for the next generation.[64]

Tax reform had appeal on policy grounds, as well, since it provided a means of furthering the agenda first outlined in the 1981 tax cuts. Stockman maintains that the concept of tax reform was first sold to the president during a golf game with Secretary of State (and former economics professor) George Shultz. After hearing Shultz argue that less government interference in investment decisions could promote long-term growth, Reagan was said to have concluded that tax reform "was a way to reduce the deficit without increasing taxes" by reaping the revenue benefits of a stronger economy.[65]

Dubbed by some within the White House as the "second installment on

Kemp-Roth," tax reform developed ideological appeal for the president and others in the administration, even though it threatened the substantial tax benefits enjoyed by important Republican constituencies. The presidential message transmitting the tax reform proposal to Congress attacked the existing revenue code as an instrument of excessive government intrusion into the marketplace, which "slows economic growth . . . by interfering with free markets and diverting productive investment into tax shelters and tax avoidance schemes."[66] The president was particularly excited about the prospects for further lowering the top tax rate. According to Treasury Secretary James Baker, when administration officials proposed providing additional tax relief to the middle class and raising the top rate in the president's plan from 35 percent to 40 percent, the president responded: "Absolutely not. I want real tax reform, I don't want to just diddle around with the margins . . . a top rate of 40 percent means it's anti-growth." Were it politically possible, Baker explained, the administration would have preferred "a flat 10 percent rate across-the-board—figure out what our income is, send 10 percent in and go on about our business, but unfortunately the political system is not such that we can do that."[67]

A final virtue of tax reform, in the administration's eyes, was that it challenged the fiscal underpinnings of active government at every level. The income tax deduction for state and local taxes was as old as the federal income tax itself, as was the exclusion of interest earned on tax-exempt municipal bonds. Despite their relevance to a balanced system of fiscal federalism and their relationship to funding the administration's own initiatives for devolution, both provisions were curtailed or eliminated under the president's tax reform plan.

The motivation for this was partly fiscal, since the elimination of deductibility alone provided an additional $33 billion in federal revenues to help fund lower tax rates. Yet the president made clear from the beginning that the elimination of deductibility also was intended to undermine the revenue base of fiscally active states and localities. In his first speech to rally citizens' groups around his tax plan, he denounced the deduction for state and local taxes as "one of the major pressures pushing up the tax rates of the American people" and an unfair tool to "subsidize the big-spending policies of a few high tax states."[68]

The Politics of Tax Reform

The underlying consistency between tax reform and the president's commitment to limited government was only one important aspect of the Tax

Reform Act of 1986. Equally important, from a political perspective, is how this sweeping legislation survived countless obituaries and achieved enactment at all. In the process, the focus of tax politics shifted abruptly from narrowing the deficit to broadening the tax base. Like congressional tax reformers before him, from Senator Bill Bradley, Democrat of New Jersey, to Representative Jack Kemp, Republican of New York, the president insisted on "revenue neutrality" in his proposal in order to focus attention on reform rather than raising revenues.

The confluence of interests between the president and congressional reformers like Senator Bradley emerged most clearly after tax reform passed the House and arrived in the Senate. After one of reform's nearest brushes with political demise, Senator Robert Packwood of Oregon, the Republican chairman of the Senate Finance Committee, jettisoned his own beleaguered proposal and advocated a new and radically different approach modeled after the Bradley-Gephart "fair tax act."

This had both substantive and political implications. Substantively, it had the effect of strengthening many of the president's original policy goals. Bradley-Gephardt was a relatively pure piece of legislation, designed by economists to portray an ideally reformed system. Because economists' prescriptions for reform had much in common with the president's objectives, though often for very different reasons, using Bradley-Gephardt as a model strengthened the administration's hand. It not only accepted the condition of revenue neutrality, it also reduced tax preferences dramatically and thus reduced federal interference in the marketplace. And because the political appeal of lower tax rates provided the incentive for eliminating special preferences, Bradley-Gephardt foreswore a progressive rate structure and offered dramatically lower tax rates. In the end this combination of bipartisan support, powerful presidential backing, and the imprimatur of "good government" economics proved sufficient to hold a coalition together in the anarchic Senate and produce a bill surprisingly to the president's liking.

Intergovernmental Dimensions of Tax Reform

The shift to a relatively pure tax reform approach, combined with the high-profile politics of a major presidential initiative, had important implications for provisions of the tax code that bear most directly on state and local governments. This was particularly true of tax-exempt municipal bonds, which were significantly restricted by the Tax Reform Act.

The legal basis for exempting interest on state and local bonds from federal taxation originated in the nineteenth century, and this practice has been part of the federal income tax code since it came into being in 1913. Since then, tax-exempt bonds had been the principal device used by localities for financing long-term capital projects like schools, roads, and government facilities. After 1970 such traditional borrowing was supplemented by a proliferation of nontraditional bonds for housing, economic development, pollution control, and hospitals. In many jurisdictions such subsidized borrowing established the financial basis for an explosion of "public-private partnerships."

Despite their long heritage and importance to state and local governments, tax-exempt bonds were under constant attack throughout the 1980s as an inefficient subsidy and unacceptably large drain on federal revenues. The revenue loss totaled $20.4 billion in 1983. This was more than triple the revenue forgone just five years earlier, and it made the interest exclusion on bonds by far the fastest growing federal "subsidy" to state and local governments.[69] Although Congress played a key role in restricting bonds in 1982 and 1984, a far more sweeping assault was proposed by the president's tax reform plan. The initial tax reform plan developed by the Treasury Department in 1984 advocated the complete elimination of interest exemption for all bonds, including traditional governmental issues. While this plan was modified in the final proposal sent to Congress five months later, the restrictions on bonds remained so severe that they were estimated to reduce total bond issuances 62 to 80 percent.[70] Despite further modification of these proposals in Congress, the final tax reform bill reduced tax-exempt issuances by as much as 60 percent and cut federal revenue losses by approximately $4 billion over five years. Ironically, given the president's rhetorical commitment to federalism, nontraditional bonds issued by state and local governments fared far less well than similar bonds issued by colleges, nonprofit hospitals, and other nongovernmental entities.

The president's attack on the deductibility of state and local taxes was even more extreme and, given the scope of revenues involved, potentially even more significant. Again the president followed the advice of Treasury Department economists. They believed that deductibility was an economically inefficient subsidy, and they wanted to use the revenues captured by its elimination to lower overall tax rates. Thus the president proposed the total elimination of deductibility for state and local sales and income taxes, which produced a five-year revenue gain of $149 billion to the federal treasury.[71]

Some charged that, in making this proposal, the president sought more than increased federal revenues and greater tax equity. They regarded the elimination of deductibility as a vehicle for exporting the "Reagan revolution" to the states, eroding their capacity to finance responsibilities devolved by the federal government.[72] Assistant Treasury Secretary Ronald Pearlman seemed to support this view when he stated, "We agree there will be more pressure [against raising state and local taxes] from those who no longer benefit from the deduction. That's as it should be."[73] Even the president contributed to this interpretation when, in a 1986 fund-raising letter, he attacked Democratic governors who "turned right around and increased state sales and income taxes, wiping out the tax cut given to you by our Administration."[74] By thus seeking to reduce taxes and government revenues at all levels of government, Reagan made clear his philosophical differences with Nixon with respect to New Federalism.

Whatever the aims, these proposals were serious and partly successful. The final tax reform bill passed by Congress and signed by the president contained the first significant limitations on deductibility since the tax code was created, eliminating the deduction for state and local sales and personal property taxes for a five-year savings of $17 billion. Because the discriminatory effect of this partial repeal of deductibility may weaken support for preserving the remaining taxes, especially at a time of continuing need for further federal revenues, some believe this was only the first step toward the president's original request: the total elimination of deductibility.

Conclusion

In a speech to the National Association of State Legislatures in 1981, Ronald Reagan declared that "with our economic proposals, we're staging a quiet federalist revolution."[75] Taken collectively, the tax and budgetary policies propounded by the new administration did indeed constitute a broad but implicit strategy for intergovernmental reform. The dramatic tax and budget reductions developed by the White House were designed to reduce substantially the federal government's profile in domestic affairs, to alter those budgetary priorities that remained, and to stem the tide of new domestic initiatives. The president's tax policies were intended both to ensure the implementation of these budgetary aims and to eliminate federal subsidies for governmental activism at the state and local levels. Thus these fiscal policies leave no doubt that Nixon's philosophy of decentralized activism was far different from Reagan's view that traditional forms of governmental activism were inappropriate throughout the public sector.

These distinctive views were expressed in quite different political environments. In contrast to the political fragmentation that overwhelmed many of Nixon's initiatives, Reagan's fiscal policies swept through Congress in 1981 on a wave of unparalleled Republican unity and a reenergized conservative coalition. This highly visible, majoritarian pattern was the institutional manifestation of the reactive politics that candidate Reagan exploited in seeking office.

This pattern of policymaking did not survive intact beyond 1981 although elements of it, most notably the heightened levels of party unity and partisan-based agenda setting and coalition building, did persist on important pieces of legislation. Even so, the initial policies adopted were sufficient to restructure the subsequent policymaking environment, institutionalizing a fiscally interdependent policy agenda that precluded a return to the politics of the fragmented, incremental expansionism that had prevailed in the 1970s. The fiscal policies of 1981 ushered in a new era of rationalizing politics, forcing policymakers to cope with the effects of policies previously adopted. And, as the president intended, this new pattern of politics had important implications for intergovernmental relations.

At the broadest level, the new rationalizing politics struck at the heart of the congressional activism that had driven the intergovernmental system for two decades. In the new era of zero-sum budgetary politics, the opportunities for successful policy entrepreneurship were substantially reduced. Fewer bills were introduced in Congress. Fewer bills were passed. Fewer amendments were introduced and voted on. The business of Congress was focused more narrowly on budgetary issues. Although signs of entrepreneurial adaptation reemerged by the 99th and 100th Congresses, the redistributive budgetary politics of the 1980s had become institutionalized.

Reagan's policies had direct effects on intergovernmental relations as well. Federal aid to state and local governments was significantly affected by the politics of budgetary constraint. Overall levels of aid were reduced in competition with other budget sectors, and priorities among federal aid programs were altered. These and other explicit dimensions of Reagan's intergovernmental policies are reviewed in chapters 8 and 9.

CHAPTER 8

Federal Aid: Budgets and Block Grants in the 1980s

REAGAN ADMINISTRATION budget and tax policies constituted a far-reaching though implicit strategy for restructuring the federal government's role in the federal system and its relations with state and local governments. But Ronald Reagan had an explicit federalism agenda as well. Especially during the first two years of his administration, federalism reform was given a prominence on the nation's policy agenda unparalleled since the days of Richard Nixon.

Both before and after becoming president, Reagan left little doubt that federalism reform would be a priority of his administration. The need for a comprehensive restructuring of intergovernmental roles and responsibilities had been a central theme of his 1976 campaign for president, and he saw to it that federalism reform was a plank in the 1980 Republican platform. Upon election he devoted time to discussing this issue in his first inaugural and State of the Union addresses. A complex proposal for sorting out intergovernmental functions and "returning" to states billions of dollars of federal programs and tax sources was made the centerpiece of his 1982 domestic program. These federalism initiatives were "even closer to the heart of Ronald Reagan than the budget cuts," reported presidential assistant Robert B. Carleson, an architect of the president's federalism strategy. "The budget cuts became the first priority because of the economic situation we inherited, but the president has been calling for these changes in the federal system throughout his entire political career."[1]

Reagan's explicit reform strategy consisted of four parts. First Reagan proposed to reduce, and alter the priorities among, federal grants-in-aid. Whereas the macro budget policies were designed to alter the broad financial profile of the national government within the federal system (see chapter 7), specific changes in grants-in-aid to state and local governments had more immediate and obvious effects on the intergovernmental system by reducing national involvement in traditional state and local responsibilities. Thus the president recommended, and obtained, the first absolute decline in federal aid expenditures since the 1940s and a 2.5 percent reduction in the number of federal assistance programs. The administration's budgets also altered the priorities among remaining programs. Particularly significant was the termination of the general revenue sharing program—the crown jewel of the Nixon administration's New Federalism strategy. Also terminated was the public jobs component of the Comprehensive Employment and Training Act (CETA) program, which was enacted under Nixon and expanded under Gerald Ford and Jimmy Carter.

Block grants were the second component of Ronald Reagan's federalism reform strategy. In his first six years in office, Reagan submitted thirty-one proposals for new or substantially revised block grants. Although he was initially more successful than Nixon had been in securing block grants—nine were enacted in 1981 and one in 1982—he made little progress in this area after 1982. Unlike Nixon, however, Reagan did not advance the block grant as a managerial device or as a useful end in itself. Rather, block grants were intended to help the federal government disengage itself from what were considered to be traditional state and local functional responsibilities.

The third element in the president's federalism reform strategy was a sweeping "sorting out" initiative—a grand design for permanently restructuring intergovernmental roles and responsibilities (see chapter 9). Under this 1982 proposal, the federal government was to assume total financial responsibility for the $19 billion state share of the medicaid program, while turning back to the states more than forty other federal aid programs—including aid to families with dependent children (AFDC) and, initially, food stamps—along with a number of excise tax sources that were to pay for them. Despite its bold outlines and high political profile, Reagan's proposal was never formally sent to Congress. Efforts to mobilize the nation's governors and reach an agreement on a compromise bill broke down because of differing objectives, logical and fiscal inconsistencies in the proposal, divisions within the administration, and strong opposition from Congress and the affected interest groups.

The fourth component of Reagan's federalism strategy was regulatory relief (see chapter 10). Here, as in the block grants, Reagan sought both continuity and change. His was the first administration to recognize intergovernmental regulation explicitly as a unique and significant form of federal regulation, and it undertook a series of initiatives designed to redress federal regulatory burdens on state and local governments. Yet, apart from regulatory changes adopted in the context of the 1981 block grants, most of the Reagan administration's deregulatory efforts were achieved through unilateral administrative action that was vulnerable to reversal in the future. Deregulation, however, was only part of the story. More telling, and far more in keeping with past federal practices, was the Reagan administration's consistent willingness to support and promote new federal regulatory initiatives—from uniform trucking standards to changes in local affirmative action policies—when they served the larger social and economic objectives of the president. Indeed, more new mandates were enacted in the 1980s than were adopted in either the 1960s or the 1970s.

Owing to the widely divergent outcomes of Reagan's efforts, from unprecedented success in the early block grant proposals to the premature failure of the swap proposal, as well as the inconsistency between the president's rhetorical goals and his actions, evaluations of his New Federalism program have been mixed. Some saw it as the central accomplishment of his first administration, dwarfing his achievements on the federal budget.[2] Others questioned whether it had any long-term significance. They note that the sorting out plan was never even introduced and that, apart from 1981, no new block grants were enacted or further significant cuts made in intergovernmental funding.[3]

Both interpretations contain an element of truth. The Reagan administration's achievements fell far short of the president's goals, but they were certainly significant when measured by historical standards. Reagan's policies altered and accelerated downward trends in federal aid spending, realigned national priorities, and placed intergovernmental issues and federalism reform prominently on the policy agenda. Yet far from being divorced from the president's budgetary priorities, many of the administration's most lasting and significant intergovernmental accomplishments were achieved within the context of budgetary policy. This combination had a powerful though often indirect effect. After eight years of concerted effort on both the budgetary and federalism fronts, the Reagan administration succeeded in capping opportunities for national policy entrepreneurship that were straining for release in the Bush and early Clinton administrations.

Intergovernmental Budget Policy: De Facto New Federalism?

Conventional wisdom suggests that Ronald Reagan substantially reduced total domestic spending while rapidly increasing spending on defense and interest payments. In truth, overall domestic spending measured in both current and constant dollars continued to increase during the Reagan administration, although the rate of growth diminished. But this overall growth masked important changes in domestic spending priorities. Some spending, such as direct payments to individuals and interest on the debt, increased throughout the 1980s, whereas spending on civilian payrolls and natural resources declined.

No area was harder hit by budget reductions than federal grants-in-aid; within grants, payments to governments for the provision of services were most deeply cut. The growth rate in current spending for grants-in-aid not only slowed dramatically during the 1980s, but it actually declined in fiscal 1982 and 1987 (see table 8-1). These were the first absolute declines in federal aid levels since the 1940s. Real spending on federal grants also declined from 1980 to 1987, in sharp contrast to the preceding thirty years of rapid growth. All this was part of a deliberate strategy by the administration to reorder federal spending priorities and eliminate or reduce "ineffective" and nontraditional federal programs.[4]

The budgetary treatment of different grant programs varied widely as well. In some cases, such as grants to states for the support of individuals, spending continued to grow during the Reagan years, although again at a slower rate. Indeed, grants for payments to individuals grew more rapidly during this period than overall spending for direct entitlements such as veterans' assistance, social security, and medicare (see table 8-2). More than 60 percent of this increase was due to higher outlays for the medicaid program. Real AFDC spending actually fell slightly during Reagan's first term, despite an increase in poverty.

By far the largest reductions were in the category of federal grants to governments. Real outlays expended on grants to state and local governments fell by 33 percent between 1981 and 1987, and the decline would have been even greater if additional highway aid stemming from the 1982 increase in the federal gas tax had been excluded. The largest reductions occurred in general-purpose assistance, economic development, employment and training, and social services (see table 8-3). With one major exception, the most severe cuts occurred early in Reagan's first term, in fiscal 1981 and 1983. Real spending for many of these programs actually

Table 8-1. *Growth Rates in Federal Aid Spending, Selected Fiscal Years, 1955–87*

Amounts in billions of dollars

Year	Current dollars		1972 dollars	
	Amount	Percent change	Amount	Percent change
1955	3.2	...	5.6	...
1959	6.5	103	10.0	79
1960	7.0	...	10.8	...
1964	10.1	44	14.7	36
1965	10.9	...	15.5	...
1969	20.3	86	24.2	56
1970	24.0	...	27.0	...
1974	43.4	82	37.9	40
1975	49.8	...	39.2	...
1979	82.9	66	48.1	23
1980	91.5	10.4	48.2	0.2
1981	94.8	3.6	46.1	–4.4
1982	88.2	–7.0	40.4	–12.4
1983	92.5	4.9	40.7	0.7
1984	97.6	5.5	41.3	1.5
1980–84	...	6.6	...	–14.2
1985	105.8	8.6	43.1	4.4
1986	112.4	6.1	44.5	3.0
1987	108.4	–3.6	41.7	–6.3
1985–87	...	2.4	...	–3.5

Sources: Based on U.S. Advisory Commission on Intergovernmental Relations, *Significant Features of Fiscal Federalism, 1985–86*, M-146 (Government Printing Office, 1986), p. 19; and *Budget of the United States Government, Historical Tables, Fiscal Year 1989*, table 12.1.

increased modestly in fiscal 1985, in anticipation of the 1984 election. The exception was general revenue sharing, which was repeatedly slated for termination in the president's budgets and allowed to expire at the end of fiscal 1986. This single step reduced federal grant outlays to local governments by approximately $5 billion in fiscal 1987.

Three trends in federal aid spending under Reagan are notable. First, federal aid reductions did not constitute a complete reversal of earlier patterns of intergovernmental fiscal relations. Rather, they accelerated

Table 8-2. *Index of Change in Constant Dollar Outlays for Selected Expenditure Categories, Fiscal Years 1980–87*

Category	1980	1981	1982	1983	1984	1985	1986	1987
Total U.S. budget outlays	100	104	107	113	115	123	124	123
National defense	100	107	118	128	133	142	148	152
Direct payments to individuals	100	106	110	117	114	117	120	122
Net interest	100	119	137	140	166	187	191	189
Total grants to state and local governments	100	94	82	82	84	92	91	85
Payments to individuals	100	105	101	106	109	120	123	127
Other grants	100	88	72	70	70	76	74	67

Sources: Lillian Rymarowicz and Dennis Zimmerman, *The Effect of Tax and Budget Policies in the 1980s on the State-Local Sector,* Report 86-2E (Congressional Research Service, 1986), p. 51; and *Budget of the United States Government, Historical Tables, Fiscal Year 1989,* table 6.1.

trends that had already begun in the waning years of the Carter administration. Second, those programs targeted for the deepest cuts by the Reagan administration were the professionally administered services at the core of the Great Society. Reagan shared Nixon's dislike of the "service strategy" of the 1960s and chose to attack it head on rather than obliquely by promoting direct aid to individuals. Third, block grants and general revenue sharing, which were central to Nixon's New Federalism, were targeted for deep cuts and eventual elimination by the Reagan administration.

Trends in Intergovernmental Spending

By most relative measures, federal grants to state and local governments reached their zenith in fiscal 1978, the second year of the Carter administration: federal aid accounted for 26.5 percent of total state and local outlays, 17.0 percent of the federal budget, and 3.6 percent of the total economy (see table 8-4). Although federal aid in current dollars continued to rise until fiscal 1982, by each of these relative measures it had begun to subside in the later years of the Carter administration.

This was particularly evident in fiscal 1981, when the final budget policies achieved by the outgoing Carter administration were combined with additional midyear reductions implemented by Reagan. Before Carter left office, Congress eliminated the state share of general revenue sharing and

Table 8-3. *Selected Grant Outlays to State and Local Governments, by Function and Program, Fiscal Years 1980, 1985*
Millions of 1980 dollars unless otherwise specified

Grants	1980	1985	Percent change, 1980–85
Total for all functions[a]	59,524	45,513	–23.5
Transportation	13,087	13,027	–0.5
Highways	8,676	9,548	10.0
Mass transit	3,129	2,547	–18.6
Airports and other	1,282	932	–27.2
Community and regional development	6,486	3,905	–39.8
Economic development	452	275	–39.2
Local public works	860	6	–99.3
CDBG	3,902	2,896	–25.8
Urban renewal grants	1,047	351	–66.6
Education, training, and social services	21,783	14,405	–33.4
Compensatory education	3,370	3,192	–5.4
Social services	2,763	2,081	–24.7
Human development	1,548	1,449	–6.4
Community services	547	285	–47.8
Temporary employment assistance	1,797	0	0
Training and employment	6,924	3,729	–68.8
Other	4,834	3,767	–22.1
General purpose assistance	8,478	4,658	–45.1
General revenue sharing	6,829	3,478	–49.1
Other	1,649	1,170	–29.0
All other grants to governments	9,690	9,420	–2.8

Source: Rymarowicz and Zimmerman, *Effect of Federal Tax and Budget Policies*, p. 11.
a. Excludes grants that provide payments to individuals.

substantially reduced CETA public employment grants. Carter also made the first significant use of the budget reconciliation process. However, federal grant outlays as a percentage of all federal spending had already declined 9 percent between fiscal 1978 and 1980, and federal aid as a percentage of GNP had declined 5 percent. Indeed, some advocates of greater federal social spending were aware by the early 1980s that a reversal of prior growth trends was inevitable. As one put it, "Changes in the economy [would] have foretold an end to the earlier rate of growth in social welfare spending, regardless of who ha[d] been in office."[5]

Table 8-4. Federal Grants as a Percentage of Total State-Local Outlays, Total Federal Outlays, and Gross National Product, Selected Fiscal Years, 1955–87

| | Federal grants as a percentage of | | |
Year	Total state-local outlays	Total federal outlays	Gross national product
1955	10.2	4.7	0.8
1960	14.5	7.6	1.4
1965	15.1	9.2	1.6
1970	19.0	12.3	2.4
1975	22.6	15.0	3.3
1976	24.1	15.9	3.5
1977	25.5	16.7	3.5
1978	26.5	17.0	3.6
1979	25.8	16.5	3.4
1980	25.8	15.5	3.4
1981	24.7	14.0	3.2
1982	21.6	11.8	2.8
1983	21.3	11.4	2.8
1984	20.9	11.5	2.6
1985	20.9	11.2	2.7
1986	20.5	11.3	2.7
1987	18.2	10.8	2.5

Source: ACIR, *Significant Features of Fiscal Federalism, 1988* (GPO, 1988), vol. 2, p. 15.

Assault on the Service Strategy

If the direction of budgetary change was not a surprise to many informed observers, the magnitude of cuts in certain areas was. By far the largest cuts recommended and adopted by the Reagan administration were concentrated in the areas of community and economic development, education, social services, and employment and training (table 8-3). While total aid declined 8 percent and all aid to governments fell 24 percent between 1980 and 1985, real outlays for community and regional development were reduced by nearly 40 percent; real outlays for education, employment and training, and social services were cut by one third. Particularly hard hit were many of the hallmark programs of the Great Soci-

ety: community services, the descendant of the community action program, was cut nearly in half; local public works and regional development
grants were practically eliminated; urban renewal and training and employment services were cut by two-thirds. Within education, the largest
cuts occurred in the 1960s programs of bilingual education, compensatory education, and the small stimulative grants consolidated into the chapter two education block grant.[6]

The proponents of the Great Society devised these programs to break
the cycle of poverty, to raise educational standards, and to promote regional economic development—not by giving the poor and unemployed
cash or a government-sponsored job, but by delivering carefully planned
and coordinated professional services prescribed by professional norms
and the latest social science research. As Samuel Beer observed:

> The Great Society acquired a special character by its emphasis upon
> spending for services provided largely by state and local governments.
> . . . To a pronounced degree there was a professionalization of re-
> form. In the fields of health, housing, urban renewal, highways, wel-
> fare, education, and poverty, the new programs drew heavily upon
> specialized and technical knowledge in and around the federal bu-
> reaucracy [and] . . . enhanced [the] importance of scientifically and
> professionally trained civil servants at all levels of government.[7]

It was precisely such programs that were most objectionable to Reagan
and the right wing of the Republican party. Both viewed them as forms of
government-sponsored "social engineering" that undermined traditional
values and social relationships. During his 1976 drive for the presidency,
Reagan complained that "thousands of towns and neighborhoods have
seen their peace disturbed by bureaucrats and social planners."[8] Earlier,
while he was governor, Reagan denounced the war on poverty as "a match-
less boondoggle," which "abandoned tried and true principles" and replaced them with the judgments of "a self-appointed group of experts
operating out of either Washington or Sacramento [who] cannot have all
the answers to the problems that beset us." He pointed, as an example, to
an antipoverty project he had vetoed because it employed seven administrators to provide employment services to seventeen unemployed individuals. Such programs, Reagan declared, amounted to little more than "the
arrogant misuse of poverty funds for political nest-building."[9]

This last objection has prompted some observers to interpret Reagan's attack on the service strategy as more than a disagreement over methods and as part of a conscious strategy to "defund the left." As one reporter observed during the budget cuts of 1981, "One of the fondest conservative dreams is that the federal budget cuts will 'defund the left'—bankrupt the social action, civil rights, and other liberal groups that depend so heavily on federal funds."[10]

That dream flowed partly out of the president's conviction that liberal activists were dependent on a Washington power base for support. "It is far easier for people to come to Washington to get their social programs," he observed in early 1981. "All their friends and connections are in Washington."[11] But some of the president's conservative supporters went further in their political diagnosis. They argued that federal programs directly subsidized the administration's liberal opponents, and that the key to conservative success lay in "eliminating the power of the federal bureaucracy . . . to subsidize activist organizations which are working . . . to render irrelevant the election returns."[12]

The conservatives' perception was not entirely fanciful. A few interest groups representing public service clients and providers were forced to make drastic personnel and operational reductions when the administration severed federal contracts with them.[13] Most were not dependent on direct subsidies, however, and were targeted in other ways.

Ironically, it was state and especially local government associations, as a group, that were most dependent on federal subsidies and were most seriously affected by Reagan's cutbacks. These very organizations the Nixon administration had consciously sponsored and assisted in order to provide lobbying assistance and technical support for common interests in the first New Federalism. Conservatives in the Reagan administration, however, viewed these same organizations as "wily stalkers of federal aid" or "merely [another] leg of that 'iron triangle.'"[14] Between 1981 and 1983 the National League of Cities lost $3.6 million in federal contracts and training grants (one-half of its total budget) and was forced to fire 58 percent of its staff. The U.S. Conference of Mayors lost over $1.5 million in federal contracts in this period and made similar staff reductions. Federal contract reductions and mismanagement drove the National Association of Counties to the brink of bankruptcy and necessitated massive personnel and organizational changes. The National Conference of State Legislatures lost one-third of its budget and a similar share of its staff. Only the National Governors' Association escaped relatively unscathed, in part because of the administration's intergovernmental biases.[15]

In addition to eliminating direct grants and contracts to Washington-based interest groups, the administration attempted to undercut indirect subsidies and programmatic support for federally oriented "liberal" organizations. Reagan repeatedly sought to defund or eliminate the Legal Services Corporation and the community services program, legacies of the Great Society's attempts to represent and organize the poor. Both had earned reputations for challenging established institutions and practices, governmental and private.[16]

The administration also attempted to alter regulations governing federal contract audit procedures in ways that would have severely restricted contract recipients from publicly promoting policy positions, particularly through congressional testimony. These proposed regulations were significantly modified, however, in response to strenuous congressional objections and opposition from defense contractors and other unintended targets of these rules changes. The White House was more successful in removing policy-oriented advocacy groups from participating in the federal government's version of the United Way, thus channeling the charitable giving of federal employees toward more traditional service-oriented organizations.

Most important, the administration used block grants to disrupt, if not "defund," the left. Block grants were intended to force interest groups to focus their activities away from Washington and thus move the center of policy decisionmaking to new and presumably unfamiliar terrain at the state and local levels.

This was expected to have two results. First, it would alter the kinds of interests involved in policy decisions, thus affecting the shape of specific policies. As Robert Carleson observed: "We have consciously set out to force political decisions and the struggles that accompany them down to the state and local level. The so-called iron triangles in Washington for too long have had a virtual monopoly on political influence in Congress and in the agencies."[17] Second, the structural changes imposed by block grants were expected to reduce the overall magnitude of public sector activity. Administration strategists assumed that if the "iron triangles" were disrupted, the supporters of domestic social programs would be less able to maintain spending and programmatic activities at existing levels. "The block grant is the ideal vehicle for permanently reducing the growth of spending," argued Carleson. Or, as the president himself observed, "It would be a hell of a lot tougher [for social programs] if we diffuse them and send them out to the states."[18]

Budgetary Implications of the Reagan Administration's Block Grants

Reagan's use of block grants to reduce the scope of the public sector and advance conservative social policy objectives was very different from Nixon's. Although not unaware of the potential merits of block grants as a political device for restructuring policymaking arenas and altering program priorities, most Nixon administration officials viewed block grants as a worthwhile end in themselves. They favored block grants as an efficient administrative mechanism for combining the federal government's revenue-raising capacity with state and local knowledge of local needs and service delivery infrastructure. In contrast, the Reagan administration saw block grants as an effective transitional device for weakening the "Washington establishment" and providing a "halfway house" on the road to total federal withdrawal from affected policy areas.[19] As the president observed in a speech to the National Conference of State Legislatures, "The ultimate objective . . . is to use block grants . . . as only a bridge, leading to the day when you'll have not only . . . the programs that properly belong at the state level, but . . . the tax sources now usurped by Washington . . . ending the round trip of the people's money to Washington, where a carrying charge is deducted, and then back to you."[20]

Reagan's budgetary treatment of block grants also differed from Nixon's. As earlier chapters have shown, the Nixon administration demonstrated a consistent willingness to accept higher spending levels for block grants in order to ease the administrative transition to these grants and enhance political support for them in Congress. In contrast, Reagan's major block grant proposals embodied large reductions in spending as well as changes in program structures. Such cuts were not entirely without justification, given the economic conditions at the time and potential administrative savings for states resulting from reductions in application, compliance, and paperwork requirements. For these reasons, the nation's governors had offered to accept a 10 percent reduction in budget authority for programs consolidated into block grants. Yet they were hardly prepared for the budget request that accompanied the president's initial block grant proposals in 1981. In his fiscal 1982 budget Reagan proposed creating seven sweeping new block grants and reducing their budget authority almost 25 percent below fiscal 1981 spending on the programs proposed for merger. Thus, rather than rewarding block grants with favored budgetary treatment, as Nixon had done, Reagan recommended them for some of the deepest spending cuts in his entire budget. As table 7-1 showed, block grants were recommended for deeper cuts than total federal aid, whereas most other major segments of the budget were to have increases. This harsh budgetary treatment was not confined to fiscal 1982. Although block grants enjoyed less prominence in later administration budgets and far fewer were enacted, budget cuts were almost always part of the package. As part of its fiscal 1986 budget, for example, the administration proposed terminating one block grant and cutting the budget of another by 10 percent. The message to state and local governments remained consistent and clear: the president would continue to support the general goal of grant reform, but—in contrast to alternative objectives like national defense, tuition tax credits, and urban enterprise zones—Reagan would not adjust his fiscal priorities to advance this cause.

The president's budgetary treatment of GRS was similar and ultimately had far more devastating consequences. Whereas revenue sharing had been the centerpiece of Nixon's New Federalism and the federal program most dear to state and local governments, Reagan held a far more hostile view of efforts to harness the federal tax apparatus to provide funds for state and local governments. In fact, the president proposed terminating or severely modifying revenue sharing on several occasions. In 1975 and again in 1982, Reagan advocated folding GRS into a broad package of federal program and revenue turnbacks to the states. In late 1981 he proposed a 12 percent cut in GRS spending as part of a broader across-the-board reduction in federal domestic expenditures.[21]

The White House, however, had to back down temporarily in 1983, when strong lobbying by local government officials forced it to agree to reauthorize GRS at its existing funding level for another three years. In its fiscal 1986 budget the Reagan administration returned to more drastic solutions and proposed terminating GRS in October 1985, one year before it was to expire. Continued large deficits led the administration to argue again that "the Federal government can no longer afford general revenue sharing."[22] In 1985 this argument carried the day in Congress, which, after exploring various options, agreed to let the program expire in October 1986.

Block Grant Politics

In 1981, under unceasing prodding from the administration, Congress consolidated seventy-seven categorical programs into nine block grants, a one-year total that surpassed the combined total of all previous enactments. Reagan's early success stemmed from new tactics—he tied grant reform tightly to new budget procedures—and new political resources. Subsequently, however, only one block grant was enacted as Congress—reinforced by stronger partisan and ideological suspicions of block grant objectives—reverted to its historic pattern of opposition and held block grants in a budgetary stalemate.

Reagan's Proposals and Early Congressional Reactions

The new parliamentary tactics used to push through the 1981 block grants altered the ground rules of grant consolidation politics. Early in the year, when the president's proposals were being considered individually by congressional committees, the prospects for significant grant reform seemed dim. Committees in the Republican-controlled Senate made substantial alterations in the president's proposals, and committees in the Democratic House threatened to block them altogether. Things changed dramatically, however, when block grants were linked to the president's budget proposals through the reconciliation process. This shifted decisionmaking from committees to the floor and reframed the issues on the president's terms.

Originally, the president proposed consolidating more than eighty programs into seven new block grants in the fields of education, health, social services, and community development. In elementary and secondary education, he proposed consolidating forty-three programs into two: a local education block grant, composed of major programs for disadvantaged, handicapped, and special needs students, and a state block grant, composed of thirty-three mostly small programs for purposes like metric and environmental education and desegregation assistance (see table 8-5). Two block grants also were proposed in public health: a preventive health care block grant that was to replace ten programs ranging from family planning to rat control, and a health services block grant consolidating seventeen categoricals like community health centers and maternal and child health grants. The social services proposal merged twelve programs, including the existing Title XX block grant, most community action programs, and child welfare and adoption services. An emergency assistance block grant combined only two grants—low-income energy assistance and emergency welfare assistance. Finally, the president proposed easing restrictions on the existing community development block grant (CDBG)

Table 8-5. *Number of Categorical Grants Proposed for Consolidation by Administration and Enacted into Block Grants by Congress, 1981*

Proposed block grant	Programs consolidated	Enacted block grant	Programs consolidated
Local education	10	State education	37
State education	30		
Health services and mental health	17	Preventive health and health services	6
		Alcohol, drug abuse, and mental health	10
Preventive health	10	Maternal and child health	9
		Primary health care	1
Social services	12	Social services	1
		Low-income energy assistance	1
Emergency assistance	2	Community services	7
Community development	1	State community development	3
Total	85	Total	77

Source: David B. Walker, Albert J. Richter, and Cynthia C. Colella, "The First Ten Months: Grant-in-Aid, Regulatory, and Other Changes," *Intergovernmental Perspective,* vol. 8 (Winter 1982), pp. 8–9.

and turning the federally administered portion of the program for small communities over to the states. He also proposed terminating several categorical programs like planning and weatherization grants and rehabilitation, allowing state and local governments to pick them up if they desired with block grant funds.

Structurally, these block grant proposals were very bold. They ignored virtually every feature that had contributed to the success of block grants in the past. No attempt was made to construct consolidations in areas of professional consensus or to focus on politically vulnerable programs. Nor was any effort made to respect Congress's traditional concern with maintaining fiscal accountability and protecting basic national purposes. Rather, the Reagan proposals resembled and expanded upon Nixon's unsuccessful concept of special revenue sharing. Within the broad range of eligible activities specified in each proposal, most of the Reagan block grants gave to state recipients nearly unlimited discretion—without planning, application, or detailed reporting requirements. As one city lobbyist remarked, they "made general revenue sharing look restrictive" by comparison. Earlier block grant enactments were also very expensive. They consistently had higher appropriations than the programs they replaced, in order to prevent most recipients of existing programs from losing funds in the shift to a new block grant formula. But there was no such attempt to "buy" consolidation under the Reagan proposals. Rather, they generally cut funding levels 25 percent below expected spending levels.

Finally, most CETA and CDBG funds had gone directly to local governments on a formula basis, in part because these governments had more influence in Washington than states did in the early 1970s. Although some of Reagan's proposals required the states to "pass through" some revenues to local governments, they sent no funds directly to local governments, even in program areas of principally local concern. Instead, they sent all the block grants—and their attendant cuts—to the states, greatly "upping the ante" on the governors' prior offer to accept modest reductions in federal aid in exchange for greater administrative flexibility.

Thus initial congressional and interest group responses to the Reagan block grant proposals were sharply negative. Throughout the spring of 1981 congressional committees in both the House and Senate deleted controversial provisions—and entire programs—from the president's proposals. In the Republican-controlled Senate, for example, defections by key moderate Republicans on the Labor and Human Resources Committee stalled progress on the administration's health and education bills for weeks. When compromise legislation finally was reported from committee, the largest and most sensitive education programs had been saved from consolidation, and the health proposals had been reworked into three less ambitious block grants. The Senate also retained legal services as a separate program, substantially scaled back the social service block grant, and restructured community action grants into a separate block grant. In short, although the Senate eventually acceded to considerable program consolidation, this occurred only after lengthy and difficult negotiations that concluded with substantial amendments to the president's proposals.

During this initial period, the president fared even worse in the Democratic House, where most of the proposed block grants were bottled up or killed entirely in their respective committees. As one senior aide with the Subcommittee on Health and Environment recalled, "The block grants were window dressing to disguise budget cuts. And many health programs historically were not funded by the states. Some, like family planning, were simply not negotiable. So the president's proposals were rejected out of hand."[23] Similarly, Education and Labor Committee chairman Carl Perkins (Democrat of Kentucky) charged that the president sought to "dismantle programs" rather than reform them,[24] while Representative William Ford (Democrat of Michigan) likened the education block grant to sending "bags of money to a State" in a Brinks truck. "We cannot send a check to Michigan addressed to: 'To whom it may concern' and hope somebody will cash it and divvy it up properly," he said.[25]

As Representative Ford's statement suggests, the issue of consolidation was of greater concern to many senior Democrats than were the Reagan budget cuts. Operating on the assumption that many of the president's cuts were popular and unavoidable, Democratic strategists attempted instead to "protect the [categorical] delivery systems."[26] This would protect Democratic priorities in the long run and permit rapid program recovery under a later Democratic administration.

The president's block grant proposals also came under scathing attacks from affected clientele and interest groups outside of Congress. Many saw the block grants merely as a thin disguise for drastic budget cuts. Others, like the Ad Hoc Coalition on Block Grants (representing more than 100 separate groups and professional associations), focused on consolidation as "a radical transformation in the relationship between citizens and their government." In a letter sent to all members of the House, the coalition charged that the president's proposals would

> repeal landmark legislation, eliminate essential programs, undermine principles of fiscal accountability and lay the groundwork for confusion, neglect, and new bureaucracy at the state level. . . . These proposals will certainly mean . . . less assistance to those in genuine need . . . and a brutal political struggle at the state level where the most vulnerable . . . are almost certain losers.[27]

During congressional hearings, witnesses drew ties between the administration's budgetary and block grant strategies. In testimony before the Senate, the executive director of one group concluded that "the problem with block grants . . . is that by removing the targeting [to specific clienteles], you remove the constituency for funding. Pretty soon you can pretend there was no need for funding at all."[28]

Even many state and local government officials—the presumed beneficiaries of grant consolidation—appeared lukewarm or hostile toward the president's proposals. Most state officials reacted tentatively to the block grants, supporting the concept but acting wary of the large budget cuts proposed and the rapid transfer of program responsibility. Local officials' attitudes were even less favorable toward the new grants, since they were anxious about both the budget cuts and state control. Mayor Richard Hatcher of Gary, Indiana, then president of the U.S. Conference of Mayors, spoke for many when he condemned the proposals as "deep budget cuts dressed up to look like block grants and sent to state capitals, where we'll have to go through another layer of bureaucracy to find them."[29] Consequently, much of the hoped-for support for the block grants by the intergovernmental lobby was dissipated in guerrilla warfare between states and cities over block grant funding, eligibility, and design.

Therefore, prospects in early 1981 for enactment of Reagan's block grant proposals seemed very dim. One respected journalist covering their progress in Congress concluded only one week before House passage of the Omnibus Budget Reconciliation Act that "the political furnace required to melt categorical grants together into large, simple blocks hasn't reached the critical temperature yet, even in this year's overheated congressional atmosphere."[30] This view was shared by many academic experts as well. "I don't think the block grant proposals will pass Congress," said Professor Frederick Mosher.[31]

Passage of the Omnibus Reconciliation Act

These expectations were dramatically reversed on June 26, 1981, when the House passed its version of the Omnibus Budget Reconciliation Act of 1981. As amended by the so-called Gramm-Latta II amendment, the reconciliation act:

—established nine new or revised block grants for public health, social services, elementary and secondary education, and community development—consolidating or terminating 139 categorical programs in the process;

—reduced funding for the consolidated programs by 25 percent;

—terminated the public service employment titles of the Comprehensive Employment and Training Act; and

—eased federal restrictions on several large education and urban programs, including CDBG and Title I education grants for educationally disadvantaged students.

In addition to reducing the number of federal aid programs by one-quarter and reducing funds for consolidated programs by a similar amount, the new block grants greatly strengthened the role of states as grant recipients—to the marked detriment of local nonprofit agencies, local school districts, and small municipalities.

The politics of the reconciliation act have already been discussed in chapter 7. In the case of grant consolidation, members of the House were offered a stark choice between two multibillion-dollar packages of budget cuts, program changes, and grant reforms. The House Budget Committee package contained an estimated $37.7 billion in reductions from fiscal 1982 outlays for current services. These cuts stemmed from legislative changes devised by each House committee, but the changes did not include any of the president's new block grant proposals. The only additional block grants in the House Democrats' package were four narrowly defined and tightly controlled block grants in public health, one of which consisted of a single program. An alternative budget package was presented in Gramm-Latta II, the substitute amendment devised by the administration and House conservatives that reduced projected fiscal 1982 outlays by $38.2. billion and established eight new block grants. Although there were some differences, these block grants were patterned closely on the president's recommendations.

The normal rules of block grant politics broke down in the confrontation over reconciliation. Key decisions about program structure were removed from the arena of individual committees, often dominated by sponsors and beneficiaries of categorical programs, and placed before Congress and the country as a whole, where they became part of a litmus test of support for the president's program. In the process the fundamental legislative issue was transformed from "Does each specific program change make sense to program specialists and supporters?" to "Do you support the economic recovery plan of a highly popular president?"

Under the latter formulation, block grants became for many a secondary issue, obscured in a massive and hurriedly compiled 1,000-page bill and nearly overshadowed by a host of competing budgetary and structural issues in defense, transportation, energy, and entitlements. As one moderate Democrat complained on the House floor: "We are dealing with more than 250 programs with no hearings, no deliberation, no debate."[32] "Normally this package would be one hundred different bills," observed a congressional staff member, "and Congress would spend months on each one." At the end of it all was a simple up or down vote on the total package with no exceptions or deletions.

The House Democratic leadership did not want the issue to be cast in such stark terms, even in the context of reconciliation. The leadership-controlled Rules Committee proposed that reconciliation be brought to the floor under a rule allowing five different votes on major sections of the reconciliation bill. Rather than let the Republicans offer a single omnibus amendment to the Democrats' bill, the rule required that the Gramm-Latta substitute be brought up in separate pieces. The hope was to isolate several politically popular programs in each amendment and force the president's supporters to go on the record voting for specific cuts in college student aid programs, food stamps, social security and medicare, energy and public health programs, and cost-of-living adjustments for federal workers.[33]

Not surprisingly, Republicans bitterly fought this attempt to disrupt their strategy, the success of which depended on a single yes or no on the president's economic package. They charged that the allowable amendments ignored subsequent changes in their package that made it more attractive politically. In fact, the Republican minority leader called the amendments "bastards of the worst order for which we disclaim any parental responsibility."[34]

More surprising than Republicans' opposition was the outcome. The Republicans won their fight on the rule, and the leadership's attempt to structure debate on the Democrats' terms was defeated. In a show of conservative support and extraordinary Republican unity, 27 Democrats joined all 189 Republicans in supporting a substitute Republican rule that required a single vote on the Gramm-Latta II reconciliation amendment. This procedural vote virtually guaranteed adoption of the Gramm-Latta amendment, since the House leadership expected to attract more support on the less visible and arcane procedural issue than on the substantive budget cuts themselves.

THE BROYHILL AMENDMENT. The major exception to this pattern of Republican victories on reconciliation involved programs under the jurisdiction of the House Energy and Commerce Committee. Here as elsewhere both parties had prepared differing budget proposals affecting energy, environmental, and health care programs including competing plans for new health care block grants. The Democrats prevailed with their proposal containing the four narrow health grants described earlier, which retained many strings and earmarks and consolidated only twelve programs rather than the twenty-five requested by the president. The Republicans proposed a substitute that contained three broader block grants and deeper spending cuts in several areas.

This Republican substitute was initially folded into the omnibus Gramm-Latta amendment and would have been adopted with the rest of Gramm-Latta II. But these provisions were taken out of the package and prepared as a separate amendment when two "boll weevils" on the Commerce Committee informed the administration that they could support Gramm-Latta only if their committee's provisions were removed.[35] Desperate for every vote, the administration and House Republican leaders agreed to separate from the rest of Gramm-Latta II the Broyhill amendment, named after the ranking Republican on the House and Energy Committee. Despite original intentions, the amendment was never offered for a separate vote on the floor. Thus, by default, the Democrats' provisions on health care and other energy and commerce issues went unchallenged and remained in the bill.

THE 1981 RECONCILIATION CONFERENCE. Even with its loss on the Broyhill amendment, the administration had won a historic victory. Gramm-Latta II allowed it to advance its economic agenda in the Democratically controlled House. The House and Senate, however, passed different versions of reconciliation legislation. The president's modified budget and block grant proposals were to be sent to a conference committee to iron out those differences. Fearing that its policy goals would be diluted further during this conference or that a way might yet be found to stymie them entirely, the administration requested that the Republican-controlled Senate simply pass the House version of the reconciliation bill and avoid such a conference.[36] Senate Republican leaders angrily refused to engage in such an unprecedented sacrifice of their legislative prerogatives, and the largest House-Senate conference in history was assembled. More than 250 members of Congress representing 59 different House and Senate subcommittees assembled to reconcile differences affecting over 200 federal programs.[37]

As with earlier versions of omnibus reconciliation, many of the most controversial issues in conference, such as the sale of Conrail and the placement of an annual cap on federal medicaid payments to the states, had nothing to do with grant consolidation. Once again, however, health grants were the exception. Because the Broyhill amendment was never offered, the House and Senate took widely divergent positions on block grants. The Senate passed three block grants for health care that consolidated twenty-five different grants—including three extremely controversial programs for family planning, community health centers, and migrant health care. All three sustained deep budget cuts. The House passed four smaller, tightly earmarked, and regulated block grants and retained all three of these programs as separately authorized grants.

These structural differences created obstacles to agreement. As one House committee staffer recalled, "There were two entirely different concepts involved. It took time for the Senate to realize they couldn't get a big block grant for health. Once they realized that, then there were logical ways that programs broke down into pieces."[38] In the end the conference reported the four health care block grants that the House had passed, but with modifications in their budgets and with nine additional programs folded in. For example, the preventive health and health services block grant was enlarged, its budget was reduced, and the reporting and structural features of the four block grants were standardized. But the House refused to consolidate several controversial programs, particularly family planning grants, with the result that the primary care "block grant" consisted of one program and was made so restrictive that only a single state chose to participate.

In health care, the conference followed the usual pattern of blending provisions from the House and Senate bills, leaving a group of block grants broader than the House's version and narrower than the Senate's. In other areas, a more obvious effort was made to weaken the block grants, much as Stockman had feared when he sought to avoid a conference committee. In social services, for example, programs that were included in one but not both House and Senate versions of this block grant were deleted, including grants for community services, child welfare, foster care, child abuse prevention, and runaway children. This left the final social services block grant (SSBG) program smaller and narrower than either the House or Senate versions—and not very different from the existing Title XX social services block grant, apart from substantial budget cuts. Similarly, when it emerged from conference, the low-income energy assistance block grant consolidated only a single existing program.

In education, few restrictive modifications were adopted in conference, primarily because neither chamber had passed an expansive block grant to begin with. Both rejected the administration's proposal that the two largest federal education programs—which provided grants for teaching handicapped and educationally disadvantaged children—be included in a separate local education block grant. As a result, the conference focused on similar plans for consolidating thirty-seven mostly small discretionary federal grants into a modest state education block grant.

Despite these modifications, it would be a mistake to conclude that the president failed in his quest for block grants. Senate supporters of the president claimed that he had won 70 to 80 percent of his initial budget requests.[39] As table 8-5 shows, Congress consolidated seventy-seven categorical programs into nine new or revised block grants, which was not too far off the president's goal of consolidating eighty-five programs into seven grants. Compared with earlier block grant efforts, this alone was a spectacular achievement. In one year, in a single law, the Reagan administration had obtained the enactment of more block grants and the consolidation of more programs than had been accomplished in the preceding twenty-five years of grant reform initiatives. Despite the fact that outlays for block grants in fiscal 1982 were 15 percent below fiscal 1981 spending levels, the proportion of the federal aid budget devoted to "broad-based" assistance—mainly block grants—rose by more than one-fifth under Ronald Reagan, going from 11.3 percent in 1981 to 14 percent by 1987.

Post-1981 Politics

These successes were never repeated. Only one additional block grant was enacted after 1981, the Job Training Partnership Act of 1982, which revised and restructured the existing CETA block grant. Even this modest achievement was counterbalanced in 1985 by the repeal of the primary care block grant, which eliminated the little-used block grant option provided for states under the community health centers program.

This decline in fortunes was not for want of trying on the president's part. In the five years after 1981, the Reagan administration issued twenty-four additional block grant proposals, several of which were recommended to Congress on repeated occasions (table 8-6). Yet few were seriously considered. Some failed even to obtain a sponsor to introduce them in Congress.[40]

There were several reasons, both substantive and political, for this reversal of fortunes. Substantively, many of the most obvious and politically tenable candidates for consolidation were folded into block grants in 1981. Several of the remaining programs proposed for subsequent consolidation—such as family planning and migrant health grants—had already been considered and firmly rejected by Congress. In other instances, the administration simply failed to present a convincing case. It proposed con-

Table 8-6. *Reagan Administration Proposals for New
or Expanded Block Grants, Fiscal Years 1983–87*

Block grant proposal	Number of programs proposed for consolidation
1983	
Child welfare block grant	4
Rental rehabilitation grants	2
Combined welfare administration	3
Vocational and adult education	3
Handicapped education	2
Rehabilitation services	3
Primary care block grant	3
Maternal and child health	1
1984	
Indian community development and housing	1
Indian housing	1
General nutrition assistance	3
Older Americans programs	3
Primary care block grant	3
State fiscal assistance block grant	22
Local fiscal assistance block grant	2
Transportation block grant	6
Rural housing block grant	4
1985	
Science and math education	1
Older Americans programs	4
Nonschool nutrition programs	2
Primary care block grant	3
1986	
Primary care block grant	3
1987	
Pollution control block grant	7
Highway and transit block grant	6
Primary care block grant	3

Source: Based on Sandra S. Osbourn, "Block Grants: Inventory and Funding History," Congressional Research Service, November 21, 1986.

solidating the women, infants, and children (WIC) nutrition program into the maternal and child health block grant, even though this promised at least temporary dislocations in what was widely considered to be one of the most successful of all federal aid programs.[41] Similarly, a proposal to consolidate funding for the regionally targeted black lung health clinics into a nationally distributed primary care block grant clearly spelled the termination of a unique program rather than a structural change in its administration.

Several political factors made matters even more difficult for block grants. To begin with, the administration used block grants to obtain budget cuts in 1981, and, as George Peterson has pointed out, "Subsequent proposals . . . failed in large part because they [became] identified politically as instruments of domestic budget cutting."[42] Consequently, block grants were no longer considered management-oriented devices deserving of bipartisan support but were perceived as a political and budgetary tool of conservatives. Therefore, traditional supporters of block grants among state and local officials grew wary of further proposals by the administration. Governor Jerry Brown of California complained that the Reagan approach to block grants was part of "a shell game" designed to "shift the burden to state and local governments."[43] Local officials, including Republicans like Indianapolis mayor William Hudnut, condemned the administration's strong bias toward block grants to states rather than local governments. "We do not want to be administrative provinces of either the federal government or the state," he declared.[44]

In addition, the president had fewer political resources available in subsequent years. Although reconciliation continued to be an integral part of the budget process, Congress refused to use it again for authorizing such wholesale changes in legislation. Even during 1981, Democrats condemned reconciliation as the most "brutal and blunt instrument . . . since Nixon used impoundment," while Republicans confessed that "nobody is particularly happy about this procedure."[45] A top Budget Committee aide said simply, "I don't think we'll do it again. Period."[46] Moreover, as noted in chapter 7, the president's voting strength in Congress declined after 1981 because conservative Democrats returned to their party fold on key votes and moderate Republicans increased their willingness to support existing federal aid programs. The loss of twenty-six Republican House seats in the 1982 election further weakened the president's political support in that chamber. Any one of these factors might have been sufficient to erode the narrow margin of support for block grants in the Congress. In combination, they proved simply overwhelming.

The only departure from this pattern of post 1981 defeats—the Job Training Partnership Act of 1982 (JTPA)—was an exception that proved the rule. Unlike the president's 1981 block grants or subsequent proposals, JPTA was enacted in an atmosphere of consensual, bipartisan block grant politics reminiscent of the early 1970s.

Much as Nixon's block grants reflected dissatisfaction with earlier Great Society programs, the new job training block grant stemmed from widespread disillusionment with CETA. Yet in 1973, when CETA was enacted, it was considered a major achievement of Nixon's New Federalism. It consolidated seventeen highly fragmented categorical programs into a single job training block grant, created a new program of public service employment, and established a new system for delivering job training services at the local level. During the 1974–75 recession, a large additional public service employment title was added.

Although CETA provided jobs for more than a million unemployed persons and job training and work experience for thousands more, by 1978 the program had become for many a "dirty four letter word." Stories of corruption and mismanagement—directed mainly at CETA's public employment titles—undermined support for the entire legislation. Moreover, careful evaluations of CETA training programs often failed to detect substantial improvements in the future earnings of trainees.[47] In response to these problems, Congress substantially amended the program in 1978, tightening up program controls and eligibility and reducing funding. In 1981 Congress returned to CETA and terminated the public employment titles of the legislation. These changes helped curb the most flagrant abuses and direct more employment assistance to the neediest clients, but they also dampened support for the program among both clients and local governments.

Against this backdrop of disillusionment with CETA, which in any case was scheduled to expire on September 30, 1981, three major replacements were introduced in Congress in 1982. The bills all featured improved linkages between the private sector and government training programs and less reliance on public employment. But they differed widely on other issues, from funding levels to how services would be delivered.

The administration's bill contained sharply reduced funding for training programs and a much narrower range of services and eligible clients. At the same time the measure gave the states and private industry councils a larger role in designing and delivering training services. Only localities with populations over 400,000 (compared with 100,000 under CETA) would have been permitted to operate their own programs under this bill.

At the other extreme was H.R. 5320, sponsored by Augustus Hawkins, chairman of the House Employment Opportunities Subcommittee. This proposal retained many CETA services and much of the existing operating structure. It also raised authorizations for training programs above 1982 levels and included a new $1 billion public jobs program for areas with high unemployment.

The bipartisan Senate bill, S. 2036, sponsored jointly by Senators Dan Quayle of Indiana and Edward M. Kennedy of Massachusetts, occupied a middle ground. Eligibility for local designation as a service delivery area (SDA) was increased to populations of only 200,000, and a roughly equal partnership between industry councils and local elected officials was established. Although stipends and wages were retained as allowable local expenditures, support services and administration were limited to 30 percent of program costs, and some of the least efficient uses of training funds were restricted or prohibited.

The new law was largely patterned after this bipartisan compromise. In deference to the administration, subsidies and allowances for trainees were sharply reduced, and the roles of state governments and the private sector were expanded. Other provisions followed the Senate bill to a large extent:

—CETA's system of local prime sponsors was abolished, and instead local units of government with populations above 200,000 were designed as service delivery areas.

—New private industry councils were established in each SDA to develop a training plan and to determine the use of training funds, subject to approval by the local chief elected official of the SDA. In cases of disagreement, governors were given power to arbitrate.

—The level of funding was more than $3 billion a year, of which 78 percent was distributed to state and local governments on the basis of unemployment and poverty; the Senate limit of 30 percent on administration and support services was retained.

—The transition year for phasing out CETA and phasing in the new block grant was to be 1983.

Conclusion

When Ronald Reagan entered the White House, he and his entourage of close aides brought with them a radical intergovernmental agenda cloaked in continuities from the past. In the realm of intergovernmental spending, for example, Reagan's budgets did not mark an absolute reversal of past policies; rather, they rapidly accelerated the downward trends in the growth and relative significance of federal aid that had begun during the Carter administration. With respect to policy instruments, Reagan relied even more heavily than Nixon on block grants to promote his New Federalism. These continuities, however, disguised fundamental differences with the first New Federalism as well as the Great Society.

That Reagan's budgets should conduct a frontal assault on the programmatic heritage of Lyndon Johnson should come as no surprise. Reagan's hostility to programs like community action services went back to his days as governor of California. The extent of his attack was less predictable, however, particularly for state and local governments and their associations in Washington.

At the core of the Great Society was the service strategy, which the Reagan administration frowned upon in virtually all respects. Both the traditionalist and libertarian factions of modern conservatism opposed the service strategy because they believed that it drained public resources and sponsored dependency on government by establishing elite cadres of social engineers who reject traditional social values. The greatest impact of the administration's numerous initiatives to reverse or eliminate such policies was felt by state and local governments. With their large educational and social service bureaucracies, state and local governments had become the foot soldiers of the service strategy. They suffered accordingly when federal grants for education, training, and social services were reduced between 1980 and 1985 by as much as 33 percent, which is far in excess of the cuts incurred by all federal aid or domestic spending in those years.

State and local government lobbies suffered just as much. Thanks in large part to the policies of the Nixon administration, they were unusually dependent on federal contracts and subsidies for staff and resources. Although the Reagan administration sometimes worked with them as allies, it was far more apt to view these organizations as just another interest group. Indeed, to some extent, their dependency was all the more objectionable because it symbolized their decline from proud and independent "co-sovereigns" to submissive supplicants of federal aid. When the administration moved aggressively to "defund the left" and reduce or eliminate direct subsidies to social lobbying associations, state and local government associations as a whole received the largest cuts of all, which forced them to reduce their staffs and operations drastically.

Other programs with roots in the Nixon administration suffered sizable and sometimes startling cuts as well. General revenue sharing was reduced, then capped, and finally abolished. Welfare benefits for the working poor were cut back sharply. Perhaps even more than the attacks on the Great

Society, these departures from policies adopted in the Nixon administration reveal the extent to which Reagan intended to break with the past.

Through block grants, in particular, the president sought to achieve a new and radical objective: elimination of federal participation in a vast array of domestic activities. Since this goal was not immediately realizable in many instances, block grants constituted a politically viable "halfway house" to termination, with the first installment represented by cuts of 25 percent in block grant budgets.

The irony of Reagan's radical approach was that it was more ambitious than Nixon's approach yet initially it was more successful. This paradox can be explained by the very different political strategy with which Reagan pursued his block grants. Rather than build a consensus for reform on each affected issue, the Reagan administration hitched consolidation proposals to the high stakes and polarized politics of his budget policies.

This tactic produced striking results in the short term but at the expense of long-term gains. In essence, the polarization of block grant politics poisoned the well for future consolidations, as was evident from the rapidly diminishing returns reaped by this strategy once the unusually propitious political circumstances of 1981 evaporated. After 1981 only one additional block grant was enacted out of twenty-four new proposals. This was the Job Training Partnership Act of 1982, which reflected the more consensual style of block grant politics that had reached its zenith under Richard Nixon. The conflictual strategy of 1981, however, superseded this tradition and put it, perhaps permanently, to rest.

CHAPTER 9

Comprehensive Federalism Reform: The Missing Chapter

$$T$$HE MOST DRAMATIC intergovernmental reform proposal of the Reagan presidency was its sweeping federalism initiative of 1982. This proposal was so bold that one respected scholar predicted that, if fully implemented, it would have returned intergovernmental fiscal relations to the days before the New Deal.[1]

Specifically, the president's initiative envisioned a comprehensive restructuring of the federal government's relationships with states and localities in "a single bold sweep." In his State of the Union address, Reagan proposed to nationalize health care financing for the poor, terminate the federal role in welfare, and return to the states forty-three major federal grant programs along with $28 billion in federal excise tax sources to pay for them.

Although it was the centerpiece of the president's agenda, the 1982 initiative was never introduced as legislation in Congress. The nation's governors were intensely interested in the plan and negotiated actively with the White House on a joint proposal. Anticipating strong resistance from Congress, the administration was reluctant to proceed with the plan without the support of state and local governments, but the policy differences between them were sizable and difficult to overcome. Moreover, it became apparent during these negotiations that important sources within the administration opposed the federalism plan as well. David Stockman, the director of the Office of Management and Budget (OMB), accepted it initially only as a means toward deficit reduction. Once it became clear that the governors would support it only on a revenue positive or neutral basis, OMB and eventually the White House backed away from the proposal, and a compromise was never reached.

Although the federalism initiative was central to the president's 1982 budget and although its outlines were largely crafted by OMB, the proposal was never mentioned in Stockman's memoirs of his five years at OMB. His book skips from the events of 1981 directly to those of 1983. Similarly, the bold federalism plan left surprisingly little trace in subsequent budgets or legislative proposals by Reagan. In substance as well as literary style, the president's bold initiative was truly the "missing chapter" in Reagan federalism.

The Origins of the "Sorting Out" Plan

Although it was a bold departure from existing policy, President Reagan's plan for sorting out governmental functions did not spring spontaneously onto the political scene. It had a substantial intellectual history based on a series of explicit policy proposals developed over the previous thirteen years. Moreover, the plan built upon the president's own distinctive and long-held views about the proper assignment of functions in a federal system.

Public finance economists had long maintained that governmental functions could be divided among the different levels of government in a rational and systematic fashion.[2] For example, services and activities that command the resources of the nation as a whole, such as management of the economy, belong clearly to the federal government. So, too, do those policies that govern public goods with substantial geographic "externalities," where policy impacts spill across state and local boundaries and affect citizens in other states and regions. Economists generally assign responsibility for income redistribution to the national level as well. They reason that public and private resources vary widely among the states, and an optimum level of redistribution is unlikely to be achieved at the state level because states will compete to keep taxes and benefits low.

By the same token, economic logic suggests placing other governmental activities at the state and local levels. Most other policies are "allocational" in nature and reflect differences in local tastes and preferences for levels of publicly provided goods. Because local decisions on these policies do not affect citizens in other jurisdictions, they can be safely left to local discretion. At the same time, overall public welfare can be maximized because mobile citizens can shop for a community offering a preferred mix of public goods and taxation. Most developmental policies are also deemed to be properly subnational in character because they promote economic growth within a single state or local community. These jurisdictions have full incentive to pursue such policies independently, to the extent supported by local residents.[3]

The U.S. Advisory Commission on Intergovernmental Relations (ACIR), a federally sponsored body of federal, state, and local public officials, developed one of the first serious proposals for rationally sorting out governmental responsibilities. In 1969 it recommended that the national government assume full financial responsibility for public assistance programs—including medicaid and general assistance. That same year it recommended that state governments assume greater fiscal responsibility for local education.[4] The commission reaffirmed these positions eight years later and then in 1981 expanded upon them.[5] It recommended federal assumption of financial responsibility for income maintenance programs and a reduction or termination of federal involvement in areas of primary concern to state and local governments.

Similar recommendations were advanced by other organizations during this period as well. Following ACIR's lead, the National Governors' Conference endorsed greater federal funding of welfare programs in 1969. In 1980 and 1981 the governors again endorsed full federal assumption of financial responsibility for income maintenance programs in exchange for states assuming more responsibility for public safety, education, and transportation programs.[6] Also in 1980 President Jimmy Carter's Commission on a National Agenda for the Eighties called for "clarification of the present confused division of labor in the federal system" and endorsed reforms along the lines advocated by ACIR and state officials.[7] The following year the governors stepped up their efforts for reform, joining with the National Conference of State Legislatures on a shared sorting out strategy. Following the 1981 budget and tax reductions, they called for negotiations with the administration on a more rational division of governmental resources and responsibilities.

All of these recommendations were prompted by a similar set of policy concerns. Initially, the focus was on the advantages of nationalizing income maintenance programs. The ACIR, most state officials, and many policy analysts believed such a policy would narrow interstate disparities in benefit levels; reduce incentives for migration to high-benefit states and away from high-tax states; recognize the high correlation between poverty rates and national economic conditions; and reduce income disparities by harnessing the relatively more progressive federal income tax.[8] To many these arguments for the federal assumption of income maintenance financing were reinforced in the late 1970s, when perceptions of dysfunctions in the intergovernmental system became more widespread. By 1980 many intergovernmental analysts believed that the federal aid system deserved poor marks on all of the principal criteria used for assessing its performance: efficiency, effectiveness, equity, and accountability. In words later used by the president in his State of the Union address, the ACIR concluded that the intergovernmental system had grown "more pervasive, more intrusive, more unmanageable, more ineffective, more costly, and above all, more unaccountable."[9]

While such developments formed a general context for the 1982 initiative, the concept held a uniquely personal appeal for the president. Reagan had long advocated sorting out governmental functions, though with a distinct difference. Rather than seeking to rationalize intergovernmental responsibilities, Reagan saw sorting out as a means of returning to the states most of the federal government's domestic responsibilities—including welfare. Indeed, in his race against Gerald Ford for the 1976 Republican presidential nomination, he unveiled an ambitious plan to turn back $90 billion in federal programs as the core of his domestic policy platform.

Decrying the "crushing weight of central government" that had turned states and localities into "little more than administrative districts, subdivisions of Big Brother government in Washington," Reagan urged a "systematic transfer of authority and resources to the states."[10] Specifically, he argued that eliminating federal programs for "welfare, education, housing, food stamps, medicaid, community and regional development, and revenue sharing, to name a few," would reduce federal spending by up to $90 billion annually. These savings, he urged, could then be put to use by balancing the federal budget, retiring a portion of the national debt, and reducing personal income taxes by 23 percent—thus creating "tax room" for states and localities to pick up the terminated programs if they so desired.

Gerald Ford aggressively attacked Reagan's plan, calling the mass transfer of programs "unrealistic" and "irresponsible."[11] Because the plan appeared to require state tax increases, it was particularly controversial in tax conscious New Hampshire, where it contributed to Reagan's unexpected defeat in that state's presidential primary. Although Reagan subsequently backed off the plan, veteran Reagan watcher Lou Cannon concluded that it "prevented Reagan from winning the Republican nomination of 1976."[12] Due in part to this inauspicious attempt, the concept was not revisited until 1982.

Developing Reagan's Federalism Initiative

When the federalism concept was revisited, the process was almost hap-hazard. As is often the case with major presidential initiatives designed around a State of the Union address—including Nixon's 1971 New Feder-alism proposals—the Reagan administration's decision to develop a ma-jor federalism initiative emerged late in a confused and protracted White House decisionmaking process. Other options, ranging from a major new tax and budget package to a welfare block grant, were explored by ad-ministration officials during the second half of 1981, but with few tan-gible results. By one account, the administration's planning process was in "disarray" by mid-November.[13] By that point, decisionmaking options were increasingly constrained by worsening economic conditions, gloomy budgetary projections, and growing restlessness among state and local offi-cials, some of whom were calling for a "domestic summit" with the presi-dent in December to head off a feared second round of massive domestic budget cuts. Since the president did not approve even the general thrust of his federalism proposal until December 23, 1981, it is no surprise that the plan was viewed as a "last minute addition" to his agenda for 1982.[14]

Work on a federalism component for Reagan's 1982 domestic agenda actually began in the summer of 1981. In August word was leaked to the press that the administration was seriously considering a block grant for the aid to families with dependent children (AFDC) program and possibly medicaid, thus making good on a long-term goal of the president and his White House aide Robert Carleson. In his outgoing address as president of the National Governors' Association (NGA), Georgia governor George Busbee announced that, after dealing with the White House, he was "con-vinced a major effort will be made . . . to transfer responsibility for income maintenance programs to the states," and he declared the NGA "should serve notice that we will oppose block grants for AFDC or Medicaid."[15] Two days later Carleson confirmed that a "general decision" had been made to convert AFDC to a block grant, but he said "the timing and form depend a lot on the budgetary situation and they are very important."[16] Within a month, however, strong opposition from the states and from Congress combined with budgetary obstacles to sidetrack the welfare block grant proposal. "It's not dead," observed one White House official, "but it's very, very much on the back burner."[17] Carleson, meanwhile, was taken to the woodshed for leaking the controversial idea.

Lower profile work on a broader federalism reform proposal continued under the auspices of White House intergovernmental assistant Richard Williamson and policy adviser Martin Anderson. This work, however, "went slowly and failed to produce a plan that seemed both viable and sufficiently ambitious."[18] The focus of attention for new initiatives shifted largely to budgetary and tax policy. Stockman reports that he and other top administration aides met with the president throughout much of early November 1981 and attempted to hammer out a comprehensive plan of further budget cuts and excise tax increases that would reduce the deficit by approximately $80 billion in fiscal 1983.[19] Backed by Secretary of the Treasury Donald Regan, however, the president rejected any effort to raise taxes. Any remaining hope to fashion the 1982 agenda around an aggressive program of deficit reduction was permanently foreclosed on December 4 when the president "stubbornly" rejected a final appeal by Stockman and White House Chief of Staff James Baker to include a tax increase in the new budget. Following this incident, the president lamented to close aide Michael Deaver that "some of my people don't believe in my program the way I do."[20]

Thus very late in the year the process for developing the president's 1982 agenda was, in the words of White House aide Richard Darman, in serious "disarray."[21] Faced with serious economic and budgetary issues in the year ahead but with little hope of being able to meet them head-on, Darman argued in a memo to the Communications Strategy Group that the administration needed a coherent and positive initiative to "advance right through the '82 elections."[22] Seeking an agenda that combined "low cost/high payoff initiatives" with "the lift of a driving dream," Darman recommended a program of small stimulative federal grants that would promote "states as laboratories" of policy innovations. As Laurence Barrett explains, "that idea died because one of [New] Federalism's real goals was to reduce government activity . . . at all levels, not to stimulate it."[23] But the proposal helped to refocus White House attention on federalism as a positive issue around which different factions in the administration could coalesce and adapt to their own ends. As Williamson recalls:

> Darman became persuaded that if we were going to make the cuts we were agreeing to in the budget meetings, we had to have some major budget initiative so it didn't look like the President was just scorching the earth.[24]

Over the next month a small group of White House staff worked on developing a comprehensive proposal to restructure program responsibilities among the federal government and the states. Given Reagan's long-held interest in the federalism concept, they knew he not only would endorse this agenda but enthusiastically support it. For presidential counselor Edwin Meese and Robert Carleson, it provided an opportunity for going beyond a welfare block grant and returning responsibility for AFDC entirely to the states. Although Carleson resisted the political price of such a turnback—nationalizing certain other programs—he had little opportunity to say so. "After his bullshit at the Governors' Conference [announcing a welfare block grant], he was called out to California and told he could no longer make public statements," said Williamson. "Carleson first read about [the federalism initiative] in the papers, though some of his ideas were included."[25]

For his part, Williamson believed the governors might accept the welfare trade as part of a balanced swap. The governors had already publicly proposed a fiscally neutral exchange of program responsibilities and a return of federal tax sources to the states. Governors Bruce Babbitt, Democrat of Arizona, and Lamar Alexander, Republican of Tennessee, had made a similar proposal to Williamson in private.

Stockman was quick to see the potential fiscal dividends of such a plan in his campaign to reduce the deficit. Like block grants, a structural reform concept attractive to the states could be used as a vehicle for budget cuts that they would otherwise resist. At the same time the president might buy tax increases tied to a desirable goal like an excise tax trust fund to be returned to the states. Finally, a bold federalism initiative would meet the requirement of James Baker and Michael Deaver for a positive program that would maintain the administration's political momentum and "jazz up an otherwise grim State of the Union Message." "It's important," said one, "that we have something to say besides budget cuts, budget cuts, and more budget cuts."[26]

With OMB's resources at his disposal, Stockman assumed major responsibility for translating the concept of a federalism initiative into a workable proposal. With help from the Treasury Department and White House, OMB worked in almost total secrecy on the plan, and there were surprisingly few leaks about it to the press.. Cabinet members were totally excluded from the process, and even within OMB only a tiny handful of career staff had input into designing the proposal.[27]

Out of this process Stockman and Williamson distilled a sweeping plan with two main components. First, they proposed a $20 billion program "swap": the federal government would return to states full responsibility

Table 9-1. *Original Design of Reagan's 1982 Federalism Initiative for Fiscal Year 1984*
Billions of dollars

Federal responsibilities	Cost	State responsibilities	Cost
	Swap component		
Assume state share of		Assume federal costs of	
medicaid	19.1	AFDC and food stamps	16.5
	Turnback component		
Establish federalism trust fund			
Windfall profit tax on oil	16.7	...	...
Excise taxes from alcohol,		Assume responsibility	
tobacco, gasoline, and		for 43 federal programs	
telephones	11.3	returned to states	30.2
Total	47.1	Total	46.7

Source: Executive Office of the President, "The President's Federalism Initiative: A Basic Framework," press release, January 26, 1982, pp. 3, 10.

for funding AFDC and food stamps in return for federal assumption of state contributions to medicaid. Second, the plan included a temporary $28 billion trust fund or "super revenue sharing" program to replace approximately forty-three federal aid programs for education, health, social services, community development, and transportation (see tables 9-1 and 9-2). Initially, each state would have the choice of retaining specific programs in categorical form or accepting unrestricted monies from the trust fund in their place. After four years the trust fund and the federal taxes supporting it would begin to be phased out, leaving states the option of replacing federal taxes with their own and continuing the terminated programs or allowing both to cease altogether.

As expected, the president approved the general thrust of this plan when it was first presented to him on December 22 and 23, 1981.[28] At that time Stockman had won agreement from other principal administration aides— James Baker, Edwin Meese, and Donald Regan—to fund the trust fund portion of the plan by doubling federal excise taxes for gasoline, alcohol, telephones, and tobacco. By raising these taxes immediately but not "returning" them to the states for four years, this approach provided the additional revenues Stockman sought in a way that appeared integral to the plan's success. When Reagan gave general approval to this plan in

Table 9-2. *Programs Slated for Turnback to States under Reagan's Federalism Initiative*
Billions of dollars

Programs by category	Estimated 1984 expenditure
Education and training	3.3
Vocational rehabilitation	
Vocational and adult education	
State education block grants	
CETA	
Work incentive and training	
Low-income energy assistance block grant	1.3
Social, health, and nutrition services	8.0
Child nutrition, child welfare	
Adoption assistance	
Foster care, runaway youth	
Child abuse, legal services	
Social services block grant	
Community services block grant	
Preventive health block grant	
Primary care block grant	
Maternal and child health block grant	
Alcohol, drug abuse, and mental health block grant	
Black lung clinics, family planning	
Migrant health centers	
Women, infants, and children nutrition program	
Transportation	6.4
Airport grants	
All noninterstate highways	
Interstate transfer	
Appalachian highways	
Urban mass transit grants	
Community development and facilities	6.4
Water and sewer grants and loans	
Community facilities loans	
Community development block grant	
Urban development action grants	
Wastewater treatment grants	
General revenue sharing	4.8
Estimated total for 43 programs	30.2

Sources: Executive Office of the President, "The President's Federalism Initiative: Basic Framework," press release, January 26, 1982, p. 8; and "Fact Sheet: Federalism Initiative," press release, January 27, 1982.

December, including the tax increase, OMB proceeded to develop and refine its programmatic and fiscal details.

One month later, however, just days before the State of the Union address was to be delivered, the tax increase issue threw the initiative into yet another crisis. When a more detailed version of the plan was presented to Reagan for final approval on January 20, 1982, conservatives challenged the idea of raising any form of taxes through the plan. The president reduced or eliminated some of the proposed excise tax increases, but agreed to replace them with other increases on luxury goods and corporations.[29] When word of this decision leaked the following day, the increases were bitterly attacked by the Chamber of Commerce and key conservatives in the House such as Jack Kemp of New York and Trent Lott of Mississippi. The following day Reagan reversed his decision to include any tax increase, telling close aides that "I haven't been able to sleep because of this. I just can't do it. I just let you think I agreed with you so you'd leave me alone."[30] Thus, only five days before presenting his plan to the Congress and the country, the president eliminated over $16 billion in revenues from it and forced OMB to scramble to make the plan add up. In the end this was done through the expedient of placing $16.7 billion in corporate energy taxes—the temporary windfall profits tax—into the trust fund to make up the difference.

With this version in hand, the president went before the Congress and the country proposing to comprehensively restructure the intergovernmental system in "a single bold stroke." He condemned the existing "maze of interlocking jurisdictions and levels of government" and the "jungle of grants-in-aid" and promised to "make government again accountable to the people, to make our system of federalism work again." Reflecting the still incomplete condition of his complex proposal, however, he declared that "its full details will . . . [be] worked out only after close consultation with congressional, State, and local officials."[31]

Political Reactions to the Federalism Initiative

If the administration expected to dominate the 1982 agenda with its bold proposal, it was soon disappointed. The reactions to the president's speech varied greatly. Many governors and state legislators approved of the idea of sorting out governmental functions and spent much of the year negotiating with the administration on a mutually acceptable proposal. Reactions from other quarters were generally less favorable. Many local officials expressed concern about diminished federal aid and severed federal ties under the plan. Members of Congress and affected interest groups objected to turning back the specific programs covered by the trust fund. Virtually all parties raised questions about the lessened federal role in welfare. Looming over these responses were the shadows of a lengthening recession and ballooning budget deficits. As the federalism plan quickly bogged down in secret and protracted negotiations with the governors, these economic conditions swept it from public attention and eventually dominated the politically charged election year agenda.

Responses from the States

Most state officials—Republicans and Democrats alike—applauded the thrust of the president's proposal but questioned specific provisions of the plan. Governor Richard Snelling of Vermont, then chairman of the National Governors' Association, said the president "deserves enormous praise for putting the subject on the table."[32] Governor Bruce Babbitt of Arizona called the proposal "elegant and imaginative."[33] Both governors raised critical questions about appropriate federal-state roles, however. Governor Hugh Carey of New York was less positive, calling the proposal "hastily conceived and poorly designed."[34]

Much of the controversy focused on the welfare provisions. Giving states full responsibility for AFDC was a longstanding goal of the president and several of his advisers. As he declared in his 1975 federalism speech:

If there is one area of social policy that should be at the most local level of government possible, it is welfare. It should not be nationalized—it should be localized.[35]

Seven years later, in his 1982 State of the Union address, President Reagan reiterated this position, arguing that full state responsibility for AFDC and food stamps "will make welfare less costly and more responsive to genuine need because it will be designed and administered closer to the grassroots and the people it serves."[36] In supporting this claim, the administration pointed to welfare reforms implemented in California in the early 1970s as an example of what could be accomplished by the states. This experience led Robert Carleson, director of the California Department of Social Welfare during Reagan's governorship, to comment:

With federal regulations eliminated, the states would be able to provide relief to the taxpayer and, at the same time, would increase benefits to those who are truly in need.[37]

Considering the president's firm support for reducing the federal role in welfare, administration officials argued that the federalism initiative made a major concession to the states by offering to assume the full costs of medicaid. This move would benefit states, they said, because medicaid costs were rising much faster than AFDC expenses. Moreover, because medicaid served large numbers of elderly patients, they argued that the move would benefit program users by consolidating federal responsibility for programs aiding senior citizens.[38]

State officials strongly supported federalizing medicaid finance, but they opposed picking up the full costs of AFDC and food stamps. As Governor William Winter of Mississippi declared: "True federalism in this enlightened time must recognize that . . . we cannot split ourselves up into 50 states, contending regions, rich and poor, skilled and unskilled, white and black."[39] State officials argued that some form of national public assistance program had been advanced by every recent president of either party, including Nixon, Ford, and Carter. Finally, they questioned the rationale for dividing responsibilities for welfare and medical assistance to the poor. According to Wisconsin State Representative Tom Loftus, this would mean that "you would be an American when you are poor and sick, but a Texan when you're just poor."[40] States were especially concerned about termination of the federal food stamp program because of its unique role in narrowing disparities in welfare benefits among the states.

Magnified by dire economic conditions and resulting state budget shortfalls, the fiscal aspects of the New Federalism also concerned state officials. When the federalism initiative was announced, the country was entering the throes of a severe recession that significantly cut into state revenues. In fiscal 1982 and 1983, state year-end budget balances averaged only 2.1 percent of state general fund expenditures compared with an average of 7.7 percent for the previous four years.[41] Certain states had even more difficult problems. Despite balanced budget requirements in virtually all states, nine ran budget deficits in one or both of those fiscal years, whereas only four states had done so during the entire period from 1978 to 1981. Many others found that to avoid such problems they had to raise taxes and reduce government services in the midst of the recession. Thus even some potential supporters feared the president's plan had come "at the worst possible time." "We may all be so anemic by the end of the year that the states won't be able to function as partners," said Governor Scott Matheson of Utah.[42] California legislator John Vasconcellos added, "We are in the red, on the verge of bankruptcy, and there's nothing we could pick up."[43]

Although the president described his initiative as a financially equal swap, many state officials feared that it would cost them extra money in the long run, and growing fiscal problems left them little room for accommodating additional expenses. Ironically, the administration had worked hard to make sure that its proposal minimized financial winners and losers among states. For example, the costs to some states of assuming the federal contribution for food stamps and AFDC would outweigh their savings from the federal assumption of medicaid. Other states, however, would gain from this exchange. Therefore, these disparities were to be evened out by contributions from the federalism trust fund. States gaining from the welfare-medicaid swap would have their trust fund allocations reduced by that amount. Loser states would receive additional allotments from the fund to compensate. Eventually, the administration claimed that most states would gain slightly from the federalism initiative because medicaid costs were projected to rise faster than welfare costs.

Despite assurances that there would be no "winners or losers," many state officials remained leery of the fiscal consequences of the plan. To begin with, administration estimates of the costs of state assumption of AFDC and food stamps assumed that these programs should and could be scaled back as the administration proposed in its fiscal 1983 budget. Without these reductions, the Congressional Budget Office (CBO) estimated that states as a whole would initially pay $1.5 billion more to assume welfare programs than they would save from the federalization of medicaid.[44] States also raised questions about the medicaid portion of the swap. Medicaid benefits varied enormously from state to state. A totally national program would presumably have more uniform benefit levels—higher than those in low-benefit states but lower than in high-benefit states. Some states in the latter category would have felt compelled to continue supplementing federal medicaid payments, thereby reducing any fiscal dividend for them because of the swap.

Finally, state officials raised questions about the trust fund portion of the initiative. Using CBO baseline figures, Governor Carey maintained that the cost of the programs suggested for inclusion in the trust fund would total $37 billion by fiscal 1984, not $30 billion as calculated by

OMB.[45] The administration's figure was based on the assumption that the substantial budget cuts recommended for those programs would be adopted before the federalism plan was implemented. Moreover, both the trust fund and the federal excise taxes supporting it were to begin phasing out in fiscal 1988. Although states would have the option of assuming these tax sources themselves, the distribution of "tax room" would not be uniform throughout the country. Per capita revenues from cigarette excise taxes would be much smaller in Utah than in neighboring Nevada, for example, and only a fraction of states would have access to the sources of the windfall profits tax on oil. For these reasons, the NGA and the National Conference of State Legislatures argued for a financing system that would provide general federal revenues and some degree of equalization among states with differing needs and taxing capacities.

Other Reactions

State officials were hardly alone in questioning the federalism initiative. Although public opinion polls showed considerable support for the New Federalism concept,[46] the plan encountered a barrage of criticism from members of Congress, local governments, affected interest groups, and the press. Like state officials, other groups objected most to the "swap" elements of the plan.

The plan had barely been announced in the State of the Union address before it was criticized in newspaper editorials. The *New York Times* likened it to "turning back the clock." Although the paper acknowledged the need for some sorting out of functions, it questioned: "Where is the logic in Federalizing one poverty program but turning back others? Do poor people get equally sick in different places but not equally hungry."[47] The *Washington Post* called the proposal "an alarming retreat" from Washington's responsibilities for basic income maintenance and concluded that the poor would be worse off under it.[48]

To no one's surprise, many advocates of social programs felt threatened by the plan. The AFL-CIO charged the New Federalism initiative would "cripple facilities and services on which all Americans depend and jeopardize the health and welfare of millions of the poor."[49] "The worst thing you can do," said Andrew Mott of the Coalition on Block Grants and Human Needs, is to decentralize "responsibilities you know will be neglected because of lack of political will."[50]

Local officials were also wary. Many local governments were deeply suspicious of turning major program responsibilities over to the states, thereby severing their direct funding link to Washington. "The pass-through [issue] is the number 1 problem" with the president's plan, said one urban representative.[51] A state legislator from New York observed that county governments in his state were "clearly afraid of being bankrupted in the name of the new federalism."[52]

All of these opposing views were fully represented in Congress, where one observer reported that the "long knives are out," ready to kill the initiative if introduced.[53] Governor James Thompson of Illinois, who had been invited to the Capitol to hear the president's State of the Union address, reported afterward that "at least two members of my congressional delegation turned around [during the speech] and said to me: 'Over our dead bodies.'"[54]

Even some strong congressional supporters of the sorting out concept were troubled by specific features of the president's plan. Senator David F. Durenberger of Minnesota, the chairman of the Senate Intergovernmental Relations Subcommittee, openly questioned the programmatic logic of the swap initiative, even after the administration agreed in April to retain food stamps at the federal level:

> I am not happy with the outcome. . . . What sense does it make to have Social Security, Medicare, Medicaid, Food Stamps, and housing assistance all at the federal level and leave dependent children with the states?"[55]

In addition to supporting full federal responsibility for basic income maintenance programs, the senator proposed allocating trust fund revenues on an equalizing basis. "It is time for the federal government to recognize a responsibility for equalizing the fiscal capacity of places," he observed.[56]

But the most serious political obstacle confronting the federalism initiative may well have been worsening economic conditions. Many members of Congress simply dismissed the proposal as a diversion from more pressing economic problems, or they perceived it as a backdoor means of cutting social programs. Within days of the president's address, a congressional newsletter reported that the federalism plan was "sinking into a sea of economic problems of greater importance."[57] A few months later the *New York Times* reported the proposal had "become entangled in the [budget] stalemate."[58] "Budgetary problems are taking more and more of Congress's attention, and elections are coming on," agreed one administration adviser.[59] With the fate of the economy affecting almost every federal, state, and local official and distorting the spending estimates on which the federalism plan was based, the timing of the plan became a hurdle in itself.

Negotiations on Federalism

Initial negative reactions and hostile economic conditions notwithstanding, the administration proceeded to negotiate with state and local officials on a specific legislative proposal. From the beginning, the president had indicated that the details of his federalism initiative were tentative and that representatives of state and local governments would be consulted about changes. The strong disagreements sparked by the federalism initiative made it all the more necessary to present a united front before Congress and drove the administration and state officials to seek a joint legislative proposal on federalism reform. The structure, salience, and intensity of these negotiations, although they were unsuccessful ultimately, and the scope of the issues at stake were unprecedented in the history of intergovernmental relations.

In late February, before the start of these formal negotiations, the governors attempted to refine their position on sorting out while making some concessions to the president's position. They dropped their bid for the immediate nationalization of all income maintenance programs, suggesting instead that consideration of changes in AFDC and food stamps be deferred. They announced support for the creation of a federalism trust fund and a willingness to negotiate over the president's list of programs targeted for inclusion. They also emphasized their support for the federal assumption of medicaid costs. But the governors' position differed with the president's in several respects. Because it would remove AFDC and food stamps from the plan, their proposal was more limited in scope and contained a much smaller trust fund component. The governors also urged that trust fund allocations be made on the basis of state fiscal capacity.[60]

In order to deal with the substantial number of points still at issue, the White House, states, and localities established negotiating teams to resolve differences and distill a compromise proposal. The administration team was headed by top White House aides Richard Williamson, James Baker, Edwin Meese, and David Stockman, backed up by an eleven-member technical working group drawn from the major domestic departments, OMB, and the Executive Office of the President. The governors and state legislators appointed bipartisan negotiating teams with six members each, while local governments were represented by a single group of mayors, county officials, and one township representative.[61]

During late February and March, following the governors' winter conference, high administration officials, often including the president, held eight major meetings with these state and local officials in an effort to resolve remaining differences. The high-level meetings were supplemented by "dozens" of additional meetings between Williamson and other members of the White House Intergovernmental Affairs Office and the staffs of state and local public interest groups in Washington.[62] Both sides hoped that these meetings would produce a specific legislative proposal by early April 1982.

This April target date passed amidst a flurry of reports that the negotiations were in danger of collapsing.[63] The administration and the states remained at loggerheads over the assignment of welfare responsibilities, while local governments opposed any plan lacking safeguards for direct federal-local grants returned to the states. Fear of outright failure prompted renewed bargaining, however, and all sides began making major concessions. On April 14 the administration agreed to retain food stamps as a federal responsibility, while continuing to insist that AFDC be turned over to the states. The governors accepted this basic formulation, with some further revisions, and in early May, Governor Snelling announced that "a compromise has been engineered, but not formally approved by either side."[64] According to Snelling, the governors believed they had obtained the administration's commitment to support a minimum national floor for state AFDC benefits, establish a "safety net supplemental" fund for states suffering temporary economic crisis or chronically low fiscal capacity, and refrain from making automatic downward readjustments in food stamp benefits when state welfare payments increased. In return, the states were prepared to accept full responsibility for AFDC and to include additional categorical programs in the federalism trust fund to pay for the above concessions. The major remaining issue to be decided, said Snelling, was the level of federal medicaid benefits under a nationally financed program. Many states were concerned that if national benefits were set too low, added costs would be imposed on states with high benefits.

Despite this hint of success, succeeding weeks brought conflicting trends of further progress in some areas and deadlock and backpedaling in others. In late May the National League of Cities lent new momentum to the initiative by reversing its earlier position and endorsing state assumption of AFDC under conditions similar to those the governors were proposing. This gave impetus to new suggestions that a joint legislative proposal would be sent shortly to Capitol Hill.[65] Such an agreement seemed close, but it was never reached. The treatment of medicaid proved more difficult to resolve than expected, and with the prolonged negotiations shaky agreements began to unravel. For example, Williamson reports that by May there was "active resistance" from OMB to the medicaid provisions of the initiative:

> The critics' charge that this was Stockman's Trojan Horse for cuts had a ring of truth to it. There was a constant effort by OMB at that time to stall. They didn't want to do it. It had become an albatross. I had to get the President to personally call Stockman twice. Dave would say, "yes Mr. President" and then not do anything.[66]

Other opposition resurfaced in the White House from Robert Carleson, who reemphasized his basic philosophical objections to any increase in federal responsibilities.[67] By the time that senior White House officials met with state negotiators on June 23, the administration had backed off earlier concessions or clarified its opposition to several of the items that the governors had thought were settled, including the "unhitching" of AFDC and food stamps.[68]

When the state and local governments saw that the administration was only becoming more disorganized and inflexible, their enthusiasm dwindled. Hoping that an endorsement of the new initiative would give it renewed momentum, the president described the outlines of a modified administration proposal in a July speech to the National Association of Counties. Although the plan contained several key concessions to state and local interests, support for it was so weak that a resolution endorsing the general concept had to be withdrawn for fear that it would fail.[69] Similarly, a report from the state legislative negotiating team to the NCSL executive committee in late July was distinctly cool, noting that "at no time have we either endorsed or approved the initiative as a whole" and that, if a proposal is sent to Congress at the conclusion of negotiations, "normal policy procedures will be followed by NCSL to determine the formal NCSL response."[70]

The strongest rejection came from the governors at their annual summer conference. Disappointed that no final agreement had yet been reached and frustrated because the fast-approaching midterm congressional elections precluded sending Congress a proposal in 1982, the governors in essence gave up. They formally resolved to focus their future efforts on developing an independent federalism initiative rather than attempt to settle remaining differences with the White House. As Governor Snelling, the outgoing chairman of the NGA, reported to the organization's executive committee: "It no longer seems prudent to pin our hopes for a new federalism on the outcome of any negotiations with the White House."[71] He laid much of the blame for the failure to reach a final agreement on remaining differences over how to implement the federal takeover of medicaid.

In a formal sense this gubernatorial revolt was short-lived. Following a "White House power play" two days after the position was adopted, the governors reversed themselves and agreed to continue discussions with the administration while developing their own proposal.[72] Nevertheless, by this stage the handwriting for a joint proposal on federalism was clearly on the wall.

After a final meeting with the president in late September, which sought to identify areas of agreement for the future, the two sides went their separate ways. In a letter to the president on November 19, 1982, the Executive Committee of the NGA outlined the governors' operating position on federalism reform. As they had done ten months earlier, the governors proposed deferring action on AFDC and food stamps. They suggested instead that attention focus first on medicaid, with the federal government assuming full responsibility for the program in exchange for state assumption of up to eighteen existing federal grant programs. In order to ease passage of this proposal, the governors suggested medicaid could be divided into three components: acute care for federally aided elderly poor, acute care for AFDC-eligible recipients, and long-term care. The federal government could choose to assume any or all of the components, turning back a specific group of federal programs with each component. A revolving fund for balancing winning and losing states was also proposed, but no method for dealing with long-term fiscal disparities was indicated.[73]

For its part, the administration focused its subsequent efforts on developing a fiscal 1984 budget proposal with four megablock grants, which collectively would have consolidated thirty-four major federal aid programs totaling $21 billion. Specifically, it proposed consolidating: twenty-two education, social service, and health service programs into a massive block grant to states; two programs (revenue sharing and CDBG) into a large local block grant; six highway and transit grants into a transportation block grant; and four programs into a rural housing block grant. None was ever seriously considered by Congress or the states. By December, before the budget was even announced, the governors had rejected the concept of megablocks and declared that the president's federalism initiative was "dead."[74] The new agenda for the states, declared NGA chairman Scott Matheson, would be "budget, budget, budget."[75]

Both sides conceded that the negotiations had failed primarily because of the income maintenance issue. Even after it was agreed that food stamps would remain a federal responsibility, three welfare-related issues stalled the bargaining: the fiscal relationship between federal food stamp and state AFDC benefits; the provision of a "safety net fund" to ensure adequate AFDC benefits in poor states; and the treatment under medicaid of "medically needy" individuals, whose high medical bills would bring their incomes close to welfare levels.[76] As Richard Williamson later observed, "Each side . . . misjudged its ability to find common ground on income maintenance. Neither side appreciated how firmly committed the other was to its position."[77]

Administration disunity was another complicating factor. Some members of the White House staff, like Robert Carleson, were philosophically uncomfortable with federalizing any income maintenance responsibilities, and as the pressure to do so mounted during negotiations with the states, they began to object to the way that the plan was evolving. Others, like Stockman and to some extent Baker, bought into the federalism initiative because it had the potential to reduce the federal deficit. They lost enthusiasm and even became obstructionist when the president removed any tax increases from the federalism trust fund and the negotiating process made clear that state and local governments would not allow other portions of the plan to become a vehicle for hidden budget cuts.

These concerns about the fiscal effects of the federalism initiative also contributed to the plan's demise. For both the federal government and the states, uncertainty about the long-term fiscal implications of the proposal was heightened by the immediate budgetary shortfalls stemming from the 1982 recession. In the end these basic considerations left both sides unwilling to forge a compromise.

Conclusion

The failure of the federalism initiative—when considered in the context of Reagan's other policy decisions—illustrates the limits of the president's own commitment to federalism reform, even though he had placed it at the top of his policy agenda and seemed willing to negotiate on certain points in order to gain acceptance of his proposal. Throughout his presidency, Reagan demonstrated an underlying ambivalence toward his goal of strengthening federalism—even as he defined it. Although his many policy objectives were frequently compatible, whenever Reagan had to choose between the goals of his federalism agenda and competing budgetary and philosophical objectives, he consistently fell short of his federalism aims.

Nowhere was this clearer than in his reaction to budgetary issues associated with the sorting out plan. Initially, the president proposed a plan that appeared to be revenue neutral, although it presupposed substantial reductions in federal aid to state and local governments. The president's "obsession over short-term budget considerations" immediately put state and local governments on guard and slowed initial progress on negotiations.[78] Moreover, it fortified suspicions that the president had agreed to federalize medicaid merely to gain the control he needed to reduce the program. Although the administration's concern over the federal deficit was certainly understandable, it was never an obstacle to other costly initiatives in defense, supply side tax policy, or even urban enterprise zones. There is little doubt that Reagan could have achieved an agreement with the governors on a common federalism plan if he had been willing to devote additional federal resources to their concerns, just as Nixon had done before him. Although some important concessions were made, notably on food stamps, the president could not bring himself to sacrifice either his budgetary or his welfare goals for the sake of federalism reform:

> As much as the president wanted to strike a deal with the governors, and walk in step with them to Capitol Hill, the philosophical gap proved to be too wide. To move state and local officials, the president needed a bigger carrot than in good faith he felt he could offer.[79]

In the final analysis this ambivalence was the real "missing chapter" in the story of the 1982 initiative. It contributed greatly to the president's failure, although other serious obstacles would have been waiting in the Congress even if the intergovernmental negotiations had been successful. Moreover, the story was repeated in other areas of the president's agenda, especially regulation.

CHAPTER 10

Regulatory Federalism under Reagan

D EREGULATION was an important plank in Ronald Reagan's New Federalism program. According to an early report by the Presidential Task Force on Regulatory Relief, "Regulatory relief is a major part of the president's efforts to revitalize federalism. As we . . . return many of the responsibilities currently held by the Federal Government to state and local government, reduction in bureaucratic red tape and the unduly burdensome regulations is a key component."[1] This high-level attention to the regulatory dimensions of federal-state-local relations was unprecedented, and it signaled a major change in the nature of intergovernmental relations.

Until the 1970s intergovernmental relations meant, for all practical purposes, a complex administrative network for the disbursement of federal grants-in-aid to state and local governments. In the context of federalism, the purpose of federal regulations was to ensure that federal aid was properly planned, budgeted, and accounted for. Whenever the question of federal aid reform arose, it was usually because of the need to deal with the consequences of multiple and competing funding sources.

As discussed in chapter 5, this one-dimensional framework changed dramatically in the 1960s and 1970s with the proliferation of new and more intrusive types of intergovernmental regulations, along with the rapid growth of tax "subsidies" for state and local governments. Some of the new regulatory devices continued to be attached to grants, which were handy vehicles for new forms of federal influence, but others were independent of federal aid. They all differed from traditional administrative requirements, however, in their techniques and intensity of influence (see table 10-1), and they differed from the more traditional forms of economic and social regulation in their uniquely intergovernmental focus. The new devices regulated state and local governments directly or enlisted them as agents to regulate the private sector.

Table 10-1. *Typology of Intergovernmental Regulatory Programs*

Program type	Description	Major policy areas
Direct orders	Mandates state or local actions under the threat of criminal or civil penalties	Public employment, environmental protection
Crosscutting requirements	Applies to all or many federal assistance programs to ensure broad coverage	Nondiscrimination, environmental protection, public employment, grants management
Crossover sanctions	Threatens to terminate aid provided under one or more specified programs unless the requirements of another program are satisfied	Highway safety and beautification, environmental protection, health planning, handicapped education
Partial pre-emptions	Establishes federal standards, but delegates administration to states if they adopt standards equivalent to national minimum requirements	Environmental protection, natural resources, occupational safety and health, meat and poultry inspection

Source: U.S. Advisory Commission on Intergovernmental Relations, *Regulatory Federalism: Policy, Process, Impact, and Reform*, A-95 (Government Printing Office, 1984), p. 8.

The politics of these new regulatory instruments often differed as well. Many originated in congressional committees outside the traditional funding sources for state and local governments, or they were the products of new, symbolically driven forms of intergovernmental politics.[2] Collectively, the new regulatory federalism implied a very different model of intergovernmental interaction, and it added considerable complexity to intergovernmental relations.

These differences were not fully recognized until the early 1980s, although questions had begun to arise in the late 1970s. The first to note the intrusiveness of federal regulations were state and local government officials; even liberal Democratic mayors found themselves publicly denouncing the pernicious effects of the federal government's "mandate millstone."[3] Anecdotes about seemingly absurd cases of federal regulatory excess were frequently exposed by the news media.

Although both regulatory burdens and regulatory reform became matters of heightened public interest and presidential activity starting with the Nixon administration, such reform efforts focused on the economic impact of regulation, particularly on private businesses and individuals. Before the 1980s few people recognized that state and local governments were often the explicit targets of federal regulations or that they were key participants in their implementation. Furthermore, few saw the implications of this situation for both federalism and regulatory reform. This appeared to change with the election of Ronald Reagan, who made regulatory reform a central plank of his economic and New Federalism programs.

This chapter explores three dimensions of Reagan's regulatory policy. The first is the administration's explicit program for intergovernmental deregulation. It developed two strategies for this purpose, administrative and legislative. Substantive changes in pending regulations were studied and in some cases implemented administratively through the Presidential Task Force on Regulatory Relief. In addition, some administration-proposed changes in intergovernmental legislation had regulatory implications, particularly those covering the 1981 block grants.

Second, it is important to recognize the intergovernmental implications of the administration's broader deregulatory program. Although the administration had established a centralized regulatory review process in the Office of Management and Budget, sensitivity to the unique character of intergovernmental regulation appeared to be missing within OMB. The consequences of this omission far outweigh those of the president's modest agenda for intergovernmental regulatory reform.

The third point to consider is the nature of regulatory expansion under Reagan. Such expansion had two sources: Congress and the administration. During the president's first term, his administration attempted to persuade Congress to roll back regulatory statutes. Yet it succeeded only in preventing the enactment of major new additions to the existing pool of regulatory statutes during this period. That stalemate began to break down after 1985, when the 99th Congress adopted important and costly new requirements affecting state and local governments, mainly in the field of environmental protection.

More telling was the administration's own willingness to support expansions of federal regulatory authority over state and local governments when such authority was consistent with its broader economic and ideological aims. Federal regulatory expansion was advocated or endorsed by the administration in areas such as trucking, state workfare, national product liability insurance, coastal zone management, local taxicab and affirmative action policies, and the nationwide minimum drinking age.

Thus, in regulation as elsewhere, the Reagan administration left a complex but often disappointing legacy when measured against its original objectives. Although the administration recognized the intergovernmental impact of federal regulation early on, its long-term commitment to this goal proved surprisingly superficial, and its deregulatory accomplishments did not extend beyond its first two years in office. Furthermore, an intergovernmental perspective was never incorporated into the principal regulatory review process established in the Executive Office of the President. On the contrary, the Reagan administration, like its predecessors, found it difficult to resist the temptation to establish new intergovernmental regulations when such requirements provided a convenient method of achieving the president's social and economic goals.

Substantive Deregulation and the New Federalism

When Reagan took office in 1981, deregulation was a major concern. In order to defuse what OMB director David Stockman identified as a "ticking regulatory time bomb,"[4] the administration launched a series of far-reaching regulatory initiatives: it immediately froze hundreds of pending rules and regulations; created a presidential task force to review these regulations and recommend cost-cutting modifications; formed a strict regulatory review and clearance process within OMB, on a par with the agency's existing budget and legislative clearance functions; and systematically placed staunch, antiregulation conservatives in key positions within federal regulatory agencies.

These initiatives were designed to curb the growth in federal regulatory activities that occurred in the 1960s and 1970s. Most available indicators of regulatory activity—especially the number of federal regulatory agencies, federal spending on regulatory activities, and pages of rules published in the Federal Register—showed rapid increases in the 1970s (see table 10-2). Although less precise, estimates of the economic costs imposed on business and society by these regulations also showed rapid growth. As a result, federal regulatory expansion had become a national concern by the time Reagan was elected. Although new federal requirements continued to be added during their presidencies, Richard Nixon, Gerald Ford, and Jimmy Carter all tried to improve the analysis of regulatory costs imposed on society and to coordinate the regulatory initiatives of federal agencies.

Table 10-2. *Growth in Federal Regulation, 1970–78*

Expenditures in millions of current dollars

Year	Number of major regulatory agencies	Federal expenditures on economic regulations	Federal expenditures on "social" regulations	Pages in federal register
1970	20	166	1,449	20,036
1971	23	196	1,882	25,447
1972	23	246	2,247	28,924
1973	26	298	2,773	35,592
1974	27	304	3,860	45,422
1975	28	427	4,251	60,221
1976	28	489	5,028	57,072
1977	28	544	6,383	65,603
1978	28	608	7,576	77,497
Addendum				
Percent increase, 1970–78	25	266	425	267

Source: "Regulatory Policy: The First Three Waves of Rules," document prepared for the Regulatory Policy Seminar, Federal Executive Seminar Center, Kings Point, N.Y., March 1986.

This expansion of federal regulatory activity was accompanied by the development and expansion of regulations aimed specifically at state and local governments (see chapter 5). The U.S. Advisory Commission on Intergovernmental Relations (ACIR) identified new and more intrusive types of federal regulation that were designed to regulate state and local governments directly or enlist them as federal agents to regulate private individuals or businesses. Significantly, these new types supplemented the more traditional federal grant requirements, which also became more numerous, more detailed, and more specific during this period.[5]

According to David Beam, the number of significant intergovernmental regulations increased from ten to thirty-six in the 1970s.[6] The cumulative costs of just six of these regulations in seven jurisdictions accounted for almost 20 percent of all federal aid received by these communities.[7] Thus it is not surprising that more than two-thirds of the nation's mayors in 1981 considered it "urgent" or important for the federal government to reduce regulatory burdens in at least seven program areas, from environmental protection to access for the handicapped. A majority of mayors agreed that in "most or all cases" standards mandated by the federal government were "unrealistic" or overly specific.[8]

By the early 1980s careful observers of intergovernmental regulation had concluded that "during the 1960s and 1970s, state and local governments for the first time were brought under extensive federal regulatory controls," and that "these . . . have altered the terms of a long-standing intergovernmental partnership."[9] As one scholar pointed out,

The federal government . . . has vastly extended its control over the states and cities through a large—but largely unnoticed—system of public sector regulation. Federal regulations have grown to define not only who should benefit from government programs but how states and cities must run those programs: what accounting standards they must follow, what environmental effects they must measure, who can be hired under the programs, and how much they must be paid.[10]

Early Intergovernmental Responses

The Reagan administration tried to tackle this problem in its earliest deregulation initiatives. Thus deregulation was one of four items given top priority in Reagan's original New Federalism program.[11] Murray Weidenbaum, chairman of the president's Council of Economic Advisers, wrote in 1981,

Our policy of regulatory reform is designed to strengthen the federal system. The elimination of ineffective regulations and insistence on sound justification for all regulatory actions will substantially reduce burdens on state and local budgets. . . . Regulatory reform will also . . . increase the discretion—and the responsibility—of states and local governments.[12]

The administration adopted two broad strategies to provide substantive relief from specific regulatory burdens: unilateral administrative actions by the executive branch and legislative proposals for changes in regulatory statutes. Both strategies had important implications for intergovernmental relations.

Administrative Responses

The president took the first administrative action in this direction on his second day in office, when he established the Presidential Task Force on

Regulatory Relief. To give the group visibility and influence within the executive branch, Reagan appointed Vice President George Bush as chairman and called upon high-ranking officials from the White House and the cabinet to serve as members. The group was asked to study the possible impact on the economy of federal rules that were still in the proposal stage, to review existing rules identified as particularly burdensome, and to propose changes in regulatory statutes where appropriate. More generally, the task force was to "provid[e] leadership" in regulatory matters and to serve as a "court of appeals" in agency disputes with OMB in the newly created regulatory review process.[13]

The group's first act was to obtain a presidential order freezing pending federal regulations for at least sixty days and blocking the issuance of new regulations for a similar time period. The order was designed to prevent the implementation of the so-called midnight regulations promulgated by the Carter administration on the eve of Reagan's inauguration. This gave the new administration time to subject the regulations to cost-benefit analysis. Although many of the affected rules were not intergovernmental, as a result of this process the administration withdrew the proposed federal rules for expanding bilingual education, prohibiting discrimination in the dress code of local schools, and requiring that states and public utilities provide certain fixed services in the performance of residential energy audits.[14]

Then in March 1981 the Bush task force invited state and local governments and the private sector to identify problems created by existing federal regulations. The major governmental associations surveyed their members and presented the task force with nearly 500 recommendations for changes in federal rules and regulations.[15] The task force subsequently selected 111 rules for intensive review and modification, of which one-quarter were intergovernmental in character. Significant actions providing regulatory relief to state and local governments included revisions in the so-called Davis-Bacon regulations, which were designed to give local governments more flexibility in the calculation of "prevailing wages" paid in federally supported construction projects; changes in the regulations governing public transportation of the handicapped to give local authorities greater freedom to provide less costly means of access; and reductions in the reporting and accounting requirements in the national school lunch program. The task force estimated that these and the remaining twenty-four regulatory actions it undertook would reduce the regulatory compliance burden on state and local governments by 11.8

million work hours a year. These actions were also said to save approximately $2.0 billion dollars a year in recurring costs and $4 billion to $6 billion in one-time capital costs.[16]

Other administrative actions with substantial intergovernmental implications occurred in the "partial preemption" programs, which are now common in the areas of environmental regulation, public health, and occupational safety. Under such programs the federal government legally preempts the right to regulate an area that has traditionally been a state responsibility and to establish minimum federal standards therein. States, however, may remain active by assuming the responsibility for enforcing federal standards and by supplementing them, if they wish, with stricter state requirements. Typically, some states choose to participate as intergovernmental agents of the federal government, whereas others prefer to let the federal government administer the program directly with its own administrative apparatus.

During Reagan's first term, the federal government's formal delegation of regulatory authority to states increased rapidly in several partial preemption programs, and federal oversight of state performance was relaxed. For example, the Reagan administration was responsible for 78 percent of the federal approvals for the first phase of state hazardous waste programs and for more than half of the state surface mining programs receiving final or conditional approval by the federal government.[17] This led some analysts to conclude that state and local governments were "the big winners" under deregulation.[18] State and local governments quietly captured some of the most important and enduring victories of the president's regulatory relief campaign, argued the author of one major study.[19] In the Clean Air Act, for example, the administration implemented new policies that gave states more power to make minor changes in their state implementation plans without detailed federal oversight and review.

Despite the bold claims about winning big, many of these program delegations appeared to be a normal part of program life cycles and had little to do with the administration in office. Similar bursts of delegation had occurred under other administrations at similar stages in program operations as states acquired the experience and resources needed to handle regulatory programs themselves. Indeed, Michael Fix acknowledged that the approvals in the Resource Conservation and Recovery Act "represented a continuation of policies set in motion under the Carter administration."[20] Moreover, in areas like surface mining and occupational safety and health, cutbacks in personnel and inspections in federally operated programs were so severe under Reagan that the delegation of greater authority to state-run programs may have produced more regulatory activity in some states.[21]

Legislative Responses

Although administrative deregulation was favored because it could be implemented quickly and unilaterally, the Reagan administration discovered early on that there were limits to what it could accomplish through administrative means. The Clean Air Act was a case in point. This statute is hundreds of pages long and, like many other intergovernmental regulatory statutes, is highly detailed in many key areas. If the law leaves little discretion to the implementing agency, there is little latitude for administrative rule changes. As a result, the Reagan administration originally planned to supplement its strategy of administrative deregulation with proposals for altering the legislative basis of regulatory programs. With the exception of its 1981 block grants, however, the administration proved unable to develop specific legislative proposals, or it encountered stiff resistance from Congress and affected interest groups.

These failures were highlighted by the administration's ill-fated attempts to rewrite the nation's environmental statutes. This was initially a high priority of the new administration, and the prospects for success seemed bolstered by strong support from the business and labor communities and by the fact that the Clean Air Act was to expire in 1982. Despite considerable efforts, the administration was unable to develop a specific legislative proposal for congressional consideration. Instead it submitted to Congress a list of eleven general principles to be considered in revising clean air laws. The administration's credibility with respect to environmental issues was further undermined by scandals at the Environmental Protection Agency (EPA) and by highly publicized gaffes by the secretary of the Interior, James Watt. Since Congress itself was deeply divided on the question of relaxing environmental regulations, the administration's disorganization merely ensured that the legislative stalemate on the issue would continue throughout Reagan's term in office.[22]

In regulation, as in many other areas, the major exception to this pattern of legislative failure was a product of the 1981 Reconciliation Act and the creation of nine new block grants. Although these grants did not affect the newer forms of intergovernmental regulation, they gave the administration an opportunity to condense and simplify the traditional grant requirements attached to the seventy-seven programs consolidated into the block grants—and the administration took full advantage of it. In education, for example, the merger of thirty-three separate programs into a single block grant allowed the administration to replace 667 pages of regulations governing the old programs with a single, twenty-page set of requirements affecting the new block grant.[23] Reductions in other block grants were equally dramatic. The regulations covering the implementation of the new health care block grants filled just six pages in each case and did little more than restate the limited conditions placed on the use of these funds in the statutes themselves.

OMB estimated that the 1981 block grants reduced the paperwork imposed on state and local governments by 5.9 million work hours, or 91 percent.[24] The administration estimated that the seven block grants under the jurisdiction of the Department of Health and Human Services alone saved the states $52 million in paperwork costs.

Deregulation through Procedural Reforms

The Reagan administration also introduced reforms designed to alter the content of federal regulations by changing the processes that produce them. The new procedures and institutions established in the Executive Office of the President to oversee the rule-making process quickly became the focus of Reagan's deregulation effort.

The most important procedural reform, Executive Order 12291, was instituted in February 1981. This order required that, where laws permit, agencies must identify and adopt the most cost-effective methods of regulation when considering new regulatory actions; they must select alternatives in which the social benefits outweigh the social costs; and they must submit proposed regulations to OMB for review and comment before they are issued or published in the Federal Register. This last development constituted a major expansion of presidential authority over executive branch decisionmaking, on a par with OMB's budget review and legislative clearance functions. OMB created a new unit with a sizable staff of economists and lawyers—the Office of Information and Regulatory Affairs (OIRA)—to accommodate its new oversight responsibilities. To ensure that OMB's regulatory analysts could influence the design of new regulations at a sufficiently early stage, the administration supplemented the review process by Executive Order 12492, which required agencies to publish a calendar of the rules that they expected to propose during the coming year and to act only on the regulations so identified.

The new OMB review process quickly became a highly controversial part of Reagan's deregulation effort. OMB statistics show that 13 percent of all regulations submitted to OMB for review in 1981 were revised and that by 1986 this proportion had risen to almost 32 percent.[25] According to OMB, many of the changes—approximately one-third—were needed to correct minor grammatical problems or to clarify sentences here and there. Others—such as those affecting cotton dust standards of the Occupational Safety and Health Administration (OSHA)—were substantive. In addition, OMB delayed some rules for long periods of time, and never even completed its review of others.[26] Partly as a result, the number of proposed rules declined by 2,000 from 1980 to 1986, and the number of final rules issued declined by 3,000 over the same period. This means that the number of pages published in the Federal Register each year during this time span fell by 46 percent—or over 39,000 pages.[27]

The number of rules issued and pages published in the Federal Register are at best imprecise indicators of changes in regulatory policymaking. Conceivably, fewer but broader rules could have greater scope and impact. Nonetheless, most observers believe that the OMB review function altered the regulatory process in fundamental ways. Indeed, some charged that OMB reviews provided a secret channel through which industry could exert influence on federal regulation.[28] Agency officials also began to anticipate OMB's reactions when developing new regulatory proposals, and therefore they tried to soften proposed rules before submitting them to OIRA. As one official of the Environmental Protection Agency admitted, "Staff people start to say 'we shouldn't do this rule because we'll never get it through OMB.' It happens on a regular basis."[29] As a result, many scholars and members of Congress believed that the new procedures were responsible for a large and possibly unprecedented expansion of presidential authority over the regulatory process.

Although deregulation was a central element of the administration's New Federalism, and OMB played an important role in regulatory relief, intergovernmental issues were largely overlooked in the OMB process. One comprehensive study of the Reagan administration's regulatory relief effort concluded that OMB review was of marginal benefit to state and local governments.[30] Some cynics have suggested that the OMB process was designed primarily to protect the administration's constituencies in the business community and that issues of federalism were at best incidental and often in conflict with such concerns. As one intergovernmental lobbyist observed, "When our problems are business's problems, then we get action. By the same token, when we are business's problem, we feel the heat."[31]

Deregulation and Intergovernmental Management

Structural and procedural changes within OMB have drawn attention away from the intergovernmental dimensions of much federal regulation. The Reagan administration reorganized or abolished organizational units and institutional processes within OMB that once dealt with intergovernmental coordination and management, so the agency now has little institutional capacity for handling issues in these areas. The Nixon administration had established virtually all of these structures and procedures to improve intergovernmental management. By eliminating and downgrading them, Reagan signaled a thoroughly different orientation toward federalism and intergovernmental relations.

The Reagan administration wasted little time in getting the reorientation under way. The system of standardized Federal Regional Councils established in 1969 to coordinate and simplify the diverse regional operations of different federal departments and agencies was first pared down and then abolished in 1983. The Intergovernmental Affairs division in OMB was also abolished in 1983, after its personnel and functions had been allowed to dwindle for two years. The division's remaining responsibilities—streamlining administrative operations in the field, overseeing auditing and financial management practices in federal grants, and monitoring implementation of the formal intergovernmental consultation process—were divided among three disparate units remaining within OMB. According to one analysis, "The traditional activities of OMB in intergovernmental management have been overshadowed, if not superseded, by . . . a new and very different intergovernmental agenda. Vestiges of the old OMB intergovernmental management functions and structure are still in place, but it is not clear that they are significant any more."[32]

The relationship between deregulation and OMB's changing intergovernmental role can be seen in the transformation of the "A-95" process of intergovernmental consultation. This process was established in 1969 to implement provisions of the Demonstration Cities Act of 1966 and the

Intergovernmental Cooperation Act of 1968. The latter law was passed in response to state and local complaints about the proliferation of Great Society grant-in-aid programs. States and localities maintained that the federal government was establishing new programs in their jurisdictions unbeknownst to elected officials, and in many cases was giving these programs to different local agencies or nonprofit organizations for competing or overlapping purposes. To remedy this situation and improve coordination, the budget office issued OMB Management Circular A-95, which required that state, regional, and local governments be notified and allowed to comment on applications for federal aid within their jurisdictions, and that governors be allowed to review state plans required under federal programs. A system of regional and statewide "clearinghouses" was established throughout the country, and federal agencies were instructed to comply with the notification and review procedures.

After a time serious questions arose concerning the usefulness of the consultation process, and some state and local governments proposed that it be modified. Yet almost all intergovernmental observers were surprised when the Reagan administration proposed to abolish the process as part of its regulatory relief program. The administration claimed that the consultation process, created to assist state and local governments, now constituted a major regulatory burden imposed by the federal government. It was replaced with a vague new process that left virtually all procedural and implementation issues up to the discretion of the individual states. Few outside the administration judged the new process to be an improvement over the past one.[33]

Interestingly, administration officials praised the A-95 revision as "the most sweeping change made in federal government philosophy and procedures in regulating the intergovernmental system."[34] Yet this process, touted as the best of Reagan's New Federalism, eliminated the very organizational structures and personnel in the Executive Office of the President that could contribute an intergovernmental perspective to federal policymaking. Moreover, as a purely administrative change, it left untouched existing statutes that required regional coordination in federal programs. The result was confusion about the differences between the new administrative procedures and established law. Indeed, the A-95 changes epitomized the Reagan administration's disdain for the administrative methods of intergovernmental reform favored by the Nixon administration.

Regulatory Expansion

Despite presidential rhetoric championing regulatory relief as a pillar of the New Federalism, intergovernmental concerns had a lower priority in the new regulatory review process than the administration had intimated. In fact, during Reagan's eight years in office, regulatory expansions took place in several areas. In this period twenty-seven major new federal mandates were enacted—a number that surpassed the previous record-setting pace of the 1970s. As figure 10-1 shows, the Reagan and early Bush years failed to alter the trend of accelerating use of federal mandates that began in the 1960s. The principal departure from the past was a negative one for states and localities. The mandates enacted in the 1980s tended to be the most coercive varieties: direct orders and crossover sanctions.

In some areas—especially environmental regulation—Congress initiated the expansion. After several years of stalemate between the White House and Capitol Hill, the Clean Water and Safe Drinking Water acts were reauthorized by the 99th Congress. These renewals imposed substantial new regulatory burdens on state and local governments. For example, municipalities were now required to monitor "nonpoint" pollution from thousands of storm sewers and to implement costly testing for seventy-seven additional chemicals in municipal water supplies.[35] Similarly, local school districts were required to identify asbestos hazards and then to remove them from local schools at an eventual cost of more than $2 billion.[36]

Apart from indicating the bipartisan revival of support for new environmental regulations in Congress, these congressional initiatives said little new about the politics of regulatory expansion. They simply showed that scientific advances made it possible to identify new environmental hazards and that Congress was willing to translate political concerns about such hazards into legislation that imposes high costs on third parties that are required to deal with them. In contrast, the cases in which Reagan supported the expansion or retention of federal regulatory authority over state and local governments had some interesting implications. His administration consistently avoided devolution whenever this policy conflicted with competing administration goals of reducing regulatory burdens on the private sector or advancing its conservative social policy agenda.

The designers of the administration's deregulation program foresaw that this policy might conflict with the devolutionary goals of New Federalism. Murray Weidenbaum pointed out in 1981, "Shifting regulatory re-

Figure 10-1. *The Growth of Regulatory Federalism:*
New Programs and Major Amendments per Decade, 1931–90

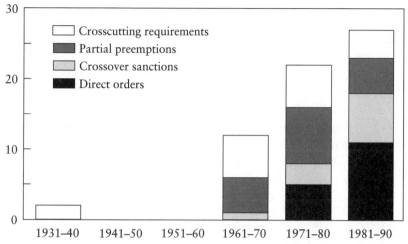

Source: U.S. Advisory Commission on Intergovernmental Relations, *Federal Regulation of State and Local Governments: The Mixed Record of the 1980s*, A-121 (Government Printing Office, 1993), fig. 3-1.

sponsibility to states and localities is rarely welcomed by business, because of their concern over the diversity of regulatory requirements, restraints, and prohibitions that can result."[37] As Weidenbaum suggests, when it comes to regulation, business generally prefers not only fewer requirements to more, but uniformity to diversity. Yet in recent years the states—like the federal government—have become increasingly active regulators in more and more policy areas, from consumer and environmental protection to occupational and product safety. Often such activity is built upon federal regulatory foundations, as in the case of environmental programs in which the states are required or strongly encouraged to enforce federal minimum regulatory standards but are permitted to supplement or exceed them. In other cases, states have chosen to develop their own regulatory activities. In either case, private industry has repeatedly asked the federal government to restrict state regulatory activities beyond the minimum national standards or to preempt state regulatory authority in a given field entirely. According to one business spokesperson, the "national interest cannot be subjected to the parochial interest of localities."[38]

Such concerns about regulatory expansion were not ignored by the

Reagan administration, which sided again and again with business interests. In a recent study of proposed federal preemptions, the administration was found to have supported moves to take regulatory powers from the states in nine out of the twelve cases studied.[39] A similar finding was reported in an analysis of Reagan administration briefs to the Supreme Court:

> The Administration . . . doesn't hesitate to give states' rights a back
> seat. . . . In each instance [examined], the issue, broadly framed, concerned states' rights, and . . . the Administration argued that Federal
> regulation should prevail. . . . Cynics might suggest that . . . the
> Administration's preference for big business is so strong that it will
> override conflicting concerns for federalism.[40]

Several cases involving transportation, energy, and product liability regulation illustrate this point.

Product Liability

In the case of national product liability legislation, "result oriented reformers [in the Reagan administration] won out over those who would have adhered to . . . the [federalist] principles of the framers."[41] Historically, state laws have governed manufacturers' liability for injuries resulting from defective products. By the 1980s, however, business interests voiced growing concerns about the difficulties resulting from differing and often increasingly stringent state laws in this area. Many called for preemptive federal legislation to correct these problems.

Backed by the Product Liability Alliance—a coalition of more than 200 trade and business organizations—legislation to this effect was introduced in Congress in 1982 by Senator Robert Kasten (Republican of Wisconsin). The Kasten bill would have superseded state product liability laws but, in order to avoid overloading already crowded federal court dockets, retained state court jurisdiction to try liability cases and interpret federal law. Thus, in the words of one analyst, the bill represented "a new approach to centralization that borders on state conscription."[42]

Confronted with a difficult choice between the concerns of manufacturing interests and its own federalism proclivities, the Reagan administration "agonized" for several months over whether to support national product liability legislation. The strongest support for national legislation came from Commerce Secretary Malcolm Baldrige and from regulatory reform advocates in the administration. As one supporter of preemption in the administration wrote, conflicting state liability laws have created "significant burdens on interstate commerce" and "tremendous uncertainty for manufacturers."[43] However, others in the administration, including Attorney General William French Smith and Labor Secretary Raymond Donovan, argued that such a position was not consistent with the president's recently announced federalism initiative. Moreover, opponents pointed to practical difficulties in the Kasten approach. For example, denying federal courts jurisdiction to resolve likely differences in statutory interpretations by fifty state judicial systems was hardly the way to guarantee uniformity in the domain of product liability. Nevertheless, when the issue was put to the president for resolution, "Reagan overrode the objections . . . that any endorsement of federal legislation would run counter to the administration's 'federalism' drive" and agreed to support the Kasten bill preempting state authority.[44]

Federal Trucking and Drinking Age Standards

Two new and highly visible federal regulations affecting transportation were also enacted with the support and encouragement of the Reagan administration. Like several other pioneering intergovernmental regulations enacted in the 1960s and 1970s, both requirements threatened states with the reduction of federal aid if they did not comply. Specifically, federal highway aid would be reduced if states did not adopt uniform federal standards on truck size and a minimum drinking age.

The trucking industry had long hoped to preempt state restrictions on truck length, width, and weight and by this means to expand the use of highly efficient double trailer trucks. Although these trucks were permitted in most areas of the country by 1982, they were still prohibited by fourteen states and the District of Columbia because of concerns about their safety and their destructive effects on highways.[45] Against this backdrop of concerns about crumbling infrastructure and deteriorating highways, the Reagan administration launched an initiative in May 1982 to alter this situation. To help fund additional highway renovation, Secretary of Transportation Drew Lewis proposed increasing the federal gasoline tax and raising truckers' fees, but he combined these new levies with provisions for establishing higher, uniform truck size and weight requirements to appease truckers who were unhappy about the new rates.[46] Under this proposal, states that refused to comply with the new standards would lose federal highway funds. For a time the president backed away from the Lewis initiative because many states and the trucking industry were opposed to it, and he himself felt uneasy about its sizable tax increases. When the president again endorsed the need for new transportation revenues following the November 1982 elections, however, a lame-duck session of Congress complied. Legislation along the lines of Lewis's proposal was enacted in the waning days of the 97th Congress.[47]

Having helped write uniform truck standards into law, the administration pushed preemption to its limits in subsequent regulations. The administration decided to permit the large new trucks, not only on interstate highways, but on an additional 140,000 miles of primary and access highways—38,000 miles more than state highway departments had deemed suitable for large trucks. This action infuriated officials in many states, including some of those that had long permitted double trailer trucks on their major highways. In response to state criticism, the Federal Highway Administration eventually removed 17,000 miles of roads from its initial designation, but it added another 19,000 miles of highways to its list and moved to quash outstanding lawsuits against its actions.[48]

Less than two years later President Reagan reversed an earlier position and endorsed a second major highway-related regulatory expansion. On July 17, 1984, in the face of rapidly growing public pressure, he signed legislation designed to compel all states to adopt a minimum drinking age of twenty-one or face reductions of 10 percent in federal highway aid by 1987. Initially, the president had been reluctant to support such a heavy-handed approach, preferring instead to continue an existing program of incentives for state actions against drunk driving. Indeed, stronger federal action on this issue appeared to be unnecessary, since twenty states had raised their drinking age since 1980 and only eight still permitted alcohol consumption at age eighteen.[49] Moreover, legislation in this area seemed firmly fixed within the sphere of state responsibilities, both by tradition and the wording of the Twenty-First Amendment.

If raising the drinking age proved to be a popular cause in most state legislatures, it became almost irresistible in Congress. In the wake of emotional publicity and effective lobbying by families victimized by drunk drivers, strong support emerged in Congress for an immediate, uniform approach to the problem. Faced with the possibility that Congress might enact preemptive legislation despite his own misgivings about it, and urged to change his mind by Transportation Secretary Elizabeth Dole, the president reversed his position on June 13, 1984, and came out strongly for federal sanctions to enforce a national drinking age.[50] With this policy reversal, the legislation sailed through Congress and was signed by the president a month later. "The problem is bigger than the individual states," he proclaimed at the signing ceremony. "With the problem so clear-cut and the proven solution at hand, we have no misgiving about this judicious use of Federal power."[51]

Regulating Social Policy

Social policy has always offered fertile ground for intergovernmental conflict, and the Reagan administration did not escape this problem. Most areas of social policy have come under state and local jurisdiction, so it has been possible to adapt policy to the diverse cultural and social traditions of different regions. Yet issues that arise in this area tend to revolve around fundamental principles and values. As a result, not only is compromise difficult to achieve, but policy advocates—conservatives and liberals alike—are tempted to seek a single national solution.

Conflict between the Reagan administration's social policy and federalism objectives created implicit and explicit tensions. Implicit conflicts were most evident in education policy, where the president argued strongly that the federal role in education had grown dangerously large and intrusive. Reagan, however, found it hard to resist using his office as a "bully pulpit" for advocating his own vision of educational reform. By appointing a highly visible educational reform commission and lobbying for tuition tax credit legislation, he legitimized the concept of national leadership in educational improvement.

Conflicts between the administration's social policies and its devolutionary objectives also have been explicit. For example, the administration wanted to mandate state-implemented workfare programs for welfare recipients and to regulate medical care for handicapped infants. Most dramatic, however, were its efforts to overturn local governments' affirmative action programs.

In an attempt to force changes in affirmative action hiring plans instituted by local governments, the Reagan administration even took state and local governments to court. Such a litigatory approach was not entirely without precedent; the administration had already used it when trying to enforce handicapped infants' rights. In addition, the Federal Trade Commission had campaigned to eliminate local government restrictions on the taxicab industry. Indeed, many of the affirmative action plans in question were originally imposed on municipalities by lawsuits undertaken by earlier administrations. Yet by the mid-1980s these policies were accepted by most of the cities involved and by their employees, who resented yet another wave of federal intervention.

This controversy stemmed from the U.S. Supreme Court's ruling in *Fire-Fighters Local Union 1784* v. *Stotts*. In this 1984 decision, the Court ruled that contractually established seniority rights assumed precedence, in making layoffs, over the rights of black employees hired later through a court-ordered affirmative action plan. Since then lower courts have interpreted the *Stotts* ruling narrowly, in part because it was a statutory interpretation of the Civil Rights Act of 1964 and not a constitutional interpretation.

Rather than wait for further clarification and stronger constitutional footing before challenging locally supported plans, the Reagan Justice Department took *Stotts* to be a mandate against "quotas and reverse discrimination."[52] It sought reversal of consent decrees in fifty-six localities and, meeting strong resistance from many of these, it took Indianapolis to court. To the Republican mayor of that city, and many less involved observers, such actions appeared inconsistent with the president's New Federalism. In the words of columnist Neal Peirce: "By initiating expensive legal action, Justice also makes something of a joke of the 'New Federalism' ideal of returning power to the grassroots."[53]

Conclusion

The Reagan administration came into office proclaiming that deregulation was a critical component in its comprehensive federalism reform strategy. Despite the bold beginnings, this promise was not realized where state and local governments were concerned. The administration's explicit program of intergovernmental deregulation—implemented administratively through the Presidential Task Force on Regulatory Relief and legislatively through the 1981 block grant regulations—was forcefully pursued only in the first two years of Reagan's initial term. Within its ongoing regulatory relief apparatus and procedures, the Reagan administration's commitment to addressing intergovernmental regulatory issues was often lukewarm and haphazard. It succeeded in tempering Congress's appetite for new regulations only temporarily, and the politics of budgetary stringency appeared to promote greater congressional interest in regulation as a relatively low-cost method for financing new program initiatives.

Most important, given its federalism and regulatory reform rhetoric, the Reagan administration was a surprisingly important source of new intergovernmental regulatory initiatives. This underscores the degree to which Reagan's views on federalism served to advance other, more deeply held values. In each case of regulatory expansion examined in this chapter, the administration was confronted with difficult policy decisions. Forced to choose between policies supportive of its federalist objectives (devolution, enhanced autonomy for states, and balanced intergovernmental relationships) and those supportive of other presidential priorities (such as easing regulatory burdens on the private sector and pursuing conservative social policy objectives), the administration decided to pursue a course that was openly or implicitly contrary to its stated intergovernmental goals.

To be sure, some of these decisions were reached reluctantly. Some may have been the product of bureaucratic momentum and political compromise more than calculated strategy. Also, certain cases did go the other way: in 1983 the Department of Transportation declined to preempt local airport noise restrictions despite calls for uniformity from the airline industry; although it ultimately relented, the administration long resisted legislative efforts to preempt state pesticide regulations; and in 1986 the president supported western demands that the federal fifty-five-miles-per-hour speed limit on rural highways be raised. Nonetheless, in the truly difficult decisions, the overall thrust of the administration's regulatory policy seemed to bear little resemblance to the president's rhetoric on intergovernmental reform.

In part this pattern of regulation is the natural expression of power and position. As former Nixon economic aide Herbert Stein has written: "Even conservative governments when in office do not want to limit their own powers."[54] Yet it also has deeper implications for our understanding of Reagan's view of federalism. For Reagan, strengthening federalism was an instrument rather than a policy objective in itself. In this respect he resembled his more liberal predecessors by his willingness to sacrifice his federalism goals whenever they conflicted with other, more deeply held policy objectives.

CHAPTER 11

Reform Interregnum:
The Bush and Early Clinton Years

B Y THE TIME President Ronald Reagan left office in 1989, little vitality was left in the intergovernmental reform agenda he had launched during his first term. Over the years Congress had added new earmarks and constraints to the block grants Reagan had established in 1981. Moreover, block grants' share of federal aid funding had declined 21 percent from its peak during Reagan's first term, as both the number and financial dominance of categorical grants began rising once again.[1] On the regulatory front, Reagan's ambitious reform agenda had given way to new federal mandates and preemptions.[2] Even his most prominent second-term initiative—the executive order on federalism—had proved to be ineffective.[3]

This erosion in the federalism reform agenda continued under President George Bush. Bush's modest agenda focused on smoothing the rough edges off the Reagan years—particularly in education and environmental policy. In the regulatory realm, the Bush administration helped formulate and enact two of the most significant federal mandates since the 1970s: the Americans with Disabilities Act of 1990 and the Clean Air Act Amendments of 1990. On the fiscal side, net federal outlays—for mandatory and discretionary programs—rose more during the four years of the Bush administration than in eight under Reagan. During Bush's presidency, fiscal federalism was influenced far more by the rapid growth of medicaid spending and coverage, fallout from the 1991 recession, and the fiscal constraints of the Budget Enforcement Act of 1990 than by Bush's own initiatives. He did attempt to advance a modest grant reform proposal in his fiscal 1992 budget, but it did not succeed. The legacy of the Bush administration was Desert Storm, not federalism reform.

Federalism reform did not assume center stage at the beginning of

Clinton's first term either. In his administration, however, the option was more consciously considered and rejected. During the 1992 campaign, the president read and contemplated Alice Rivlin's compelling book *Reviving the American Dream*, which argued for a comprehensive sorting out of governmental functions between the federal government and the states.[4] Although the president recruited Rivlin to serve as deputy director (and later director) of the Office of Management and Budget (OMB), he rejected her recommendation that the national government's responsibilities in education, job training, law enforcement, and economic development be devolved to the states. On the contrary, an expanded federal role in all of these areas became a major feature of the president's domestic agenda. So, too, did a sweeping reform of the nation's health care system. Although it expanded the welfare state, a larger federal role in health care was consistent with Rivlin's prescription for an ailing federal system. Thus, as happened during Bush's term, competing features of the president's agenda far overshadowed his modest smorgasbord of reforms in the intergovernmental arena.

From 1988 to 1994, then, fundamental federalism reform was far from the center of policy deliberations in the nation's capital. Beneath the surface of policy debates in Washington, however, fissures widened in the foundations of American politics. Bush's laissez-faire economic policies, Clinton's legislative failures, and congressional scandals and excesses eroded Americans' confidence in their government. As the following chapter makes clear, this emerging crisis of governmental legitimacy sparked a purported "revolution" in American politics and a major new reform initiative.

Regulatory Trends: Renewed Momentum for Mandating

The accelerated adoption of new federal mandates, which began in Reagan's second term, continued under Presidents Bush and Clinton. Six prominent new mandates were enacted between 1990 and 1994, imposing significant administrative requirements and billions of dollars of new costs on state and local governments. In addition, federal agencies promulgated costly new rules to implement previously enacted regulatory statutes. Combined with the existing base of intergovernmental regulations adopted in the 1960s and 1970s, these actions lifted federal mandate reform to the top of state and local governments' priority list by 1994.

New Enactments

Significant intergovernmental regulations enacted during the Bush and Clinton administrations included not only the Clean Air Act Amendments and the Americans with Disabilities Act, but also the Civil Rights Restoration Act, the Family and Medical Leave Act, the National Voter Registration Act, and mandated expansions in coverage under the federal medicaid program. Of this group, the clean air and disabilities bills had the most far-reaching effects. Both were advanced with the active encouragement and support of President Bush. In contrast, the expansions in medicaid coverage and the civil rights legislation were primarily congressional initiatives, pushed at times over the opposition of the Bush administration. Finally, the family leave and "motor voter" acts were supported and signed by President Clinton in 1993. Each had been opposed and vetoed by President Bush.

Together, the new regulations placed a variety of administrative duties and fiscal burdens on state and local governments. A brief listing of the major provisions of the three most significant programs underscores their importance. The Clean Air Act Amendments of 1990 reauthorized and expanded the nation's principal air pollution control legislation and contained significant new requirements and timetables for dealing with urban smog, acid rain, hazardous and toxic air pollutants, and ozone-destroying chlorofluorocarbons. Although many provisions were directed at private and industrial sources of pollution, the Clean Air Act has long been one of the most prescriptive and intrusive intergovernmental regulatory statutes, and the 1990 amendments strengthened this dimension.[5] The legislation contained new mandates and requirements affecting state and local governments, including tough new "hammer" provisions requiring federal implementation plans if state air pollution plans proved inadequate; new controls on municipal waste incinerators and sewage treatment plants; acid rain control requirements for publicly owned utilities; new emissions and fuel standards affecting public transportation vehicles and fleets; and mandated state assistance programs for small, privately owned sources of air pollution. Intergovernmental sanctions for violating clean air requirements included prohibitions on new construction and drinking water supplies in noncomplying jurisdictions and the withholding of state highway and air pollution assistance grants.[6]

The Americans with Disabilities Act is widely considered to be one of the most important recent federal mandates affecting state and local governments.[7] According to its congressional sponsors, the act was intended to establish

> a clear and comprehensive national mandate for the elimination of discrimination against individuals with disabilities . . . to provide clear, strong, consistent, enforceable standards, . . . and to invoke the sweep of congressional authority . . . in order to end such discrimination.[8]

Although many of the act's provisions are directed at the private sector, other provisions affect the public sector by expanding handicapped individuals' access to public transportation and facilities. For example, all fixed-route public transportation systems must be made accessible to the handicapped, all new buses and transit facilities must be equipped with wheelchair lifts and other equipment to make them fully accessible, and paratransit services must be provided to those who are unable to take advantage of accessible public transportation. Politically, the Americans with Disabilities Act, like the Clean Air Act, enjoyed early and strong support from the Bush administration.

Legislated expansions of medical coverage in 1988, 1989, and 1990 added an estimated $2.56 billion to state medicaid bills by fiscal 1992.[9] President Bush did not assume the same leadership role on health care requirements that he did on the Clean Air Act Amendments; Democrats in Congress claimed that role. But in his budget proposals the president did call for certain medicaid expansions, and he and his predecessor signed legislation putting these medicaid mandates into effect.

In particular, the 1990 Budget Enforcement Act—which was designed primarily as a deficit reduction measure—mandated that states gradually phase in medicaid coverage to *all* poor children between the ages of six and eighteen. Previously, most states had set the eligibility cutoff for medicaid at income levels below the official poverty line. By 1995 the new requirement had added an estimated 700,000 children to the program, at a five-year cost of about $1 billion to both the federal government and the states.[10] An additional mandate in the budget act required that states cover the medicare expenses of elderly beneficiaries with incomes below the poverty line—at a cost of several hundred million dollar over five years. All told, the new requirements—together with rapid inflation of overall health care costs—helped to increase the proportion of state spending budgeted for medicaid from 9 percent in 1980 to 14 percent in 1990.[11]

Growing Regulatory Costs

Medicaid was not the only mandate to impose new costs on state and local governments. In addition to presenting states and localities with new administrative responsibilities, many of the mandates entailed significant financial burdens as well. Pursuant to its responsibilities under the State and Local Cost Estimates Act, the Congressional Budget Office (CBO) estimated the costs of the new laws before their enactment. According to CBO's best estimates at the time, the Americans with Disabilities Act would impose as much as $1 billion in additional costs on states and localities; the Clean Air Act Amendments would impose new costs of $250 to $300 million annually; and the cost of implementing the motor voter law would reach $100 million over five years.[12]

New laws were not the only source of additional mandated costs during this period, however. Federal agencies were also busy promulgating new rules to implement earlier regulatory statutes. Table 11-1 lists six rules issued between 1989 and 1992 that were estimated to have significant effects on intergovernmental costs. According to the agencies' own "regu-

Table 11-1. *Fiscal Impact of Six Federal Rules Issued between 1989 and 1992*
Billions of 1992 dollars

Title of rule	Total lifetime projected cost for state and local governments
Criteria for filtration and disinfection of surface water and national primary drinking water regulations for microbiological contaminants	3.3
National oil and hazardous substances pollution contingency plan (NCP) revisions	0.7
Medicare and medicaid: requirements for long-term care facilities	0.4
Transportation for individuals with disabilities	6.9
Maximum contaminant level goals and national primary drinking water regulations for lead and copper	2.3
Criteria for municipal solid waste landfills	4.2
Total	17.9

Source: Marcella Ridlen Ray and Timothy J. Conlan, "At What Price? The Costs of Federal Mandates in the 1980s," *State and Local Government Review*, vol. 28 (Winter 1996), p. 10.

latory impact analyses," these six rules were expected to impose lifetime costs of nearly $18 billion. Such costs were often higher than first anticipated during legislative consideration of the authorizing statutes. For example, CBO's state and local cost estimate for the Americans with Disabilities Act was admittedly vague, but overall costs were deemed to be less than $1 billion.[13] Yet when the Department of Transportation later attempted to estimate the costs of specific rules designed to comply with the act, it anticipated additional long-term costs of almost $7 billion for public transit alone.

Fiscal Federalism

To assess changes in American federalism, social scientists have traditionally focused on fiscal developments rather than regulatory developments. Like regulatory trends, fiscal indicators suggest modest recentralization in American federalism during the early 1990s under President Bush as well as President Clinton. By virtually every measure, federal aid to state and local governments increased in relative importance compared with what it had been at the end of the Reagan era (see table 11-2). Modest reform efforts by both presidents failed to alter this outcome. Although four new block grants were enacted, block grant spending declined relative to total federal aid, and the number of categorical grants increased by 20 percent.

Table 11-2. *Cost Comparison of Federal Aid, Fiscal Years 1990 and 1995*
Outlays in billions of dollars

Expenditure item	1990	1995	Percent increase
Grant outlays in current dollars	135	225	67
Medicaid	41	88	115
Nonmedicaid	94	137	46
Grant outlays in constant 1987 dollars	119	173	45
Medicaid	36	68	88
Nonmedicaid	83	105	26
Federal aid as a percent of total federal outlays	11	15	36
Federal aid as a percent of state and local expenditures	20	23	15

Source: *Budget of the United States Government, Analytical Perspectives, Fiscal Year 1998.*

Federal Aid Trends

When George Bush moved into the Oval Office in 1989, there was support for a more active federal role in domestic policymaking. After real and perceived retrenchment during the Reagan years, opinion polls showed the public favored more federal spending on a variety of social policy issues. By 1990, 75 percent of Americans believed the nation was spending "too little" on education and protecting the environment, 72 percent said the same about health care, and two-thirds agreed that too little was being spent on "assistance to poor" (though only 24 percent said the same about "welfare").[14] The year 1990 marked the contemporary apogee in public support for more federal spending in each of these areas.

Although this support was built on a shaky foundation of weak public confidence in Washington's ability to carry out its responsibilities effectively, politicians in Washington responded to the warmer climate of public opinion. President Bush signaled his intention to steer a more activist course in domestic policy in his inaugural address: "[Our] purpose today . . . is to make kinder the face of the nation and gentler the face of the world."[15] Although the president acknowledged that fiscal limitations would constrain the scope of forthcoming federal initiatives, he ended a litany of problems to be addressed on an activist note: "Our funds are low. . . . we have more will than wallet, but will is what we need."

Upon taking office in 1993, President Clinton envisioned a rebirth of federal activism that began where Bush left off. Although he had portrayed himself during the campaign as a "new Democrat" unlike his "tax and spend" Democratic predecessors, Clinton pursued an activist role for the federal government once he was elected. His ambitious domestic agenda included new initiatives to combat crime, invest in education, and "grow the economy." Above all, he staked the prestige of his office on a plan to complete the welfare state legacy of the New Deal and extend health insurance coverage to all Americans.

These presidential initiatives, and the greater scope their activism afforded to entrepreneurial activity in Congress, quickly registered on the federal government's balance sheet. By the early 1990s every important indicator of fiscal federalism reflected new growth in federal spending, a trend that began under Bush and continued through Clinton's first two years in office. Measured in current dollars, federal grant outlays increased more in four years under George Bush ($58 billion) than in eight years under Ronald Reagan ($42 billion), and they rose another $31 billion during Bill Clinton's first two years.[16]

Figure 11-1. *Federal Aid to State and Local Governments, 1980–95*

Billions of constant dollars

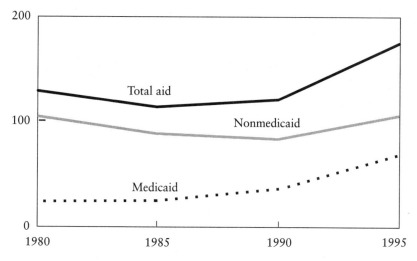

The changes in fiscal federalism under Bush and Clinton are most apparent in measures that hold constant the effects of inflation and other spending. As figure 11-1 shows, real spending on federal aid actually declined 6 percent during the 1980s. If the rapidly growing medicaid program is taken out of the picture, the real decline in federal aid was a much steeper 20 percent. In contrast, total aid spending increased 45 percent between 1990 and 1995; even excluding medicaid, inflation-adjusted grant outlays rose 26 percent during this period.

A similar portrait emerges if one looks at federal aid as a percentage of total federal outlays or state and local outlays. As a percentage of all federal spending, federal grant outlays declined by over one-third during the Reagan years, falling from 15 percent to 11 percent of federal expenditures (see figure 11-2). This lost ground was regained under Presidents Bush and Clinton, however. By 1995 the grant-in-aid share of the federal budget had returned to its 1980 level of 15 percent. Federal aid's share of total state and local expenditures made a similar but less complete recovery during the early 1990s. After falling by nearly one-third between 1980 and 1990, federal aid as a percentage of total state and local spending increased from 20 percent to 23 percent between 1990 and 1995.

An examination of trends in grant program structures rather than bud-

Figure 11-2. *Relative Indicators of Federal Aid to State and Local Governments, 1980–95*

Percent

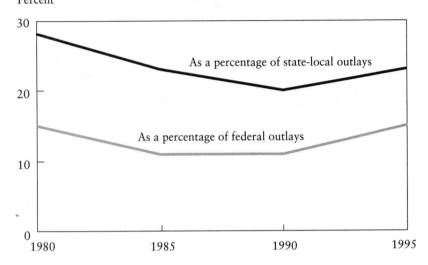

gets reveals weaker but similar trends toward modest recentralization in the grant system. After falling by one-fifth under Ronald Reagan, the numbers of categorical grants began rising again. The number of categorical grants increased from 478 in 1990 to more than 600 under Clinton, an increase of approximately 25 percent.[17] Although the vast majority of these new programs were small, "pygmy" grants received by only a fraction of state and local governments, this growth reestablished the trends of the 1960s and 1970s toward a more elaborate and complex grant system.

Grant Reform Efforts in the Early 1990s

Modest grant reforms under both Bush and Clinton, even though they never attained the status of major presidential initiatives, deserve passing mention in a review of intergovernmental relations during this period. It is also worth noting that, on a set of separate parallel tracks, Congress enacted three new block grant programs for child care, transportation, and low-income housing. Taken together, these modest actions acquire significance. In particular, the mere fact that presidents and congressional leaders of both parties, who had so little interest in federalism reform issues, felt inclined to offer such initiatives at all illustrates the degree to which federalism reform had become an institutionalized feature in modern intergovernmental relations.

The capstone of President Bush's reform efforts was a "surprise section" of his 1991 State of the Union address in which he invited the nation's governors to help him design a major new block grant initiative. According to an illustrative proposal outlined in his fiscal 1992 budget, between $15 billion and $22 billion in federal funding from approximately twelve existing programs would be "turned over" to the states in the form of a single large, highly flexible block grant.[18] Programs suggested for elimination and turnover included four block grants: the community development block grant (CDBG), the social services block grant, the Chapter 2 education block grant, and low-income energy assistance. All were budgeted by the president for stable or declining funding in future years, and they presumably met one of two tests proposed by OMB director Richard Darman for inclusion: they were deemed to be programs of value to the states but declining priority to the federal government, or they were appropriate for flexible management by the states. Regardless, the president and budget director went out of their way to label the list as tentative and to invite active participation by the states in designing a concrete plan.

This invitation spurred a flurry of activity on alternative block grant proposals, but none of these plans attracted serious consideration by Congress. The governors "welcomed" the president's initiative and promptly went to work devising their own proposal.[19] By April 1991 the National Governors' Association (NGA) had reached agreement on a $14 billion plan to consolidate forty-two categorical programs into seven block grants. At about the same time the National Conference of State Legislatures (NCSL) came forward with its own proposal to consolidate eighty-five existing programs into twelve block grants. Although these plans had some common goals and objectives, they had substantial programmatic differences. The number of consolidated programs varied from twelve to eighty-five, and the number of block grants ranged from one to twelve. The functional focus of the plans differed as well. The governors did not include in their plan any programs in criminal justice, community development, or transportation; the legislators omitted health and human services but included transportation. Funding was also an issue. In particular, the president anticipated declining funding for his block grant package, reflecting anticipated cuts and freezes in the incorporated programs. By contrast, state officials proposed a funding stream that would grow with inflation.

The whole initiative proved to be an exercise in futility. Almost as soon as the president announced his plan, congressional Democrats and local government officials voiced their objections to it. Democrats denounced the proposal as a ploy to cut federal spending, while mayors attacked it for diverting funding away from needy cities to the states.[20] Within three months of its unveiling, the president's reform initiative was considered "dead."[21]

New Block Grants in the 1990s

Despite the failure of the president's reform initiative, three new block grants were established during the early 1990s for child care, housing, and multimodal transportation. The first two, however, were block grants by default, driven by legislative bargaining rather than intergovernmental reform principles. They resulted from compromise between congressional Democrats, who favored new federal programs targeted to specific needs, and the Bush administration, which opposed new programs in these areas. The outcome was passage of relatively flexible formula grants that fit the technical definition of block grants, although they consolidated no existing programs and hardly represented a bow wave of intergovernmental reform.

This process of creating incidental block grants is best illustrated by the child care grant. After years of hard-fought legislative battles, a major child care assistance block grant was enacted in 1990 as part of the fiscal 1991 Omnibus Budget Reconciliation Act (P.L. 101-508). The legislation established a five-year, $2.5 billion block grant program to the states to enhance the availability and quality of child care services to low-income families, and it expanded direct federal tax credits for child care expenses. The final program represented a compromise between the Bush administration, which opposed creating a new federal aid program for child care services, and congressional Democrats, who generally preferred a categorical program designed to establish national child care standards.

The issue of national child care standards had been an important point of controversy for several years and one of the factors obstructing earlier attempts to enact federal child care legislation. Such standards were an integral part of the Act for Better Child Care (ABC) bill that the Senate debated in 1988. They were necessary, said the bill's chief sponsor, to avoid "indirectly subsidizing a form of abuse, and that's what it is if we don't have minimum health and safety standards."[22] Opposing national standards were the administration, the nation's governors, and congressional conservatives, who charged that they would create "another money-eating bureaucratic sinkhole."[23]

Conflict over national standards strengthened the political hand of state officials because their support was critical if child care grants were to be enacted over conservative opposition. Thus, when the Senate passed new ABC legislation in 1989, uniform health and safety standards had been replaced by a requirement that states establish and enforce their own standards, supplemented by a separate grant program for improving the quality of child care. This legislation was supported by the nation's governors and state legislators.[24]

For its part, the House passed a bill fashioned by the tax-writing Ways and Means Committee. The House bill combined tax credits, as urged by the president, with a child care grant program folded into the existing Title XX block grant, which also fell within the committee's jurisdiction. Unable to reconcile the competing ABC and Title XX grant mechanisms, the House-Senate conference committee invented yet another funding approach: a new child care block grant within the Title IV public assistance portion of the Social Security Act. By combining state-prescribed standards with tax credits and a smaller budget, the legislation was made acceptable to the administration and state and local opponents of national standards. Thus a block grant solution, which was originally favored by neither the proponents nor opponents of federal child care funding, became the vehicle that enabled passage of a new national initiative.

Grant Reform in Clinton's First Two Years

Modest intergovernmental reform initiatives were proposed and partially implemented during the first two years of Clinton's presidency. At least twice during the 1992 presidential campaign, Clinton rejected sweeping proposals for comprehensive federalism reform. As noted earlier, Alice Rivlin's brief for sorting out federal, state, and local roles failed to deter the president's commitment to expand the federal role in traditional local functions like education and law enforcement.[25] A subsequent proposal by government "reinvention" guru David Osborne recommended eliminating 100 federal aid programs and consolidating and devolving control over 400 others. It was transformed into a set of modest demonstrations.[26]

Instead, President Clinton's principal intergovernmental initiatives took place under the banner of a broader administrative reform agenda: the National Performance Review (NPR). The logic of the NPR did not lead directly to the fundamental restructuring of intergovernmental relationships, as originally advocated by Rivlin and Osborne. Rather, the NPR sought to improve governmental management and performance. For intergovernmental programs it implied greater state and local flexibility but with a catch. The federal government would closely monitor performance by state and local governments granted greater flexibility and would stand ready to reassert control as needed. As expressed by presidential adviser William Galston, the first principle of Clinton federalism was an ambivalent combination of "federal leadership with state and local flexibility."[27]

The administration outlined an array of intergovernmental reform initiatives that could have proved significant if they had been aggressively and systematically implemented. In the initial NPR report on "strengthening the [intergovernmental] partnership," the NPR staff recommended a program that included state-initiated "bottom-up" program consolidation initiatives, unfunded mandate relief, and a $13 billion proposal for "state flexibility" block grants, designed jointly by the National Governors' Association and the National Conference of State Legislatures.[28]

The administration's performance in this area, however, fell far short of its promises. No progress was made on enacting legislation to implement bottom-up program consolidation, nor did Congress take any action on the NGA and NCSL block grant proposals. The administration's ambivalence and hostility from senior Democrats on Capitol Hill stymied mandate reform legislation in Congress until Republicans gained control in 1995. Accordingly, David Walker judged the Clinton administration's record on intergovernmental reform to be "unexceptional." Indeed, Clinton's overall record on federalism fit into a general pattern of modest accomplishments dubbed "small change" by David Stoesz.[29] Considering Clinton's broader record of more categorical grants, two significant new mandates, and concerted (if only partially successful) attempts to expand the federal government's role in health care, education, job training, and law enforcement, the real direction of policy change in this period was toward more complexity in Washington, not less.

Political Trends

By almost any measure of fiscal and regulatory policy, the Bush administration and Clinton's first two years as president represented an unmistak-
able pause in the intergovernmental reform agenda. Their haphazard reform
initiatives were largely unsuccessful and were overshadowed by powerful
fiscal and regulatory trends. It was a period not of rampant recentralization,
but of "slouching toward Washington," to use David Walker's graphic
phrase.[30]

These policy trends, built on a weak and unsteady foundation of political support, were volatile. During the late 1980s and early 1990s, public
trust in the federal government continued to decline, small but growing
segments of the population questioned its very legitimacy, and public support for devolutionary policies grew. Together these developments paved
the way for a new and ambitious wave of federalism reform initiatives in
the 104th Congress (1995–97).

Declining Confidence

One of the most striking trends in public opinion since the 1960s has
been the decline of public confidence in the federal government. In 1964,
76 percent of Americans polled said they felt they could "trust the government in Washington to do the right thing" "just about always" or "most
of the time." As figure 11-3 shows, confidence in the federal government's
performance fell sharply through the late 1960s and 1970s, providing a
popular foundation for Ronald Reagan's devolutionary policies in the
1980s. Trust in Washington recovered somewhat during the Reagan years,
but it resumed its decline under Presidents Bush and Clinton. By 1995
public trust in the national government had returned to the abysmal levels
reached in 1980.

As many analysts have observed, the federal government was not alone
in suffering an erosion of public confidence. Confidence in almost all
American institutions declined after 1965.[31] Yet the downward trend was
much steeper for Washington than for state and local governments. In
1972, for example, the national government still retained higher levels of
public confidence than states or localities; by 1992 it had the lowest levels
and they were still falling.[32] Confidence in state government performance
showed volatility over this period but no pattern of erosion comparable to
Washington's.

Figure 11-3. *Public Confidence in Federal Government, 1972–96*
Percent expressing a "great deal" or "fair amount" of confidence

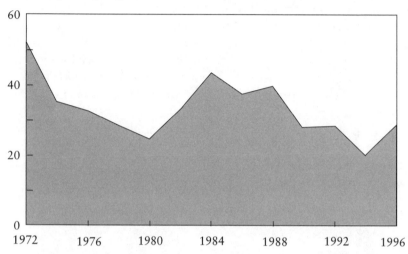

Source: American National Election Studies, various years.

Figure 11-4. *Changing Public Views about Federal Power, 1964–95*
Percent

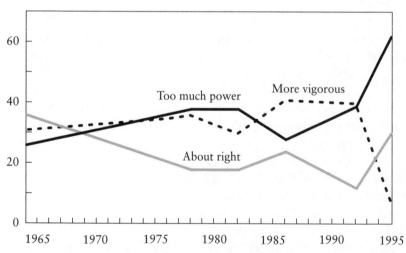

Sources: Lloyd Free and Hadley Cantril, *The Political Beliefs of Americans: A Study of Public Opinion* (Rutgers University Press, 1967); U.S. Advisory Commission on Intergovernmental Relations, *Changing Public Attitudes on Government and Taxes,* various years; Gallup Poll, August 11–14, 1996, *Public Perspective,* vol. 8 (April–May 1997), p. 57.

Table 11-3. *Public Attitudes toward Federal and State Governments, 1994–95*

Question	Percent of responses
"Think about relations between the states and the federal government. Does the federal government have too much power, do the state governments have too much power, or is the balance about right?"	
Federal too much	48
States too much	6
About right	38
"What if some of the tax dollars that go to the federal government now went to your state government instead. Generally, speaking, do you think that would result in better government services, in worse government services, or wouldn't it have much impact on the quality of government services?"	
Better	53
Worse	4
Little impact	32
"Would you favor or oppose having your state government assume many of the governmental powers and functions now exercised by the federal government in Washington?"	
Favor	59
Oppose	32
Not sure	10

Sources: Surveys by CBS News/*New York Times*, February, 1995; *Los Angeles Times*, January 1995; and Time/CNN, September 1994, reprinted in "How Much Government?" *Public Perspective*, vol. 6 (April–May 1995), p. 28.

Statistically unchanged were public attitudes toward local governments. Whereas 64 percent of the public expressed confidence in local governments two decades ago, 60 percent continued to do so in the early 1990s. As a result, local governments—which evoked the least amount of public trust and confidence in 1972—summoned the most in 1992. Similarly, in 1989 respondents rated local governments most highly in terms of governmental responsiveness. When they were asked which level of government "responds best to your needs," 40 percent chose local government; 21 percent, state government; and only 18 percent, federal government.[33]

Figure 11-5. *Public Support for a Greater State Role, 1995*

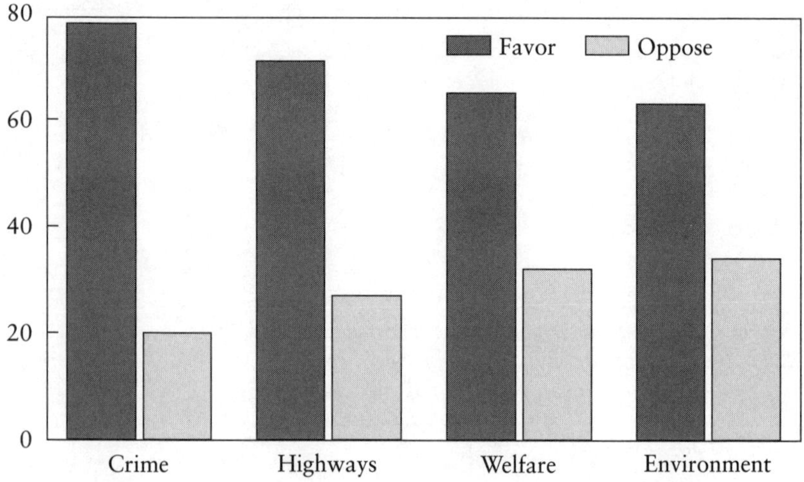

Source: "How Much Government?" *Public Perspective*, vol. 6 (April–May 1995), p. 29.

These changing public attitudes had important implications for public policy. By 1994 and 1995 most Americans believed that the federal government had grown too powerful and needed to be cut back. As figure 11-4 shows, there was a rapid rise in the mid-1990s in the percentage of Americans who believed that the federal government had too much power. From 1964 to 1992, there was a relative balance between the numbers of Americans who thought the federal government had grown too powerful and those who thought it needed to exercise its powers more vigorously to redress problems in society. The portion of the population concerned about governmental power was ascendant in the late 1970s and early 1980s, while renewed support for governmental activism emerged at the end of the Reagan era. After 1986, however, support for the more conservative position increased once again, dramatically so in the mid-1990s. By 1995, 62 percent of the public shared the belief that the federal government had too much power.[34]

Large majorities of Americans also believed that the federal government spent taxpayers' money less efficiently than did states and localities, and most supported sending more of their dollars to the states than to Washington (see table 11-3). Indeed, by January 1995 majorities of Americans said that they favored giving the states—as opposed to the federal government—more control over virtually every area of domestic activity, including welfare, environmental protection, highways, and crime prevention (see figure 11-5).

Thus by the mid-1990s a foundation for substantial policy devolution had been laid in public opinion. Confidence in the national government's leadership and performance had fallen to levels that seemed to portend a "legitimation crisis."[35] As the following chapter describes, when this secular decline of confidence in Washington was combined with a sharp spike of disgust with the Democratic Congress in 1993 and 1994, an accelerating Republican realignment in the South, and successful party building efforts by the Republican party, conditions were ripe for an electoral shock to the political system—and for a bold new agenda of intergovernmental reform.

CHAPTER 12

A Devolution Revolution?
Federalism in the 104th Congress

"T HE ERA of big government is over."[1] Nothing more clearly symbolized the rightward shift in American politics during the 104th Congress than this stark assertion by President Bill Clinton in his 1996 State of
the Union address. During his first two years in office, Clinton's top domestic priority had been a national health care reform plan. If enacted, the
president's proposal for universal health insurance would have been the
most dramatic expansion of the nation's welfare state since the 1960s.
Instead, the plan's failure to win strong public support or enactment by
the Democratic Congress helped spark a sudden shift to the right in the
public agenda.[2] In the midterm elections of 1994, Democrats lost control
of both houses of Congress for the first time in forty years, and the new
Republican majority moved quickly to launch initiatives to shrink rather
than expand the welfare state.

The new congressional agenda had far-reaching implications for American federalism. The Republicans' program centered on a bold plan to reduce federal spending, cut federal taxes, trim federal regulations, and
balance the federal budget within seven years. A reduced federal role would
be made permanent by amending the Constitution to require balanced
budgets each year in the future. To help implement this budget strategy
and further reduce federal policy influence, the new majority embraced
the use of block grants with unprecedented zeal. In the early stages of
congressional deliberations, the new majority weighed plans to consolidate 349 existing programs—totaling $217 billion—into just ten broadly
defined block grants![3] Finally, the new agenda included a comprehensive
assault on the federal regulatory state, including but not limited to direct
federal mandates affecting state and local governments.

Had it been successfully enacted and implemented, this Republican agenda would have launched a true "devolution revolution."[4] But the American political system resists most revolutionary impulses, as David Stockman—Ronald Reagan's director of the Office of Management and Budget (OMB)—had learned a decade earlier. With their stringent budget and plans to devolve federal power to state and local governments, the Republicans exceeded their electoral mandate even more than Clinton had with his health care proposal. They might still have succeeded had they controlled the White House as well as Congress. But they did not, and their revolution was doomed once Clinton became convinced that most Americans questioned or opposed key elements of their program. By the time the 1996 elections were held, President Clinton was no longer sounding his State of the Union theme "the era of big government is over." Instead, he had successfully amended it to something along these lines: "the era of big new expansionary initiatives may be over for now, but let's preserve medicare and medicaid and do a little more for education and the environment."

Although the 104th Congress failed to achieve a devolution revolution, its actions still comprised a record of federalism reform not seen since the presidencies of Richard Nixon and Ronald Reagan. Given the inherent difficulty of promoting a coherent policy agenda from the normally factious and multiwilled Congress, this was no mean achievement. Accomplishments included the enactment of comprehensive welfare reform, unfunded mandates reform, and reductions in federal discretionary appropriations. Most important, perhaps, Congress had shifted the focus of political debate and moved the public agenda's center of gravity well to the right. Republicans' success in maintaining control over both houses of Congress in the 1996 elections promised to institutionalize this shift in the years ahead.

Prelude to Revolution: Politics and the 1994 Election

The attempted Republican revolution was made possible by the startling midterm congressional elections of 1994. The Democrats' long dominance in the House of Representatives had become so institutionalized that many Washington insiders scarcely imagined it would change in their lifetime. One scholarly book about House Republicans even characterized them as the "permanent minority."[5] Yet, literally overnight, seemingly healthy Democratic majorities in both houses of Congress were erased.

Republicans registered a net gain of fifty-three House seats. Thirty-five Democratic incumbents in the House were defeated, and a comparable number of open seats were lost. Remarkably, not a single House Republican seeking reelection was defeated. Republicans even won a majority of House seats in the South for the first time since Reconstruction. The trend toward southern partisan realignment, evident in presidential politics since 1964, had gathered new momentum in congressional races. Since 1986 the Republicans' share of votes cast in House elections in the South had risen sharply with each subsequent election, reaching more than 52 percent by 1994.[6] This steady trend allowed Republicans to cement their hold on power in the House after the election by enticing a number of conservative Democrats to switch parties rather than face the prospect of defeat the next time they ran.

Reinforcing the impact of their victories in the House, Republicans scored substantial gains in virtually all other races as well. They regained control of the Senate for the first time since the 99th Congress (1985–87), picking up a net gain of eight seats in that chamber. As in the House, no Republican incumbents were defeated in the Senate. At the state level, the party picked up eleven new governorships, including statehouses in most of the nation's largest states. Republican gains in state legislatures were notable as well. In short, it was a smashing electoral victory for the party nationwide.

The ideology of the newly elected Republicans was almost as important as their numerical gains in Congress. The freshmen Republicans were an unusually conservative and ideologically committed group.[7] Many had been recruited, trained, and substantially financed by national party committees, Newt Gingrich's own GOPAC, or conservative organizations like the Christian Coalition.[8] For more than half of the new members, Congress was their first elective office.[9]

Right from the Start: The Contract with America

The political influence of the Republican majority was enhanced by its ready-made policy agenda. Many newly elected leaders are ill equipped to legislate; once in office they suddenly must grapple with the difficult question "Now what?" But House Republicans had prepared a detailed answer to this question and were ready to "hit the ground running." In a most unusual campaign initiative, 367 House Republican candidates endorsed a specific legislative agenda: ten major items that they promised to bring to a vote in the first one hundred days of a Republican-controlled House.

Dubbed the "Contract with America," this agenda was as much a campaign marketing device as a guide to governing. All ten items chosen were politically popular and relatively noncontroversial. Public opinion polls showed that most of them were supported by at least 70 percent of the general population. Divisive conservative issues like school prayer were deliberately left out. To attract maximum public attention, the Republicans widely publicized their Contract. A full-blown media extravaganza was held on the steps of the U.S. Capitol in September 1994 followed by full-page ads in *TV Guide*. Equally important for its later policy impact, each item in the Contract was backed up by specific and often detailed pieces of legislation. All were crafted to demonstrate the party's seriousness about its policy pledges.

Although it was an unusually comprehensive and detailed preelection agenda, the Contract with America had no federalism reform plank per se. A general statement in the preamble pledged "the end of government that is too big, too intrusive, and too easy with the public's money," but federalism and devolution were not directly discussed in the actual Contract.[10] Nonetheless, many of the items in the document had clear implications for the distribution of power and responsibility in the American federal system. Included in this category were the balanced budget amendment to the Constitution, congressional term limits, welfare reform, federal regulatory reform, and limits on unfunded federal mandates. Individually and collectively, these provisions comprised a broad-gauged assault on Washington's fiscal, regulatory, and political influence, and this assault was fully understood by the Contract's advocates and opponents.

For example, adoption of a balanced budget amendment to the Constitution was intended to restrain federal activism in several ways. First, it would limit future federal spending growth to the rate of revenue inflow. Although raising taxes is politically difficult under the best of circumstances, the Contract promised to increase this difficulty by requiring a supermajority of House members to pass any increase in federal taxes. Indeed, the Contract promised to tighten the squeeze on federal spending with hundreds of billions of dollars of federal tax cuts, ranging from capital gains reductions to per-child tax credits.

Astute supporters of the balanced budget amendment recognized that it would change the politics of federal budgeting. By providing political "cover" for difficult budgetary decisions, it would strengthen the hand of federal budget cutters. Advocates of spending cuts could argue that they didn't *want* to hurt beneficiaries, but "the Constitution made us do it." In this context supporters of federal spending programs would be placed in a virtual "state of nature"—a war of all against all. Advocates of each program would be forced to defend their share of a stable or shrinking pie against all other claimants. One Republican strategist even argued that the resulting zero-sum budgetary game would be "a dagger through the heart" of the Democratic party. "The balanced budget hurts the Democratic Party for the next decade. It will force budget cuts vs. tax increase fights, and that's good for us."[11]

Term limits were intended to strike another mortal blow at the political establishment in Washington. The Contract itself spoke in rather tame language about "replacing career politicians with a citizen legislature," but many conservative Republican advocates were more expansive.[12] One freshman House Republican argued during congressional debate that term limits were needed to break the grip of "the current system," which "allows certain people to spend a lifetime in Washington . . . fall out of touch with their constituents and consolidate the power . . . to ensure continued success in passing wasteful and pork barrel programs."[13] Conservative columnist and presidential candidate Pat Buchanan was even more graphic, arguing that congressional term limits were necessary to "drain the fetid swamp of political corruption that is Washington, D.C."[14]

Leading supporters of regulatory reform in the new Congress were equally vociferous. One claimed to be seeking "the demise of the modern era of government regulation." Another, House Republican whip Tom DeLay of Texas, bluntly stated that "we are ideologues. We have an agenda. . . . I want to repeal the Clean Air Act."[15] In point of fact, the new majority sought regulatory changes far beyond environmental issues. The Contract had two titles that dealt with regulatory reform. One, the Job Creation and Wage Enhancement Act, required that all federal regulations undergo risk assessment and strict cost-benefit analysis, strengthened the Regulatory Flexibility Act, and included unfunded mandate reform legislation. Another bill, the Common Sense Legal Reform Act, preempted state product liability laws, imposed "loser pays" requirements to reduce lawsuits, and limited punitive damages in various tort cases. Overall, the effects of such provisions would be to "bind the hands of regulators."[16]

Great Expectations, Modest Results in the 104th Congress

In the Congress moving beyond a stated agenda to producing actual results is a very big step. In 1995 and 1996 the Republican Congress developed big plans, got off to a strong start, and proceeded farther than many observers thought possible. But its results, compared with its ambitious goals, were surprisingly modest. The 104th Congress cut domestic discretionary spending by a small amount, reformed welfare programs, placed restraints on future federal mandates, and changed the tenor of political debate. Its most sweeping legislative goals were stymied by the innate conservatism of the Madisonian system, however. Many policy proposals that survived the legislative process encountered roadblocks on Pennsylvania Avenue as President Clinton used his veto to blunt the Republicans' assault on Washington.

The remainder of this chapter sketches a brief outline of the major policy actions of the 104th Congress.[17] The following chapter provides more detailed case studies of two important intergovernmental accomplishments: welfare reform and the Unfunded Mandates Reform Act.

Banking on the Budget

Apart from some of the regulatory reform initiatives, most of the key legislative initiatives of 1995 were developed and implemented through the congressional budget process. As Allen Schick observed:

In 1995 almost all legislative roads led to the congressional budget process. Efforts to balance the budget, cut federal taxes, terminate or curtail hundreds of programs and agencies, redesign farm price supports, change medicare and medicaid, renegotiate the relationship between Washington and the states—all were driven by [the] budget resolution.[18]

There were several reasons why the new Republican majority adopted this strategy. Substantively, of course, many of its policy objectives—tax cuts, a balanced budget—were fiscal in nature. But the Republicans wanted to shrink the size and scope of government, not just balance the budget. Cutting federal spending programs could help accomplish this aim. Moreover, from a tactical perspective, the budget framed political debate in terms favorable for the reformers. Balancing the federal budget was a

Table 12-1. *Tentative Block Grant Initiative by House Republican Leaders, January 1995*

Proposed block grant	Number of current federal programs	1995 appropriations (billions of dollars)
Food and nutrition	10	38.0
Cash welfare	7	17.2
Child care	45	11.8
Social services	33	6.6
Child welfare and child abuse	38	4.3
Employment and training	154	24.8
Housing	27	17.5
Health	22	5.1
Total	336	125.3

Source: Barbara Vobejda, "GOP Outlines Broad Welfare Reform: Proposal Would Replace Federal Programs with Block Grants to States," *Washington Post*, January 7, 1995.

popular, easily communicated objective. As Reagan discovered, combining hundreds of specific spending cuts in one large omnibus package tended to drown out the appeals of individual beneficiaries and draw attention instead to the popular overarching objective. Finally, legislating through the budget process carried important procedural advantages that limited the minority's opportunities for obstruction, especially in the Senate.

BLOCK GRANTS AND BUDGET CUTS. A related strategy of the new majority was to rely heavily on block grants to implement many of its policy goals.[19] Early in the 104th Congress Republican leaders outlined a tentative plan to consolidate over 300 federal programs, totaling $125 billion, into eight block grants (see table 12-1). Ultimately, the House budget resolution included twelve new block grants designed to consolidate hundreds of programs and save tens of billions of dollars.

Even among Republicans in Congress, a block grant strategy was controversial. Some proposed alternative plans that would have completely abolished federal involvement in some fields while increasing it in others. For example, in a plan reminiscent of President Reagan's approach in 1982, Senator Nancy Kassebaum of Kansas proposed that the federal government assume all costs of the medicaid program while turning full responsibility for aid to families with dependent children (AFDC) and food stamps over to the states. "It isn't just a question of sending money to the states and letting them, with a block grant, have the flexibility to run it," she argued on "Meet the Press." "I would sever Washington's involvement."[20] Although Senator Kassebaum was regarded as a moderate in the Senate, sorting out federal-state responsibilities was favored by some conservatives as well. Jeffery Eisenach of the Progress and Freedom Foundation, a group with close ties to Speaker Gingrich, argued that "complete devolution approaches really and truly get the federal government out of it." In contrast, Congress would find that "block grants are a temptation to micromanage."[21]

Certainly many congressional Republicans were uncomfortable with the notion of giving up too much control over block grant funds, just as their Democratic predecessors had been. Representative Bill Goodling of Pennsylvania, the new chairman of the House Opportunities Committee, asserted: "I'm not just for block granting money back and saying, 'Here, do your thing.' There has to be a purpose and goals . . . and oversight to see what's happening."[22] Or, as one conservative advocate of mandating tough restrictions on welfare put it: "If we impose the taxes at the federal level, why shouldn't we control the program?"[23]

But the new House leadership quickly decided to support a package of bold, flexible block grants in a variety of welfare and social service-related fields, within the context of a comprehensive balanced budget plan. They did so for several reasons. To begin with, block grants were strongly favored by most of the nation's governors. Following their sweep of virtually all of the nation's most populous states, Republican governors had been catapulted into a place of unusual prominence within the party. Their support of any proposed legislation was deemed to be crucial to the enactment of a broad balanced budget package. If governors worked with their congressional delegations to fight budget provisions that reduced funding to their states, the entire package would be in jeopardy. In addition, this marriage of block grants and budget reductions made intellectual sense to many in the new congressional majority, since both tools had the apparent effect of reducing the scope and influence of the federal government.

Finally, block grants had another important political advantage: they obscured and deferred much of the political pain associated with many of the proposed budget cuts. As a former Democratic aide on the Senate Budget Committee explained: "Block grants are one of the best ways to cut the budget. The cuts are so ethereal. You don't have to specify what will really happen to people and programs. You just give the states less money and let them decide."[24] Until actual cuts were made in specific activities, interest groups could not fully mobilize their supporters to oppose the changes. This, some conservatives hoped, would set in motion a continued cycle of cuts, leading to the eventual phase-out of federal involvement:

> You start by saying, 'you'll get a block grant with all the flexibility, but I'm going to cut funding by 15–20 per cent'—whatever you can get away with. Then the pressure is on Congress to look for ways of cutting that back further over time.[25]

FORGING A BUDGET RESOLUTION. None of this implies that the budgetary strategy was easily implemented. The congressional budget process can be as daunting as the overland trails of the old West. Completing the journey takes many months, and steep obstacles are encountered along the way. At times the trails diverge as different parties take different paths only to regroup again.

The first milestone on this legislative journey was the passage of a budget resolution by both houses of Congress. This resolution established targets for total federal revenues and overall levels of spending in major budget categories. These targets were then supposed to be met by the House and Senate Appropriations Committees and the authorizing committees with jurisdiction over the affected areas.

The budget resolution passed by the House on May 18, 1995, would have launched a true "devolution revolution" if it had been fully implemented. Instead, it represented the high-water mark of reforms in the 104th Congress. It proposed to cut projected federal spending by more than $1 trillion over seven years. This included real cuts of $190 billion in nondefense discretionary spending (a category that includes many federal grant programs as well as direct federal operating expenses). This figure would have reduced such discretionary spending by 12 percent below 1995 levels and 30 percent below the baseline level of projected federal spending in 2002, assuming regular program growth for inflation, population increases, and the like.[26] Other cuts included $187 billion in previously scheduled medicaid spending over seven years, $288 billion in medicare, and $35 billion in cuts to various welfare programs, with part of the proceeds intended to go toward tax cuts of $353 billion over seven years.[27]

In sheer fiscal terms this budget proposed major changes in federal finances. Yet the true magnitude of the proposal was most evident in its intended changes in federal program structures and operations. In the words of Budget Committee chairman John Kasich of Ohio, "Our vision is to take the power and the money and control and influence from people in this city and give it back to the men and women in every city and town and village."[28] Although the budget resolution could not dictate how its fiscal targets would be accomplished, much consultation transpired between the House Budget Committee and other committees before setting the overall spending targets. Examples provided in the Budget Committee's report illustrated the types of legislative changes that were being anticipated. The budget resolution proposed to

—create over a dozen new block grants affecting medicaid, cash welfare, child protection, nutrition, Native Americans, job training, education, housing, law enforcement, and rural development;

—abolish three federal departments—Energy, Education, and Commerce;

—terminate fourteen other federal agencies, including the Appalachian Regional Commission, the Economic Development Administration, the Legal Services Corporation, and the Tennessee Valley Authority;

—eliminate sixty-nine commissions, including the Advisory Commission on Intergovernmental Relations and the Administrative Conference of the United States;

—consolidate or eliminate 283 federal programs, including bilingual education programs, summer youth employment programs, the low-income energy assistance block grant, and the Davis-Bacon Act; and

—reduce the budgets of several block grants by 20 to 50 percent, including the community development block grant (CDBG), maternal and child health, and the preventive health block grant.[29]

The full House adopted this dramatic proposal on a nearly party-line vote of 238 to 193. All but one Republican voted for the budget resolution; only eight Democrats voted for it.

The Senate passed its version of the budget resolution on May 25, 1995. The overall shape of the package was similar to that passed by the House, but significant elements of the House budget were moderated in the Senate. The Senate's tax cut package was smaller, as were its medicare and medicaid cuts. Moreover, fewer federal programs were slated for elimination, consolidation, and structural reform. For example, only one department (Commerce) was targeted for elimination, fewer programs were suggested for termination (100 compared with 283), and fewer block grants were detailed in the committee report.[30]

The House-Senate conference split down the middle many of the differences between the two chambers' resolutions. The agreed-upon tax cuts, medicare reductions, and medicaid cuts were about halfway between the House and Senate figures. Both chambers had agreed to seek cuts of approximately $190 billion in discretionary spending, but they differed in how they planned to achieve these reductions. Both chambers agreed to eliminate the Department of Commerce, but they "agreed to disagree" about eliminating the Energy and Education departments. Disagreements remained concerning intergovernmental programs as well. But the compromise budget resolution continued to assume that funding for many grant-in-aid programs (including CDBG, preventive health, the Appalachian Regional Commission, and mass transit operating subsidies) would be deeply cut or eliminated. In addition, the final budget resolution agreed to create new block grants for medicaid, welfare, rural development, public housing, and job training.

Appropriating unto Themselves

For all the energy and attention that went into it, the budget resolution was only that: a promise that Congress made to itself. The real challenge of translating these promises into law fell to the Appropriations Committees, which were responsible for meeting the reduced discretionary spending targets, and to various authorizing committees responsible for making substantive changes (such as welfare reforms and entitlement cuts) in their areas of jurisdiction. As in 1981, these provisions would be gathered into a giant omnibus reconciliation act designed to permanently alter the scope and structure of federal responsibilities.

THE RESCISSION DECISION. The Appropriations Committees began working on their part of the assignment before the budget resolution was even adopted. The new majority was eager to begin cutting the budget, and the appropriations process provided a speedy vehicle. The House and Senate Appropriations Committees revisited spending decisions made by the previous Congress for the fiscal year already under way. They produced "rescission" bills that reduced previously authorized spending levels for scores of federal programs from A (the Animal and Plant Inspection Service in the Department of Agriculture) to V (medical care and construction projects in the Department of Veterans' Affairs).[31] These cuts were not spread evenly throughout the government, however. By one estimate, 62 percent of the rescissions were made in programs serving people with low incomes.[32]

The biggest cuts were made in low-income housing ($7.2 billion), job training grants ($1.3 billion), and low-income energy assistance grants ($319 million). Overall, the total cuts in spending authority amounted to $13.3 billion. This was only about 5 percent of all domestic discretionary spending, but a few programs were zeroed out entirely (homeless adult literacy grants, summer youth employment grants), and the effects on other programs were felt more deeply because the fiscal year was already half over.

THE CUTTING EDGE. The rescission bill was only an opening salvo. The big battles in appropriations occurred later in the year as Congress struggled to piece together and pass the thirteen regular appropriations bills that determine federal discretionary spending. Some of the deepest cuts were in the spending bill for the Labor, Health and Human Services (HHS), and Education departments. The House-passed version of this bill cut fiscal 1996 spending by the Department of Labor $1.6 billion below the 1995 level of appropriations, a cut of 19 percent. This figure was $2.8 billion (29 percent) below the president's request.[33] Nonmedicare spending by the Department of Health and Human Services was cut $8 billion (6 percent) below 1995 levels, and Education spending was reduced $3.2 billion below prior year appropriations.

The House-approved cuts on the Labor, HHS, and Education spending bill tended to be deeper than in the Senate. The two chambers never reached agreement on a compromise appropriations bill for these functions. But the Senate, like the House, followed the pattern of cutting spending below 1995 levels—and well below the president's fiscal 1996 request. And the record was the same on other domestic appropriations bills where the two chambers passed a compromise bill. For example, spending for housing and urban programs in H.R. 2099, which passed both chambers, was cut nearly 25 percent ($6.1 billion) below postrescission 1995 levels. The Environmental Protection Agency budget was cut by 21 percent in the same bill. Similarly, the conference agreement on the Commerce-Justice-State appropriations bill reduced Commerce Department spending 15 percent below fiscal 1995 levels and 27 percent below the president's request.[34]

THE POWER OF ZERO. Budget cuts were the most visible part of the Republican majority's appropriations strategy in 1995. It also used the appropriations process to force structural changes in government by terminating program funding, attaching legislative riders, and even by writing new legislation in appropriations bills.

The most straightforward approach to making new policy in appropriations bills involved "zeroing out" program budgets. A program or agency's authorization might remain on the books, but the lack of funding would effectively terminate it. "All we have to do is put a zero next to a particular line in an appropriation bill," said House Appropriations Committee chairman Robert Livingston. "It doesn't matter what the Senate or what the President does. . . . We may not have the power to spend money, but we do have the power to withhold it."[35] And many, mostly small, programs and agencies were zeroed out. The Advisory Commission on Intergovernmental Relations, for example, was forced to close down when its funding was eliminated—even though its authorizing statute was not repealed. The same fate befell other small agencies like the Administrative Conference of the United States, the Office of Technology Assessment, and the National Commission on Employment Policy. Programs like the Urban Parks and Recreation Fund, the pension fund partnership program, and the dropout prevention demonstration program became history as well.

The termination strategy was carried to its fullest extent in the House-passed version of the Labor-HHS appropriations bill, which zeroed out eleven programs in the Department of Labor, sixty-six programs in the Department of Health and Human Services, and ninety-three programs in the Department of Education.[36] But despite its appeal to self-styled revolutionaries, the limits of this termination strategy soon became apparent. Enacting appropriations bills with these budget levels required approval by the Senate and the president. This proved difficult to secure. For example, the fiscal and policy changes in the Labor-HHS appropriations bill were so controversial that the Senate failed to pass its version of the bill, much less reach agreement with the House and the president.

Indeed, so much was attempted with so much controversy that by the October 1, 1995, deadline—the beginning of the new fiscal year—Congress had enacted few appropriations bills. This forced it to pass a short-term continuing resolution to fund the government while appropriators worked to pass regular funding (or "defunding") bills for the year. By the time the continuing resolution expired in November, only six of the thirteen regular appropriations bills had been signed into law. Most of the rest were in serious trouble. President Clinton vetoed several when they were sent to him in December, including the Commerce, Justice, State, Judiciary bill; the Interior Department appropriation; and the Veterans' Affairs, Housing and Urban Development, and independent agencies appropriation. He vetoed them because of disagreements over spending levels and conflicts over policy issues like the termination of the Commerce Department and changes in environmental programs. These vetoes, when combined with the Senate's failure even to pass the Labor, Health and Human Services, and Education appropriations bill, had serious consequences: more than half of all federal domestic activities lacked legal spending authorization well into the fiscal year.

If the Republicans' political strategy had been successful, this failure might actually have advanced their cause. As the earlier statement by Appropriations Committee chairman Livingston indicated, the "revolutionaries" hoped that a House refusal to fund particular programs would be definitive. But the president refused to sign bills that contained unacceptable provisions, even at the risk of shutting down entire agencies. And without signed appropriations bills, entire departments and agencies were forced to shut down when temporary spending bills expired.

Government shutdowns occurred not once but twice between November 1995 and January 1996. In the interim, public anger at the government's failure to perform its most basic tasks was directed at the Republican Congress, which had claimed, after all, to be promoting revolution. By January the shutdown strategy was acknowledged to be a failure, and it was eventually replaced by negotiations on an omnibus appropriations act for all of the remaining unpassed appropriations bills. This omnibus bill, H.R. 3019, was signed by the president on April 26, 1996—halfway through the fiscal year—and it marked an end to the bitter financial battles of the 104th Congress.

In the end what did the new Congress accomplish on the appropriations front? Republicans did not achieve a revolution, but they did succeed in cutting federal domestic discretionary spending for the first time in three decades. Appropriations for nondefense programs were cut almost $22 billion in fiscal 1996 from the original fiscal 1995 level—a reduction of 9 percent, not including inflation. After two years, budget authority for fiscal 1997 remained below fiscal 1995 levels.[37]

According to the House Appropriations Committee, 207 separate programs or projects were terminated in fiscal 1996, including more than seventy grant programs. Almost all of the terminated programs were very small, however. For example, the seventy-three grants that were eliminated saved only about $2.3 billion dollars combined. Most of them averaged $10 million or less. Other grant programs were cut rather than terminated. The low-income energy assistance program (LIHEAP) was cut by 31 percent; state student incentive block grants were cut in half, and the social services block grant, mass transit formula grants, and homeless assistance grants suffered double-digit cuts. Still, it was hardly a revolution. Appropriations for numerous programs favored by the president—including the women, infants, and children (WIC) nutrition program, crime prevention programs, and school to work grants—increased, and major targets for elimination—including cabinet departments and programs like the Appalachian Regional Commission and the Economic Development Administration—survived.

DEFUNDING THE LEFT—AGAIN. Appropriations bills were also used to influence policy in ways that went beyond adjusting spending levels. This is not unheard of in the legislative process, but it is always controversial. Normally, the authorizing committees in Congress guard their legislative prerogatives jealously. Appropriations bills are meant to set program and agency budgets, but, presumably, they are not supposed to determine how an agency is structured or who receives the funding. Yet in 1995 the leadership sanctioned the use of appropriations bills to rewrite laws and alter policy. As House Republican whip DeLay explained: "We didn't have time to legislate through the normal process."[38]

The idea was to incorporate some of the most controversial policy changes in "must pass" legislation like appropriations bills. The president would then be forced to sign them, the Republicans thought, to avoid shutting down the government. For example, the Justice Department appropriations bill passed by the House abolished several crime prevention programs and a presidential initiative for hiring local cops and replaced them with a new law enforcement block grant. Similarly, the Senate created a new rural development block grant within its agricultural appropriations bill.

One of the most visible attempts to legislate on an appropriations bill was the amendment by Representative Ernest Istook (Republican of Oklahoma). This was the latest in a string of conservative efforts to "defund the left" by restricting political advocacy by nonprofit entities that received federal grants.[39] As had been true in the Reagan years, many conservatives believed that the activities of their liberal opponents were being subsidized by federal funds. The Istook amendment was intended to halt such activities by

—expanding the existing prohibition on lobbying Congress with federal funds to preclude executive branch lobbying at any level of government or participation in lawsuits involving the government;

—barring nonprofit organizations from receiving federal funds if they spent 5 percent or more of their nonfederal grants funds on political advocacy in any one of the past five years;

—limiting federally funded groups from entering coalitions with other organizations that spend at least 15 percent of their funds on lobbying and advocacy;

—including coverage of indirect federal grants that are passed through state and local governments; and

—licensing "bounty hunters" to help enforce the new restrictions, allowing them to bring lawsuits against federal grantees up to ten years after alleged violations and authorizing them to collect 25 percent of any resulting fines and penalties.

The Istook amendment was part of a broader pattern of legislative initiatives to defund the left during the 104th Congress. Within the Congress "legislative service organizations," many of which had a strong liberal orientation, lost their funding, staff, and office space as new rules adopted by the House prohibited members from pooling funds from their individual office allowances to support special interest caucuses. "Among those defunded," noted political scientist Roger H. Davidson, "were the Democratic Study Group, the black, Hispanic, and women's caucuses, and groups promoting the arts, the environment, human rights, arms control, and federal employees."[40] Majority Leader Dick Armey of Texas "wrote a letter to dozens of corporate executives blasting them for giving money to liberal public advocacy groups." Tom DeLay reportedly refused to talk with one company's lobbyist, saying, "You need to hire a Republican. . . . We don't like to deal with people who are trying to kill the revolution. We know who they are. The word is out.'"[41]

As had been true under Nixon and Reagan, some conservatives also advocated block grants as a way to "smash the power of national groups that supported the 'welfare state.'" Devolution and grant consolidation would break interest groups' ties to Washington policymakers and force them to scratch for reduced funding in what were presumed to be less hospitable state capitals. "For the Gingrich group," argued Elizabeth Drew, "breaking the power of the political infrastructure of the welfare state was at least as important . . . as the issue of where the [block grant] funds went."[42]

The Istook amendment became the symbol for the new attack on liberal groups, however. It was included in the Labor-HHS appropriations bill after a strenuous debate within the House Appropriations Committee, where most Democratic members strongly opposed it. The Republican chairman of the Labor-HHS subcommittee, Representative John Porter of Illinois, also opposed it, arguing that substantive policy should not be written in an appropriations bill. "This bill has a great deal of baggage on it," he complained, which "is going to bring this bill down."[43] Full committee chairman Robert Livingston initially opposed the provision as well, complaining to Gingrich that "you guys are piling a lot of crap on my bill."[44] But the leadership insisted on keeping the provision in the bill, and they backed up their support when the appropriations bill came to the floor. A Democrat's attempt to strip the provision from the bill was defeated on a mostly party-line vote, as the leadership pulled out all stops to keep Republicans on board.[45] The House went on to pass the full appropriations bill by a comfortable margin, but the bill with its amendments stalled in the Senate and never encountered the certain presidential veto that awaited it.

Irreconcilable Differences

An equally dismal fate lay in store for many of the GOP's budget and policy priorities. Despite the instances of legislating in appropriations bills, most attempts at comprehensive program restructuring and changes in entitlement programs were undertaken by the authorizing committees of jurisdiction. Their reforms were packaged in a broad reconciliation bill that included the major fiscal policy objectives of the new Congress—tax cuts and medicare savings—as well as program restructuring and policy changes. In particular, the reconciliation bill adopted by the Congress in November 1995 proposed to create seven full or partial block grants, including comprehensive restructuring of welfare, medicaid, and child protection programs.

PARALYSIS ON PENNSYLVANIA AVENUE. As noted earlier, the Republican strategy to use the budget process to advance these reforms had procedural advantages. In particular, Republican leaders believed that they could use the budget as leverage to force presidential acceptance of policy changes that he would otherwise reject. "We are prepared to shut the government down," the House Budget Committee chairman, John Kasich of Ohio, publicly warned the president.[46] Speaker Gingrich was even more emphatic in late September 1995, when he warned that Congress was willing to send the federal government into default by refusing to extend the debt ceiling unless the president accepted Republicans' fiscal priorities. "I don't care what the price is. I don't care if we have no executive offices, no bonds for 60 days. What we are saying to Clinton is: Do not assume that we will flinch, because we won't."[47]

And the Republicans did not flinch. They sent the president a bill to increase the debt ceiling temporarily, but it was adorned with provisions that were unacceptable to the president, and he vetoed it.[48] Artful but legal juggling of trust fund accounts by Treasury secretary Robert Rubin kept the government from defaulting on its financial obligations.

Avoiding default was not enough to keep the federal government operating, however. Annual appropriations bills are needed to pay for ongoing programs, personnel, and overhead in each major field of government. As noted, many of these bills had not been passed by the October 1 deadline. A short-term continuing resolution kept the federal government operating until mid-November, but the extension passed by Congress had more "poison pills" unacceptable to the president. When Clinton vetoed the continuing resolution, the first of two government shutdowns occurred on November 14, 1995. Days later Congress sent President Clinton the reconciliation bill described earlier. It contained the welfare reform and medicaid block grants, medicare reforms and cuts, sweeping tax cuts, and elimination of the Commerce Department. The president promptly vetoed the reconciliation bill as well. Only when he agreed to negotiate with the Congress on a balanced budget package on the Republicans' terms did Congress pass a new continuing resolution to reopen the government until December 15.

By this date no agreement had been reached. Those portions of the government operating without signed appropriations—including most or all of the departments of Commerce, Education, Labor, Interior, and Health and Human Services—were forced to close again. Employees were sent home without pay over Christmas, and the public was denied access to the federal services involved. During these protracted disputes over budget and reform issues, large portions of the federal government closed down two times for a total of nearly four weeks.

This outcome showed the vulnerability of the Republicans' budget strategy for enacting reforms. Unexpectedly (to congressional leaders), the president took the risk of negative public opinion by vetoing crucial funding bills and allowing the government to close down. He was vindicated politically when Republicans received most of the blame for causing the crisis.

This was a turning point in the Republicans' reform efforts. If the president could not be "blackmailed" into accepting their legislation by closing down the government, they lacked an alternate strategy for obtaining their policy goals. Accordingly, much of their agenda was defeated in this way. When the president vetoed the Republicans' reconciliation bill in November 1995, many of their policy goals came to a dead end. Proposals to reform and cut medicare, to create a medicaid block grant, to cut federal taxes, to eliminate the Department of Commerce, and to establish a law enforcement block grant were all killed by presidential vetoes (see table 12-2). Of the Republicans' major goals, only welfare reform legislation survived the legislative gauntlet after the great showdown of late 1995. As discussed in the following chapter, it gained enactment in the election-year atmosphere of July 1996. For conservatives, however, this victory was counterbalanced that summer by decidedly nonrevolutionary enactments, such as legislation to increase the federal minimum wage and to expand health care coverage and portability.[49]

THE OBSTACLE COURSE ON CAPITOL HILL. The dramatic conflict between the president and Congress did not tell the whole story of devolution's dismal fate in the 104th Congress. Many intergovernmental reforms in the initial House budget resolution never reached the president's desk. Some died a quiet death in authorizing committees; others were caught in struggles between the House and Senate. Similar difficulties encountered during the expansion of the federal government's role in the 1950s and 1960s led one earlier observer to liken the legislative process to an "obstacle course on Capitol Hill."[50] During the mid-1990s, a comparable struggle to shrink the federal government's role encountered similar institutional rigidities. Not even the extraordinary discipline and unity of congressional Republicans in the 104th Congress could overcome the manifold challenges of the legislative process.

In regulatory reform, only a handful of the Republicans' priorities survived the tortuous process. Bipartisan legislation on mandate reform legislation passed Congress, as did a moderate reform of the Safe Drinking Water Act. But for the core reforms of regulation in the Contract with America, it was a different story. A comprehensive regulatory reform bill (S. 343), sponsored by Senate Majority Leader Bob Dole of Kansas, was filibustered to death in the Senate. A sweeping moratorium on new federal regulations (H.R. 450) and a controversial relaxation of the Clean Water Act also died in the Senate. Major rewrites of the superfund program and the Endangered Species Act of 1973 failed to pass even in the House. Product liability and tort reform legislation made it through both

Table 12-2. *Disposition of Major Reform and Block Grant Proposals, 104th Congress*

Block grant reform proposals in house budget resolution	Actions by House and Senate	Final outcome
Welfare reform: Convert AFDC into TANF block grant (temporary assistance to needy families).	Passed by House and Senate; included in 1995 budget reconciliation bill sent to president.	Vetoed twice by president, amended version signed by president in July 1996 (P.L. 104-193).
Child care: Consolidate nine child care programs as part of welfare reform.	Passed by House and Senate; included in 1995 budget reconciliation bill sent to president.	Vetoed twice by president, amended version signed by president in July 1996 (P.L. 104-193).
Child protection and family services: Consolidate twenty-three programs as part of welfare reform.	Passed by House; rejected by Senate.	Dropped from final conference version of bill. Block grant provisions died in Congress.
Medicaid: Convert from an individual entitlement to a capped block grant to states.	Passed by House and Senate; included in 1995 budget reconciliation bill sent to president.	Vetoed by president. Not included in final welfare reform bill.
Food stamps: Optional block grant for states.	Passed by House and Senate; included in 1995 budget reconciliation bill sent to president.	Vetoed twice by president. Not included in final welfare reform bill.
Nutrition: Consolidate seven school and family nutrition programs into two block grants.	School nutrition block grant passed by House, opposed by Senate; optional, experimental block grant for seven states included in 1995 reconciliation bill sent to president.	Vetoed twice by president. Not included in final welfare reform bill.
Rural development: Consolidate five to seven rural development programs and terminate four others.	Senate Agriculture Appropriations bill consolidated eight rural programs. No comparable House provision. Senate receded on consolidation effort in appropriations bill.	Modest reorganization of rural development programs included in 1996 farm bill (P.L. 104-127).

(table continues)

Table 12-2 (continued)

Block grant reform proposals in house budget resolution	Actions by House and Senate	Final outcome
Job training: House budget resolution assumes consolidation of 64 to 100 programs into at least one job training block grant.	Different versions passed both House and Senate.	Bogged down in conference. Bills died in Congress.
Housing: Consolidate major public housing programs into one or more block grants.	House and Senate passed different versions. House bill contained two local housing block grants, Senate bill contained one.	No House-Senate conference. Bills died in Congress.
Justice assistance: Establish a block grant to replace categorical programs for community policing, drug courts, and local crime prevention programs.	House passed block grant in early 1995, but bill stalled in Senate. Block grant passed as part of fiscal 1996 Commerce, Justice, and State appropriations bill.	Appropriations bill including law enforcement block grant vetoed by president. Provision dropped from final continuing resolution.
Governors' Education block grant: Consolidates six modest education programs.	No action in either chamber.	Died in Congress. Some small education programs terminated.
Native American block grant.	No action in either chamber.	Died in Congress.
Eliminate Department of Commerce.	Passed by House and Senate. Included in 1995 reconciliation bill sent to president.	Vetoed by president.
Eliminate Department of Education.	Passed by House. Excluded from Senate Budget Resolution.	Never advanced to reconciliation. Provision died in Congress.
Eliminate Department of Energy.	Passed by House. Excluded from Senate budget resolution.	Never advanced to reconciliation. Provision died in Congress.

chambers of Congress only to be vetoed by the president. By the end of the 104th Congress, the conservative agenda for relaxing and reforming federal regulations lay in tatters.[51]

The fate of several block grants proposed by the new majority was much the same. The budget resolution passed by the House in May 1995 presumed that over a dozen new block grants would be created by authorizing committees in Congress. Yet one-third of them never made it to the Oval Office, where the president was ready to veto them. Congress took no significant action on proposed consolidations of education and Native American grant programs. In other areas, like job training and housing, conflicting block grant proposals were passed by the House and Senate. Strong political and policy differences between the two chambers kept them from agreeing on a common program and sending it on to the president.

Job Training: Fast Track to Nowhere

Congress's failure to reform federal job training programs was particularly significant, underscoring the difficulties of the legislative process even under favorable circumstances. Despite bipartisan support for consolidating a welter of training programs, Congress was unable to pass a new block grant. Although the House and Senate each passed a reform bill, differences between the two chambers, partisan and intergovernmental squabbles, and vociferous opposition from right-wing groups blocked passage of final legislation.

This outcome was unexpected. At the beginning of the 104th Congress, job training seemed to be on a fast track to success. There was widespread agreement on the need to reform and streamline existing programs. The General Accounting Office had identified 154 separate programs in the field of employment and training, and it argued that differences in the eligibility criteria of these multiple programs "hampered the delivery of services" to needy clients and made it "difficult for program staff to coordinate activities and share resources."[52] Accordingly, President Clinton's fiscal 1996 budget proposed consolidating seventy of these programs. In language similar to the GAO's, the president's budget stated that "existing [job training] programs have conflicting rules and administrative structures, confuse the people they are intended to help, add bureaucracy at every level, and waste taxpayer money."[53]

Not surprisingly, legislation for creating a new, more comprehensive job training block grant got off to a strong start in the 104th Congress. Passage of such legislation was assumed in the budget resolution adopted by Congress in 1995; the grant was expected to produce savings of 20 percent from existing spending levels in this area.[54] Committees in both the House and Senate held hearings and developed legislation to put this commitment into effect.

In May the House Opportunities Committee adopted a bill to consolidate more than one hundred job training and vocational education programs into four block grants to the states: for youth and education, adult training, vocational rehabilitation, and adult education. The bill passed with strong bipartisan support, although many Democrats were unhappy with the level of funding and the inclusion of vocational rehabilitation programs.[55] The bill (H.R. 1617) was passed by the full House in September 1995 by a vote of 345 to 79, after the House accepted a major modification.[56] A bipartisan amendment was adopted that removed vocational rehabilitation programs from the consolidation bill on grounds that disabled clients should not be forced into general purpose, "one-stop" career centers. With this change, the House bill created a total of three block grants, merging about one hundred remaining programs.

The Senate passed a bill that was quite different. It consolidated about ninety programs into a single block grant. The stated goal of the Workforce Development Act of 1995 (S. 143) was to enable each state to develop a single, unified system of job training and training-related education activities. Although there were disagreements about which programs to include and how much federal oversight to continue, the block grant concept enjoyed even stronger support in the Senate, where the bill passed by a vote of 95 to 2, than it had in the House.[57]

As the House and Senate moved to conference to reconcile their distinctive reform bills, prospects for success seemed unusually good. One journalist captured the climate of expectations with the following upbeat assessment: "In a display of amazing bipartisanship for these politically divisive times, the House and Senate—with the blessing of the Clinton Administration—have agreed to meld more than 80 disparate job training and vocational education programs into a system of block grants." But she raised a prophetic cautionary flag: "now comes the politically devilish task of negotiating the details."[58] That turned out to be far more difficult than the lopsided votes for passage suggested. As noted, the House and Senate bills melded different groups of programs into different block grant structures. The Clinton administration complicated things further, siding with the House in support of training vouchers and siding with the Senate on funding levels. Authorized funding levels in the House bill were $3 billion lower than in the Senate, and House appropriators proposed even deeper cuts. Many Democrats and the Clinton administration insisted that higher levels be provided.

Other differences among the conferees reflected interests outside of Congress. As often occurs on block grant legislation, governors, state legislatures, mayors, and state education agencies were divided over who should control the funds at the state level and how much money should be earmarked for particular uses. In a new twist to the block grant story, some external conservative groups—which normally support the block grant concept—became vocal opponents of the legislation, lobbying conservative members of Congress to follow suit. Prominent groups, including Phyllis Schlafly's "Eagle Forum" and the Family Research Council, were concerned that federal performance standards and school-to-work provisions would amount to hidden federal control of local education.

In truth, none of these issues was beyond compromise, and none should have doomed the bill. But they seriously slowed the legislation's progress, bottling it up in conference committee for months. A compromise bill was not reported out of conference until the summer of 1996, well into the season of partisan electoral politics. By this point, too many participants were using the bill to score political points rather than to secure legislative change. Prospects for passage had faded. Labor secretary Robert Reich complained that the bill had been "kidnapped by the extreme right," while Senator Nancy Kassebaum accused Democrats of wanting to "protect the status quo."[59] With time running out and accusations flying, the revised bill was deemed too controversial to bring up for final consideration in the 104th Congress.

The sad end of the job training block grant illustrates the pitfalls and obstacles of the legislative process. Even a reform with powerful momentum succumbed to the overheated political climate of the 104th Congress. Many supporters of reform were sorely disappointed. As one Republican aide said,

> Employment and training shows the difficulties of the process. It was the most important one [to fail]. There is a ton of money and over 100 programs, so if conservatives wanted to judge whether there has been a revolution, you could point to that. You are ending over 100

programs! It looked like a done deal. God, I was so excited! Then it hit a huge roadblock by the name of Phyllis Schlafly.[60]

A long-time Democratic staffer agreed it was an opportunity lost: "The ironical thing is that of all the block grants [the Republicans proposed], this is the one they could have had. Unfortunately, they screwed up."[61]

Conclusion

What became of the "devolution revolution?" Certainly, legislative outcomes in the 104th Congress did not live up to the proponents' initial expectations. Hopes for consolidating hundreds of large and small federal programs were dashed when Congress failed to pass, or the president refused to sign, proposed block grants for medicaid, food stamps, employment and training, housing, law enforcement, and other functions. No federal departments were eliminated, and many programs and agencies criticized by conservative opponents survived. By the end of 1996, the National Endowment for the Arts, the Corporation for Public Broadcasting, the Appalachian Regional Commission, and the Economic Development Agency still lived, albeit somewhat shrunken and battered.

Conservatives lost political momentum as well. They had misinterpreted the results of the 1994 elections, believing that the public at large shared in their overweening hostility to governmental activism. Yet even in early 1995, when opinion polls showed strong support for many conservative policies, cautionary signs of public ambivalence could be detected. For example, a survey by the Luntz group in January 1995 showed that most Americans believed the federal budget could be balanced painlessly by cutting "waste." When Congress tried to accomplish this objective by restraining the growth and benefit levels of medicare, medicaid, nutrition assistance, and other popular programs, the negative public reaction surprised only the self-styled "revolutionaries." In the end Republicans were forced to support some very unrevolutionary programs. Hoping to retain political control of the House in the 1996 elections, the Republican Congress raised the minimum wage, expanded health care portability, and increased spending on education.

The majority party, however, did accomplish some of its objectives: more than 200 small programs, projects, and agencies were terminated, a major welfare reform package was enacted, procedural restraints were placed

Figure 12-1. *Real Federal Spending, Fiscal Years 1962–96*
Billions of constant 1992 dollars

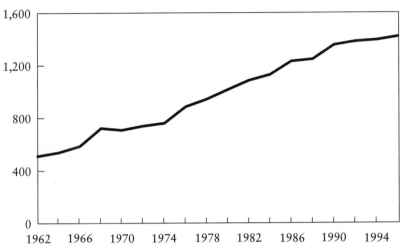

Source: *Budget of the United States Government, Historical Tables, Fiscal Year 1998*, table 8.2.

Figure 12-2. *Federal Domestic Discretionary Spending, Fiscal Years 1962–96*
Billions of dollars

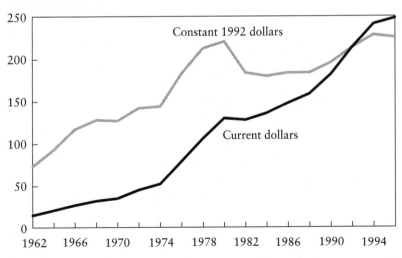

Source: *Budget of the United States Government, Historical Tables, Fiscal Year 1998*, tables 8.7, 8.8.

on the adoption of new federal mandates, and the tenor of political debate was altered. Federal spending was restrained, although accomplishments on the fiscal front again fell short of initial goals, underscoring the complex legacy of the 104th Congress.

Figure 12-1 shows trends in overall federal spending in constant dollars from 1962 to 1996. Although the growth rate of real federal spending was greatly slowed in the 1990s, the Republican Congress did not succeed in reducing total federal spending. This was entirely the result of spending on entitlement programs. Federal discretionary outlays were reduced— from $546 billion in fiscal 1995 to $534 billion in fiscal 1996.[62] This was the first absolute decline in federal discretionary spending in twenty-five years.[63] The overall decline in discretionary spending was exaggerated, however, by ongoing reductions in defense spending. When one looks only at nondefense discretionary spending, the picture is less dramatic.

In current dollars, nondefense discretionary outlays declined only $1.9 billion between fiscal 1995 and fiscal 1996. The decline in constant dollars was larger, falling from $233 to $225 billion over this period. But the results were hardly revolutionary. As figure 12-2 shows, a much steeper decline in real discretionary spending occurred in the early Reagan years. As the following chapter attests, a case can be made for evolutionary devolution in the 104th Congress. The revolution was still on hold.

CHAPTER 13

Evolutionary Devolution:
The Saga of Mandates
and Welfare Reform

T HE TWO MOST significant intergovernmental enactments of the 104th Congress were the Unfunded Mandates Reform Act of 1995 (UMRA) and the Personal Responsibility and Work Opportunity Reconciliation Act of 1996 (welfare reform). The first was a relatively simple procedural reform; the second was a lengthy, complex bill that fundamentally altered the nation's social contract. The two bills were distinctive politically as well as substantively. The mandates reform act—one of the first enactments of the Republican Congress—was passed with unusual speed. Moreover, it was adopted by overwhelming majorities in both houses of Congress and quickly signed by the president. Passage of welfare reform, on the other hand, remained in doubt until very late in the 104th Congress. Twice vetoed by President Clinton, the bill was ensnared in high stakes politics until the bitter end, as many of the president's allies lobbied for a veto on the third try as well. Overwhelming majorities of House Democrats voted against welfare reform bills on each occasion.

Beneath the surface, however, these two reforms also had important similarities. Both were present on the political agenda before the Republican revolution, and versions of each might have passed in the 104th Congress even if the Democrats had retained control. The mandates act came close to passage in the prior Congress, and welfare reform had powerful momentum. The president was on record in support of both concepts—although his efforts to pass each reform were often tepid—and he had introduced his own welfare bill in 1994.

From an intergovernmental standpoint, these two reforms shared a substantive similarity as well. Both were evolutionary in their impacts on the intergovernmental system. UMRA was explicitly so, comprising one of the milder approaches available for dealing with the mandate issue. The Personal Responsibility and Work Act affected the clients and structure of the welfare system more dramatically, but its devolutionary thrust was heavily compromised in passage. Although it gave states new flexibility over many aspects of welfare eligibility, funding, and services, it imposed strict new mandates in many other areas. Whatever its pros or cons as social policy, it was, at best, a halting move toward devolution that did little to change the intergovernmental system as a whole.

The Unfunded Mandates Reform Act

The Unfunded Mandates Reform Act (P.L. 104-4) marked an important event in the history of regulatory federalism. Among other things, this legislation created new procedures in Congress to restrict the enactment of future unfunded mandates; it required that additional information about the projected costs of proposed regulatory statutes and agency require-ments be provided before congressional and executive agency action; and it restricted the implementation of unfunded or underfunded regulatory requirements.

The politics of the new law may have been more noteworthy than its substance. For the first time state and local government officials made issues of federal regulation—rather than federal aid subsidies—their top priority in Washington. They organized a concerted political campaign against intergovernmental regulations, which was capped by "National Unfunded Mandates (NUM) Day" in October 1993. They worked closely with Democrats and Republicans in Congress throughout 1994 to de-velop mandate relief legislation. When that effort fell short, they were well positioned to take advantage of Republican gains in the 1994 con-gressional elections. By the time the 104th Congress convened on January 4, 1995, mandate reform had become the first legislative priority of the Senate and a key provision of the Contract with America in the House.

Mandates on the Public Agenda

The era of regulatory federalism had its origins in the 1960s, when Con-gress began to develop new regulatory instruments to supplement prolif-erating grant-in-aid programs. In legislation ranging from the Civil Rights

Figure 13-1. *The Changing Mix of Intergovernmental Grants and Regulations, 1951–90*
Percent of all major intergovernmental enactments

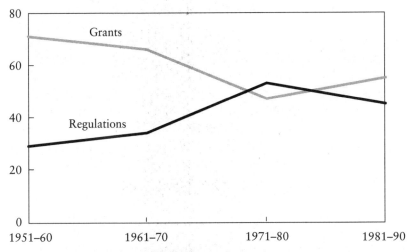

Source: Author's tabulations derived from David R. Mayhew, *Divided We Govern: Party Control, Lawmaking, and Investigations, 1946–1990* (Yale University Press, 1991), table 4.1.

Act of 1964 to the Wholesome Meat Act of 1967, the federal government established new and more intrusive regulatory relationships with state and local governments.[1] As seen in chapter 5, this trend did not end with the passing of the Great Society. The pace of intergovernmental regulatory enactments accelerated during the 1970s, with programs like the Clean Air Act Amendments of 1970 and the Education for All Handicapped Children Act of 1975. Moreover, such regulatory statutes encompassed a greater share of all intergovernmental legislation in the 1970s. If one looks only at "major" intergovernmental laws enacted between 1951 and 1990, the number of regulatory statutes surpassed the number of new spending programs during the 1970s (see figure 13-1).[2]

The widely publicized deregulation initiatives of the early 1980s did not halt Washington's affinity for passing new federal mandates. New laws during the Reagan-Bush years mandated national standards for alcohol consumption, underground storage tanks, and trucking standards, required the removal of asbestos from local schools, and tightened the restrictions of the Clean Air and Safe Drinking Water acts. By the close of the 1980s, the number of major new intergovernmental regulatory provisions enacted during the decade surpassed that of any previous period.[3]

The costs of federal mandates escalated with their numbers. New rules promulgated between 1983 and 1992 cost state and local governments at least $10.85 billion, and this does not include costly requirements adopted before or after this period.[4] Looking solely at environmental regulations imposed since 1970, the EPA estimated that compliance with federal pollution requirements cost local governments $19 billion in 1987, and this was projected to rise to $32 billion by the year 2000.[5] "Federal mandates are putting a stranglehold on state budgets," maintained the head of the National Association of State Legislatures (NCSL) during the early 1990s, when recession choked off state and local revenues as the bills were coming due for recently enacted health, environment, and handicapped requirements.[6]

Such complaints gave rise to growing state and local efforts to resist new mandates. Between 1991 and 1993, jurisdictions in many states began to assess the costs of local mandate impacts and to protest the growing burden of federal requirements.[7] In addition to these independent efforts, action was taken by national associations of state and local governments. The most influential of these initiatives was the National Unfunded Mandates (NUM) Day initiative in 1993 sponsored by the U.S. Conference of Mayors and National Association of Counties. More than 300 cities and 128 counties participated in a nationwide effort to measure the costs imposed by major federal regulations. Jurisdictions submitted self-assessments of local mandate impacts, which were compiled by the accounting firm of Price-Waterhouse. When extrapolated to all other jurisdictions, the studies estimated that mandates imposed additional costs of $6.5 billion *annually* for cities and $4.8 billion for counties.[8]

The NUM Day methodology was flawed by the absence of any independent verification of local submissions and a nonrandom sample of participating jurisdictions.[9] From a political perspective, however, NUM day served its intended purpose. For the first time the topic of federal mandating was raised from the specialized discourse of the intergovernmental community and placed upon the broader public agenda. As figure 13-2 shows, there was an explosion of media attention devoted to unfunded mandates leading up to and following NUM Day. The number of newspaper articles discussing "unfunded federal mandates" jumped from 22 in 1992 to 836 in 1994—providing a classic illustration of Anthony Downs's "issue attention cycle."[10]

Figure 13-2. *Salience of Unfunded Federal Mandates in the Press, 1989–94*

Number of newspaper articles

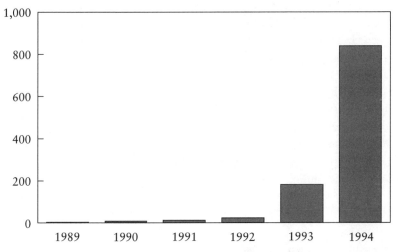

Source: These data were produced by searching the newspaper database of Nexis for the words "unfunded federal mandates" and "unfunded mandates." As mandate reform legislation was being debated in Congress in 1995, the number of stories rose to 1,050 in just the first two months of the year.

Too Little, Too Late in the 103d Congress

Following the tremendous response to NUM Day, some local officials sought to make mandate reform a political litmus test for the 1994 congressional elections. As the president of the U.S. Conference of Mayors put it: "Some mayors will tell you that it's the penultimate issue, and they won't support a candidate if he comes down the wrong way on it."[11] That perspective was not universally shared, but it was sufficiently widespread to transform intergovernmental politics. For the first time federal *regulations* rather than federal *spending* became the preeminent intergovernmental issue for many state and local officials and their national associations. Although the political influence of these officials had diminished with the decline of party conventions and other changes in the electoral system, the public interest groups could still exert considerable influence on mandate legislation when they were active and united.[12] And they were united against mandates to a degree that had "never, ever happened before," according to the National League of Cities chief lobbyist.[13]

The broad and insistent intergovernmental coalition now demanding mandate relief had its intended impact on the Congress. Thirty-two mandate relief bills were introduced in just the first session of the 103d Congress, including nine bills that required some form of federal reimbursement. Even more important, two of these bills were cosponsored by a majority of members in their respective chambers: S. 993, introduced by Senator Dirk Kempthorne, a Republican from Idaho, where he had been the mayor of Boise; and H.R. 140, sponsored by Representative Gary Condit, a Democrat from California.

Momentum developed fastest in the Senate, where the issue was championed by freshman senator Kempthorne. On May 20, 1993, he introduced the Community Regulatory Relief Act, a brief, five-page bill that advanced a "no money, no mandate" approach to mandate reform. It specified that

> a statute or regulation that requires a State or local government to (A) take certain actions . . . or (B) comply with certain specified conditions in order to receive . . . federal assistance . . . shall apply . . . only if all funds necessary to pay the direct costs incurred . . . are provided.

This was one of the more extreme responses to the mandate problem to be advocated in Congress, but Senator Kempthorne combined it with a pragmatic negotiating posture. He wanted to enact a bill, not just strike a pose. As his administrative assistant put it:

> As a freshman who was number 99 in seniority, Sen. Kempthorne needed a simple message to draw attention to what he considered the most important issue he had faced as a mayor—and to get a seat at the [legislative] table. The pressures to go partisan with this were very acute. We were pushed to get a vote and go down to defeat. But we wanted to solve a problem, and we knew our original bill had a fatal flaw. We could not develop how it was supposed to work on our own.[14]

This attitude was welcomed by John Glenn of Ohio, the chairman of the Senate Governmental Affairs Committee with jurisdiction over most mandate reform legislation. According to one of his committee aides, Glenn was feeling "enormous grassroots pressure" to cooperate on this issue because local governments in Ohio—led by the city of Columbus—had been in the vanguard of the antimandates movement. Moreover, Glenn knew that the issue was popular in the Senate, where Kempthorne's bill had fifty-three cosponsors, and that President Clinton favored some type of mandate reform legislation.

Glenn held hearings on the subject in November 1993, shortly after NUM Day, and then commenced negotiations with Kempthorne on a compromise bill. Several thorny issues had to be resolved to turn Kempthorne's skeletal bill into a viable solution. The legislation required a more precise definition of federal mandates—particularly a way to deal with onerous grant conditions in programs like medicaid. Many senators were also concerned about creating a mandatory funding requirement in an era of large federal deficits. As the bill currently stood, even guarantees of basic civil rights would not apply unless they were accompanied by federal funding. Thus most Democrats wanted an escape clause from the mandatory funding provision. Finally, it was clear to all that the legislation needed a workable enforcement mechanism.

After lengthy negotiations with state and local interest groups and representatives of the Clinton administration, Senators Glenn and Kempthorne produced a compromise bill. It was offered as a substitute to the original S. 993 and adopted, with mostly modest amendments, by the Governmental Affairs Committee. The substitute established a new definition of "federal intergovernmental mandate" that explicitly exempted civil rights, accounting, and auditing requirements and applied to grant conditions only in large entitlement programs providing at least $500 million annually to state and local governments.[15] For enforcement purposes, the substitute developed a new point-of-order mechanism in the Senate that could be used to block future unfunded mandates. In general, bills containing intergovernmental mandates could no longer be considered on the Senate floor unless they were accompanied by a cost estimation report from the Congressional Budget Office (CBO). Intergovernmental mandates with estimated direct costs above $50 million annually would have to be accompanied by an authorization for funding, although this provision could be waived by a majority vote of the Senate. After adopting a major amendment requiring CBO to produce comparable regulatory cost estimates for "private sector mandates" over $200 million, the committee passed S. 993 by a unanimous voice vote on June 16, 1994. Progress on a mandate reform bill in the House was much more grudging. There was broad and growing support for Representative Condit's "no money, no mandate" bill, which by August 1994 was cosponsored by more than one-half of all House members.[16] On August 11 the House Intergovernmental Affairs Subcommittee approved a companion bill to S. 993, and the chairman of the full Governmental Operations Committee, Representative John Conyers, Democrat of Michigan, promised further action. But there was strong resistance in the House from powerful senior members. The chairmen of many other House committees and subcommittees, as well as the Democratic leadership, viewed the mandate reform legislation as a direct threat to their policy agenda and institutional prerogatives. If the mandates legislation were to pass, warned Representative Henry Waxman (Democrat of California), "we could no longer pass essential laws to address urgent social problems or to protect human health and the environment."[17] Coalitions of environmental, health, and safety groups also opposed the mandates legislation.[18]

With liberals waging a rearguard battle to block the legislation in the House, last-minute efforts to move the bill proved to be too little, too late. The legislation's chief advocate in the House, Representative Condit, launched a discharge petition drive to try to force his bill out of committee. Responding to this threat, the House Government Operations Committee approved an alternative bill, H.R. 5128 (a slightly modified companion to the Glenn-Kempthorne bill) on October 5, 1994. Perhaps by design, this was too late in the session to proceed. Congress adjourned before the bill could move to the floor.

In the Senate, after weeks of wrangling over health care reform and Republican filibusters on other bills coming to the floor, members voted 88 to 0 to consider S. 993 on October 6. Because it was "one of the last trains leaving the station," however, members began offering nongermane amendments in a last-ditch effort to get them passed.[19] As a result (or, some claimed, as an excuse), Majority Leader George Mitchell of Maine pulled the bill off the floor, and it was allowed to die.

Success in the 104th Congress

On November 8, 1994, Republicans gained control of the House and Senate for the first time in forty years. Overnight the prospects for quickly enacting mandate reform legislation improved dramatically. After being treated like an awkward stepchild by the Democratic 103d Congress, mandate reform was heartily embraced by the Republican 104th. It became the number one legislative priority of the Senate and a key provision of the House Republicans' Contract with America.

This sudden change in fortunes confronted supporters of the legislation with a strategic decision. Should they go back and rewrite the legislation to make it stronger, or should they take advantage of the bill in hand and rush it through the open window of opportunity? Sentiment for taking the first course was strongest in the House.[20] The compromise bill in the 103d Congress had been fashioned mainly by the Senate, and it was designed in part to accommodate a defeated power structure that was no longer in control. Moreover, the mandate reform provision in the Contract with America—while generally patterned after S. 993—contained a new and powerful provision termed the "agency backstop." This provision was intended to limit agency implementation of mandates that lacked full funding by Congress.[21]

A radical redesign of unfunded mandates legislation was rejected, however, after active negotiations among key actors in the new Republican Congress and representatives of major interest groups representing state and local governments. This outcome was partly determined by technical and legal obstacles to designing a stronger bill. A full-fledged agency backstop provision would delegate tremendous policy discretion to agency officials and would likely engender a constitutional challenge. Moreover, a viable reimbursement program would be extraordinarily difficult to design, given widely varying fiscal and accounting systems at the state and local levels and the difficulties of accurately measuring mandated costs. Above all, however, the incremental strategy was dictated by the politics of the Senate, where the issue of mandate reform had suddenly become linked to larger fiscal and political goals.

The balanced budget amendment was considered by all parties at the time to be the linchpin of the Republican party's domestic agenda. Yet after the election in November, Republican governors warned that the amendment would not be ratified by the states unless it was joined to mandate reform. As one put it, "if you don't get rid of the mandates, it's not going to happen."[22] The governors feared that Congress would seek to balance the federal budget by imposing costly new mandates on the states. Thus the strategy of Republican leaders, especially in the Senate, was to pass quickly a mandates reform bill and then turn immediately to the balanced budget amendment. Since Democrats were seriously threatening to filibuster a much stronger bill, and since state and local officials had supported the Glenn-Kempthorne bill in the past, that became the logical vehicle.

SENATE STRATEGY. To underscore the new priority given to mandate reform, the prospective majority leader—Senator Bob Dole of Kansas—agreed to designate the revised Kempthorne-Glenn bill S. 1. The plan was to rush a little changed and uncontroversial S. 1 through the Senate in the first week of legislative business, and then have an identical bill passed by the House and sent to the president. The Senate would then promptly move on to the budget amendment.

It was a sensible strategy, but the best-laid plans can be thwarted by the rules and ancient folkways of the Senate, as generations of doleful legislators have learned. On its way to swift and easy passage, the mandates bill got caught for several weeks in what came to be known as "Byrdlock." The dean of Senate Democrats, Senator Robert Byrd of West Virginia, objected to the lack of careful deliberation. He organized delay and filibuster tactics that prevented passage of the mandates bill—or virtually anything else—until the end of January.

Things began well enough. Senator Kempthorne introduced his bill on the opening day of the new Congress, and the Governmental Affairs Committee held hearings on it the next day. The bill reached the Senate floor the following week. That is when Byrd began to object:

> Senate Rules require . . . a report to be available for 48 hours before proceeding with a bill. You simply say that you are not going to file a report. Then you proceed to the bill . . . the next day. . . . Why all this hurry? Why all the rush? It is the 17th day of January. We have 11 months and 14 days to go yet this year.[23]

Although Senator Byrd was no fan of the mandates bill, he, like Dole, had bigger fish to fry. As one reporter observed, Byrd "has served notice that he has a broader goal—to keep Republicans from 'jamming and ramming' their whole legislative program through the Senate."[24] The former chairman of the Senate Appropriations Committee was an implacable foe of the balanced budget amendment and the line-item veto, which he believed would radically reduce the power of Congress. By holding up the mandates bill, he hoped to rally Democratic opposition to these broader issues.

Thanks in large part to Byrd's admonition that his party "show some guts," Democrats resisted efforts to cut off debate on S. 1.[25] Instead, they proposed a slew of amendments—forty-four in all—to allow state and local governments to tax out-of-state mail order sales, to require reports concerning the effects of mandates on homeless children, and so on. Although some amendments were proposed by Republicans, Majority Leader Dole complained that Democrats were "cleaning out their wastebaskets trying to find amendments."[26] In response, Republicans showed remarkable party unity, voting unanimously on amendments in thirty-nine of the forty-four votes.[27] In twenty-six cases a majority of Democrats opposed the Republican phalanx but to little effect. On January 27, after more than two weeks of debate, a little changed S.1 was passed by the Senate on a vote of 86 to 10. Although only a handful of Democrats opposed the bill on final passage, the subsequent failure of the balanced budget amendment appeared to vindicate Byrd's larger strategy.

A HOUSE DIVIDED. Even with its more streamlined rules of procedure, the House was unable to pass mandate reform legislation without surprising delays as well. H.R. 5, the House companion to S. 1, was reported by the newly named Government Reform and Oversight Committee without hearings and rushed to the floor in hopes that it might be passed before President Clinton's State of the Union address. But when House debate began on January 20, the legislation faced a mountain of amendments. Hoping to put Republicans on the record, Democrats demanded roll-call votes on amendments to exempt dozens of activities from the mandates bill, including disposal of nuclear waste, child support enforcement, and health care for the disabled.

Because of the slow pace, Republicans were forced to temporarily pull their bill from the floor in order to pass the balanced budget amendment. Then on February 1, 1995, after defeating scores of mostly Democratic amendments to the mandate reform legislation, Republicans won passage of H.R. 5 by a vote of 360 to 74.

Despite the temporary delays, passage marked a dramatic change in fortunes for a bill that had been throttled in the previous Congress. The change from Democratic to Republican control of the House was the overriding factor in this change, as the leadership went from bottling up the bill to pushing it aggressively. Moreover, the Republicans' discipline in voting on the bill and amendments to it was extraordinary. The party was virtually unanimous on vote after vote, breaking ranks only on an amendment to substantially strengthen the bill.

Democrats, on the other hand, demonstrated sharp divisions on many issues during the debate. Sixty-five percent voted for final passage of the mandate reform bill, but on many amendments a majority of Democrats voted to weaken the bill. Research indicates that ideology was the most important correlate of Democratic voting on the mandate bill.[28] Conservative Democrats repeatedly voted to support mandate reform, while liberal Democrats were the most consistent supporters of efforts to weaken the mandate reform act—a response that is unsurprising given the origins of many of the environmental, health, and safety laws that could be affected by the new law.

CONFERENCE COMMITTEE ACTION. The original legislative strategy called for the House to pass a bill identical to the Senate's. This would avoid the need for a conference committee and allow the bill to be sent directly to the president's desk. Nothing in the saga of P.L. 104-4 could be so simple, however. The House bill was different—and "tougher"—than S. 1 in two key respects. First, H.R. 5 permitted judicial review of federal agency performance under the act. This meant that outside parties could challenge agencies' cost-benefit analyses in federal court. The Senate bill specifically precluded this, since Senate Democrats believed that this could tie up regulations in the courts for years. Senator Glenn threatened to kill the bill unless this House provision was removed.

For their part, House conservatives were skeptical of the "Byrd amendment" in the Senate bill. The amendment attempted to deal with the problem of inadequate appropriations for a mandate. If an agency estimated that a mandate was underfunded, the Byrd amendment required that the agency come back to Congress for more guidance in an expedited process. Byrd maintained that he was trying to ensure that Congress, rather than an agency, retained responsibility for setting policy. House Republicans were understandably concerned about his motives.

The House and Senate differences proved difficult to reconcile. As the disputes dragged on for over a month, participants began to fear a deadlock. "There were times in conference when I thought it was all over," one participant confessed. But such prospects always concentrate the mind, and in classic conference style a compromise was found. A limited form of judicial review was permitted in the conference bill. Under the agreement, courts could consider whether an appropriate analysis of mandate costs was done, but they could not second guess its quality. The Byrd amendment was accepted by the House as members came to believe that it improved the bill.

For once, the rest proved easy. The Senate passed the conference report on March 15, 1995, by a vote of 91 to 9. The House approved it the next day by an equally overwhelming vote of 394 to 28.

Unfunded Mandates Reform and the Future of Regulatory Federalism

The Unfunded Mandates Reform Act of 1995 was a victory for the intergovernmental lobby and an important legislative product of the 104th Congress. Was it also a bill that "ma[de] history," as President Clinton declared when he signed it?[29] Or was the president's description a mere flourish of Rose Garden rhetoric? The implementation of P.L. 104-4 to date sends conflicting signals about the legislation's long-term significance.

The law does make it somewhat harder to enact direct order mandates and selected conditions of aid in the future. The legislation's point-of-order procedures allow individual members of Congress to block consideration of unfunded or underfunded mandates unless the funding requirement is specifically waived by a majority of the House or Senate. Moreover, Congress began receiving better information about the estimated fiscal costs of proposed requirements. To comply with the law, the Congressional Budget Office expanded its staff resources for preparing mandate cost estimates and developed a more sophisticated data-gathering network at the state and local levels. Finally, federal agencies were constrained from carrying out underfunded mandates without clear congressional sanction (see box 13-1).

These new procedures and resources were put into effect in the 104th Congress. According to one CBO analyst, the agency prepared cost estimates for about 900 bills and amendments during the act's first twenty months of operation, and about 10 percent of these identified mandates.[30] Only twelve of the estimates found mandates in legislation with direct costs over the $50 million threshold set by the law, which allowed the point-of-order procedures to come into effect. Half of these involved different bills dealing with the same issue: raising the national minimum wage. About 100 other bills for which estimates were prepared imposed "other" costs on state and local governments, primarily new grant conditions that were not defined as mandates in the legislation.

Did the new congressional rules and information have any influence over the content of actual legislation? The early evidence indicates that it did. Three major bills were modified in 1996 to avoid having a point of order raised that might block or complicate consideration on the floor.[31] Most congressional observers agree that the mandate reform bill had the biggest impact on telecommunications legislation. Different versions of the Telecommunications Reform Act of 1996 passed by the House and Senate before UMRA took effect prohibited state and local governments

Box 13-1. *Highlights of the Unfunded Mandates Reform Act of 1995*

Legislative accountability and reform

Defines federal intergovernmental mandates as legislation or regulations that impose a legally binding duty on state, local, or tribal governments. Exempts mandates that protect civil rights, provide disaster relief, are designated as emergency legislation, or are related to social security programs.

Congressional authorizing committees must submit mandate bills to the Congressional Budget Office (CBO) for an estimate of the mandate's costs. CBO must estimate and report the effects of any intergovernmental mandate that would cost $50 million or more and private sector mandates above $100 million.

Any House or Senate member can raise a point of order against a new congressional action that contains an intergovernmental mandate without a CBO cost estimate, or one that exceeds the $50 million threshold, unless the mandate is fully funded. The full funding requirement can be waived by a majority vote of the House or Senate.

Points of order against reauthorizations are allowed in cases of decreasing financial assistance for existing mandates or increasing costs without additional federal money.

Regulatory accountability and reform

Federal agencies must determine whether they have sufficient funds to carry out a federal mandate and propose alternatives to the Congress if funds are insufficient. If the Congress does not act within sixty days, the mandate is unenforceable.

Federal agencies must consult with states and localities before imposing mandates.

Federal agencies must adopt the least burdensome rules and regulations or publish an explanation of why they did not.

Review of federal mandates

ACIR is required to report on the role of federal mandates and their effects, make recommendations on easing the burden of mandates, and report annually to the Congress.

Judicial review

Judicial review is limited to allowing courts to compel agencies to conduct required cost-benefit analyses; standing to sue is limited to 180 days after publication of a rule.

Source: Timothy J. Conlan, James D. Riggle, and Donna E. Schwartz, "Deregulating Federalism? The Politics of Mandate Reform in the 104th Congress," *Publius,* vol. 25 (Summer 1995), p. 40.

from imposing taxes and license fees on communications companies and exempted the siting of certain telecommunications facilities from local zoning authority. As a result of UMRA, both provisions were modified before the conference bill was brought to the floor. Other major bills that were modified in similar ways included immigration reform legislation, securities reform legislation, mental health care amendments to the Health Care Portability Act, and the Safe Drinking Water Act Amendments of 1996.[32]

Still, obituaries for the era of regulatory federalism would be premature. The Unfunded Mandates Reform Act did not impose a total ban on federal mandating: important escape clauses remained. Either implicitly or explicitly, the act excluded many intergovernmental mandates from coverage, including protections for civil rights—including the Americans with Disabilities Act; federal accounting and auditing requirements; most conditions attached to federal aid; federal restrictions that impose nonfinancial costs on state and local governments, or costs that fall below the $50 million threshold; and existing federal mandates.

Some of the UMRA-induced legislative modifications mentioned above simply took advantage of these exclusions. In the case of immigration reform, for example, states were given more time to comply with the bill's requirement that all state drivers' licenses be altered to include social security numbers. This allowed the annual costs of state compliance to fall below the $50 million threshold of the mandates act. Similarly, some of the new requirements added to the Safe Drinking Water Amendments were simply converted from direct orders to conditions of aid.

In spite of UMRA, the 104th Congress adopted several significant new mandates. Its first deficit reduction initiative—H.R. 1158, the Fiscal 1995 Appropriations Rescission Act—cut $1.3 billion in previously appropriated federal wastewater treatment grants, a clear violation of the spirit if not the letter of the mandate reform act.[33] Other mandates adopted by Congress in 1996 and 1997 included increases in the federal minimum wage, estimated to cost state and local governments $1.3 billion over five years; mandated expansions of state medicaid coverage, and several of the modified reform bills mentioned earlier. Even some of the block grants proposed in the 104th Congress contained new federal policy directives, although they also tended to provide states with greater flexibility in other respects. For example, the new welfare reform law restricts states' ability to determine the length of welfare eligibility, places stringent and costly demands on states for putting welfare recipients to work, and requires states to take additional actions to determine the welfare eligibility of legal immigrants. Finally, in the case of child support, the new welfare law:

commandeer[s] state laws and bureaucracies to achieve national child support goals. States are essentially directed to track new hires by employers, match them against parents with child support orders, and then obtain and process withholdings of support payments from employers. Moreover, states are required to suspend driver's and other occupational licenses of individuals overdue in support payments.[34]

In short, congressional mandating and preemption continued in the conservative 104th Congress just as it did during the Reagan years of the 1980s. As Paul Posner observed in the wake of UMRA, "the march of mandates continues."[35]

To explain this march, Posner examined congressional roll-call votes on mandate-related issues in the second session of the 104th Congress. He found forty-two roll-call votes involving mandate or preemption issues and discovered that both Republicans and Democrats voted in support of new mandates or preemptions more than 50 percent of the time. The types of mandate that each party tended to support were quite different, however: "Republicans supported mandates to achieve national welfare, moral policy, immigration and business preemption goals. Democrats . . . supported mandates to [advance] the party's labor and housing agendas."[36]

In sum, the Unfunded Mandates Reform Act in the early stages of implementation appeared to influence congressional behavior. The new law deterred Congress from mandating in a handful of instances and prompted it to modify its behavior in others. But Congress's propensity for mandating remained strong in the Republican Congress as it had in prior Democratic Congresses. The policy aims had changed, but the instruments had remained the same. If a revolution occurs in intergovernmental relations, it will not be as a result of UMRA.

Welfare Reform

Until 1996 few policy goals seemed more elusive in the preceding thirty years than enacting comprehensive welfare reform. Virtually every president since Richard Nixon had made reforming the nation's welfare system an important part of his policy agenda at one time or another. All had failed.[37] These reform proposals had important implications for the intergovernmental system, as well as for the millions of people who were directly dependent on them.

The principal welfare program of the modern era—aid to families with dependent children (AFDC)—was one of the oldest federal aid programs, while medicaid, the principal program of health care for the poor, was the largest grant program by far. Altering either could affect the entire intergovernmental system, which is why welfare reform was often integrated into the broader federalism reform initiatives examined in this book.

As federalism reform evolved from the 1970s to the 1990s, so did the definition of what it meant to "reform" welfare. In Nixon's family assistance plan, welfare reform meant in part the creation of a uniform, minimum national standard of welfare support, which stood in stark contrast to the decentralizing features of revenue sharing and block grants in Nixon's program. In Ronald Reagan's 1982 sorting out proposal, welfare reform meant devolving the program entirely to the states in exchange for federal assumption of medicaid. Before and after Reagan, Presidents Jimmy Carter and Bill Clinton had proposed stand-alone reform plans of their own.

One of the few things all of these plans had in common was their failure to be enacted. Although the idea of "reforming welfare" was immensely popular, putting the concept into practice raised so many complicated issues and encountered so many policy "traps" between conflicting objectives that legislation failed in the legislative arena time after time.[38] During 1995 and much of 1996, it appeared likely that this dismal history would repeat itself. Once again a bold plan to redefine the contours of American federalism encompassed major changes in the structure and financing of federal assistance to the poor. And once again it appeared that the plan would fall short of enactment, having confronted two presidential vetoes and persistent Democratic opposition.

Thus it was a notable accomplishment of the 104th Congress when, on August 12, 1996, President Clinton signed a long awaited and hotly debated welfare reform bill: the Personal Responsibility and Work Opportunity Reconciliation Act of 1995. Although the bill's chief House sponsor, Florida Republican Clay Shaw, exaggerated when he called it "the most important piece of legislation to come out of Congress this century except for declarations of war," the legislation was, by all accounts, landmark legislation.[39] It converted the principal federal welfare program from an open-ended entitlement to a capped block grant, temporary assistance to needy families (TANF); it altered the terms of eligibility for recipients, establishing a lifetime limit on benefits of five years and a limit of two years at any one time; and it cut dramatically the welfare benefits available to legal immigrants and their families.

From the standpoint of welfare policy, these were very significant changes. From a devolutionary perspective, however, the act's accomplishments were mixed. The TANF block grant structure gave states new flexibility in defining who would be eligible for cash welfare benefits, the level and form of those benefits, the structure of related work and training programs, application procedures, and many other administrative issues. The act also eliminated state matching requirements and gave states more flexibility to transfer funds between cash support, child care, and work preparation programs. Yet the welfare law contained new federal mandates governing the maximum length of federally supported welfare benefits, stringent targets for placing welfare recipients in jobs, and intrusive child support enforcement procedures. Moreover, provisions in earlier reform proposals that would have maximized the states' flexibility and policy discretion by converting the food stamp and medicaid programs into additional block grants were dropped from the final legislation. Although the new law dramatically altered the structure for providing cash welfare in the United States, it did not constitute a revolution in American intergovernmental relations.

Too Little, Too Late: The Clinton Welfare Reform Plan

President Clinton came to office committed to reforming the nation's welfare system. In 1988, while he was chair of the National Governors' Association, Clinton had helped craft the Family Assistance Act. By 1992 he had made welfare reform a major plank in his policy platform. His pledges to "end welfare as we know it" and to establish a two-year time limit on non–work-related benefits—"two years and you're off"—were highly salient in the campaign. "Our pollsters told us that 'two' was the single most memorable number of the 1992 campaign," observed David Ellwood, one of the chief architects of Clinton's welfare reform plan. These positions on welfare served a crucial political purpose because they helped to distinguish Clinton as a "new Democrat" in his efforts to lure disgruntled voters back to the party fold.

Despite the president's high-profile commitment to welfare reform, the Clinton administration was slow to introduce its version of reform legislation in the 103d Congress. The president's plan was not sent to Capitol

Hill until June 1994. By then proposals already before Congress—including health care reform and anticrime and gun control legislation—took precedence on the legislative calendar, and welfare reform joined the logjam of bills brought to a halt by the extraordinary partisan rancor that preceded the 1994 elections. Many observers believe that this delay ensured the failure of welfare reform in the 103d Congress and contributed to the election of the Republican Congress in November 1994.[40]

Reflecting and expanding on his campaign pledges, Clinton's bill—the Work and Responsibility Act—had four major elements: a time limit on benefits, work incentives, child support enforcement, and teen pregnancy prevention. It limited welfare benefits to able-bodied recipients to two years. By providing child care, job training, and subsidized jobs if necessary, the bill emphasized the transition from welfare to work. Improvements in the earned income tax credit, the proposed adoption of universal national health insurance, and expanded child care benefits would create incentives for working over welfare and would help keep low-wage workers employed.

The bill strengthened the nation's system of child support by requiring hospitals to establish paternity at birth, by mandating centralized child support registries in every state, and by instituting automatic wage withholding and stronger penalties to enforce child support orders. To discourage teen pregnancy, the bill required teen-age welfare recipients to live at home and remain in school and once they completed school to begin work. The provision requiring hospitals to establish paternity at birth and the inclusion of teen fathers in the child support enforcement system were also intended to discourage teen pregnancy. Finally, the bill established a series of state demonstration grants.[41]

Many of these concepts had considerable support in Congress and among the public; many were incorporated in the final welfare reform bill enacted in 1996. But the structural changes promoted by the president were far less dramatic than those Congress ultimately adopted. Under the president's bill, for example, AFDC remained an individual entitlement, and recipients could still receive support after the two-year limit as long as they were *willing* to work. Subsidized jobs for welfare recipients were included in the plan, and the reforms were to be phased in gradually to help participants—and the system—cope.

Despite general support for the concept of welfare reform, the president's plan was criticized from all sides. Conservatives condemned its cost and complexity. "Making work pay" and providing subsidized jobs for hard-to-employ welfare recipients were expensive propositions—far more costly than simply sending welfare checks to people. Finding funds to pay for these features in a budget constrained by deficit reduction initiatives proved to be difficult and was one of the reasons why the president was so slow in sending his bill to Congress. Liberals in and out of Congress joined the chorus of opposition. A coalition of eighty-nine liberal interest groups lobbied against the idea of time limited welfare while the president's plan was being written, and liberal members of Congress criticized this and other features after the bill was introduced.[42] For all these reasons, the president's bill died a quiet death in the 103d Congress. But the politics of welfare reform had just begun.

Welfare Reform and the Contract with America

Republicans were also at work on welfare reform legislation in the 103d Congress. Their proposals evolved in response to the president's positions, as each side sought political advantage on this highly charged issue. Indeed, this competition encouraged a process of policy escalation that ultimately produced a more conservative approach to welfare than anyone had anticipated when the president first seized the issue in 1992. Equally important in shaping the Republicans' proposals was the need to adjust reform to the competing goals of different but overlapping factions within the party. Welfare specialists in the Republican party initially supported the president's emphasis on transitioning to work. Governors and "new federalists" favored devolution and state flexibility. Social conservatives sought to mandate federal policies intended to discourage teenage illegitimacy and the breakdown of the family. And fiscal conservatives advocated budget savings above all else. These competing goals could be combined in varying formulations but not all could be obtained simultaneously. Social policy mandates conflicted with state flexibility, although each could generate budget savings. Transitioning from welfare to work could be encouraged through new spending on training and support services or through penalizing poorly performing states. The resulting process of adjustment was inherently unstable: constituencies who lost favor in one legislative version fought to obtain their goals in the next.[43] Along the way devolution of power to the states became one—but only one—objective whose fortunes rose and fell as the welfare debate continued.

The initial Republican offering, cosponsored by the entire House Republican caucus and introduced in November 1993, shared important features with the president's bill, but it was less costly for the federal government and tougher on welfare recipients. Written mainly by two moderate Republicans on the House Ways and Means Committee, Clay Shaw of Florida and Nancy Johnson of Connecticut, this bill included strict time limits on individual eligibility for welfare benefits, and it preserved the entitlement status of cash welfare (although it did provide for an optional block grant at states' discretion.) Most important, it shared the president's focus on work, seeking to "provide welfare families with the education, training, job search, and work experience needed to prepare them to leave welfare within 2 years."[44] This was a popular but expensive goal at odds with fiscal conservatives' hopes for cutting welfare spending. To bridge the gap on spending more for training and child care benefits while still reducing overall welfare spending, H.R. 3500 placed a 2 percent cap on the growth of future spending on welfare-related entitlements, denied benefits to legal resident aliens, and converted food and nutrition programs into a block grant. Finally, it sought to increase states' flexibility in designing and implementing welfare programs by encouraging waivers of federal regulations and by authorizing a laundry list of state options, including denial of AFDC benefits to minor parents, denial of benefits to additional children, modification of certain income rules, and the option to convert AFDC into a block grant.

The development of H.R. 3500 was guided by Representatives Shaw and Johnson, who had developed expertise on welfare issues from their service on the House Human Resources Subcommittee—the Ways and Means subcommittee with primary jurisdiction over the core welfare programs.[45] Increasingly, however, social conservatives in the Republican party advocated an alternative approach. They urged a shift in the focus of welfare reform from encouraging work to discouraging illegitimacy. This would address what they viewed as the more urgent problem of family disintegration, and it would not require increased spending on training and employment assistance.

The revised version of the welfare reform bill that was introduced on the first day of the 104th Congress reflected social conservatives' influence over the welfare component of the Contract with America. No longer a bill that highlighted education and job training for welfare recipients, H.R. 4 promised "to restore the American family, reduce illegitimacy, control welfare spending, and reduce welfare dependence." Like much of the Contract with America, major changes in the relationship between the federal government and state and local governments were implicit in the bill, but its explicit focus was on social and fiscal policy. The legislation was now replete with conservative policy mandates: prohibiting states from paying AFDC benefits to mothers who failed to establish their child's paternity; prohibiting states from paying additional benefits for children born while the mother was already receiving welfare benefits; prohibiting welfare payments to teenage mothers who did not live with their parents; requiring that states take additional efforts to determine paternity; requiring that states inform the Immigration and Naturalization Service about suspected illegal immigrants; requiring drug testing and treatment for welfare recipients; and capping the annual growth rate of federal welfare expenditures. Balanced against these new mandates were provisions consolidating federal food stamps and child nutrition programs, allowing states to transfer a portion of food stamp funds into job subsidy programs for welfare recipients, and providing for an optional welfare program block grant at each state's discretion.

Welfare Reform in the 104th Congress: New Players and New Politics

The environment shaping welfare reform changed radically after the November 1994 elections. Suddenly, conservative Republicans went from being minority outcasts to being in charge—not only in Washington but in thirty-one state houses across the nation. Republicans had won a net total of fourteen additional governorships and now controlled the executive mansion in nine of the ten most populous states. This gave them an opportunity to reconsider many of the bargains struck in the original design of H.R. 4.

REPUBLICAN GOVERNORS AND WELFARE REFORM. From an intergovernmental perspective, one of the most remarkable features of the policymaking process on welfare reform was the degree to which Republican governors helped shape the contours and write the details of this legislation. The intergovernmental lobby had been a major player in the legislative process in the past, but the governors' role in 1995 was unique. Previously, the power of the intergovernmental lobby had been greatest on issues, like revenue sharing, that united the nation's governors, mayors, and county officials in a common cause. In the welfare reform debate, however, local government officials and other groups traditionally active in the welfare policy arena were excluded or ineffectual, especially in the House. Even the National Governors' Association, which was deeply split along partisan lines, was "sidelined" in 1995.[46] Instead, a handful of Republican governors and their key staff members assumed center stage. Working closely with congressional leaders in the back rooms of the House and Senate, state welfare officials helped draft the actual language of the legislation considered in committee. Although many state-favored provisions were cut back or modified as the legislation proceeded through the House and Senate, welfare reform remained a remarkable chapter in the politics of intergovernmental relations.

The roots of this gubernatorial involvement went back to a meeting between the new leadership of the 104th Congress and the Republican governors shortly after the 1994 elections. At the Republican Governors' Conference in Williamsburg, Virginia, the two groups decided to rely on block grants to implement their party's welfare agenda. Elizabeth Drew reported on Speaker Newt Gingrich's account of the session:

> The governors made us much bolder than we would have been without them. . . . When we were in the meeting with the governors . . . they said to us, "If you'll block-grant [welfare] and get the federal government out of the way, we don't need any more money." And my ears perked up and I said, "You literally would accept a flat line for five years if you were in charge?" And they said yes. But they all agreed they had to have a real freedom to manage the programs. And I said, "Fine. We're in charge, let's do it." . . . That actually was the first big step toward thinking we could balance the budget. Because you would suddenly have a model for dramatically lower costs and for dramatic reform . . . [for] reshaping the entire federal government.[47]

"After Williamsburg," said Speaker Gingrich's press aide, Tony Blankley, "everything else was detail."[48] Perhaps, but it was vital detail with far-reaching policy implications. To all concerned, the decision to block-grant welfare meant more than changing the rules of the AFDC program. It required the conversion into block grants of even larger low-income entitlement programs, particularly medicaid and food stamps, along with the freedom to transfer funds among them. To balance the budget, congressional leaders as well as the governors understood the need for capping and blocking all of the largest low-income entitlement programs. As a result of the Williamsburg agreement, welfare reform became inextricably linked with the Republicans' overall fiscal strategy.

The depth of change became evident in late December and early January, when congressional leaders contemplated folding as many as 336 programs into only eight block grants.[49] Among the programs considered for consolidation were Head Start, Title I education grants, and the food stamp program. Weeks of negotiations by key congressional actors and core Republican governors winnowed down this ambitious agenda, but it still produced a very different version of H.R. 4 than the one that had been introduced in early January. The new bill was constructed around five broad block grants for cash welfare assistance (temporary assistance for needy families or TANF), child protection (including foster care and adoption assistance), child care, school-based nutrition assistance (including school lunch and related programs), and family nutrition assistance (including the WIC program for women, infants, and children). Although the bill retained strict time limits on benefits and provisions aimed at reducing illegitimacy, it offered states unprecedented flexibility in several respects. States were given great latitude in determining the actual structure of their welfare programs. There was no longer any state match or maintenance of effort requirement. States, which contributed 30 percent to 50 percent of total welfare benefits under AFDC, could dramatically reduce their own spending if they liked. Funds could be transferred among block grants to suit differing state needs and priorities.

These provisions were not accidental. They reflected unprecedented input into welfare policy from a handful of key Republican governors. Some, like Michigan governor John Engler and Wisconsin governor Tommy Thompson, were involved in many key strategy sessions with the new congressional leadership. Engler had a particularly close relationship with Gingrich because of their long collaboration in GOPAC, a political action committee that recruited, trained, and helped fund conservative candidates for elective office.[50] According to one account, Governor Engler visited Gingrich's office so often that he seemed "like a member of the Speaker's staff."[51] Gerald Miller, Michigan's director of social services, and many other gubernatorial aides spent days in the back rooms of congressional committees helping to write the House welfare reform bill. "It has been a very real partnership," Miller observed. "We were sharing drafts back and forth. We were able to write language. It was a very meaningful, open process."[52] The staff director of the House Human Resources Subcommittee offered a similar assessment:

I bet this is the closest the Governors and Congress ever worked together in the history of this institution. Gerry Miller and I must have met or talked 50 times in the course of writing this legislation. Same with LeAnn Redick [Michigan's Washington lobbyist]. And we must have talked forty times with people from Wisconsin. When we made the big decisions, they were always in the room.[53]

All in all, it was a remarkable exercise in intergovernmental lobbying.[54]

SIDELINED PLAYERS. Not all governors were granted such policymaking access in 1995. Initially, the bipartisan National Governors' Association sought to join Republican governors in shaping policies in the 104th Congress. In early January 1995, NGA staff put together a draft proposal for the new Congress dubbed "A Plan to Consolidate Federal Categorical Grants to States." The NGA proposed consolidating almost 400 programs totaling $96 billion into only eighteen block grants.[55] Instead of becoming a blueprint for reform, this proposal fell by the wayside as partisan divisions threatened to destroy the NGA.

Democratic governors felt particularly excluded from the new consultative process, which was closely tied to Republicans' efforts to deliver on campaign promises and become the undisputed majority party in American politics. Governor Howard Dean of Vermont, the Democratic chairman of the NGA, denounced the emerging GOP welfare plan as something written by "extremists" who were out to "starve children and kick old people out of their houses."[56] He said Democratic governors were "furious, furious" about being frozen out of negotiations with Congress and were discussing canceling NGA's winter meeting and dismantling the organization. In the end the meeting was held, but the consensus was that the "NGA has been paralyzed" and "sidelined in the welfare debate."[57]

Democrats in Congress were also sidelined as the welfare reform locomotive picked up steam. This was a dramatic reversal of party politics. "Ten years ago," complained a Republican aide, "we didn't have a handful of goddamned Republicans who could spell AFDC. Democrats know the programs, it was their constituency, but we didn't."[58] Suddenly the Democrats were out of the loop. "Everybody is so stunned by defeat we have become incoherent," acknowledged Charles Rangel (Democrat of New York), a senior member of the Ways and Means Committee.[59] Struggling to influence welfare reform, the Democrats assumed the role of the opposition. They scored political points by criticizing the nutrition block grant in the Republican bill for cutting back the school lunch program and by denouncing the welfare block grant as "weak on work." But Democrats on the Ways and Means Committee had difficulty moving beyond mere opposition. They were too divided among themselves to unite around an alternative proposal in committee.

Democrats were not the only ones left on the sidelines during the welfare debate. Groups traditionally active in shaping welfare policy—those representing welfare professionals, nonprofit service providers, and advocates for the poor—were shunted aside as Republicans crafted their approach. "There wasn't even a perfunctory effort to listen to us," complained a representative for Catholic Charities. "We had to fight to testify, and when we did it was after 8 o'clock at night after almost all the members and all the press had gone, despite the fact that Catholic Charities is the largest provider of services in the country."[60] Such groups and the views they represented were displaced by welfare analysts from conservative Washington think tanks.

THE HOUSE BILL. As reported by the major committees with jurisdiction over key components of H.R. 4—the Ways and Means, Education and Economic Opportunities, and Agriculture committees—welfare reform consisted of multiple block grants married to social policy mandates. Major provisions of the bill were designed to

—convert AFDC into a block grant for cash assistance to poor families, with funding capped at the same level for five years. States were granted wide latitude in defining welfare eligibility and services and were guaranteed set funding for five years. The federal entitlement of assistance to individuals was eliminated;

—impose strict time limits on the receipt of welfare financed by block grant funds and deny federally funded support for unmarried mothers under eighteen and for children born to current recipients (the "family cap");

—establish two food and nutrition block grants: one replacing the school lunch, breakfast, and other school-related programs and the other replacing nonschool nutrition programs, including WIC;

—create a new block grant for welfare-related child care programs;

—consolidate child welfare, adoption, and foster care programs into a new block grant;

—offer states that established electronic benefit transfer programs the option of receiving food stamp funds in the form of a block grant;

—cap annual food stamp expenditures and restrict benefits to non-disabled, nonworking adults to ninety days;

—strengthen the nation's child support system by requiring hospitals to establish paternity at birth, establishing centralized state child support registries, and instituting automatic wage withholding and stronger penalties to enforce child support orders;

—restrict eligibility for supplemental security income (SSI) payments to severely disabled children; and

—deny food stamps, SSI, medicaid, and welfare block grant funds to most legal immigrants.

This version of welfare reform passed the House on March 24, 1995, with relatively few changes after three days of acrimonious debate. Majority Leader Dick Armey of Texas defended it as the best hope "for reforming a system of despair." One Democrat likened its impact on poor people to the Nazi holocaust![61] The conversion of AFDC from an individual entitlement to a state block grant, along with the imposition of a "family cap" and other restrictions on eligibility, were major points of contention during floor debate. Opponents charged that these changes would plunge millions of children deeply into poverty; President Clinton denounced the Republican bill as "tough on kids" and "weak on work."[62]

Democrats in Congress finally united around a substitute reform proposal offered by Nathan Deal of Georgia, a conservative southerner who later joined the Republican party. The Deal amendment rejected the block grant approach and retained the individual entitlement for cash benefits and nutrition programs, but it imposed strict time limits on benefits, imposed stiff work requirements, and cut aid to legal immigrants. This conservative approach was supported by every Democratic House member, but it went down to defeat when all Republicans but one opposed it.[63]

As with the Deal amendment, party affiliation was the principal factor that determined final passage of H.R. 4. The House passed the bill by a vote of 234 to 199. Only nine Democrats voted for it; five Republicans opposed it. A supercharged atmosphere of partisanship in the House characterized voting on this and other elements of the Contract. Other factors that normally would have played a role, such as region and ideology, exerted little influence.

In particular, interstate disagreements over formula allocations under the welfare block grants were simply brushed over. Yet a massive formula fight could have occurred because of the way welfare funds would be distributed under the TANF block grant. States were essentially locked into the same share of federal funds as they received under the prior matching grant formula. This seemed fair from one perspective, but the system of open-ended matching grants had produced wide disparities in federal assistance from state to state. The federal government matched whatever states were paying in welfare, so wealthier or more generous states could receive much larger shares of federal aid. When these shares were maintained under the block grant formula, the resulting allocations bore no relationship to need. Mississippi, with a 1993 poverty rate of 24.7 percent, was scheduled to receive a block grant worth $302 per poor child, while Connecticut, with a poverty rate of only 8.5 percent, would receive a share worth $1,566 per poor child![64] Altering the block grant formula so that every state received an equal amount per child would have required cutting the grants for several northern states in half while doubling the grants to many southern states—home to virtually all the leaders of the 104th Congress. Yet what could have been a ferocious formula fight, severe enough to endanger reform, never materialized. It was perhaps the greatest testament to the new majority's discipline and ideological fervor.

THE SENATE RETREATS. The House-passed welfare reform bill was constructed around five new block grants. Along with an optional food stamp block grant and another one contemplated for the medicaid program in the House Budget Resolution, this was the high point of the block grant strategy in the 104th Congress. From this point on, the block grant approach to welfare reform was cut back, even as Republican conservatives and moderates fought over the extent of the mandates that would be imposed on beneficiaries.

In the Senate Republican governors again pushed for extensive use of broad, flexible block grants. The draft welfare bill they submitted to the Senate Finance Committee included block grants for AFDC, food stamps, child protection, and child care, and they were at work on a proposal for medicaid. They also sought to loosen the mandated restrictions in the House bill on federally supported aid to young unwed mothers, legal immigrants, and welfare families with new children, arguing that these decisions should be left as state options.[65] The Republican governors returned to the principles they had espoused during deliberations in the House. "Conservative micromanagement is just as bad as liberal micromanagement," Governor Engler had declared in earlier hearings. "States must have the freedom, with no strings attached, to implement change."[66]

Virtually all factions in the Senate—moderate and conservative Republicans as well as Democrats—took issue with aspects of Engler's approach. Denying benefits to young unwed mothers was "punitive," argued moderate Republican senators John Chafee of Rhode Island and Nancy Kassebaum of Kansas.[67] Conservative Republicans, like Phil Gramm of Texas and Lauch Faircloth of North Carolina, were just as adamant that such mandates were needed to discourage out-of-wedlock births. "I am never going to consider this bill to be complete until we have language that denies additional cash benefits to people who have more and more children on welfare," declared Senator Gramm.[68] Without federal mandates on issues like this, argued Senator Dan Coats (Republican of Indiana), too many states would just "repeat the same mistakes as federal officials."[69]

Most Democrats opposed the entire block grant approach, preferring to retain welfare as an individual entitlement. "If the states want to make all of the decisions, no strings attached, let them raise the money," said Senator Kent Conrad of North Dakota during Finance Committee hearings on the issue.[70] The implications of a five-year funding cap under the block grant worried senators from states with growing populations, particularly in the South and Southwest. They lobbied vigorously for adjustments to their future needs.

Given the slim margin of GOP control in the Senate and the minority party's greater clout, these crosscurrents stalled welfare reform for months. When agreement was finally reached, the Senate bill looked quite distinctive. The Senate had moderated several of the most conservative features of the House plan. The five welfare-related block grants in the House bill had been reduced in the Senate bill to two: for family assistance and child care. The two nutrition block grants, which had been effectively attacked by Democrats for "cutting" popular programs like school lunches, were dropped, as was the child protection block grant. Although AFDC was converted from an individual entitlement to a capped block grant, with strict time limits and work requirements, more funding was included for child care and a new maintenance of effort requirement was imposed on the states. Whereas the House block grant allowed states to make any reductions they wished in their own spending on welfare, the Senate bill required them to continue spending at least 80 percent of their 1994 level of funding on welfare. Finally, the Senate bill converted the family cap and limits on teen mothers into state options, and it modified the cutbacks in SSI and aid to legal immigrants. Combined, these changes reduced the budgetary savings in the Senate bill substantially—from $62 billion over five years to $39 billion.[71]

These concessions were enough to give the Senate bill much broader support than in the House. The Senate's version of H.R. 4 passed by a vote of 87 to 12, with 35 Democrats joining 53 Republicans in voting for the bill. A number of liberal Democrats denounced the legislation for jeopardizing children on welfare; Senator Ted Kennedy of Massachusetts called it "legislative child abuse." Nevertheless, only eleven Democrats voted against the Senate bill after the president said that he would sign similar legislation.

There were warning flags, however, signaling rough waters in conference committee. Although only one conservative Republican opposed the bill for backing away from tougher social policy mandates, several warned that they expected the legislation to move in the House's direction in conference.[72] At the same time the president's spokespersons warned that he would veto a bill that looked like the House version. The stage was set for further conflict.

Death and Transfiguration

Conflict erupted with a capital C once House and Senate conferees agreed on a compromise welfare plan and folded it into the omnibus balanced budget package discussed in chapter 12. Welfare reform and budget policy had often been linked together. One reason the Clinton administration had been slow to offer its own reform plan in the 103d Congress was its inability to find new funding, and pressure to achieve budgetary savings had shaped the Republicans' reform plan in the 104th Congress. Indeed, the hope of budgetary savings helped to explain the block grant strategy, as well as the decision to include controversial cuts in food stamps, benefits for legal immigrants, and SSI and medicaid. These policy linkages were now reinforced by legislative strategy considerations. Welfare reform would have to pass Congress as part of the omnibus budget plan, and, if successful, it would be presented to the president in this form.

Inevitably, the conference report produced by House and Senate negotiators blended elements of the two bills. In the process, state flexibility was restricted in some areas while it was maintained in others. The House provisions for school nutrition and child protection block grants were dropped, although the Senate option for a food stamp block grant was retained. The conservative House provisions for a family cap and restrictions on benefits to teen mothers were retained only as state options, and a state maintenance of effort requirement was imposed.

Most important from a political standpoint, though not unexpected, was the decision to fold welfare reform into the balanced budget package. In the process even the high-profile issue of welfare was overshadowed by the larger drama of governmental shutdowns, medicare reforms, tax cuts, and political summitry. President Clinton vetoed the Republican package on December 6, 1995, killing welfare reform along with the rest of the bold budgetary gambit. Congressional leaders made a half-hearted attempt to revive welfare reform in January 1996, once they realized that budget talks with the president had collapsed for good. Knowing that he was unlikely to sign such a bill, especially if it still included deep cuts in future spending on medicaid and food stamps, they introduced the legislation in hopes of creating a political issue for the upcoming presidential campaign. If the president vetoed welfare reform once again, after it was detached from the unpopular budget bill, they reasoned that he would be vulnerable on the issue in the fall campaign. As expected, Clinton vetoed this bill as well, emphasizing its changes to the medicaid program.

At this point history appeared to have repeated itself: welfare reform looked as if it would die in the 104th Congress just as it had in the 103d. Republican legislators in Congress who had worked hardest to pass a bill were sorely disappointed. They wanted a bill, not a sound bite. Governors, too, were in a quandary. Unwisely, perhaps, many had counted on fiscal savings and greater flexibility in welfare programs while designing their own budgets. Now they were about to begin their legislative sessions with none of these savings in sight.

This forced another amazing twist in the saga of welfare reform and a new flurry of gubernatorial involvement—this time on a bipartisan basis. Led by Tommy Thompson, who had been a major player in earlier negotiations and was now chairman of the NGA, Republican governors worked with their Democratic counterparts on a bipartisan reform plan. At their winter meeting in February 1996, the governors agreed on the outlines of a plan to overhaul both welfare and medicaid. State executives of both parties agreed to support the conversion of welfare to a block grant, but with more generous federal funding for child care and employment activities. Unlike the failed congressional legislation, though, the governors' plan preserved medicaid as an individual entitlement, albeit with provisions to enhance state flexibility.

Initial reactions to the governors' proposals were positive, and the volume of partisan bickering was suddenly reduced. Both President Clinton and congressional leaders praised the governors' efforts. Speaker Gingrich even predicted that a bill patterned after the governors' proposal could be passed by the House within a month.[73] Yet this initial optimism soon passed. The governors' plan consisted of a short, relatively vague outline, only a few pages long. As efforts were made to flesh out the details, ruptures reappeared. Conservatives were dissatisfied with the elimination of anti-illegitimacy mandates and the shrinking budget savings. By one congressional estimate, the governors' plan reduced federal spending by just $10 billion over five years, as opposed to $40 to $50 billion in earlier versions.[74] Liberals in and out of Congress were dissatisfied with the plan's attempts to loosen mandatory medicaid coverage for certain demographic groups and by the conversion of AFDC to a block grant. Before long, much of the governors' agreement had unraveled, and their hopes for a rapid breakthrough had vanished.

Once again Republicans in Congress faced a dilemma: they could have a law or a campaign issue but not both. If they passed a stand-alone welfare bill similar to what the Senate had passed earlier, the president seemed committed to sign it. If they passed a bill including welfare mandates and a medicaid block grant, he was sure to veto it once more. For many the issue was decided by pure politics. Majority Leader Bob Dole, who was on his way to capturing his party's presidential nomination, sought a third presidential veto of a welfare bill. He needed issues to use against a resurgent president in the fall campaign, and he hoped that politics might imitate baseball: three strikes and you're out.

Dole's colleagues in Congress, however, were not sure a presidential veto of a welfare bill was in their best interests. Congressional Republicans' political position had weakened dramatically over the course of 1995. Their ratings in opinion polls had plummeted, while the president's popularity had surged. Most of the public blamed them for shutting down the government. Republicans were subjected to an unprecedented barrage of withering television ads by organized labor, and Democrats caricatured the 104th Congress as a "do-nothing" Congress. In response, members who had earlier embraced the role of uncompromising "revolutionary" began to act more like politicians who feared losing their majority status in Congress and possibly their own seats as well.

This led to a dramatic turnabout in the tactics of the Republican Congress. In the space of a few months, it rejected ideological purity and passed a number of "big government" initiatives, including a 20 percent increase in the minimum wage, health care and insurance protections for new mothers and for people who change jobs, and new pollution protections for drinking water. In the midst of this flurry of activity, Congress also passed another version of welfare reform. It was designed to meet many of the president's stated positions defining the type of bill he could sign. All of the earlier block grant provisions relating to school lunches, child nutrition, food stamps, child protection programs, adoption assistance, and medicaid were gone, stripped from the final bill. Child care funding in the bill was increased, and the states' "rainy day fund" was slightly enlarged. A state maintenance of effort provision was retained. Many of the social policy and illegitimacy mandates had been stripped or left as state options. In short, it was the most moderate version of welfare reform yet passed by the 104th Congress.

It was still a conservative reform, however. It ended the individual entitlement for cash welfare and established a block grant to the states. It replaced the system of federal open-ended matching grants, designed to stimulate state welfare spending, with a predetermined system of formula payments to each state that would remain essentially unchanged for five years. It gave states important new powers to determine welfare eligibility and program administration. It established strict new time limits and work requirements for the receipt of cash welfare benefits. It severely restricted eligibility for medicaid, food stamps, and income support payments by legal immigrants and unemployed men. And it established an invasive new federal system of child support enforcement.[75]

Passage of the revised bill put the administration in a quandary. Factions within the Democratic party—both within the administration and without—were deeply divided over how the president should respond. The new bill was similar to, and in some respects more "liberal" than, welfare reform legislation passed earlier by the Senate, which the president had signaled his willingness to sign. On the whole, the bill seemed responsive to the president's high-profile commitment to "end welfare as we know it." Yet liberal Democrats raised serious arguments against the bill. It retained many punitive provisions, from rigid time limits to strict work requirements to aid cutoffs for vulnerable groups. The administration's own studies projected that the strict time limits in the bill, among other features, would add substantially to childhood poverty as families were cut off from assistance. Administration estimates for the earlier Senate bill suggested that 1.1 million additional children would be forced into poverty once all the provisions took effect.[76]

From an intergovernmental perspective, the most serious objection to the welfare block grant concerned its formula structure. Federal incentives under the old funding system encouraged state welfare spending by contributing one to two federal dollars for every state dollar spent in cash benefits. By the same token, states were penalized by one to two federal dollars for every dollar they reduced their existing welfare benefits. In contrast, the new formula structure actually rewarded states for cutting back their welfare payments. States could reduce their welfare spending by up to 20 percent with no reduction in their federal payment. (The maintenance of effort requirement in the bill required that states continue at least 80 percent of their prior spending level on welfare.) In fact, states could "profit" from such cuts. Because of linkages with the food stamp program, federal food stamp allocations to a state would rise if its welfare benefits were cut.[77] Absent the prop of federal incentives for state welfare spending, many liberals feared that states would engage in a "race to the bottom" as they sought to avoid becoming "welfare magnets" for poor people while attracting economic development with lower taxes.[78]

Despite these concerns, President Clinton seemed bound by his election pledge and signed the bill on August 22, 1996, calling it "an historic opportunity to end welfare as we know it and transform our broken welfare system."[79] To appease disgruntled liberals and representatives of immigrant groups, he pledged to "fix" flaws in the bill in the next Congress. But this was not enough to dissuade three appointees in the Department of Health and Human Services—including two assistant secretaries with responsibilities for welfare policy—from resigning in disgust.

The End of Welfare As We Knew It

Why did welfare reform succeed while other initiatives of the 104th Congress failed? In one sense, its enactment was aided by the prior history of failed attempts. Unlike many other aspects of the Republican revolution, welfare reform did not spring suddenly on the agenda without warning or preparation. It had experienced a long gestation period, and key actors were prepared to grapple with it. Even more important, the legislation dealt with a singularly unpopular program and a particularly vulnerable clientele. Unlike medicare, welfare was not a program benefiting millions of middle-class voters. And unlike medicaid and food stamps, it targeted the least deserving of the "deserving poor"—single, often unwed, mothers, legal and illegal immigrants, childless dysfunctional men. In contrast, the other, more popular means-tested programs were retained as entitlements and were not converted into block grants.

Finally, the issue had been framed in a way that mitigated the effects of divided government. Clinton himself had placed the issue firmly on the policy agenda. He had made eliminating "welfare as we know it" a salient campaign promise in his election in 1992, campaigning on it far more prominently than on his weak and belated endorsement of tax cuts. Indeed, more than any other policy position, it had helped define him as a "New Democrat," different from the "tax and spend" liberals who now seemed incapable of being elected. Having made the promise of reform so central to his political identity, he felt committed—and appropriately so—to sign a bill. He could—and did—veto omnibus legislation that combined a conservative welfare reform package with unpopular changes in medicare and social spending. But once welfare reform was isolated as a stand-alone program, the president had little real choice.

Conclusion

The Unfunded Mandates Reform Act of 1995 and the Personal Responsibility and Work Opportunity Reconciliation Act of 1996 were important legislative achievements of the 104th Congress. They were also important intergovernmental reforms, although their effects on the federal system are likely to be modest. As passed, UMRA provides Congress with better information about the intergovernmental consequences of its actions. The legislation favors more meaningful legislative deliberation and greater comity between the federal government and state and local governments.[80] But as research by Paul Posner shows, the law does not appear to have made a decisive change in the policymaking process, nor in Congress's propensity to mandate.[81]

Welfare reform clearly demonstrated this regulatory propensity in the Republican 104th Congress. At the same time the legislation gave the states new avenues of flexibility.[82] The conversion of AFDC from an individual entitlement to a capped block grant fundamentally altered the incentive structure facing states in welfare policy. Without the open-ended matching formula of the past, states lost a powerful federal incentive to raise their spending on welfare. As inflation eats away at the maintenance of effort requirement, they will face little federal penalty for decreasing their own welfare expenditures.[83] It will also make states, and their welfare recipients, far more vulnerable to the effects of economic recession. Whether the welfare reform legislation will provoke a "race to the bottom" is uncertain at this point. Federal attempts to stimulate state welfare spending failed to prevent a gradual decline in the value of welfare benefits after the early 1970s, or to prompt many states to raise incredibly low benefit levels. Other factors can balance fiscal incentives. But the potential for a race—or a slide—to the bottom has been increased.

The new welfare law is an important policy change, but it is not the vaunted devolution revolution sought by governors and congressional leaders in 1994 and 1995. What it grants in terms of flexibility for the states is largely countered by policy restrictions in other areas. Politically, it was significant that the 104th Congress succeeded in gaining the president's signature on only two major acts of devolution—the two with the longest track records and most bipartisan support. As Texas governor George W. Bush said at the conclusion of the 104th Congress: "Williamsburg was the revolution . . . to redefine the relationship between the states and the federal government. But the great redefinition didn't take place."[84] Such a great redefinition was always unlikely, though not impossible. The American system of separated powers and weak political parties militates against such change, although it does not preclude it. The outcome might have been quite different had 1994 been a presidential election year, giving the Republican Congress a more sympathetic president to work with. Even then, however, the public mandate for sweeping changes was volatile and incomplete. The large entitlements for the middle class—the principal engines of domestic federal spending—were never intended for great changes in the public mind. Evolution, not revolution, remains the preference of most Americans.

CHAPTER 14

Intergovernmental Reform and the Future of Federalism

ALTHOUGH the intergovernmental reform agendas of Presidents Richard Nixon and Ronald Reagan, and of House Speaker Newt Gingrich in the 104th Congress, were shaped by similar concerns about the health of the U.S. federal system, they differed in their aims and political outcomes. Those differences chart the shifting course of conservative ideology over the past three decades and reflect broader changes in the structure of American politics.

Federalism Reform and Conservative Ideology

Richard Nixon was an "activist conservative" president who was thoroughly at ease with the idea of an energetic government, and this orientation colored his intergovernmental reform initiatives. Nixon's principal concern was how this governmental energy should be channeled and where the wellsprings of activism should reside.

Nixon's New Federalism agenda was a coherent strategy designed to address these questions. Nixon proposed a more rational sorting out of the functional responsibilities of the various governmental levels in order to make government "leaner, but in a sense . . . stronger."[1] This was a decentralizing approach, but it was not intended to be antigovernment per se. It was viewed as a "positive Republican alternative to running things out of Washington."[2] Rather than simply "getting government off the backs of the people," Nixon believed that a properly designed decentralization program would make government more effective and creative. As he wrote in the margin of one memorandum: "Decentralization is not an excuse for inaction, but a key to action."[3] In the words of one former aide,

The notion was to have the Federal Government do what it does best (levy taxes) and to have state and local governments do what they do best (administer local spending). That was intended to result in a kind of "national localism." . . . The Feds would say to the locals "do it your way," adding gently but firmly "but do it."[4]

This activist orientation was evident in the administration's reform proposals. Complex "capacity building" schedules were included in certain block grants, and additional funding for block grants and revenue sharing was provided to entice congressional support. The general revenue sharing formula rewarded the most active spenders at the state level by factoring in a measure of "tax effort." Uniform national benefits for welfare were proposed, and entitlement spending and intergovernmental regulations were expanded at unprecedented rates. Although some of these elements were concessions to congressional demands and were in keeping with the liberal temper of the times, most were consistent with the president's general philosophy of government, which guided his decisions from foreign policy to executive branch reorganization.

In sharp contrast, Ronald Reagan was highly skeptical about domestic governmental activism. This skepticism emerged clearly in his first economic report to the Congress:

We should leave to private initiative all the functions that individuals can perform privately. We should use the level of government closest to the community involved for all the public functions it can handle. . . . Federal Government action should be reserved for those needed functions that only the national government can undertake.[5]

When asked subsequently by reporters which domestic functions he would put in the last category, Reagan could think of only one: national security![6] Even at the local level, his positive vision of private communal action left little room for government. Rather, he emphasized volunteerism as "an essential part of our plan to give government back to the people."[7]

Reagan's New Federalism was an expression of this broader philosophy of government. Far from diffusing activism throughout all governmental jurisdictions, Reagan's federalism constrained it at every level. During his 1976 presidential campaign, Reagan openly rejected Nixon's managerial approach to federalism reform: "It isn't good enough to approach this tangle of confusion by saying we will try to make it more efficient or 'responsive.' . . . The problem must be attacked at its source. . . . We can and must *reverse* the flow of power to Washington; not simply slow it or paper over the problem."[8] He proposed a radical "$90 billion plan" to eliminate practically all federal aid programs and slash federal taxes by 23 percent. In this way Reagan hoped to redress what he saw as the major flaw in the intergovernmental aid system—the failure to "tie the spending and taxing functions together."

Of course, this very "flaw" lay at the heart of Nixon's New Federalism. In Reagan's view, however, this separation of functions was responsible for the government's uncontrolled growth and spending, which "blurs the difference between wasteful states and prudent ones, and . . . destroys incentives toward economy." Citizens in fiscally conservative states, he argued, are "called upon to pay in federal taxes and inflation for other states that don't curb their spending." In short, because the root of the problem was profligacy at all levels of government, an intergovernmental solution was needed. To "put an effective lid on spending," it was necessary to dismantle stimulative federal programs and return "tax room" to the states. "When tax increases are proposed in state assemblies and city councils," Reagan explained, "the average citizen is better able to resist and to make his influence felt."[9]

Reagan never returned to this specific plan once he took office. Although he toned down his rhetoric, his federalism reform initiatives continued to reflect a general hostility toward governmental activism at all levels. The administration's domestic spending program singled out federal grants for state and local government services for the deepest cuts among all the major budget categories. Unlike Nixon, Reagan did not use block grants to harness the federal fisc to state and local priorities. Instead, the president and his top advisers considered these grants "a step toward total withdrawal of the Federal Government from education, health and social services programs which . . . are properly the responsibility of state and local governments."[10] This withdrawal strategy was pursued even further in the ill-fated federalism initiative of 1982. It proposed turning back to the states more than $30 billion in federal aid programs, along with aid to families with dependent children (AFDC) and food stamps. The administration also favored eliminating the major indirect subsidies provided through the tax code—yet another avenue of attack on the funding base of state and local governments.

In short, from program structure to budget to tax policy, the Reagan administration waged a comprehensive assault on the intergovernmental dimensions of public sector activism. Federalist rhetoric notwithstanding, Reagan consistently favored federal over state and local authority whenever the former was more supportive of free markets or private sector interests. This pattern was repeated in cases ranging from interstate trucking standards to product liability insurance. The Reagan administration even took local governments to court when they implemented objectionable policies involving affirmative action and taxing cab licensing. It was this tension between intergovernmental deference, implied by the president's devolutionary rhetoric, and the antigovernment implications of his broader philosophy that gave rise to Reagan's unique brand of instrumental federalism.

Intellectually, Georgia Republican Newt Gingrich, elected Speaker of the House in 1995, distinguished himself from both Nixon and Reagan by attempting to develop a comprehensive philosophical critique of the welfare state. Whereas Reagan often expressed a visceral dislike for government, Gingrich, the former college professor, placed great emphasis on the role of ideas in public policy. "Things that are wrong in America," he said shortly after the 1994 elections, "are wrong because we've had a bad set of ideas that haven't worked."[11] And while Reagan railed against the heavy hand of big government, he vowed to preserve a "safety net" of programs for the poor. Indeed, most of the "safety net" entitlements for the poor and middle class—the heart of the welfare state—continued to grow during most of his presidency.

Gingrich, on the other hand, spoke and wrote openly about the need to "replace the welfare state . . . thoroughly, from the ground up." Far from preserving a safety net for the poor, he took special aim at poverty programs: "They are a disaster. They ruin the poor, they create a culture of poverty and a culture of violence, which is destructive of this civilization."[12] The very ideas that underlay such programs were fundamentally flawed: "It is impossible to take the Great Society structure of bureaucracy, the redistributionist model of how wealth is acquired, and the counter-culture value system," Gingrich said, "and have any hope of fixing it."[13]

Since the welfare state could not be fixed, Gingrich sought to "remake the Government of the United States." The great challenge was to "replace the welfare state with opportunity," to become an "opportunity society."[14] The Speaker's definition of what would constitute an opportunity society varied in different contexts, but supportive policies would need to expand individual choice, reduce the federal government's size and influence, and decentralize power and decisionmaking. As he said in his nationally televised address to the nation on April 17, 1995:

> We have to do a number of things to become an opportunity society. We must restore freedom by ending bureaucratic micromanagement here in Washington. . . . We've got to return power back to you—to your families, your neighborhoods, your local and state governments. We need to . . . reduce regulation, taxation, and frivolous lawsuits.[15]

Although Gingrich's vision of an opportunity society had important implications for the distribution of power in American federalism, he made it clear that devolving power to state and local governments was only a partial step. As he explained in remarks to the Republican National Committee:

> We have to decentralize power out of Washington, D.C., and disperse power. Let me make this very clear, because they are two very different words. . . . We want to decentralize power. That means we get it out of Washington. Governors hear that and they love it. . . . But we also want to disperse power. That means it actually goes back to the people from whom it comes. So the people should decide. . . . We want the people to have the maximum . . . choices, so in your home town, in your family, in your community, you can have the maximum impact on the life you want to lead.[16]

Following the Republicans' legislative disappointments in the 104th Congress, their narrow escape from losing control of the House in the 1996 elections, and the subsequent turmoil in the Speaker's office, some observers detected an end to the latest cycle of devolutionary politics. "The revolution has given way to the era of Republican incrementalism, gradualism, caution," asserted columnist E. J. Dionne.[17] There was clearly a change in Republicans' rhetoric and behavior in the 105th Congress (1997–99) compared with the 104th (1995–97). For example, the 105th Congress reached agreement with President Clinton on a balanced budget plan that involved only superficial cuts in many domestic programs and a significant expansion in health care coverage for children.

Early in 1998, however, Speaker Gingrich urged a reduction in the relative size of American government—federal, state, and local combined—to pre–Great Society levels. One of the "goals for a generation," he argued, should be to reduce government's total share of the economy to 25 percent of GDP, a figure well below the current government share of 35 percent of GDP.[18] This would squeeze the public sector to levels about 3 percent below the average of the 1950s and almost 30 percent below current levels—a significant change considering the demographic shifts and growth in health care costs that have occurred in the intervening years. In practice, should such a goal be achieved, the end result would be a transformation of intergovernmental roles as well as changes in the size and instruments of contemporary government.

Paradoxical Politics

Political responses to the reform initiatives of Nixon, Reagan, and Gingrich (and to the political coalitions they constructed to achieve their goals) differed as much as their objectives. Paradoxically, the activist and nationally oriented Nixon was hindered by the centrifugal parochialism and fragmentation of the 1970s. In contrast, Reagan, the antigovernment crusader, won crucial victories through his mastery of national politics. Gingrich rose to power within the Republican party as a conservative maverick, yet once he became Speaker, he was able to get House Republicans in the 104th Congress to vote with near unanimity on dozens of key issues. Such a record of party loyalty has rarely been seen in this century.

Nixon proposed a coherent and consistent program of federalism reform. Nonetheless, Congress addressed the proposals in a segmented and individualized fashion, as can be seen in its treatment of Nixon's block grants. Political responses were primarily shaped by the particular interests of each affected policy subsystem. The pattern of idiosyncratic politics was repeated across the entire range of Nixon's reform agenda. General revenue sharing, for example, caused sharp divisions within Congress that cut across party lines. As Beer has shown, it generated its own unique coalitions, structured by the "categorical phalanx" on the one side and the pressures of "distributive localism" on the other.[19] The politics of the family assistance plan (FAP) were different yet again, although crossparty cleavages were present here too. In the House the plan attracted broad bipartisan support, largely in deference to the president and the influential chairman and ranking member of the Ways and Means Committee. In the Senate, however, the family assistance plan twice collapsed when conservatives and liberals joined forces to fight its provisions for precisely the opposite reasons.

The politics of Reagan's New Federalism evolved in two distinct phases, each characterized by a far higher degree of policy interdependence than was evident in the 1970s. The first phase was marked by the president's budget and tax victories of 1981. In that single year the fragmented subsystem politics that hampered Nixon's reform efforts gave way to a highly visible, majoritarian style of presidential policy leadership. President Reagan successfully constructed a conservative phalanx that pushed much of his fiscal policy through Congress more or less intact. The highly polarized and unified partisan coalitions in Congress proved critical in key votes on the president's program, and the overall levels of party voting in Congress remained high throughout the 1980s.

This majoritarian style of leadership lost effectiveness after 1981, but intergovernmental policymaking did not return to the fragmented patterns of the 1970s. Rather, the fiscal policies adopted in 1981 ushered in a new phase of rationalizing politics—a "new politics of deficits."[20] The domestic policy agenda became preoccupied with the fiscal, institutional, and policy consequences of the 1981 initiatives. New budgetary procedures were implemented that integrated diverse spending and authorization issues on the president's terms. Opportunities and incentives for entrepreneurial initiatives were reduced as zero-sum budgeting increased policy interdependence. The numbers of new laws introduced and passed declined, and those proposed and adopted were often altered by the new policymaking environment.

For his part, Gingrich helped to engineer extraordinary party unity in the 104th Congress as Republicans voted in near lockstep on most Contract with America items and on many budget issues. The average party unity score for congressional Republicans was well above levels commonly seen in the postwar era.[21] The degree of unity Speaker Gingrich achieved from rank-and-file Republicans in 1995 has even been compared to that seen at the turn of the century under Speakers "Czar" Reed and Joseph Cannon.[22]

There was irony in this. During most of his career in Congress, Newt Gingrich was no favorite with party regulars in Congress—on either side of the aisle. He led a band of conservative insurgents in the House who were more interested in fashioning wedge issues and obstructing the Democratic majority in Congress than in passing laws and drafting legislation. He opposed Republican presidents on high-profile issues like tax reform in 1986 and the budget summit in 1990. Even his election as Republican whip in 1989 was hotly contested: he overcame the leadership's candidate by a single vote.[23]

Gingrich was skilled, however, at grass-roots party building and at using highly visible media tools like the Contract with America. The Republican takeover of the House in 1994 was widely considered his doing. As a result, he acquired firm and faithful support from senior members and newly elected freshmen alike. And, having won a Republican majority in the House, he was freed of the need to rely on conservative Democrats the way President Reagan had.

From the beginning Gingrich's style of leadership in the 104th Congress was compared to leadership in a parliamentary system. "Gingrich seems to think of himself as a kind of prime minister," observed former senator and presidential candidate Eugene McCarthy.[24] Early in his career, Gingrich said he wanted to "make the House the co-equal of the White House."[25] This ambition may have led to his greatest failing in the 104th Congress. In 1995 President Clinton vetoed its core budget proposals. This marked the end of the Republican revolution (at least for the time being) and offered stark evidence that the House of Representatives is not the House of Commons.

The Ironies of Reform

The New Federalism initiatives of Nixon, Reagan, and the 104th Congress left ironic legacies that affected not only the federal system but also American politics and policy in general. Richard Nixon sought to simplify and streamline intergovernmental relations and to produce a more decentralized federal system than the one he inherited. He left behind a system of massive intergovernmental interdependence and higher levels of fiscal and regulatory dominance by the federal government. Ronald Reagan and Newt Gingrich enjoyed more success in their efforts to refocus the policy agenda and accomplish desired changes in policy direction. Yet they, too, left behind a legacy of support for governmental activism, at least in the short term.

In his efforts to reduce the size and activity of the welfare state, Reagan accomplished more than most analysts thought likely when he entered office. From 1980 to 1988, nondefense discretionary spending declined by 29 percent as a proportion of the gross national product, and general federal revenues went down 13 percent. Entitlement growth as a percentage of GNP was limited to just 5 percent during this period, and federal aid to state and local governments was reduced by one-fourth.

Yet, in some respects, the welfare state emerged as strong as ever from the Reagan years. Reagan's agenda trimmed questionable programs and addressed public concerns about governability and uncontrolled governmental growth. As a result, public confidence in Washington actually improved during the Reagan years, notwithstanding his attacks on the "puzzle palaces on the Potomac." By 1986 American public opinion had reverted to older patterns of broad support for governmental spending, and polls indicated that Americans no longer supported substantial budget cuts in virtually any area of domestic policy.

In the 104th Congress public support for a radical change in federal-state roles, if it ever existed, evaporated once tangible programmatic decisions and budget cuts replaced political slogans. By 1996 public disapproval of Congress had grown, and support for President Clinton had increased. He won reelection by promising to do more to promote education, protect the environment, and preserve medicare and medicaid. The political search for new and creative program initiatives to deal with contemporary problems had resumed, at least for the time being, and another reform cycle appeared to have run its course.

The Intellectual Underpinnings of Federalism Reform

Over the past three decades the objectives of federalism reform evolved from the rational restructuring of intergovernmental responsibilities under Nixon's New Federalism to the goal of devolution in the 1990s, the "de-evolution" of government growth involving the return to an earlier era of smaller government and a reduced federal role.[26] This shift in goals was accompanied by a parallel shift in the intellectual underpinnings of federalism reform.

Nixon's New Federalism was based on theories of public administration and public finance. Many of his proposals were designed to improve the management and efficiency of intergovernmental programs, and they were premised on standard precepts of public administration: executive leadership, clear lines of authority, improved coordination. In recent years these precepts have receded into the background of reform initiatives, and the strongest advocates of such reforms have been quieted. Offices or committees with formal intergovernmental responsibilities in the Office of Management and Budget, the General Accounting Office, and Capitol Hill have been abolished, and by 1998 the U.S. Advisory Commission on

Intergovernmental Relations (ACIR) had been reduced to just a shadow of its former self.

The declining influence of the administrative perspective can be seen if one compares the block grant proposals of the 104th Congress with grant design criteria developed over the years by ACIR. As discussed in earlier chapters, public administration theorists had made a strong case that block grants could improve intergovernmental management and coordination. But block grants were deemed appropriate only under certain circumstances. According to the ACIR, administrative considerations supported grant consolidation under these conditions:

—a cluster of functionally related categorical programs has been in existence for some time;

—the broad area to be covered is part of the recipient's traditional range of services;

—no more than mild fiscal stimulation of recipient outlays is sought; and

—a high degree of consensus over general purposes exists among the Congress, the federal agencies, and recipients.[27]

In the past important block grant proposals generally met these conditions. Yet in the 104th Congress the most significant block grant initiatives—temporary assistance to needy families (TANF), medicaid, food stamps, and school nutrition—failed to meet *any* of these criteria. None was chiefly motivated by concerns about program fragmentation. Nor could they be justified by the level of policy consistency among federal, state, and local governments. Medicaid, food stamps, and school nutrition programs did not qualify as "traditional" services of state and local governments. On the other hand, block grant proposals that did appear to meet administrative criteria, such as employment and training, failed to be enacted or, in the case of education, failed to even receive serious attention in the 104th Congress.

Even less political support has been sustained for sorting out intergovernmental functions and rationalizing federal and state roles. This approach draws upon traditional public finance theory for guidance in designing program allocations, swaps, or turnbacks. Most public finance theorists argue that redistribution of income should be the job of the national government. Smaller jurisdictions are constrained from doing this effectively by the mobility of people and capital. Distributive or developmental programs, in contrast, are often best left to state and local governments where they can be tailored more precisely to the needs and tastes of local residents.[28] In addition, this branch of theory argues that open-ended matching grants—such as medicaid and AFDC—are the preferred mechanism for allocating federal redistributive programs because they minimize substitution effects by recipient governments and are the most efficient tool for correcting interjurisdictional spillover effects.

Nixon's New Federalism, with its proposals for nationalizing welfare and decentralizing control over many other functions through the use of block grants, was generally consistent with the prescriptions of public finance theory. Yet most reform initiatives since then have headed in the opposite direction.[29] Reagan's 1982 sorting-out plan increased federal responsibility for one redistributive program (medicaid) only to eliminate federal involvement in two others (AFDC and food stamps). Many of the major proposals advanced in the 104th Congress also contravened these prescriptions. By advocating cuts in welfare spending and the creation of capped block grants to replace open-ended matching grants for AFDC and medicaid, the Republican majority tried to reduce federal responsibility for redistributive programs rather than increase it.

Indeed, during the 1990s, politicians of both parties seemed to have little enthusiasm for a rational reallocation of the functions of government. President Clinton explicitly rejected the idea in 1992, and since then he signed a welfare block grant and encouraged an expanded federal role in several traditionally local and developmental functions: education, economic development, and law enforcement. Two of his major domestic initiatives involved efforts to raise standards and provide more funding for elementary and secondary education, as well as putting "100,000 new cops on the beat" in America's towns and cities. Congressional Republicans have offered legislation to expand federal involvement in several areas of law enforcement, such as mandating stricter sentencing procedures. They also have advocated school vouchers, a clear interference with the local administration of schools. Neither party, it would seem, is willing to sacrifice the opportunity for federal involvement in state and local activities that hold political appeal. As Martha Derthick has observed: "Sorting out has not worked. . . . Intergovernmental sharing is not going to go away. Since the 1930s it has steadily deepened. The question is how to practice it constructively."[30]

Public choice theory, the theoretical perspective most consistent with the federalism reform initiatives of the 104th Congress, differs from the traditional public finance models that informed Nixon's New Federalism. Although public choice provides a normative rationale for shrinking the public sector, downsizing the federal government, and decentralizing welfare policy, important features of the most prominent reform proposals of the Republican Congress departed from the prescriptions of this framework as well.

Controlling public sector growth and interference in the market constitute principal policy concerns for conservative public choice theorists. According to this model, government is virtually certain to exceed its optimal size because of "rent seeking" behavior by public officials and narrow special interests. Many public choice theorists advocate structural reforms in government and changes in institutional rules to alter these perverse outcomes. Thus the public choice concept of "competitive federalism" provides a normative rationale for devolution. Interstate competition can be a valuable tool for controlling the leviathan of government.[31] Whereas traditional theorists were concerned that interstate competition could provoke a "race to the bottom," public choice theorists are inclined to applaud the race and commend the "winner."

But, given this theoretical framework, even welfare and medicaid block grants were an inadequate, halfway measure. As Richard Wagner argued:

> In the current political environment, the block grant approach has been elevated to the supreme position for stimulating this competitive process. . . . While this is better than what we have, it is still a bad idea; [it] still leaves the federal government as the paymaster and regulator.[32]

Without a doubt, the intellectual underpinnings of federalism reform proposals have shifted significantly during the past thirty years. Older paradigms in public administration and finance are increasingly neglected by policymakers. Yet the newer frameworks have still to be fully embraced or implemented.

The Future of Reform

Apart from changing contributions from social science, what can be said about the future of federalism reform? Much depends on deeper trends affecting American federalism. At least two different but plausible scenarios warrant consideration. The first describes a federal system that becomes increasingly decentralized. The second scenario is one of continued federal preeminence.

The Rising Tide of Devolution

One scenario begins from the premise that significant decentralization is already under way in our system of government and is likely to accelerate in the years ahead, propelled by powerful economic, political, and social forces. "As a country we have been quietly weighting our bets toward devolution," observes one critic of this trend. "By the measures that best gauge governmental power—authority, resources, and legitimacy—the tide is flowing away from Washington."[33]

THE DECLINE OF THE NATION STATE. In this view devolution is being stimulated by economic and political trends that are both global and regional in nature. Globally, the future of the nation state itself is being questioned as country after country faces new challenges from without and within.[34] Individual nations are increasingly viewed as too small to deal with a growing list of global problems and too large to accommodate internal demands for greater regional autonomy and local self-governance.

For example, resource and environmental problems that once could be addressed locally or nationally now require solutions on an international scale. From ocean fisheries to atmospheric ozone, nations are obliged to enter into international treaties to deal with what have become global problems. Similarly, on trade and economic issues many nations are ceding power and authority to new supranational institutions, such as the World Trade Organization and the European Union, and are entering expansive regional trade agreements, such as the North American Free Trade Agreement (NAFTA).

At the same time, demands in many countries for greater local autonomy and policy devolution are strengthening subnational entities and creating pressures to establish new ones.[35] Economically, many of the same forces that are breaking down national trade barriers also are promoting greater economic decentralization. Regional attributes, such as specialized economic networks and swifter decisionmaking, appear to be gaining competitive advantage over the eroding capabilities of central governments to manage their economies and mobilize resources. Simultaneously, political forces, such as ethnic identification and a growing desire for local self-determination, are eroding central authority in many nations around the world, even prompting the breakup of some established countries into smaller, more homogeneous entities.

Many factors are contributing to these developments. The end of the cold war has lessened the salience of national defense concerns, historically the raison d'être of the modern nation state. Rapid technological changes in communications, transportation, and manufacturing have punctured national boundaries, giving rise to expanding international markets and their global spillover effects of pollution and social disruption. These trends appear to be enhancing the authority of subnational governments in countries around the world. In Germany the Länder governments have grown increasingly influential in domestic and European affairs even as the central government gives up powers to the European Union.[36] In Britain and France recent developments are strengthening the formal and informal authority of regional governments, from Scotland in the North to the Rhône-Alps region of southeastern France.[37]

THE POLICY EFFECTS OF PARTY REALIGNMENT. In the United States, according to the devolution scenario, international trends (namely the erosion of the nation state's power) are reinforced by trends in public attitudes and changes in the party system. In this view the Democratic majority in Congress, committed to a stronger and more energetic national government, gave way to an emerging Republican majority committed to reducing the size and activity of the public sector in general and the federal government in particular.

Clear evidence of movement toward party realignment developed in the 1980s, when Republicans achieved rough parity with Democrats in party identification, a seeming "lock" on the electoral college in presidential elections, and temporary control of the Senate.[38] Although this trend was questioned in the wake of President Clinton's victory in 1992, it was bolstered by the Republican sweep of 1994. "If the gains are sustained," wrote one authority on congressional elections, "1994 will mark a partisan realignment of historic proportions."[39] Republican gains largely were sustained at the congressional level in 1996, although the scope and character of realignment remains disputed. The GOP increased its margin of control in the Senate and narrowly retained control of the House in 1996. Given the advantages of incumbency and Republicans' emerging dominance in the South, a true realignment in control of the Congress may well have transpired. If the party remains committed to a platform of smaller, more decentralized government, then prospects for the devolution scenario will be enhanced.

The existence and strength of party realignment among the electorate are still disputed among political scientists, however. Voters' growing independence and weakened partisan attachments have led some to question the meaning of realignment in an increasingly "dealigned" public.[40] Others, like Everett Carll Ladd, argue that Republicans have yet to achieve majority status and that the process of party realignment is incomplete.[41] Ladd argues instead that a "philosophical realignment" occurred in the 1990s "distinguished by far greater skepticism about government. . . . The dispersion and decentralization induced by postindustrialism . . . have made central national government bureaucracy seem ever more cumbersome and out of phase."[42] Hence, in 1996, 63 percent of respondents said they favored a smaller government with fewer services, 62 percent said they believed that government was too big and too active, and 70 percent reported being angry or dissatisfied with the way the federal government works.[43] These percentages were identical to the levels recorded in 1994, the year of the "Republican Revolution," and considerably higher than levels reported on similar questions in the 1960s and 1970s. Because of the continuity between 1994 and 1996, Ladd concluded that "in the mid-1990s, the U.S. is no longer seeing significant year-to-year change in public sentiment about government and its proper role. . . . The philosophical side of the postindustrial revolution has come swiftly and decisively."[44]

FISCAL TRENDS IN THE UNITED STATES. Trends in public finance have provided another uneven but ongoing push toward devolution in the United States. As federal resources have become increasingly constrained, the states have been growing financially stronger and more energetic. The contrast can be seen in figure 14-1, which displays the long-term trends in financing American government over the course of the postwar era. Federal revenues, which experienced dramatic growth in the 1930s and 1940s, have fallen during the postwar period when measured as a percentage of total government revenues. Moreover, significant changes have occurred in the composition of federal revenues. The proportion raised by federal trust funds, and subsequently devoted to social insurance spending, has grown dramatically, at the relative expense of general fund revenues and discretionary spending. On the other hand, state and local revenues have climbed slowly but steadily from the 1950s to the present. Starting out as junior fiscal partners at the beginning of the postwar era, state and local governments were headed in the 1990s toward financial parity with the national government.

On the expenditure side, John Donahue has sketched out the scenarios

Figure 14-1. *Change in Federal, State, and Local Shares of Total Government Revenues, 1952–92*

Percent

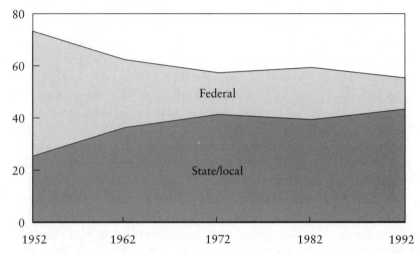

Source: U.S. Advisory Commission on Intergovernmental Relations, *Significant Features of Fiscal Federalism, 1994* (Government Printing Office, 1994), table 18.

for fiscal devolution based on projected reductions in federal spending to meet balanced budget targets:

> [One] possibility is that Washington cuts back, according to schedule, over the last years of this century and the first years of the next. [If] state and local spending continues to grow at the same average pace as it did over the 1980–95 period . . . [it] would edge out federal entitlements and debt service as the largest category of public spending.[45]

If states and localities were to *boost* their own spending enough to make up for cutbacks in federal domestic spending, the effects would be even more dramatic:

> Spending controlled by states and localities in 2002—the sum of self-funded state and local spending and federal grants to cities and states—would reach about fifteen times the level of federal domestic

spending (other than interest and entitlements). Even more than it does today, American government would wear a state and local face.[46]

THE MODERNIZATION OF STATE GOVERNMENT. Growing state and local financial parity was made possible in part by broad improvements in the organization and capacity of state governments over the past forty years. During the Great Depression, state governments were nearly written off as hopeless anachronisms of a pre-industrial era. "It is a matter of brutal record," wrote Luther Gulick in 1933. "The American State is finished."[47] This harsh judgment resulted largely from state governments' failures to meet the challenges of an urban, industrialized society. When Americans' expectations of government expanded rapidly during the 1930s, most states were ill equipped politically, administratively, or financially to meet the new demands being placed upon them. Thirty years later the civil rights movement put a different but equally unflattering spotlight on the states' role in the U.S. system of government. Responding to the bitter spectacle of state-enforced segregation in the 1950s and 1960s, William Riker wrote caustically that "one should approve of American federalism" only if "one approves of Southern white racists.[48]

In truth, throughout this period states varied enormously in their public policies and levels of performance. Innovative states typically led the way in dealing with new social, economic, and environmental challenges, and many of the federal government's own initiatives from the New Deal to the Great Society were patterned after state experiments and innovations. But during the middle part of this century, states as a whole were called upon to overcome serious deficiencies in their institutional capacity and their quality of democratic representation. To a remarkable extent, they have done so.

During the postwar era, most states have undergone sweeping institutional reforms in the legislative and executive branches of state government and in their electoral and revenue systems, leading to impressive gains in state managerial and technical capacity. Governorships have been strengthened, state legislatures have been modernized, state bureaucracies have been professionalized, and revenue systems have been broadened (see box 14-1). State electoral processes have become fairer and more representative of all citizens, thanks in large part to federal civil rights policies and a series of Supreme Court decisions. In short, by the 1980s and 1990s, most states had established the political and institutional foundation needed to respond to rapidly changing global and

---

Box 14-1. *The Modernization of State Government*

Institutional capacity

Strengthened executive authority: Governors today have longer terms and stronger professional staff support.

More professionalized legislatures: Most state legislatures have increased the length and frequency of their sessions; attracted a more educated and diverse membership; and acquired larger, more professional staffs. This allows legislatures to deal with more complex policy issues in a timely and innovative manner.

More capable bureaucracy: States have developed more professional, less politicized, and better-paid staffs. Over half the states have comprehensively reorganized their bureaucracies in the past twenty-five years to enhance coordination, accountability, and efficiency.

Finances

More balanced fiscal systems: Most states have developed well-balanced revenue systems that are adequate to fund their principal responsibilities and less vulnerable to cyclical swings in the economy. Thirty-nine states impose both individual and personal sales taxes. Only two impose neither.

Representation

Greater representation by women and minorities: In 1996 over 20 percent of all state legislators were women, up from 5 percent in 1970. Forty-seven state legislatures had a higher percentage of female representatives than did the U.S. Congress. Six percent of state legislators were African American, compared with 3 percent in 1970.

Fairer representation: The severe malapportionment of many state legislatures before the 1960s is now a thing of the past. The number of "one-party" states is declining.

---

intergovernmental conditions and to assume new responsibilities in a devolutionary era.

A NEW JUDICIAL FEDERALISM? Finally, by the mid-1990s, it appeared that the political, economic, and fiscal trends promoting devolution were being reinforced by the Supreme Court. If this, in fact, were the case, it would be a dramatic turn of events: the Court had been one of the principal agents of centralization during the post–New Deal era. As Martin Shapiro observed in the late 1970s: "Nearly all of [the Supreme Court's] most successful interventions have been primarily against state governments in areas like education, police, and morals that had traditionally been left primarily to state law."[49] At the same time the Court's expansive interpretations of the commerce clause, the spending power, the concepts of standing and class action, and of various federal statutes all served to permit or promote the growth of congressional and federal agency power vis-à-vis the states.

Beginning in the 1970s, modest efforts were made to stem or reverse the Court's centralizing proclivities. The most notable example was the Court's attempt in *National League of Cities* v. *Usery* (1976) to resurrect use of the Tenth Amendment as a constraint on congressional authority. But in 1986 the Court overturned *NLC* with its decision in *Garcia* v. *San Antonio*; the majority argued that states should no longer look to the courts to protect their interests but rather should seek to advance their aims through the legislative and political processes. *Garcia* was soon followed by other strongly worded decisions upholding broad federal authority under the spending and taxing powers.[50] It appeared that the Court's role as a centralizing institution would be maintained.

In 1992, however, a new trend of decentralizing Supreme Court decisions began, and it has accelerated over time. In *New York* v. *United States* (1992), the Court invalidated a portion of the Low-Level Radioactive Waste Policy Amendments Act of 1985, arguing that it was an unconstitutional attempt by the federal government to "commandeer" the administrative apparatus of the states. In *United States* v. *Lopez* (1995), the Court restrictively interpreted Congress's reach under the commerce clause; the federal Gun-Free School Zones Act of 1990, it ruled, was unconstitutional. In 1996 the Court invalidated portions of the Indian Gaming Regulatory Act in *Seminole Tribe of Florida* v. *Florida,* arguing that it violated the Eleventh Amendment's grant of state sovereign immunity from private party lawsuits. In 1997 the Court struck down a portion of another federal statute, the Brady Handgun Violence Prevention Act, in *Printz* v. *United States;* following the doctrine espoused five years earlier in *New York* v. *United States*, the Court held that Congress cannot commandeer the administrative apparatus of state and local governments without the state's consent. In another 1997 decision, *City of Boerne* v. *Flores*, the Court struck down another federal statute—the Religious Freedom Restoration Act—on the grounds that Congress had exceeded its powers to guarantee equal protection under the Fourteenth Amendment.

Prospects for the devolution scenario will be greatly enhanced if the

Supreme Court continues this line of cases and becomes an active partner in promoting a new direction in American federalism. The full import of the cases decided to date, however, remains to be seen. Most of the cases were decided by narrow majorities, and Congress still has powerful tools under existing Court doctrines to achieve its objectives vis-à-vis state and local governments. In particular, Congress's power to attach conditions to grants-in-aid is virtually unlimited by the Court, and this gives Congress considerable latitude, even if its powers under the commerce clause are restricted.

The Power of the Center

Not all signs in contemporary federalism point to devolution. The forces promoting centralization in the federal system have a long history, and many remain strong. All told, a variety of political, economic, and demographic factors point to continued federal preeminence in American federalism.

THE CENTRALIZING POTENTIAL OF GLOBALIZATION. As discussed above, a number of devolutionary effects have been attributed to globalization. Yet, historically, the modernization process and resulting increases in economic interdependence have had centralizing effects on political institutions.[51] Consistent with this historical pattern, the expansion of international trade, changes in international trade rules (such as NAFTA and the Uruguay Round of GATT), and other forms of global policy interdependence could result in a power shift away from state and local governments and toward Washington, toward supranational authorities, or both.

The potential federalism impacts of economic globalization were apparent in the negotiations over NAFTA and the General Agreement on Tariffs and Trade (GATT). Both agreements raised the specter of federal preemption of state and local authority as foreign trade negotiators sought to delimit the forms of labor, environmental, financial, and consumer regulations that might impinge on future trading relations. As Conrad Weiler observed:

The two agreements broadly require new federal regulation of state and local government taxation, economic development, procurement and regulation of services, professions, investments, insurance, banking and financial services, health, environmental, food, and product-safety standards, and land transportation. In addition, procedures are created whereby disputes over these new rules can be initiated and even resolved largely outside the federal courts.[52]

State and local governments' concerns about federal preemption of their powers led to the formation in 1988 of the Intergovernmental Policy Advisory Committee; the committee advised the Office of the U.S. Trade Representative about specific state and local issues during negotiations over NAFTA and GATT. While most state and local objections to these treaties were resolved, the potential for future federal and international preemption persists. Moreover, the dynamic apparent in these trade negotiations suggests that national authority vis-à-vis state and local governments can expand in an environment of proliferating international negotiations. Whatever authority the nation state may relinquish to international forums and entities, its traditional role as negotiating agent for the nation remains largely intact. Thus, Weiler concluded that globalization is likely to promote intergovernmental centralization rather than devolution:

> While the global economy may stimulate state and local economies and provide them greater resources to improve their citizens' lives, most signs point to an ever broader and more globally integrated network of rules that will alter federalism dramatically and continue the shift toward coercive federalism.[53]

THE TEMPTING OF AMERICAN CONSERVATIVES. Domestic political behavior also may promote continued centralization. Those holding power in Washington will naturally seek to use it. Because Democrats were the majority party for most of the post–New Deal era, and because a program of centralization fit comfortably with their dominant ideology, the tendency to accrue power at the center was often associated with this party. Yet conservative Republicans are often tempted to use and even expand federal authority when they have the opportunity to do so. Abundant evidence from the Nixon and Reagan administrations and the Republican-led 104th Congress indicates that ideological scruples have not stood in the way. This record makes devolution seem highly uncertain if it is premised on a Republican realignment in national politics.

The Reagan administration consistently opted to preempt, prescribe, or constrain decisionmaking by state and local governments when it faced the choice of pursuing its own policy preferences or exercising restraint and deferring to its federalist ideals. Thus it was no accident that the growth of federal mandates in the 1980s was comparable to levels in the 1960s and 1970s.

The 104th Congress had a similar record of intervention. Although the Republican majority actively promoted devolution of power to the states, this was usually confined to cases consistent with its broader policy objectives. When conservative goals could be attained more easily through federal policy prescriptions, the Congress rarely refrained from making them.

Welfare reform was a case in point. Under the Personal Responsibility and Work Opportunity Reconciliation Act of 1996 (P.L. 104-193), states were required to comply with a long list of mandates: time-limit federally assisted welfare benefits, reduce or eliminate benefits for recipients under eighteen who were not living at home or going to school, meet workforce participation requirements, establish and report the paternity and immigration status of children receiving welfare benefits, operate an automated centralized unit to collect and disburse child support payments, ensure that employers withhold payments from individuals owing child support, and maintain an electronic benefit transfer system for food stamps. These are just some of the intergovernmental prescriptions in the bill intended to constrain spending or promote conservative policy values.

Moreover, welfare reform was not an isolated example. Paul Posner examined the politics of mandating in the 104th Congress and found a pattern of policy prescription among both Democrats and Republicans. There was virtually no difference in the two parties' proclivity to rely on federal requirements to achieve their aims, but the parties did differ in the goals they sought to advance with mandates. "Republicans supported mandates to achieve national welfare, moral policy, immigration, and business preemption goals," observed Posner. "Democrats supported mandates to support the party's labor and housing agendas."[54]

A similar pattern of policy prescription appeared to be present in fiscal policy in the Republican Congress. For example, in 1997 congressional Republicans were accused of "pigging out" on porkbarrel projects in public works. As one reporter put it: "Most GOP revolutionaries are lining up at the public trough to try to steer money for roads and bridges toward their districts."[55] Similarly, the 1997 tax bill was a Christmas tree of benefits for specific groups and interests. Although President Clinton played a major part in promoting this approach, Republicans in Congress were responsible for dozens of provisions in the tax bill aimed at rewarding their constituents or advancing their policy goals. Examples include so-called Roth IRAs, a restored capital gains exclusion, $500-per-child tax credits, and changes in estate taxes.

THE AMBIVALENCE OF PUBLIC OPINION. Since at least the 1960s, opinion polls have uncovered a deep ambivalence in Americans' beliefs about their government. On the one hand, polls have shown consistent and powerful public support for many of the specific programs of an activist federal government. During most of this period, sizable public majorities have favored spending more rather than less on a broad range of program areas, including education, health care, environmental protection, and social security.[56] Yet, in terms of ideology, far more Americans call themselves conservatives than liberals. In the abstract, many espouse the classic views of limited government, particularly when compared with citizens' attitudes in other western democracies.

Public opinion analysts Lloyd Free and Hadley Cantril, who first discussed this pattern of public ambivalence during the 1960s, estimated that at that time 65 percent of the public could be classified as "operational liberals"—given their support of specific government programs—but only 16 percent could be considered liberals in terms of their expressed values and ideology. They argued that American public opinion was "schizoid," with "a large majority of Americans qualifying as operational liberals while at the same time a majority hold to a conservative ideology."[57]

Although American opinion has moved in a conservative direction on many "operational" issues since 1990, the schizoid mentality persists. In 1996 more than three-fifths of the respondents in a poll claimed a preference for "smaller government providing fewer services." Yet over 60 percent of respondents in the same poll agreed that "the federal government should see to it that every person who wants to work has a job" and that "Washington should guarantee medical care for all people who don't have health insurance."[58]

It was this duality in public opinion that Republican legislators overlooked in 1995. Seeing conservative responses to questions about the role of government, they wrongly concluded that most Americans shared their own ideological consistency. Many Republicans in the 104th Congress were surprised when their agenda was perceived as excessive or extreme, and their public support eroded.

This longstanding ambivalence in public opinion is likely to persist, and it will continue to have important political implications for American politics. It enables politicians and pollsters to elicit different results—even from the same individuals—from one poll or election to the next, depending on which ideological dimension is tapped or how the issues are framed. In the process this dichotomy may place genuine limits on the scope of devolution for the foreseeable future.

Conclusion

For more than thirty years, major federalism reform initiatives have been launched in cycles of roughly ten years. They are a natural response to problems inherent in our increasingly interdependent system of government, they speak to fundamental values in American political culture, and they conform to established patterns of partisan conflict.

Yet these cycles of reform have not been merely repetitious, replaying themselves like a broken record. The sought-after changes have become more extensive, the political responses more strident, and the strains upon our polity more evident. This escalation of reform initiatives is a significant development and, were it to continue uninterrupted, a cause for concern.

To date, these reform initiatives have produced only incremental results. Some of the forces driving intergovernmental reform, such as the federal budget deficit, have even begun to diminish. But dramatic changes and policy breakthroughs are also possible, particularly because the U.S. policymaking system has grown more open and volatile during the past thirty years.[59] The political legitimacy of the federal government has been eroded, the mediating role of the party system has been diminished, populist impulses have grown stronger and more easily expressed, and the scope of symbolic policymaking has grown more extensive. All of these changes have made the system less predictable and more vulnerable to unexpected swings in policy outcomes. Despite a record of incrementalism to date, dramatic federalism reform initiatives could be enacted with unexpected haste. Federalism reform as a goal of policy change might yet surprise us.

At the same time the very institution of federalism may counterbalance some of the new volatility in the U.S. political system. Although confidence in the national government has eroded, levels of trust in state and local government have become more stable. If confidence in government is a prerequisite for public sector activism, decentralized government may help sustain the welfare state rather than undermine it. The institution of federalism mediates public dialogue, provides an escape valve for populist sentiments, and limits the diffusion of ill-considered policies. Consequently, it may grow increasingly important as alternative forms of mediating structures lose influence. Although the future of federalism reform will ultimately depend on the values that Americans hold in highest esteem, the institution itself helps to nurture and sustain those values.

Notes

Chapter 1

1. See U.S. Advisory Commission on Intergovernmental Relations (ACIR), *The Condition of Contemporary Federalism: Conflicting Theories and Collapsing Constraints*, A-78 (Government Printing Office, 1981), chap. 3.

2. V. O. Key Jr., *The Responsible Electorate* (Harvard University Press, 1966), p. 31.

3. ACIR, *Significant Features of Fiscal Federalism, 1985–86 Edition*, M-146 (GPO, 1986), pp. 6, 16.

4. Ibid. See also David B. Walker, *Toward a Functioning Federalism* (Cambridge, Mass.: Winthrop, 1981).

5. ACIR, *Fiscal Balance in the American Federal System*, A-31 (GPO, 1967), p. 260.

6. Executive Office of President, Bureau of the Budget, "Creative Federalism: Report on Field Surveys of Problems in Administering Intergovernmental Programs," quoted in ACIR, *Improving Federal Grants Management: The Intergovernmental Grant System—An Assessment and Proposed Policies*, A-53 (GPO, 1977), pp. 11, 12.

7. Charles L. Schultze, *The Politics and Economics of Public Spending* (Brookings, 1968), p. 105.

8. Quoted in James L. Sundquist and David Davis, *Making Federalism Work* (Brookings, 1969), p. 15.

9. ACIR, *An Agenda for American Federalism: Restoring Confidence and Competence*, A-86 (GPO, 1981), p. 101.

10. Ronald Reagan, "National Conference of State Legislatures, Remarks at the Annual Convention," July 30, 1981, in *Weekly Compilation of Presidential Documents*, April 3, 1981, p. 834.

11. See Samuel H. Beer, "In Search of a New Public Philosophy," in Anthony King, ed., *The New American Political System* (Washington: American Enterprise Institute, 1978); and Everett Carll Ladd Jr. and Charles D. Hadley, *Transformations of the American Party System: Political Coalitions from the New Deal to the 1970s* (Norton, 1975).

12. Ladd and Hadley, *Transformations of the American Party System*; James L. Sundquist, *Dynamics of the Party System: Alignment and Realignment of Political Parties in the United States* (Brookings, 1973); and Sidney Verba and Gary Orren, *Equality in America: The View from the Top* (Harvard University Press, 1985), pp. 128–30.

13. Herbert McCloskey, Paul V. Hoffman, and Rosemary O'Hara, "Issue Conflict and Consensus among Party Leaders and Followers," *American Political Science Review*, vol. 54 (June 1960), pp. 406–27.

14. Samuel H. Beer, "The Adoption of General Revenue Sharing: A Case Study in Public Sector Politics," *Public Policy*, vol. 24 (Spring 1976), p. 160.

15. See Richard E. Dawson, *Public Opinion and Contemporary Disarray* (Harper and Row, 1973).

16. See Walter Dean Burnham, *Critical Elections and the Mainsprings of American Politics* (Norton, 1970); and Ladd and Hadley, *Transformations of the American Party System*.

17. Quoted by Garnett O. Horner, "Nixon Looks Ahead: 'A New Feeling of Responsibility . . . of Self Discipline,'" *Washington Star-News*, September 9, 1972; reprinted in Richard P. Nathan, *The Plot That Failed: Nixon and the Administrative Presidency* (Wiley, 1975), pp. 166, 168.

18. Ronald Reagan, *The Creative Society* (New York: Devon-Adair, 1968), p. 19.

19. See Herbert Croly, *The Promise of American Life* (Jersey City, N.J.: Da Capo Press, 1986).

20. "Address to the Congress on the State of the Union, January 22, 1971," *Public Papers of the Presidents: Richard M. Nixon, 1971* (GPO, 1972), pp. 53–55.

21. Quoted in William A. Schambra, "Progressive Liberalism and American 'Community,'" *Public Interest*, vol. 80 (Summer 1985), p. 47.

22. Reagan, "National Conference of State Legislatures," pp. 836–37.

23. Newt Gingrich, "Address to the Nation, April 7, 1995," reprinted in *Washington Post*, April 8, 1995.

24. Statement on signing the State and Local Fiscal Assistance Act, October 20, 1972. Quoted in "Nixon Goal: A Leaner but Stronger Government," *National Journal*, December 16, 1972, p. 1911.

25. Interview with the *Evening Star* and *Washington Daily News*, November 9, 1972, in ibid.

26. Ibid.

27. Quoted in "New Federalism II: Philosophy—Great Society Failures, Conservative Approach to Government Underlie New Federalism Drive," *National Journal*, December 16, 1972, p. 1916.

28. Reagan, "National Conference of State Legislatures," pp. 834–35.

29. See Ronald Reagan, fund-raising letter on behalf of the Republican Governors' Association/Republican National Committee, n.d., p. 3.

30. This literature is reviewed in Daphne Kenyon, "Interjurisdictional Tax and

Policy Competition: Good or Bad for the Federal System?" paper submitted to the U.S. Advisory Commission on Intergovernmental Relations, November 3, 1987.

31. Quoted in Schambra, "Progressive Liberalism," p. 47.

32. Newt Gingrich, "Address to the Nation."

33. Newt Gingrich, speech to the Washington Research Symposium, November 11, 1994, reprinted in "New House Speaker Envisions Cooperation, Cuts, Hard Work," *Congressional Quarterly Weekly Report*, November 12, 1994, p. 3296.

34. Anthony King, "The American Polity in the Late 1970s: Building Coalitions in the Sand," in Anthony King, ed., *The New American Political System* (Washington: American Enterprise Institute, 1978), p. 371.

35. See Lawrence C. Dodd and Bruce I. Oppenheimer, *Congress Reconsidered*, 3d ed. (Washington: CQ Press, 1985); James L. Sundquist, *The Decline and Resurgence of Congress* (Brookings, 1981); Gary Orfield, *Congressional Power: Congress and Social Change* (Harcourt Brace Jovanovich, 1975); and ACIR, *An Agenda for American Federalism: Restoring Confidence and Competence*, A-86 (GPO, 1981).

36. David Broder, *The Party's Over: The Failure of Politics in America* (Harper and Row, 1972).

37. Calculated from Kay Lehman Schlozman and John T. Tierney, *Organized Interests and American Democracy* (Harper and Row, 1985), p. 75.

38. Jack L. Walker, "The Origins and Maintenance of Interest Groups in America," *American Political Science Review*, vol. 77 (Spring 1983), pp. 390–406.

39. See Roger H. Davidson and Walter J. Oleszek, *Congress and Its Members*, 6th ed. (Washington: CQ Press, 1998), pp. 260–61.

40. Richard E. Cohen and William Schneider, "Soft Center," *National Journal*, December 14, 1996, p. 2681.

Chapter 2

1. Lawrence D. Brown, *New Policies, New Politics: Government's Response to Government's Growth* (Brookings, 1983), p. 45.

2. Edwin Harper, quoted in "New Federalism I: Return of Power to States and Cities Looms as Theme of Second-Term Domestic Policy," *National Journal*, December 16, 1972, p. 1909.

3. See James L. Sundquist, *Politics and Policy: The Eisenhower, Kennedy, and Johnson Years* (Brookings, 1968), p. 137.

4. Most of these initiatives are described in detail in U.S. Advisory Commission on Intergovernmental Relations, *Improving Federal Grants Management* (Government Printing Office, 1977).

5. Paul Studenski, "Federal Grants in Aid," *National Tax Journal*, vol. 2 (September 1949), p. 211.

320 / Notes to Pages 24-29

6. Commission on the Organization of the Executive Branch, *A Report to Congress on Federal-State Relations* (GPO, 1949), pp. 31–32.

7. This view was expressed by the Kestnbaum Commission. See Commission on Intergovernmental Relations, *A Report to the President* (GPO, 1955), p. 122.

8. See Deil Wright, *Federal Grants in Aid: Perspectives and Alternatives* (Washington: American Enterprise Institute, 1968), pp. 11, 131; Selma Mushkin and John F. Cotton, *Sharing Federal Funds for State and Local Needs* (Praeger, 1967), p. 182; and James Maxwell, *Financing State and Local Governments*, rev. ed. (Brookings, 1969), pp. 58–59.

9. ACIR, *The Comprehensive Employment and Training Act: Early Readings from a Hybrid Block Grant*, A-58 (GPO, 1977), pp. 5, 19.

10. Sar A. Levitan and Joyce K. Zickler, *The Quest for a Federal Manpower Partnership* (Harvard University Press, 1974), p. 6.

11. Personal interview, August 17, 1978.

12. Testimony of Mayor John Reading, *Manpower Development and Training Legislation, 1970*, Hearings before the Subcommittee on Employment, Manpower, and Poverty of the Senate Committee on Labor and Public Welfare, 91 Cong. 2 sess. (GPO, 1970), p. 2006.

13. James L. Sundquist and David Davis, *Making Federalism Work* (Brookings, 1969), p. 7.

14. Quoted in Deil Wright, *Understanding Intergovernmental Relations* (North Scituate, Mass.: Duxbury Press, 1978), p. 57.

15. Walter Heller, *New Dimensions of Political Economy* (Harvard University Press, 1967), p. 142.

16. Quoted in Harry Scheiber, "American Federalism and the Diffusion of Power: Historical and Contemporary Perspectives," *University of Toledo Law Review*, vol. 9 (1978), p. 661.

17. Lawrence Kirsch, "Block Grants: Methods and Implications," Budget Bureau staff paper, Washington, D.C., December 1968.

18. "Address to the Nation on Domestic Programs, 8 August 1969," *Public Papers of the Presidents: Richard M. Nixon, 1969* (GPO, 1970), p. 643.

19. See Heller, *New Dimensions of Political Economy*; and James M. Buchanan, *Fiscal Theory and Political Economy: Selected Essays* (University of North Carolina Press, 1960).

20. Paul R. Dommel, *The Politics of Revenue Sharing* (University of Indiana Press, 1974), pp. 42–52.

21. Heller, *New Dimensions of Political Economy*, pp. 169, 170.

22. Wright, *Federal Grants in Aid*, p. 11.

23. Richard M. Nixon, quoted in Richard P. Nathan, *The Plot That Failed: Nixon and the Administrative Presidency* (Wiley, 1975), pp. 16, 102.

24. *The Intergovernmental Revenue Act of 1969 and Related Legislation*, Hearings before the Subcommittee on Intergovernmental Relations of the Senate Committee on Government Operations, 91 Cong. 1 sess. (GPO, 1970), p. 155.

25. Milton Friedman, *Capitalism and Freedom* (University of Chicago Press, 1962), chap. 12.

26. Nixon, "Address to the Nation on Domestic Programs," p. 638.

27. Nathan, *The Plot That Failed*, p. 31.

28. Vincent J. Burke and Vee Burke, *Nixon's Good Deed: Welfare Reform* (Columbia University Press, 1974), p. 67.

29. Richard P. Nathan, "Special Revenue Sharing: Simple, Neat, and Correct," Washington, D.C., May 5, 1971, p. 2.

30. Memorandum, John Ehrlichman, director of Domestic Council, to Ed Harper, "OMB Staff Recommendations, January 6," January 9, 1971.

31. Dommel, *Politics of Revenue Sharing*, p. 107.

32. Ibid., pp. 107–08 (emphasis added).

33. Office of Management and Budget, Revenue Sharing Working Group, "Initial Report of the OMB Working Group on a FY 1972 Revenue Sharing Program," December 1, 1970, p. 2.

34. Interview with Richard Nathan, June 5, 1978.

35. George Shultz, director, Office of Management and Budget, "Memorandum for the President on Revenue Sharing," December 18, 1970.

Chapter 3

1. Quoted in Jonathan Cottin, "Wide-Ranging Interests Oppose Administration's Proposals," *National Journal,* April 10, 1971, p. 773.

2. Interview with Richard P. Nathan, Washington, D.C., June 5, 1978.

3. Quoted in Timothy B. Clark and others, "Drive to Return Power to Local Governments Faces Hill Struggle over Control of Programs," *National Journal,* December 16, 1972, p. 1928.

4. Representative Carl Perkins, quoted in Karen DeWitt, "Administration Revenue Sharing Plan Unlikely to Get Passing Grade from Congress," *National Journal*, March 24, 1973, p. 421.

5. Interview with Representative Albert Quie, Washington, D.C., May 25, 1978.

6. Quoted in Gary Orfield, *Congressional Power: Congress and Social Change* (Harcourt Brace Jovanovich, 1975), p. 169.

7. David Mayhew, *Congress: The Electoral Connection* (Yale University Press, 1974), pp. 49, 52, 53.

8. Ibid., p. 129.

9. Morris Fiorina, *Congress: Keystone of the Washington Establishment* (Yale University Press, 1977), p. 48.

10. Ibid., pp. 73, 74.

11. Douglass Cater, *Power in Washington* (Random House, 1964), p. 17.

12. Hugh Heclo, "Issue Networks and the Executive Establishment," in An-

thony King, ed., *The New American Political System* (Washington: American Enterprise Institute, 1978), pp. 88, 102–03.

13. For a similar analysis of the deep degree of subsystem autonomy and fragmentation in the transportation field, see John W. Kingdon, *Agendas, Alternatives, and Public Policies* (Little, Brown, 1984), pp. 124–26.

14. See Arthur Maass, *Congress and the Common Good* (Basic Books, 1983); Martha Derthick and Paul Quirk, *The Politics of Deregulation* (Brookings, 1985); and Kingdon, *Agendas, Alternatives, and Public Policies.*

15. Garth Mangum, *The Emergence of Manpower Policy* (Holt, Rinehart, and Winston, 1969), pp. 70–75.

16. Ibid, pp. 80, 81.

17. See James L. Sundquist and David Davis, *Making Federalism Work* (Brookings, 1969); and J. David Greenstone and Paul E. Peterson, *Race and Authority in Urban Politics: Community Participation and the War on Poverty* (Russell Sage Foundation, 1973).

18. See Henry Aaron, *Politics and the Professors* (Brookings, 1978).

19. Sar A. Levitan and Joyce K. Zickler, *The Quest for a Federal Manpower Partnership* (Harvard University Press, 1974), p. 50.

20. National Manpower Policy Task Force, "Improving the Nation's Manpower Effort," undated policy paper, reprinted in *The Manpower Act of 1969*, Hearings before the Select Subcommittee on Labor of the House Education and Labor Committee, 91 Cong. 2 sess. (GPO, 1970), pp. 107–09.

21. "Statement of the National League of Cities and United States Conference of Mayors," in *Manpower Development and Training Legislation, 1970*, Hearings before the Subcommittee on Employment, Manpower, and Poverty of the Senate Labor and Public Welfare Committee, 91 Cong. 2 sess. (GPO, 1970), p. 3027.

22. Martin Anderson, *The Federal Bulldozer* (MIT Press, 1964), p. 228.

23. Bernard Frieden and Marshall Kaplan, *The Politics of Neglect: Urban Aid from Model Cities to Revenue Sharing* (MIT Press, 1977), p. 126.

24. Ibid., p. 192.

25. Interview with Edward Silverman, National Association of Housing and Redevelopment Officials, Washington, D.C., August 1, 1977.

26. Quoted in "The Changing Model Cities Concept," *Nation's Cities*, vol. 8 (November 1970), p. 29.

27. William Lilley III, "Both Parties Ready to Scrap Grant Programs in Favor of 'City Strategy' Package of Aid," *National Journal*, July 3, 1971, p. 2701.

28. William Lilley III, "Capitol Hill Activists Work on Plan to Snare Policy Role from HUD," *National Journal*, January 9, 1971, p. 59.

29. *Housing and the Urban Environment*, Report and Recommendations of the Subcommittee on Housing of the House Committee on Banking and Currency, Committee Print, 92 Cong. 1 sess. (GPO, 1971), pp. 39, 41.

30. Interview with George Gross, counsel, House Subcommittee on Housing, April 1, 1978.

31. Interview with Nancy Remine, National Association of Counties, Washington, D.C., August 17, 1978.

32. Interview with William Langbehn, chief, Division of Legislation and Program Development, Employment and Training Administration, U.S. Department of Labor, August 15, 1978.

33. Memorandum, Dick Eckfield, National League of Cities, to Allen Pritchard and John Gunther, "Saving Model Cities in the Community Development Bill," February 28, 1974.

34. Interview with George Gross, House Subcommittee on Housing, emphasis in the original.

35. "Additional Views of Sen. Taft," in *Housing and Community Development Act of 1974, S. Rept. 693, to Accompany S. 3066,* 93 Cong. 2 sess. (GPO, 1974), p. 744.

36. Testimony of Percy Moore in *Manpower Development and Training Legislation, 1970,* Hearings, pt. 3, p. 2060.

37. Ibid., pt. 1, p. 117.

38. *Congressional Quarterly Almanac, 1973* (Washington: CQ, 1974), p. 7-A.

39. Quoted in *Housing Affairs Letter,* vol. 73-3, January 19, 1973, p. 3.

40. *Congressional Quarterly Almanac, 1970* (Washington: CQ, 1971), p. 51-S.

41. Dennis Fargas, quoted in Charles Culhane, "Mayors, Labor Leaders Add Political Muscle to Hill Challenge of Manpower-Training Cuts," *National Journal,* April 7, 1973, p. 499.

42. Interview with John Murphy, National Association of Counties, Washington, D.C., August 23, 1977.

43. Interview with John Sasso, National Community Development Association, Washington, D.C., August 25, 1977.

44. Interview with John Murphy.

45. Interview with William Langbehn.

46. John L. Moore, "Congress Gathers Wide Support for Reshaping Administration's Community Development Bill," *National Journal,* June 2, 1973, p. 797.

47. Interview with Anthony Valanzano, minority counsel, House Subcommittee on Housing, August 9, 1977.

48. Interview with Representative Albert Quie.

49. William Mirengoff and Lester Rindler, *CETA: Manpower Programs under Local Control* (Washington: National Academy of Sciences, 1978), p. 19.

50. Interview with David Garrison.

Chapter 4

1. Paul R. Dommel, *The Politics of Revenue Sharing* (Indiana University Press, 1974), p. 95.

2. Governors, backed by a coalition of conservative southern Democrats and Republicans in Congress, had succeeded in replacing President Lyndon Johnson's proposal for project grants to large cities with law enforcement block grants exclusively to states.

3. Dommel, *Politics of Revenue Sharing*, p. 105.

4. "A City Visits Washington," *Nation's Cities Weekly* (January 1971), pp. 24, 25.

5. Donald H. Haider, *When Governments Come to Washington: Governors, Mayors, and Intergovernmental Lobbying* (Macmillan, 1974), pp. 252, 253.

6. Dommel, *Politics of Revenue Sharing*, p. 114.

7. Quoted in Samuel H. Beer, "The Adoption of General Revenue Sharing: A Case Study in Public Sector Politics," *Public Policy*, vol. 24 (Spring 1976), p. 181.

8. Ibid., p. 171.

9. Dommel, *Politics of Revenue Sharing*, p. 162.

10. Ibid. See also Martha Derthick, *Uncontrollable Spending for Social Services Grants* (Brookings, 1975).

11. Beer, "Adoption of General Revenue Sharing," p. 187.

12. Ibid., p. 188.

Chapter 5

1. Vincent J. Burke and Vee Burke, *Nixon's Good Deed: Welfare Reform* (Columbia University Press, 1974), p. 52. This section relies heavily on their excellent account of the politics of the family assistance plan.

2. Ibid., p. 69.

3. Daniel Patrick Moynihan, *The Politics of a Guaranteed Income: The Nixon Administration and the Family Assistance Plan* (Random House, 1973), pp. 130–36.

4. Ibid., chap. 3.

5. Burke and Burke, *Nixon's Good Deed*, p. 92.

6. Ibid., p. 67.

7. Richard Nixon, "Television Address on the New Federalism," August 8, 1969, reprinted in Richard P. Nathan, *The Plot That Failed: Nixon and the Administrative Presidency* (Wiley, 1975), pp. 102, 103.

8. Congressional Quarterly, *Congress and the Nation, 1969–1972*, vol. 3 (Washington: CQ, 1973), p. 623.

9. Nathan, *The Plot That Failed*, p. 116.

10. Moynihan, *Politics of a Guaranteed Income*, p. 437.

11. Representative Philip Landrum, quoted in Burke and Burke, *Nixon's Good Deed*, p. 147.

12. Ibid., p. 165.

13. U.S. Advisory Commission on Intergovernmental Relations, *Public Assis-*

tance: The Growth of a Federal Function, A-79 (Government Printing Office, 1981), pp. 79–82.

14. "Poverty in the United States: Where Do We Stand Now?" *IRP Focus*, vol. 7 (Winter 1984), p. 6.

15. Congressional Quarterly, *Congress and the Nation, 1969–1972*, pp. 619–20.

16. U.S. Advisory Commission on Intergovernmental Relations, *Regulatory Federalism: Policy, Process, Impact, and Reform*, A-95 (GPO, 1984), p. 245.

17. This regulatory typology was first devised and elaborated in David R. Beam, "Washington's Regulation of States and Localities: Origins and Issues," *Intergovernmental Perspective*, vol. 7 (Summer 1981), pp. 8–18.

18. Donald F. Kettl, *The Regulation of American Federalism* (Louisiana State University Press, 1983), p. 34.

19. This was true of both Title IX of the Education Amendments of 1972, which prohibited discrimination against women in educational programs, and Section 504 of the Rehabilitation Act of 1973, which prohibited discrimination against the handicapped.

20. Congressional Quarterly, *Congress and the Nation, 1969–1972*, p. 756.

21. Mel Dubnick and Alan Gitelson, "Nationalizing State Policies," in Jerome Hanus, ed., *The Nationalization of State Government* (Lexington, Mass.: D.C. Heath, 1981), pp. 56–57.

22. See Alfred A. Marcus, *Promise and Performance: Choosing and Implementing an Environmental Policy* (Westport, Conn.: Greenwood Press, 1980), chap. 2.

23. Charles O. Jones, *Clean Air: The Policies and Politics of Pollution Control* (University of Pittsburgh Press, 1975), p. 203.

24. U.S. Advisory Commission on Intergovernmental Relations, *Protecting the Environment: Politics, Pollution, and Federal Policy*, A-84 (GPO, 1981), pp. 24–31.

25. J. Clarence Davies III and Barbara S. Davies, *The Politics of Pollution*, 2d ed. (Indianapolis: Bobbs-Merrill, 1975), p. 193.

26. Thomas J. Madden, "The Law of Federal Grants," in U.S. Advisory Commission on Intergovernmental Relations, *Awakening the Slumbering Giant: Intergovernmental Relations and Federal Grant Law*, M-122 (GPO, 1980), p. 17.

27. ACIR, *Regulatory Federalism*, pp. 80–81.

28. Ibid., p. 81.

29. Over time the fifty-five-mile-per-hour speed limit became viewed as inappropriate and unenforceable, and it was a lightning rod for conflict in the West. In the 1980s and 1990s it was first relaxed and then abolished.

Chapter 6

1. Ralph Widner, "State Growth and Federal Politics," *State Government*, vol. 47 (Spring 1974), p. 90.

2. U.S. Advisory Commission on Intergovernmental Relations, *Federalism in 1974: The Tension of Interdependence*, M-89 (Government Printing Office, 1975), p. 16.

3. William Mirengoff and Lester Rindler, *CETA: Manpower Programs under Local Control* (Washington: National Academy of Sciences, 1978), p. 19.

4. Donald F. Kettl, "Regulating the Cities," *Publius*, vol. 11 (Spring 1981), p. 123.

5. U.S. Advisory Commission on Intergovernmental Relations, *Catalogue of Federal Grants-in-Aid*, M-139, (GPO, 1984), p. 2.

6. James Q. Wilson, *American Government: Institutions and Policies* (Lexington, Mass.: D.C. Heath, 1986), p. 349; see also Joel Havemann, "Carter's Reorganization Plans—Scrambling for Turf," *National Journal*, May 20, 1978, pp. 788–94.

7. David S. Broder, "Reshuffling the Chaos," reprinted in *County News*, April 3, 1978, p. 4.

8. Quoted in David Rosenbaum, "President Delays Urban-Aid Rise," *New York Times*, December 18, 1977.

9. See Kay Lehman Scholzman and John T. Tierney, *Organized Interests and American Democracy* (Harper and Row, 1986), p. 326.

10. U.S. Advisory Commission on Intergovernmental Relations, *An Agenda for American Federalism: Restoring Confidence and Competence*, A-86 (GPO, 1981), p. 101.

11. See Theodore J. Lowi, "Europeanization of America? From United States to United State," in Theodore J. Lowi and Alan Stone, eds., *Nationalizing Government: Public Policies in America* (Beverly Hills, Calif.: Sage, 1978), pp. 15–29; and Stephen L. Schechter, "The State of American Federalism in the 1980s," in Robert B. Hawkins, eds., *American Federalism: New Partnership for the Republic* (San Francisco: Institute for Contemporary Studies, 1982), p. 59.

12. Ronald Reagan, "First Inaugural Address," in *Congressional Quarterly Almanac, 1981* (Washington: CQ, 1982), pp. 11-e, 12-e.

13. Samuel Beer, "Political Overload and Federalism," *Polity*, vol. 10 (Fall 1977), p. 16. See also Daniel Bell, "The Revolution of Rising Entitlements," *Fortune*, April 1975, pp. 98–135; and Michel J. Crozier, Samuel P. Huntington, and Joji Watanuki, *The Crisis of Democracy: Report on the Governability of Democracies to the Trilateral Commission* (New York University Press, 1975), chap. 3.

14. Presidential Task Force on Regulatory Relief, *Reagan Administration Achievements in Regulatory Relief for State and Local Governments: A Progress Report* (GPO, 1982), pp. i, ii.

15. For a similar interpretation, see Theodore J. Lowi, "Ronald Reagan—Revolutionary?" and James W. Ceaser, "The Theory of Governance of the Reagan Administration," in Lester M. Salamon and Michael S. Lund, eds., *The Reagan*

Presidency and the Governing of America (Urban Institute Press, 1984), pp. 29–56, 57–87.

16. For a discussion of this economic weltanschauung and its limitations, see David R. Beam, "Economic Theory as Policy Prescription: Pessimistic Findings on 'Optimizing Grants,'" in Helen M. Ingram and Dean Mann, eds., *Why Policies Succeed or Fail* (Sage, 1980), pp. 137–62.

17. Isabel V. Sawhill, "Economic Policy," in Palmer and Sawhill, eds., *The Reagan Experiment*, pp. 33, 41.

18. Theodore H. White, *America in Search of Itself: The Making of the President, 1960–1980* (Harper and Row, 1982), p. 137.

19. Calculated from Sawhill, "Economic Policy," pp. 34, 41.

20. Isabel V. Sawhill and Charles F. Stone, "The Economy: The Key to Success," in John L. Palmer and Isabel V. Sawhill, eds., *The Reagan Record* (Ballinger, 1984), pp. 80–81.

21. See Jude Wanniski, *The Way the World Works: How Economies Fail and Succeed*, rev. ed. (Touchstone, 1983); and George Guilder, *The Spirit of Enterprise* (Simon and Schuster, 1984).

22. "The concerns of . . . corporate chieftains have changed dramatically over the past decade. . . . Their greatest concerns [in 1986], by a wide margin, were 'cost containment,' 'productivity,' and the 'training and motivation of employees.'" In a similar 1976 survey, *Fortune* found the most cited problem, again by a wide margin, to be 'government.'" Robert Samuelson, "Reforming Management," *Washington Post*, April 23, 1986.

23. See Lloyd N. Cutler, "To Form a Government," *Foreign Affairs*, vol. 59 (Fall 1980), pp. 126–43.

24. Lawrence C. Dodd and Bruce I. Oppenheimer, "The House in Transition: Partisanship and Opposition," and Norman J. Ornstein, Robert L. Peabody, and David W. Rohde, "The Senate through the 1980s: Cycles of Change," in Lawrence C. Dodd and Bruce I. Oppenheimer, eds., *Congress Reconsidered* (Washington, D.C.: Congressional Quarterly, 1985), pp. 28, 44.

25. James L. Sundquist, *The Decline and Resurgence of Congress* (Brookings, 1981), pp. 367, 369, 395.

26. Dodd and Oppenheimer, "The House in Transition," p. 56.

27. U.S. Advisory Commission on Intergovernmental Relations, *The Transformation in American Politics: Implications for Federalism*, A-106 (GPO, 1986), pp. 257, 280.

28. See Jack Walker, "The Origins and Maintenance of Interest Groups in America," *American Political Science Review*, vol. 77 (June 1983), pp. 309–406; and Schlozman and Tierney, *Organized Interests and American Democracy*, pp. 74–82.

29. ACIR, *Transformation in American Politics*, p. 347.

30. Cornelius P. Cotter and John F. Bibby, "Institutional Development of Par-

ties and the Thesis of Party Decline," *Political Science Quarterly*, vol. 95 (Spring 1980), pp. 3–5.

31. David Adamany, "Political Parties in the 1980s," in Michael J. Malbin, ed., *Money and Politics in the United States: Financing Elections in the 1980s* (Chatham, N.J.: Chatham House, 1984), p. 81.

32. Joseph Califano, *Governing America: An Insider's Report from the White House and the Cabinet* (Simon and Schuster, 1981).

33. Anthony King, "The American Polity in the Late 1970s: Building Coalitions in the Sand," in Anthony King, ed., *The New American Political System* (Washington: American Enterprise Institute, 1978).

34. See Crozier, Huntington, and Watanuki, *Crisis of Democracy*.

35. Arthur Miller, "Is Confidence Rebounding?" *Public Opinion*, vol. 6 (June–July 1983), pp. 19, 20.

36. These negative attitudes toward the federal government did not remain stable throughout the 1980s. Most public evaluations of the federal government's performance reached their nadir in the early 1980s. By the beginning of Reagan's second term, public support for federal programs had generally increased, and a majority of the population responded that most domestic programs had been cut sufficiently. See David Gergen, "Following the Leaders," *Public Opinion*, vol. 18 (June–July 1985), p. 56; and "Opinion Outlook," *National Journal*, May 11, 1985, p. 1051.

37. James L. Sundquist, *Politics and Policy: The Eisenhower, Kennedy, and Johnson Years* (Brookings, 1968), p. 112. For a similar description, see Daniel P. Moynihan, *Maximum Feasible Misunderstanding* (Free Press, 1969), p. 24.

38. Moynihan, *Maximum Feasible Misunderstanding*, p. 25.

39. Samuel H. Beer, "Federalism, Nationalism, and Democracy in America," *American Political Science Review* vol. 72 (March 1978), p. 17.

40. This development has been analyzed most thoroughly by Lawrence D. Brown, *New Policies, New Politics: Government's Response to Government's Growth* (Brookings, 1983); and Samuel H. Beer, "The Adoption of General Revenue Sharing: Case Study in Public Sector Politics," *Public Policy*, vol. 24 (Spring 1976), pp. 127–96.

41. See James Q. Wilson, "American Politics, Then and Now," *Commentary*, vol. 67 (February 1979), pp. 41–46.

42. Quoted in Sawhill and Stone, "The Economy," p. 72.

43. Richard S. Williamson, "The Self-Government Balancing Act: A View from the White House," *National Civic Review*, vol. 71 (January 1982), p. 19.

44. National Conference of State Legislatures: Remarks at the Annual Convention," July 30, 1981, in *Weekly Compilation of Presidential Documents*, August 3, 1981, p. 834.

45. Eugene Eidenberg, "Federalism: A Democratic View," in Hawkins, ed., *American Federalism*, p. 112.

46. Governors Jerry Brown and Harry Hughes, quoted in Adam Clymer, "Governors Split over Reagan Proposals," *New York Times*, January 28, 1982.

47. See Reagan, "National Conference of State Legislatures," pp. 834–35.

Chapter 7

1. Executive Office of the President, *Federalism: The First Ten Months—A Report from the President* (Washington: EOP, November 1981), p. 28.

2. *Congressional Quarterly Almanac, 1981* (Washington: CQ, 1982), p.19E.

3. Dale Tate, "New Federalism No Panacea for State and Local Governments," *Congressional Quarterly Weekly Report*, April 25, 1981, p. 709.

4 . John L. Palmer and Gregory B. Mills, "Budget Policy," in John L. Palmer and Isabel V. Sawhill, eds., *The Reagan Experiment* (Washington: Urban Institute Press, 1982), p. 81.

5. David B. Walker, Albert J. Richter, and Cynthia Colella, "The First Ten Months: Grant-in-Aid, Regulatory, and Other Changes," *Intergovernmental Perspective*, vol. 8 (Winter 1982), pp. 7–9.

6. James R. Storey "Income Security," in Palmer and Sawhill, eds., *The Reagan Experiment*, p. 376.

7. John Shannon, "Federal and State-Local Spenders Go Their Separate Ways," in Jay Dilger, ed., *American Intergovernmental Relations Today: Perspectives and Controversies* (Prentice Hall, 1986), pp. 169–83.

8. Martin Tolchin, "Reagan Used Legislative Shortcut to Slash Budget: Stockman's Plan Bore Fruit," *New York Times*, June 28, 1981.

9. Richard P. Nathan, "Retrenchment in Washington Ripples across Country," *Public/Private*, vol. 1 (November 1982), p. 43.

10. Hedrick Smith, "President Attains Mastery at the Capitol," *New York Times*, July 30, 1981.

11. Representative James Jones, quoted in *Congressional Quarterly Almanac, 1982*, p. 256. See also Dennis Famey and Leonard M. Apcar, "Budget Triumph Seen Giving Ronald Reagan Firmer Grip on Economic Policy, Added Political Momentum," *Wall Street Journal*, June 29, 1981.

12. Robert Fulton, "Federal Budget Making in 1981: A Watershed Year in Federal Domestic Policy," *New England Journal of Human Services*, vol. 1 (Fall 1981), p. 26.

13. Data on this and the following votes are taken from ibid., p. 28, and from *Congressional Quarterly Almanac, 1981*, pp. 245, 257.

14. Fulton, "Federal Budget Making in 1981," pp. 29–30.

15. See Dale Tate, "Reconciliation Conferees Face Slim Choices," *Congressional Quarterly Weekly Report*, July 4, 1981, pp. 1167–69.

16. Quoted in Naomi Caiden, "The Politics of Subtraction," in Allen Schick,

330 / *Notes to Pages 118–21*

ed., *Making Economic Policy in Congress* (Washington: American Enterprise Institute, 1983), p. 117.

17. Bill Peterson, "Billions in Days: Frenzy on the Hill," *Washington Post,* June 28, 1981.

18. See, for example, Arthur H. Miller, "What Mandate for Change?" *Public Welfare,* vol. 40 (Spring 1982), pp. 9, 13; and Everett C. Ladd, "The Brittle Mandate: Electoral Realignment and the 1980 Presidential Election," *Political Science Quarterly,* vol. 96 (Spring 1981), pp. 1–25.

19. See Thomas E. Mann and Norman J. Ornstein, "Sending a Message: Voters and Congress in 1980," in Mann and Ornstein, eds., *The American Elections of 1982* (Washington: American Enterprise Institute, 1983), pp. 135–37.

20. Russell Baker, "The New Deal: It Was Time for It to Die," *Minneapolis Tribune,* August 4, 1981.

21. See Lawrence C. Dodd and Bruce I. Oppenheimer, "The House in Transition," in Dodd and Oppenheimer, eds., *Congress Reconsidered* (Praeger, 1977), pp. 21–53; and Barbara Sinclair, "Coping with Uncertainty: Building Coalitions in the House and Senate," in Thomas Mann and Norman Ornstein, eds., *The New Congress* (Washington: American Enterprise Institute, 1981), p. 220.

22. See Sinclair, "Coping with Uncertainty," pp. 204, 216; James Singer, "Labor and Congress: New Isn't Necessarily Better," *National Journal,* March 14, 1978, p. 352; and Bill Keller, "Special Interest Lobbies Cultivate the 'Grass Roots' to Influence Capitol Hill," *Congressional Quarterly Weekly Report,* September 12, 1981, pp. 1739–42.

23. *Congressional Quarterly Almanac, 1981,* pp. 36C, 19C.

24. Lou Cannon, *Reagan* (Perigee Books, 1982), p. 331.

25. *Congressional Quarterly Almanac, 1981,* pp. 30C, 10C.

26. Quoted in John White, "The Speaker Speaks: A Talk with Tip," *Party Line,* vol. 11 (November 1982), p. 7.

27. Demetrios Caraley and Yvette R. Schlussel, "Congress and Reagan's New Federalism," *Publius,* vol. 16 (Winter 1986), p. 61.

28. See Gary Jacobson, "Congressional Campaign Finance and the Revival of the Republican Party," in Dennis Hale, ed., *The United States Congress: Proceedings of the Thomas P. O'Neill Jr. Symposium on the U.S. Congress* (Leominster, Mass.: Eusey Press, 1982), p. 318.

29. See Jacobson, "Congressional Campaign Finance"; Cornelius P. Cotter and John F. Bibby, "Institutional Development of Parties and the Thesis of Party Decline," *Political Science Quarterly,* vol. 95 (Spring 1980), pp. 1–27; and Alan Ehrenhalt, "Campaign Committees: Focus of Party Revival," *Congressional Quarterly Weekly Report,* July 2, 1981, p. 1345.

30. Jacobson, "Congressional Campaign Finance," p. 319.

31. See Bill Keller, "Coalitions and Associations Transform Strategy, Methods of Lobbying in Washington," *Congressional Quarterly Weekly Report,* January

23, 1982, p. 123; and Hedrick Smith, "Taking Charge of Congress," *New York Times Magazine*, August 9, 1981, pp. 47, 48.

32. See Aaron Wildavsky, *The Politics of the Budgetary Process* (Little, Brown, 1964); and Caiden, "Politics of Subtraction," pp. 102–03.

33. Norman J. Ornstein, Thomas E. Mann, and Michael J. Malbin, *Vital Statistics on Congress, 1987–1988* (Washington: CQ Press, 1988), p. 204.

34. For example, the average page length of bills had been increasing, partly because of the growing number of reauthorizations. On the other hand, the amount of noncontroversial commemorative legislation also increased sharply, while the percentage of substantive legislation declined.

35. Because comparable data on the House are available only for the five years shown, identical years were selected for table 7-6 for the Senate. However, complete data have been compiled for the Senate from 1975 to 1986, and the averages for the years shown in the table are representative of the time periods selected.

36. Helen Dewar, "Reagan's Themes, Deficits Alter Course of Democratic Mainstream," *Washington Post*, March 9, 1987.

37. Representative Al Swift, quoted in David Maraniss, "Leaders Tailor Panels for Productivity," *Washington Post*, May 22, 1983.

38. Kay Lehman Schlozman and John T. Tierney, *Organized Interests and American Democracy* (Harper and Row, 1986), p. 155.

39. Quoted in Ward Sinclair, "Farm Relief Bill Gathers No Moss," *Washington Post*, April 23, 1987.

40. See Caiden, "Politics of Subtraction"; Allen Schick, "The Distributive Congress," in Schick, ed., *Making Economic Policy in Congress*, pp. 100–30, 257–74; and John Ellwood, "The Great Exception: The Congressional Budget Process in an Age of Decentralization," in Lawrence C. Dodd and Bruce I. Oppenheimer, eds., *Congress Reconsidered*, 3d ed. (Washington: CQ Press, 1985), pp. 315–42.

41. William Schneider, quoted in Dewar, "Reagan's Themes, Deficits Alter Course," p. A3.

42. Charles Hulton and June O'Neill, "Tax Policy," in Palmer and Sawhill, eds., *The Reagan Experiment*, p. 113.

43. Joseph A. Pechman, *Tax Reform and the U.S. Economy* (Brookings, 1987), p. 1.

44. Representative Ted Weiss, "Legislation to Repeal Gramm-Rudman," Extensions of Remarks, *Congressional Record*, daily ed., January 7, 1987, p. E31. See also statement of Senator Daniel Patrick Moynihan, *Congressional Record*, daily ed., April 24, 1986, p. S.4792.

45. David A. Stockman, *The Triumph of Politics: Why the Reagan Revolution Failed* (Harper and Row, 1986), pp. 53, 297.

46. John Shannon and Susannah Calkins, "Financing Federal Growth: Changing Aspects of Fiscal Constraints," in ACIR, *The Condition of Contemporary*

Federalism: Conflicting Theories and Collapsing Constraints (Government Printing Office, 1981), p. 143.

47. See Cannon, *Reagan*, p. 324; and Stockman, *Triumph of Politics*, p. 229.

48. Ronald Reagan, *Weekly Compilation of Presidential Documents*, August 17, 1981, p. 868.

49. William Greider, *The Education of David Stockman and Other Americans* (Dutton, 1982), p. 50.

50. John Witte, *The Politics and Development of the Federal Income Tax* (University of Wisconsin Press, 1985), p. 228.

51. Lawrence I. Barrett, *Gambling with History: Reagan in the White House* (Penguin, 1984), p. 169.

52. Quoted in Greider, *Education of David Stockman*, p. 58.

53. Stockman, *Triumph of Politics*, p. 262.

54. Ibid., p. 263; and Keller, "Special Interest Lobbyists Cultivate the 'Grass Roots,'" pp. 1739–42.

55. Witte, *Politics and Development of the Federal Income Tax*, p. 229.

56. Susan B. Hanson, "The Politics of Federal Tax Policy," in James P. Pfiffner, ed., *The President and Economic Policy* (Institute for the Study of Humane Issues, 1986), p. 197.

57. Witte, *Politics and Development of the Federal Income Tax*, p. 230.

58. Stockman, *Triumph of Politics,* p. 262.

59. Catherine E. Rudder, "Tax Policy: Structure and Choice," in Shick, ed., *Making Economic Policy in Congress*, p. 207.

60. Interview with Donald Susswein, August 14, 1986.

61. *Congressional Quarterly Almanac, 1984,* p. 143.

62. For a thorough exploration of these issues, see Timothy J. Conlan, Margaret T. Wrightson, and David R. Beam, *Taxing Choices: The Politics of Tax Reform* (Washington: CQ Press, 1990).

63. See Joseph T. Minarik, *Making Tax Choices* (Washington: Urban Institute Press, 1985); and Henry J. Aaron and Harvey Galper, *Assessing Tax Reform* (Brookings, 1985).

64. "Interview with Presidential Assistant Mitchell Daniels," *First Monday*, vol. 15 (July 1985), p. 20.

65. Stockman, *Triumph of Politics*, p. 362.

66. Ronald Reagan, "Tax Reform: Message to Congress Transmitting Proposed Legislation, May 29, 1985," *Weekly Compilation of Presidential Documents*, June 3, 1985, p. 708.

67. "Interview with Treasury Secretary James Baker," *First Monday*, vol. 15 (July 1985), p. 18.

68. "Remarks to Citizens' Groups, May 18, 1985," *Weekly Compilation of Presidential Documents,* June 3, 1985, p. 712.

69. George Peterson, "Federalism and the States: An Experiment in Decentrali-

zation," in John Palmer and Isabel Sawhill, eds., *The Reagan Record* (Washington: Urban Institute Press, 1984), p. 228.

70. Government Finance Officers' Association, "GFOA Opposes the Administration's Tax-Exempt Bond Provisions," position statement, June 21, 1985, Washington, D.C., p. 1.

71. Executive Office of the President, *The President's Tax Proposals to the Congress for Fairness, Growth, and Simplicity* (GPO, May 1985), app. C.

72. See remarks of Representative Robert Matsui, in Timothy B. Clark, "The Tax Reform Spotlight Is Falling on State and Local Tax Deduction," *National Journal*, June 29, 1985, p. 1511.

73. Quoted in "State Tax Deduction: Why and Why Not," *Tax Notes*, December 24, 1984, p. 1167.

74. Ronald Reagan, fund-raising letter on behalf of the Republican Governors' Association/Republican National Committee, Washington, D.C., n.d., p. 3.

75. "National Conference of State Legislatures: Remarks at the Annual Convention in Atlanta, July 30, 1981," *Weekly Compilation of Presidential Documents*, August 3, 1981, p. 834.

Chapter 8

1. Quoted in Claude E. Barfield, *Rethinking Federalism: Block Grants and Federal, State, and Local Responsibilities* (Washington: American Enterprise Institute, 1981), p. 61.

2. Richard P. Nathan and Fred C. Dolittle, "The Untold Story of Ronald Reagan's 'New Federalism,'" *Public Interest*, no. 77 (Fall 1984), p. 97.

3. See David B. Walker, "The Condition and Course of the System," in Lewis G. Bender and James Stever, eds., *Administering the New Federalism* (Boulder, Colo.: Westview, 1986), pp. 329–47.

4. See remarks of Donald Morgan, associate director of OMB for Human Resources, in Barfield, *Rethinking Federalism*, pp. 23, 24.

5. Jerry Turem, "Social Service Managers and Budget Cuts," *New England Journal of Human Services*, vol. 2 (Winter 1982), p. 19.

6. Congressional Research Service, "The Impact of Legislative Changes on Major Programs Administered by the Department of Education, FY 1980–1986," Report 85-551-EPW, Washington, D.C., January 31, 1986.

7. Samuel H. Beer, "The Adoption of General Revenue Sharing: A Case Study in Public Sector Politics," *Public Policy*, vol. 24 (Spring 1976), pp. 160, 162.

8. Ronald Reagan, "Conservative Blueprint for the 1970s," Speech to the Executive Club of Chicago, September 26, 1975, as reprinted in *Congressional Record*, October 1, 1975, p. 31184.

9. Ronald Reagan, *The Creative Society* (Devin-Adair, 1968), pp. 17, 20, 14.

10. Rochelle L. Stanfield, "'Defunding the Left' May Remain Just Another Fond Dream of Conservatives," *National Journal*, August 1, 1981, p. 1374.

11. Quoted in Steven V. Roberts, "Budget Axe Becomes Tool of Social Change," *New York Times*, June 21, 1981

12. Howard J. Phillips, quoted in Stanfield, "'Defunding the Left,'" p. 1374.

13. Harold Wolman and Fred Teitlebaum, "Interest Groups and the Reagan Presidency," in Lester M. Salamon and Michael S. Lund, eds., *The Reagan Presidency and the Governing of America* (Washington: Urban Institute Press, 1985), pp. 315–16.

14. See 1982 HUD Urban Policy Report, and "Statement of David A. Stockman before the Committee on Governmental Affairs, United States Senate," press release, February 4, 1982.

15. Ibid. See also Timothy J. Conlan, "Politics and Governance: Conflicting Trends in the 1990s?" *Annals of the American Academy of Political and Social Science*, vol. 509 (May 1990), p. 135.

16. See, for example, Jo Ann Boyd, "Despite Setbacks, Reagan's Assault on Legal Services Corp. Bears Fruit," *National Journal*, March 12, 1983, pp. 562–64.

17. Quoted in Barfield, *Rethinking Federalism*, p. 24.

18. Robert Carlson, quoted in Rochelle L. Stanfield, "Block Grants Look Fine to States; It's the Money That's the Problem," *National Journal*, May 9, 1981, p. 830. Ronald Reagan quoted in Roberts, "Budget Axe," p. 2.

19. Robert Carleson, as quoted in Barfield, *Rethinking Federalism*, p. 26.

20. "National Conference of State Legislatures: Remarks at the Annual Convention in Atlanta, Georgia, July 30, 1981," *Weekly Compilation of Presidential Documents*, August 3, 1981, p. 835.

21. For more details on these proposals, see David R. Beam, "New Federalism, Old Realities: The Reagan Administration and Intergovernmental Reform," in Salamon and Lund, eds., *Reagan Presidency*, pp. 431–32.

22. *Budget of the United States Government, Fiscal Year 1986*, p. 5–151.

23. Personal interview, August 18, 1983.

24. Quoted in Dale Tate, "New Federalism No Panacea for State and Local Governments," *Congressional Quarterly Weekly Report*, April 25, 1981, p. 710.

25. *Elementary and Secondary Education Consolidation Act of 1981*, Hearings before the House Committee on Education and Labor, 97 Cong. 1 sess. (Government Printing Office, 1981), pp. 61, 64.

26. Spencer Rich, "Panel Rejects Reagan Plan for Block Grants to States," *Washington Post*, May 15, 1981.

27. Ad Hoc Coalition in Block Grants, "Letter to Rep. Henry Waxman," in *Congressional Record*, June 24, 1981, p. 13785.

28. Testimony of Sandy Solomon, executive director, Coalition on Block Grants and Human Needs, *Block Grant Implementation*, Hearings before the Subcom-

mittee on Intergovernmental Relations of the Senate Committee on Governmental Affairs, 97 Cong. 2 sess. (GPO, 1982), p. 176.

29. Quoted in "The New Federalism: Where Are the Cities?" *The Mayor*, April 15, 1981, p. 2. See also "Reagan's Block Grant Proposal Pits Cities against the States," *Wall Street Journal*, May 12, 1981.

30. Rochelle L. Stanfield, "Congressional Roadblocks," *National Journal*, June 20, 1981, p. 1126.

31. Quoted in "Congress Stalls Reagan Grant Consolidation Plan," *Public Administration Times*, June 1, 1981, p. 6.

32. Representative Leon Panetta, quoted in Martin Tolchin, "Reagan Used Legislative Shortcut to Slash Budget," *New York Times*, June 28, 1981.

33. *The Omnibus Budget Reconciliation Act of 1981*, H. Rept. 97-208, 97 Cong. 1 sess. (GPO, 1981).

34. Representative Robert Michel, *Congressional Record*, June 25, 1981, p. H3381.

35. *Congressional Quarterly Almanac, 1981* (Washington: CQ, 1982), p. 264.

36. David A. Stockman, *The Triumph of Politics: Why the Reagan Revolution Failed* (Harper and Row, 1986), p. 225.

37. Robert Fulton, "Federal Budget Making in 1981: A Watershed in Federal Domestic Policy," *New England Journal of Human Services*, vol. 1 (Fall 1981), p. 29.

38. Personal interview, August 18, 1983.

39. Harrison Donnelly, "Scaled-Down Block Grants Near Enactment," *Congressional Quarterly Weekly Report*, July 4, 1981, p. 1180.

40. Sandra Osbourn, "Block Grants: Inventory and Funding History," Congressional Research Service, November 21, 1986.

41. Linda E. Demkovich, "Feeding the Young—Will the Reagan 'Safety Net' Catch the 'Truly Needy'?" *National Journal*, April 10, 1982, p. 624.

42. George Peterson, "The Block Grants in Perspective," in George Peterson, ed., *The Reagan Block Grants: What Have We Learned?* (Washington: Urban Institute Press, 1986), p. 28.

43. Quoted in David S. Broder, "States Offer Reagan a Deal on Aid Cuts," *Washington Post*, August 12, 1981.

44. Quoted in Norman J. Ornstein, "Chipping Away at the Old Blocks," *The Brookings Bulletin*, vol. 18 (Winter–Spring 1982), p. 14.

45. Representatives Richard Bolling and Barber Conable, quoted in Dale Tate, "Reagan Victory May Bring House Backlash," *Congressional Quarterly Weekly Report*, July 4, 1981, p. 1168.

46. Quoted in ibid.

47. These and other problems are discussed in U.S. Advisory Commission on Intergovernmental Relations, *Reducing Unemployment: Intergovernmental Dimensions of a National Problem*, A-80 (GPO, 1982), pp. 82–100.

336 / *Notes to Pages 170–75*

Chapter 9

1. George E. Peterson, "The State and Local Sector," in John L. Palmer and Isabel V. Sawhill, eds., *The Reagan Experiment* (Washington: Urban Institute Press, 1982), p. 168.

2. See, for example, Richard A. Musgrave, *The Theory of Public Finance: A Study in Public Economy* (McGraw-Hill, 1959); George Break, *Intergovernmental Fiscal Relations in the United States* (Brookings, 1967), chap. 3; and Wallace Oates, *Fiscal Federalism* (Harcourt Brace Jovanovich, 1972).

3. See Paul E. Peterson, *City Limits* (University of Chicago Press, 1981).

4. U. S. Advisory Commission on Intergovernmental Relations, *State Aid to Local Governments*, A-34 (Government Printing Office, 1969), p. 16.

5. ACIR, *Summary and Concluding Observations, The Intergovernmental Grant System: An Assessment and Proposed Policies*, A-62 (GPO, 1978), p. 78; and ACIR, *An Agenda for American Federalism: Restoring Confidence and Competence*, A-86 (GPO, 1981), pp. 111, 112.

6. National Governors' Association, "Agenda for Restoring Balance to the Federal System," *Policy Positions, 1981–82* (Washington: NGA, 1981), pp. 15–18.

7. President's Commission for a National Agenda for the Eighties, *A National Agenda for the Eighties* (GPO, 1980), pp. 69–72.

8. ACIR, *State Aid to Local Governments*, pp. 16–18.

9. ACIR, *An Agenda for American Federalism*, p. 101.

10. Ronald Reagan, "Conservative Blueprint for the 1970s," *Congressional Record*, October 1, 1975, pp. 31184–85.

11. *New York Times*, February 24, 1976.

12. Lou Cannon, *Reagan* (Perigee Books, 1982), p. 202.

13. Laurence I. Barrett, *Gambling with History: Reagan in the White House* (Penguin, 1984), p. 342.

14. Rochelle L. Stanfield, "President Reagan's New Federalism . . . A Budget Afterthought," *National Journal*, February 13, 1982, p. 278.

15. David S. Broder, "States Offer Reagan a Deal on Aid Cuts," *Washington Post*, August 11, 1981.

16. David S. Broder and Spencer Rich, "AFDC Shift to States Is Considered," *Washington Post*, August 13, 1981.

17. Linda E. Demkovich, "Political, Budget Pressures Sidetrack Plan for Turning AFDC over to States," *National Journal*, September 19, 1981, p. 1671.

18. Barrett, *Gambling with History*, p. 342.

19. David A. Stockman, *The Triumph of Politics: Why the Reagan Revolution Failed* (Harper and Row, 1986), p. 347.

20. Quoted in Cannon, *Reagan*, p. 348.

21. Quoted in Barrett, *Gambling with History*, p. 342.

22. Ibid., p. 393.

23. Ibid.

24. Interview with Richard S. Williamson, Washington, D.C., June 18, 1987.

25. Ibid.

26. Steven R. Weisman, "A Federalism Whose Time Is Now," *New York Times,* January 26, 1982.

27. Interview with senior career official, Office of Management and Budget, February 5, 1986.

28. Barrett, *Gambling with History,* p. 344.

29. Ibid.

30. Ibid., p. 345.

31. "The State of the Union: Address Delivered before a Joint Session of the Congress, January 26, 1982," *Weekly Compilation of Presidential Documents,* February 1, 1982, pp. 79, 80.

32. "Two State Leaders Respond to Reagan's Plan: Cautious, Optimistic, and Loaded with Questions," *State Government News* (March 1982), p. 14.

33. Bruce Babbitt, "His Plan Deserves a Chance," *Washington Post,* January 28, 1982.

34. Hugh L. Carey, "'New Federalism' Yes, But Reagan's Proposal Needs Major Revision," *New York Times,* March 14, 1982.

35. Reagan, "Conservative Blueprint," p. 31186.

36. "State of the Union: Address," p. 586.

37. Robert B. Carleson, "The Alternatives: True Reform or Federalization," *Commonsense,* vol. 3 (Winter 1980), p. 17.

38. Executive Office of the President, "Fact Sheet: Federalism Initiative," press release, January 27, 1982, p. 7.

39. Quoted in Fred Jordan, "New or 'No Federalism,' It's a Hot Topic in Seattle," *Nation's Cities Weekly,* August 30, 1982, p. 6.

40. Quoted in David S. Broder, "White House Is Warned on Its Federalism Plans," *Washington Post,* July 29, 1982.

41. The State-Local Advisory Group, "Response to the U.S. Treasury Intergovernmental Study," in U.S. Department of the Treasury, Office of State and Local Finance, *Federal-State-Local Fiscal Relations: Report to the President and the Congress* (GPO, 1985), p. 446.

42. Quoted in William Schmidt, "Three Western Governors Seem to be Potential Allies of 'New Federalism,'" *New York Times,* February 18, 1982.

43. Quoted in Jay Matthews, "States Unable or Unwilling to Shoulder 'Federalism' Burden," *Washington Post,* February 17, 1982.

44. Congressional Budget Office, "AFDC, Food Stamp, and Medicaid Exchange," January 29, 1982. See also National Governors' Association and National Conference of State Legislatures, "The President's Federalism Initiative," February 5, 1982, p. 3.

45. Carey, "'New Federalism' Yes," p. E23.

46. For example, one review of opinion surveys on new federalism concluded that it "fit the public's image of the respective roles of the Federal and state governments." "The New Federalism Outlook," *Opinion Outlook Briefing Paper,* February 12, 1982, p. 6.

47. "The New Old Deal," *New York Times,* January 28, 1982.

48. "A Great Swap Masks a Great Danger," *Washington Post,* January 27, 1982, p. A20.

49. AFL-CIO Statement Submitted for the Record, *President's Federalism Initiative,* Hearings before the Senate Committee on Governmental Affairs, 97 Cong. 2 sess. (GPO, 1982), p. 482.

50. Quoted in Neal R. Peirce, "The States Can Do It, But Is There the Will?" *National Journal,* February 27, 1982, p. 377.

51. Quoted in Rochelle L. Stanfield, "A Neatly Wrapped Package with Explosives Inside," *National Journal,* February 27, 1982, p. 360.

52. Richard Brodsky, quoted in Howell Raines, "President Seeking Counties' Support," *New York Times,* July 14, 1982.

53. Richard E. Cohen, "Meanwhile, in Congress, the Long Knives Are Out," *National Journal,* January 27, 1982, p. 381.

54. James R. Thompson, Speech before the Institute for Socioeconomic Studies' Ninth Annual Conference, New York, N.Y., May 10, 1983.

55. Quoted in Broder, "White House Is Warned," p. A10.

56. Quoted in David Broder and Herbert Denton, "Reagan's Aides Push Program Swap," *Washington Post,* January 29, 1982.

57. *Congressional Insight,* January 29, 1982, p. 1.

58. Robert Pear, "The Outlook for Reagan's 'New Federalism' Plan," *New York Times,* May 5, 1982.

59. Quoted in ibid.

60. "Despite Opposition to Budget Cuts, Governors Agree to Develop Federalism Proposal," *Governors' Bulletin,* February 22, 1982, pp. 1–3.

61. For a complete list of the members of these negotiating teams, see Richard S. Williamson, "The 1982 New Federalism Negotiations," *Publius,* vol. 13 (Spring 1983), pp. 16, 18.

62. Ibid., p. 16.

63. See Robert Pear, "White House Halts Attempts to Shift Welfare to States," *New York Times,* April 7, 1982.

64. Quoted in Bill Peterson, "White House Agreement on 'New Federalism' Announced by Governors," *Washington Post,* May 6, 1982.

65. "NLC Now Backs Takeover of Welfare by States," *Weekly Bond Buyer,* May 24, 1982, p. 25.

66. Interview with Richard Williamson. See also Williamson, "The 1982 New Federalism Negotiations," p. 27.

67. David Broder and Dan Balz, "Governors Break with President," *Washington Post,* August 9, 1982.

68. Memorandum, Jim Medas to Steve Farber, "Tentative Administration Decisions on Federalism Initiative," June 22, 1982.

69. Raines, "President Seeking Counties' Support," p. A21. The new proposal retained food stamps as a federal responsibility along with several controversial programs originally scheduled to be consolidated into the trust fund; required states to pass through to local governments sufficient funds from the federalism trust fund to cover terminated federal-local grants; and replaced the controversial windfall profits tax on oil with more reliable general revenues as a trust fund revenue source. Apart from these concessions, however, the revised plan included federal assumption only of "routine" medical care for the poor and a new block grant for costly long-term care for the elderly. It excluded medicaid coverage for "medically needy" individuals currently covered as a state option. For more details, see Ronald Reagan's "Remarks at the [National Association of Counties'] Annual Convention, July 13, 1982," *Weekly Compilation of Presidential Documents*, July 19, 1982, p. 899.

70. Ross Doyen and others, "Report to the NCSL Executive Committee," July 26, 1982, p. 3.

71. Governor Richard Snelling, chairman, National Governors' Association, "The Governors' Federalism Initiative: Report to the Executive Committee," August 8, 1982.

72. David S. Broder, "Governors Relent, to Seek Accord on Federalism with Reagan," *Washington Post*, August 11, 1982.

73. Governors Scott Matheson and Richard Snelling, "Letter to President Reagan," November 19, 1982.

74. "Reagan's Idea of Federalism Called 'Dead,'" *New York Times*, December 12, 1982. See also "Matheson Says Governors Disappointed by Draft Federalism Plan," *Governors' Bulletin*, December 17, 1982, p. 1.

75. Rochelle L. Stanfield, "Governors, Mayors Turn from Seeking More Power to Fending off Aid Cuts," *National Journal*, January 22, 1983, p. 167.

76. "Governor Snelling Foresees Reform of Federalism within a Decade," *Washington Report*, *American Public Welfare Association*, vol. 17 (October 1982), p. 2.

77. Williamson, "The 1982 New Federalism Negotiations," p. 26.

78. Ibid., p. 31.

79. Ibid., p. 26.

Chapter 10

1. Executive Office of the President, "The Task Force on Regulatory Relief: Its Impact on Federalism," *Federalism: The First Ten Months, A Report from the President* (Government Printing Office, 1981), p. 27.

2. See U.S. Advisory Commission on Intergovernmental Relations, *Regulatory Federalism: Policy, Progress, Impact, and Reform*, A-95 (GPO, 1984), chap.

3; and Robert A. Katzmann, *Institutional Disability: The Saga of Transportation Policy for the Disabled* (Brookings, 1986), chap. 2.

3. See Edward I. Koch, The Mandate Millstone," *Public Interest,* no. 61 (Fall 1980), pp. 42–57.

4. David Stockman, "Avoiding an Economic Dunkirk," reprinted in William Grieder, *The Education of David Stockman and Other Americans* (Dutton, 1982), p. 146.

5. For more on the growing intrusiveness of traditional grant requirements during this period, see Donald F. Kettl, *The Regulation of American Federalism* (Louisiana State University Press, 1983); and Paul E. Peterson, Barry G. Rabe, and Kenneth K. Wong, *When Federalism Works* (Brookings, 1986).

6. David R. Beam, "Washington's Regulation of States and Localities: Origins and Issues," *Intergovernmental Perspective,* vol. 7 (Summer 1981), pp. 8–18.

7. Thomas Mueller and Michael Fix, "The Impact of Selected Federal Actions on Municipal Outlays," in *Government Regulations: Achieving Social and Economic Balance,* vol. 5 of *Special Study on Economic Change,* Joint Economic Committee (GPO, 1980), p. 368.

8. ACIR, *Regulatory Federalism,* pp. 174, 175.

9. Ibid., pp. 245, 246.

10. Kettl, *Regulation of American Federalism,* p. xv.

11. The other three areas of emphasis were federal budget reductions, tax cuts, and block grants. See Executive Office of the President, *Federalism,* pp. 2, 7–10.

12. Murray L. Weidenbaum, "Reagan Federalism," *Journal of Contemporary Studies,* vol. 4 (Fall 1981), pp. 74–75.

13. Murray L. Weidenbaum, "Regulatory Reform: Looking Backward and Forward," paper prepared for the Urban Institute Conference on Regulatory Reform, Washington, D.C., June 15, 1993, p. 4.

14. Presidential Task Force on Regulatory Relief, *Reagan Administration Achievements in Regulatory Relief for State and Local Governments: A Progress Report* (Washington: Presidential Task Force, August 1982), p. 4.

15. Executive Office of the President, *Federalism,* p. 28.

16. Presidential Task Force, *Reagan Administration Achievements,* pp. i, ii.

17. Michael Fix, "Regulatory Relief: The Real New Federalism," *State Government News,* January 1985, p. 8.

18. Molly Sinclair, "Reagan Helps State, Local Regulators," *Washington Post,* June 27, 1984.

19. Fix, "Regulatory Relief," p. 7.

20. Ibid., p. 8.

21 "The Pitfalls of Defederalization," *Chemical Week,* June 17, 1991, pp. 34–58.

22. Weidenbaum, "Regulatory Reform," p. 5.

23. Richard S. Williamson, "A New Federalism: Proposals and Achievements of President Reagan's First Three Years," *Publius,* vol. 16 (Winter 1986), p. 25.

24. Ibid.

25. Calculated from data in Judith Havemann, "OMB Cracks Whip on Rulemaking," *Washington Post,* June 21, 1987.

26. Erik D. Olson, "The Quiet Shift of Power: Office of Management and Budget Supervision of Environmental Protection Agency Rulemaking under Executive Order 12291," *Virginia Journal of Natural Resources Law,* vol. 4 (1984), pp. 48, 49.

27. Calculated from data in Havemann, "OMB Cracks Whip on Rulemaking."

28. See testimony of Daniel Guttman and Gary D. *Bass, Oversight of the Office of Management and Budget Regulatory Review and Planning Process,* Hearing before the Senate Committee on Governmental Affairs, 99 Cong. 2 sess. (GPO, 1986), pp. 249–51, 254–55.

29. Alison Mitchell, "The Silent Shift of Power," *Newsday,* May 4, 1986, p. 24.

30. See Marshall R. Goodman and Margaret T. Wrightson, *Managing Regulatory Reform: The Reagan Strategy and Its Impact* (Praeger, 1987), pp. 106–08.

31. Quoted in ibid., p. 108.

32. Sandra S. Osbourn, "The Office of Management and Budget and Intergovernmental Management," in Senate Committee on Governmental Affairs, *Office of Management and Budget: Evolving Roles and Future Issues,* 99 Cong. 2 sess. (GPO, 1986), p. 335.

33. See Irene Fraser Rothenberg and George J. Gordon, "'Out with the Old, In with the New': The New Federalism, Intergovernmental Coordination, and Executive Order 12372," *Publius,* vol. 14 (Summer 1984), pp. 32–47.

34. Williamson, "New Federalism," p. 25.

35. Goodman and Wrightson, *Managing Regulatory Reform,* p. 206.

36. Marcella Ridlen Ray and Timothy J. Conlan, "At What Price? Costs of Federal Mandates since the 1980s," *State and Local Government Review,* vol. 28 (Winter 1996), p. 10.

37. Weidenbaum, "Reagan Federalism," p. 76. See also C. Boyden Gray, "Regulation and Federalism," *Yale Journal on Regulation,* vol. 1 (1983), pp. 93–110.

38. Quoted in Daniel Gottlieb, "Business Mobilizes as States Begin to Move into the Regulatory Vacuum," *National Journal,* July 31, 1982, p. 1342.

39. Felicity Barringer, "U.S. Preemption: Muscling in on the States," *Washington Post,* October 25, 1982.

40. Alan B. Morrison, "N[e]w Fed[e]ral[i]sm Holes," *New York Times,* September 20, 1982.

41. Alfred R. Light, "Federalism, FERC v. Mississippi, and Product Liability Reform," *Publius,* vol. 13 (Spring 1983), p. 85.

42. Ibid., p. 96.

43. Gray, "Regulation and Federalism," pp. 96, 97.

44. Caroline Mayer, "Product Liability Dispute Is Settled," *Washington Post,* July 16, 1982. Despite President Reagan's support, the bill was not adopted by Congress.

45. Ernest Holsendolph, "Lewis Offers Plan on Trucks as Exchange for a Tax Rise," *New York Times*, May 5, 1982.

46. Ibid.

47. *Congressional Quarterly Almanac, 1982* (Washington: CQ, 1983), p. 317.

48. Barbara Harsha, "DOT Sets Final Routes for Large Trucks," *Nation's Cities Weekly*, June 19, 1984, p. 2.

49. Steven R. Weisman, "Reagan Signs Law Linking Federal Aid to Drinking Age," *New York Times*, July 18, 1984.

50. Douglas Feaver, "Reagan Now Wants Twenty-One as Drinking Age," *Washington Post*, June 14, 1984.

51. Weisman, "Reagan Signs Law."

52. Eric Wiesenthal, "Municipal Affirmative Action Plans Attacked," *Public Administration Times*, June 1, 1985, p. 1.

53. Neal R. Peirce, "Republican Mayor Blasts Reagan on Civil Rights," *County News*, June 3, 1985, p. 18.

54. Herbert Stein, "The Reagan Revolt That Wasn't," *Harpers*, February 1984, p. 48.

Chapter 11

1. David B. Walker, *The Rebirth of Federalism: Slouching toward Washington* (Chatham, N.J.: Chatham House, 1995), p. 18.

2. See Timothy Conlan, "And the Beat Goes On: Intergovernmental Mandates and Preemption in an Era of Deregulation," *Publius*, vol. 21 (Fall 1991), pp. 43–57.

3. U.S. Advisory Commission on Intergovernmental Relations, *Federal Regulation of State and Local Governments: The Mixed Record of 1980s*, A-126 (Government Printing Office, 1993), chap. 3.

4. Alice M. Rivlin, *Reviving the American Dream: The Economy, the States, and the Federal Government* (Brookings, 1992).

5. Mel Dubnick and Alan Gitelson, "Nationalizing State Policies," in Jerome Hanus, ed., *The Nationalization of State Government* (Lexington, Mass.: D.C. Heath, 1981).

6. P.L. 101-549. For an elaboration of these provisions and details about their enactment, see Gary Bryner, *Blue Skies, Green Politics: The Clean Air Act of 1990 and Its Implementation*, 2d ed. (Washington: CQ Press, 1995); and Richard E. Cohen, *Washington at Work: Back Rooms and Clean Air*, 2d ed. (Boston: Allyn and Bacon, 1995).

7. See, for example, U.S. Advisory Commission on Intergovernmental Relations, *The Role of Federal Mandates in Intergovernmental Relations: A Preliminary ACIR Report* (GPO, 1996).

8. *Americans with Disabilities Act of 1990*, H. Rept. 101-485 (II), 101 Cong. 2 sess. (GPO, 1990), pp. 22–23.

9. Julie Rovner, "Governors Ask Congress for Relief from Burdensome Medicaid Mandates," *Congressional Quarterly Weekly Report*, February 16, 1991, p. 417.

10. Spencer Rich, "Benefits Grow among Budget Cuts: Deficit-Reduction Bill Expands Health Aid for Poor Children," *Washington Post*, November 3, 1990.

11. National Governors' Association, "States Feeling the Pressure for Increased Spending for Health, Transportation, Education, and Corrections," News Release, April 6, 1990, p. 1.

12. ACIR, *Federal Regulation of State and Local Governments*, p. 67; based on CBO cost estimates contained in relevant committee reports, various years.

13. *Americans with Disabilities Act of 1990*, H. Rept. 101-485 (II), pp. 50–51.

14. See Tom W. Smith, "Public Support for Public Spending, 1973–1994," *The Public Perspective*, vol. 6 (April–May 1995), pp. 1–3; and James A. Davis and Tom W. Smith, *General Social Surveys, 1972–1994: Cumulative Codebook* (Chicago: National Opinion Research Center, 1995).

15. President George Bush, "Inaugural Address," *Congressional Quarterly Almanac, 1989* (Washington: CQ, 1990), p. 8-c.

16. See Federal Funds Information for States, "Grant-in-Aid Programs: Selected Discretionary and Entitlement Comparisons, FY 1981 to 1990 and 1990 to 1993" (Washington: FFIS, 1992); and U.S. Office of Management and Budget, *Special Analyses: Budget of the United States, Fiscal Year 1997* (GPO, 1996), table 9-2.

17. Walker, *Rebirth of Federalism*, p. 16.

18. U.S. Office of Management and Budget, *Budget of the U. S. Government, Fiscal Year 1992* (GPO, 1991), p. 26.

19. See Gwen Ifill and David Broder, "Governors Welcome Bush Plan," *Washington Post*, February 4, 1991; and Bruce D. McDowell, "Grant Reform Reconsidered," *Intergovernmental Perspective* (Summer 1991), pp. 8–11.

20. Gwen Ifill, "Sasser Voices Opposition to Block Grant Proposal," *Washington Post*, February 21, 1991; and David Broder, "Mayors to Fight Bush Plan to Transfer Grant to States," *Washington Post*, February 9, 1991.

21. David Rapp, "Nervous Partners in the Block Grant Minuet," *Governing* (May 1991), p. 58.

22. Senator Christopher Dodd, Democrat of Connecticut, quoted in *Congressional Quarterly Almanac, 1989*, p. 205.

23. Senator Robert Dole, Republican of Kansas, quoted in ibid., p. 208.

24. For an excellent account of intergovernmental lobbying and the child care block grant, see Anne Marie Cammisa, *Governments as Interest Groups: Intergovernmental Lobbying and the Federal System* (Praeger, 1995).

25. Rivlin, *Reviving the American Dream*.

26. David Osborne, "A New Federal Compact: Sorting Out Washington's Proper

Role," in Will Marshal and Martin Schram, eds., *Mandate for Change* (New York: Berkley Books, 1993), pp. 237–62.

27. William A. Galston and Geoffrey L. Tibbetts, "Reinventing Federalism: The Clinton/Gore Program for a New Partnership between the National Government, States, and Localities," *Publius*, vol. 24 (Summer 1994), pp. 23–48.

28. Office of the Vice President, *Strengthening the Partnership in Intergovernmental Service Delivery* (Washington: National Performance Review, 1993), pp. 9–15.

29. David B. Walker, "The Advent of an Ambiguous Federalism and the Emergence of New Federalism III," *Public Administration Review,* vol. 56 (May–June 1996), p. 274; and David Stoesz, *Small Change: Domestic Policy under the Clinton Presidency* (White Plains, N.Y.: Longman, 1996).

30. Walker, *Rebirth of Federalism.*

31. See Seymour Martin Lipset and William Schneider, *The Confidence Gap: Business, Labor, and Government in the Public Mind* (Free Press, 1983); and Everett C. Ladd, "Americans Rate their Society and Chart its Values," *Public Perspective* (February–March 1997), pp. 2–5.

32. Timothy J. Conlan, "Federal, State, or Local? Trends in the Public's Judgment," *Public Perspective*, vol. 4 (January–February 1993).

33. U.S. Advisory Commission on Intergovernmental Relations, *Changing Public Attitudes on Government and Taxes—1989*, survey series 18 (GPO, 1989), p. 4.

34. An indeterminate share of this change may be the result of a slight change in question wording. The question asked from 1964 to 1992 was "Do you think the federal government in Washington has too much power in the United States today, about the right amount of power, or should use its powers more vigorously to solve our country's problems?" The question wording in 1995 was "Do you think the federal government in Washington has too much power in the United States today, about the right amount of power, or not enough power?"

35. James Davison Hunter and Daniel C. Johnson, "A State of Disunion?" *Public Perspective* (February–March 1997), pp. 35–38.

Chapter 12

1. William Jefferson Clinton, "1996 State of the Union Address."

2. See, for example, Theda Scocpol, *Boomerang: Health Care Reform and the Turn against Government* (Norton, 1996).

3. Paul L. Posner and Margaret T. Wrightson, "Block Grants: A Perennial, but Unstable, Tool of Government," *Publius*, vol. 26 (Summer 1996), p. 90.

4. Richard P. Nathan, "The 'Devolution Revolution': An Overview," *Rockefeller Institute Bulletin* (1996), pp. 5–13.

5. William F. Connelly and John J. Pitney, *Congress' Permanent Minority? Republicans in the U.S. House* (Rowman and Littlefield, 1994).

6. James G. Gimpel, *Fulfilling the Contract: The First 100 Days* (Boston: Allyn and Bacon, 1996), p. 32.

7. See Robert S. Erikson and Gerald C. Wright, "Voters, Candidates, and Issues in Congressional Elections," in Lawrence C. Dodd and Bruce I. Oppenheimer, eds., *Congress Reconsidered*, 6th ed. (Washington: CQ Press, 1997), pp. 132–61; and "The Frosh Factor: Spunk and Spine of the GOP Freshmen Fuel Gingrich Revolution in House," *Congressional Quarterly Weekly Report*, October 28, 1995, pp. 3251–75.

8. Paul Herrnson, "Money and Motives: Spending in House Elections," in Dodd and Oppenheimer, eds., *Congress Reconsidered*, p. 104.

9. Gimpel, *Fulfilling the Contract*, p. 8.

10. "Republican Contract with America," http://users.vnet.net/rdavis/RepubContract.html.

11. William Kristol, quoted in Elizabeth Drew, *Showdown: The Struggle between the Gingrich Congress and the Clinton White House* (Simon and Schuster, 1996), p. 119, and remarks at Brookings Governmental Studies Luncheon, 1995.

12. Ibid.

13. Statement of Representative Jon D. Fox, Republican of Pennsylvania, "Term Limits a Necessity for Good Government," *Congressional Record*, online edition, March 28, 1995, p. H3858.

14. Pat Buchanan, "Letter to Delegates of Presidency III," November 14, 1995, www.buchanan.org/pres.html, p. 1.

15. Drew, *Showdown*, p. 116.

16. Lobbyist for the Wholesale Grocers' Association, quoted in Rosemary O'Leary and Paul Weiland, "Regulatory Reform in the 104th Congress: Revolution or Evolution?" *Publius*, vol. 26 (Summer 1996), p. 27.

17. Detailed accounts of legislative activity in the 104th Congress are available from several sources. See, in particular, Gimpel, *Fulfilling the Contract*; Drew, *Showdown*; David Maraniss and Michael Weisskopf, *"Tell Newt to Shut Up"* (New York: Touchstone, 1996); and R. Kent Weaver, "Deficits and Devolution in the 104th Congress," *Publius,* vol. 26 (Summer 1996), pp. 45–85.

18. Allen Schick, "The Majority Rules," *Brookings Review*, vol. 14 (Winter 1996), p. 42.

19. For a thorough and insightful analysis of the political and policy interactions between budget policy and intergovernmental reform, see Weaver, "Deficits and Devolution."

20. Quoted in Rochelle Stanfield, "The *New* Federalism," *National Journal,* January 28, 1995, p. 229.

21. Quoted in ibid.

22. Ibid.

23. Representative Jim McCrery, Republican of Louisiana, quoted in Jeffrey L. Katz, "Members Pushing to Retain Welfare System Control," *Congressional Quarterly Weekly Report*, January 28, 1995, p. 280.

24. Interview with David Williams, March 1, 1996. For more elaboration of this argument, see Weaver, "Deficits and Devolution."

25. Stuart Butler of the Heritage Foundation, quoted in Stanfield, "The *New* Federalism," p. 229.

26. Pauline Abernathy, "Congressional Budget Plans Deep Cuts in Non-Defense Discretionary Programs" (Washington: Center on Budget and Policy Priorities, 1995).

27. See "GOP Throws Down Budget Gauntlet," *Congressional Quarterly Almanac, 1995* (Washington: CQ, 1996), pp. 2-21–2-24.

28. Ibid., p. 2-22.

29. House Committee on the Budget, *Concurrent Resolution on the Budget—Fiscal Year 1996*, H. Rept. 104-120, 104 Cong. 1 sess. (Government Printing Office, 1995).

30. Senate Committee on the Budget, *Concurrent Resolution on the Budget—Fiscal Year 1996*, S. Rept. 104-82, 104 Cong. 1 sess. (GPO, 1995); and *Congressional Quarterly Almanac, 1995*, pp. 2-24–2-32.

31. H. R. 1944 (P.L. 104-19).

32. Pauline Abernathy, "62 Percent of Enacted Rescission Bill Hits Low-Income Programs" (Washington, D.C.: Center on Budget and Policy Priorities, July 27, 1995).

33. "Omnibus Measure Covers Spending in Five Bills," *Congressional Quarterly Weekly Report*, May 11, 1996, p. 1333.

34. Ibid., pp. 1331, 1334.

35. Quoted in Jeff Shear, "Power Loss," *National Journal*, April 20, 1996, p. 876.

36. H. R. 2127, H. Rept. 104-209.

37. House Appropriations Committee, "Fact Sheet: Discretionary Spending and the Federal Budget," n.d., p. 1. See www.house.gov/appropriations/discret.htm. These figures vary slightly from the outlay figures presented later in figure 12-2, because the Appropriations Committees measure spending in budget authority (the legal authorization for government agencies to spend money, which may be spread over several years), rather than outlays (actual spending in a given year). Also, the committee data do not include subsequent "emergency" spending.

38. Quoted in Robert Wells, "House Passes Labor-HHS Bill," *Congressional Quarterly Weekly Report*, August 5, 1995, p. 2365.

39. For a discussion of similar efforts under the Reagan administration, see chap. 8.

40. Roger H. Davidson, "Out with the Old? In with the GOP," *Brookings Review*, vol. 14 (Spring 1996), p. 39.

41. Maraniss and Weiskopf, *"Tell Newt to Shut Up,"* pp. 116, 118.

42. Drew, *Showdown*, p. 84.

43. Quoted in Robert Wells, "Delving into Realm of Policy, Panel Oks Labor-HHS Bill," *Congressional Quarterly Weekly Report*, July 29, 1995, p. 2280.

44. Maraniss and Weiskopf, *"Tell Newt to Shut Up,"* p. 89.

45. See Drew, *Showdown*, pp. 259–72.

46. *Congressional Quarterly Almanac, 1995,* p. 2-21.

47. Quoted in ibid., p. 2-64.

48. These included a comprehensive regulatory reform bill that had stalled in the Senate, habeas corpus reforms designed to limit death penalty appeals, and (in the House version) termination of the Commerce Department.

49. For an overview of other centralizing enactments by the 104th Congress, see David Hosansky, "GOP Confounds Expectations, Expands Federal Authority," *Congressional Quarterly Weekly Report,* November 2, 1996, pp. 3117–22.

50. Robert Bendiner, *The Obstacle Course on Capitol Hill* (McGraw-Hill, 1964).

51. For a review of the politics of intergovernmental regulatory reforms in the Republican Congress, see O'Leary and Weiland, "Regulatory Reform in the 104th Congress."

52. U.S. General Accounting Office, *Multiple Employment Training Programs: Conflicting Requirements Hamper Delivery of Services* (GPO, 1994), p. 3.

53. Quoted in House Budget Committee, *Concurrent Resolution on the Budget—Fiscal Year 1996,* H. Rept 104-120, p. 5.

54. House Committee of Conference, *Concurrent Resolution on the Budget—Fiscal Year 1996: Conference Report to Accompany H. Con. Res. 64,* H. Rept. 104-159, 104 Cong. 1 sess. (GPO, 1995), p. 73.

55. Robert Wells, "Job Training Grant Approach Approved by House Panel," *Congressional Quarterly Weekly Report,* May 27, 1995, p. 1511.

56. Robert Wells, "House Passes Job Training Bill, Cutting Provision on Disabled," *Congressional Quarterly Weekly Report,* September 23, 1995, p. 2915.

57. See *Congressional Record,* daily ed., October 11, 1995, p. S14991.

58. Rochelle Stanfield, "Training Wheels," *National Journal,* December 16, 1995, p. 3085.

59. Quoted in Rochelle Stanfield, "Slinging Mud over Job-Training Bill," *National Journal,* July 6, 1996, p. 1485.

60. Interview with Ron Haskins, staff director, Human Resources Subcommittee, House Ways and Means Committee, August 14, 1996, Washington, D.C.

61. Quoted in Stanfield, "Slinging Mud over Job-Training Bill," p. 1486.

62. Congressional Budget Office, "Outlays for Major Spending Categories, Fiscal Years 1962–1996," Table F-8, *The Economic and Budget Outlook: Fiscal Years 1998–2007* (GPO, 1997), p. 112.

63. U.S. Congress, House, Committee on Appropriations, Homepage (www.house.gov/appropriations).

Chapter 13

1. David Beam and others, *Regulatory Federalism: Policy, Process, Impact and Reform,* A-95 (Washington: U.S. Advisory Commission on Intergovernmental Relations, 1984).

2. David R. Mayhew, *Divided We Govern: Party Control, Lawmaking, and Investigations, 1946–1990* (Yale University Press, 1991), table 4-1.

3. Timothy J. Conlan and others, *Federal Regulation of State and Local Governments: The Mixed Record of the 1980s*, A-121 (Washington: U. S. Advisory Commission on Intergovernmental Relations, 1993), p. 46.

4. Marcella R. Ray and Timothy J. Conlan, "At What Price? The Cost of Federal Mandates since the 1980s," *State and Local Government Review*, vol. 28 (Winter 1996), pp. 1–8.

5. U.S. Environmental Protection Agency, *Environmental Investments: The Cost of Clean: A Summary* (Government Printing Office, 1993).

6. John Martin, quoted in Oklahoma State Senate, *Federal Action Monitor*, vol. 11, no. 36, September 6, 1991.

7. Reports were issued by the cities of Anchorage, Alaska; Chicago, Illinois; Columbus, Ohio; and Lewiston, Maine; as well as the states of Ohio and Tennessee. These reports are briefly summarized in Philip M. Dearborn, "Assessing Mandate Effects on State and Local Governments," *Intergovernmental Perspective*, vol. 20 (Summer–Fall 1994), pp. 22–26.

8. See U.S. Conference of Mayors/Price Waterhouse, *Impact of Unfunded Federal Mandates on U.S. Cities: A 314 City Survey* (Washington: U.S. Conference of Mayors, 1993), p. 2; and National Association of Counties/Price Waterhouse, *NACO Unfunded Mandates Survey* (Washington: National Association of Counties, 1993), p. 2.

9. For a methodological critique, see Senate Committee on Environment and Public Works, *Staff Report: Analysis of the Unfunded Mandates Surveys Conducted by the U.S. Conference of Mayors and the National Association of Counties*. For alternative estimates, see Ray and Conlan, "At What Price?" and U.S. Advisory Commission on Intergovernmental Relations, *Federally Induced Costs Affecting State and Local Governments*, M-193 (GPO, 1994).

10. See Anthony Downs, "Up and Down with Ecology—The 'Issue-Attention Cycle,'" *The Public Interest* (Summer 1972), pp. 38–50.

11. Jerry Abramson, quoted in William Claiborne, "Nation's Mayors Press for Relief from Unfunded Mandates by Hill," *Washington Post*, January 29, 1994.

12. See Paul L. Posner, *The Politics of Federal Mandates: Congress on the Frontiers of Federalism* (Georgetown University Press, forthcoming).

13. Frank Shafroth, quoted in Margaret Kriz, "Cutting the Strings," *National Journal*, January 21, 1994, p. 170.

14. Comments of Buzz Fawcett, ACIR Task Force on Federal Mandates, October 24, 1994.

15. At the time this included only nine programs: medicaid, AFDC, child nutrition, food stamps, and several social service welfare programs.

16. Jeanne Ponessa, "Clinton, Congress Strain to Limit Unfunded Federal Mandates," *Congressional Quarterly Weekly Report*, August 6, 1994, p. 2239.

17. Quoted in Kriz, "Cutting the Strings," p. 168.

18. See Bureau of National Affairs, "Draft Legislative Strategy Paper Developed by Environmental Group Lobbyists," *Daily Environment Report,* vol. 50, March 16, 1994, p. E-1.

19. For example, Senator Paul Simon (Democrat of Illinois) proposed to establish an African American museum within the Smithsonian Institution, and Republican senator Phil Gramm of Texas sought to repeal the 1993 tax increases in social security.

20. Staff memo, "Options for Strengthening the Portman Contract with America Unfunded Mandates Bill," n.d.

21. U.S. Congress, House Legislative Counsel, Job Creation and Wage Enhancement Act, Title X—Federal Mandate Accountability and Reform, sec. 10502, September 23, 1994.

22. Republican governor-elect John Rowland of Connecticut, quoted in Andrew Tailor, "Governors: Don't Balance Budget without Ending Mandates," *Congressional Quarterly Weekly Report,* November 26, 1994, p. 3403.

23. Remarks of Senator Robert Byrd, *Congressional Record,* electronic ed., 104 Cong. 1 sess., January 17, 1995.

24. Helen Dewar, "Republicans Face the Bitter Truth: Divisions, Democratic Defiance Complicate Arduous Agenda," *Washington Post,* January 23, 1995.

25. Quoted in David Hosansky, "Mandates Legislation Caught in a Shifting Current," *Congressional Quarterly Weekly Report,* January 21, 1995, p. 208.

26. Ibid., p. 209.

27. In the remaining cases the largest number of dissenting Republican votes was five.

28. See Timothy J. Conlan, James D. Riggle, and Donna E. Schwartz, "Deregulating Federalism? The Politics of Mandate Reform in the 104th Congress," *Publius,* vol. 25 (Summer 1995), pp. 23–39.

29. President Bill Clinton, "Remarks by the President at the Signing Ceremony for the Unfunded Mandates Reform Act of 1995," The White House, Office of the Press Secretary, March 22, 1995.

30. Marjorie Miller, Congressional Budget Office, "The Unfunded Mandates Reform Act of 1995," remarks to conference on Implementing Devolution: Federal, State, and Local Perspectives, American Political Science Association Section on Federalism and Intergovernmental Relations, August 27, 1997, Washington, D.C.

31. Paul L. Posner, "Unfunded Mandates Reform Act: 1996 and Beyond," *Publius,* vol. 27 (Spring 1997), p. 58.

32. Ibid. See also Miller, "The Unfunded Mandates Reform Act of 1995."

33. Jon Healey, "Rescissions Negotiators Restore Some Cuts in Social Programs," *Congressional Quarterly Weekly Report,* May 13, 1995, p. 1307.

34. Posner, "Unfunded Mandates Reform Act," p. 62.

35. Ibid., p. 59.

36. Ibid., p. 66.

37. The Family Support Act of 1988 was a significant piece of welfare legislation, but it was not a comprehensive reform of the welfare system, nor was it primarily a presidential initiative.

38. See R. Kent Weaver and William T. Dickens, eds., *Looking before We Leap: Social Science and Welfare Reform* (Brookings Occasional Paper, 1995), chap. 5.

39. James G. Gimpel, *Fulfilling the Contract* (Boston: Allyn and Bacon, 1996), p. 93.

40. Mickey Kaus, "They Blew It," *New Republic,* December 5, 1994, p. 14.

41. For details, see David T. Ellwood, "Welfare Reform as I Knew It: When Bad Things Happen to Good Policies," *American Prospect,* vol. 26 (May–June 1996), p. 23 (http://epn.org/prospect/26/26ellw.html); and U.S. Congress, House, H.R. 4605, *The Work and Responsibility Act of 1994,* 103 Cong. 2 sess., 1994.

42. David Stoesz, *Small Change: Domestic Policy under the Clinton Administration* (Longman, 1996), p. 69; and Ellwood, "Welfare Reform," p. 25.

43. For more analysis of this process, see R. Kent Weaver, "Deficits and Devolution in the 104th Congress," *Publius,* vol. 26 (Summer 1996), pp. 53–64.

44. U.S. Congress, House, *H.R. 3500, The Responsibility and Empowerment Support Program, Providing Employment, Child Care, and Training Act,"* 103 Cong. 1 sess., 1993.

45. Gimpel, *Fulfilling the Contract,* pp. 81–82.

46. Jeffrey Katz, "Governors Group Sidelined in Welfare Debate," *Congressional Quarterly Weekly Report,* May 20, 1995, p. 1423.

47. Newt Gingrich, quoted in Elizabeth Drew, *Showdown* (Simon and Schuster, 1996), pp. 84–85.

48. Ibid., p. 85.

49. Barbara Vobejda, "GOP Outlines Broad Welfare Reform," *Washington Post,* January 7, 1995.

50. As Gingrich said in a speech to Republican governors in 1995, "Governor Engler has been a dear friend since he was a state senate leader and we invented the GOPAC audio tape program together." Newt Gingrich, Speech to Republican Governors in New Hampshire, November 21, 1995, http://dolphin.gulf.net/nov27-95/Gingrich.

51. David Maraniss and Michael Weiskopf, *"Tell Newt to Shut Up"* (Simon and Schuster, 1996), p. 26.

52. Barbara Vobejda and Judith Havemann, "Traditional Welfare Constituencies Put out by Lack of Input in Reform," *Washington Post,* May 21, 1995.

53. Interview with Ron Haskins, staff director, Human Resources Subcommittee, House Committee on Ways and Means, August 14, 1996. Input from officials in Michigan and Wisconsin was also apparent in the funding formula of H.R. 4. An analysis by the Center on Budget and Policy Priorities simulated the effects of

the block grant formula in the House if it had gone into effect in 1990 rather than 1995. Forty-eight states would have lost funding. The only two states that would have gained under the House formula were Michigan and Wisconsin.

54. For more details on the governors' role, see Martha Derthick, "New Players: The Governors and Welfare Reform," *Brookings Review* (Spring 1996), pp. 43–45; and John Dinan, "State Government Influence in the National Policy Process: Lessons from the 104th Congress," *Publius*, vol. 27 (Spring 1997), pp. 129–42.

55. National Governors' Association, "A Plan to Consolidate Federal Categorical Grants to States," marked "draft—for comment only," Washington, D.C., January 6, 1995.

56. Dan Balz, "Governor Assails GOP Welfare Proposal," *Washington Post*, January 9, 1995.

57. Jeffrey L. Katz, "Governors Group Sidelined in Welfare Debate," *Congressional Quarterly Weekly Report*, May 20, 1995, p. 1423.

58. Quoted in James G. Gimpel, *Fulfilling the Contract: The First 100 Days* (Allyn and Bacon, 1996), p. 79.

59. Barbara Vobejda and Judith Havemann, "Welfare Debate Moves to Capitol Hill," *Washington Post*, January 13, 1995.

60. Sharon Daly, quoted in Vobejda and Havemann, "Traditional Welfare Constituencies Put out by Lack of Input in Reform," p. A.4.

61. Representative Armey, quoted in Jeffrey Katz, "House Passes Welfare Bill; Senate Likely to Alter It," *Congressional Quarterly Weekly Report*, March 25, 1995, pp. 872–75. Democratic representative John Lewis of Georgia, quoted in Gimpel, *Fulfilling the Contract*, pp. 89, 90.

62. Katz, "House Passes Welfare Bill," pp. 872–74.

63. Ibid., p. 875.

64. Robert D. Reischauer, "The Blockbuster inside the Republicans' Budget," *Washington Post*, May 14, 1995; and House Committee on Ways and Means, *1996 Green Book*, H. Prt. 104–14, appendix 14.

65. Jeffrey Katz, "Key GOP Senators Back Giving States Leeway on Welfare," *Congressional Quarterly Weekly Report*, April 29, 1995, p 1190.

66. Quoted in Barbara Vobejda, "Republicans Open Hearings on Welfare," *Washington Post*, January 14, 1995.

67. Barbara Vobejda, "Dole Faces GOP Rifts on Welfare," *Washington Post*, September 6, 1995.

68. Ibid.

69. Quoted in Jeffrey Katz, "Senate Overhaul Plan Provides Road Map for Compromise," *Congressional Quarterly Weekly Report*, September 23, 1995, p. 2911.

70. Katz, "Key GOP Senators," p. 1190.

71. Ibid., p. 2910.

72. Ibid., p. 2911.

73. Barbara Vobejda and Judith Havemann, "Hill GOP Leaders to Study Governors' Welfare Plan: Gingrich Predicts House Will Act by Early March," *Washington Post*, February 8, 1996.

74. Interview with David Williams, Senate Budget Committee, March 1, 1996.

75. H.R. 3734, The Personal Responsibility and Work Opportunities Reconciliation Act of 1996.

76. Jeff Shear, "Looking for a Voice," *National Journal*, March 16, 1996, p. 594.

77. For a clear illustration of this, see Robert D. Reischauer and R. Kent Weaver, "Financing Welfare: Are Block Grants the Answer?" in Weaver and Dickens, eds., *Looking before We Leap*, p. 21.

78. See Paul E. Peterson, *The Price of Federalism* (Brookings, 1995); and Paul E. Peterson and Mark C. Rom, *Welfare Magnets: A New Case for a National Standard* (Brookings, 1990).

79. Bill Clinton, "Statement by the President," White House press release, August 22, 1996, The White House, Washington, D.C.

80. See Congressional Budget Office, *An Assessment of the Unfunded Mandates Reform Act in 1997* (GPO, 1998).

81. Posner, "Unfunded Mandates Reform Act."

82. For an elaboration of this, see Irene Lurie, "Temporary Assistance for Needy Families: A Green Light for the States," *Publius*, vol. 27 (Spring 1997), pp. 73–87.

83. Reischauer and Weaver, "Financing Welfare," p. 21.

84. Quoted in Dan Balz, "'Back to Basics' for GOP Governors," *Washington Post*, November 26, 1996.

Chapter 14

1. Interview with *Evening Star* and *Washington Daily News*, November 9, 1972, in "Nixon Goal: A Leaner but Stronger Government," *National Journal*, December 16, 1972, p. 1911.

2. Edwin Harper, deputy staff director, White House Domestic Council, quoted in Timothy B. Clark and others, "New Federalism: Return of Power to States and Cities Looms as Theme of Nixon's Second-Term Domestic Policy," *National Journal*, December 16, 1972, p. 1909.

3. Quoted in A. James Reichley, *Conservatives in an Age of Change: The Nixon and Ford Administrations* (Brookings, 1981), p. 70.

4. William Safire, "Newest Federalism," *New York Times*, January 28, 1982.

5. "Economic Report of the President: Annual Message to the Congress, February 10, 1982," *Weekly Compilation of Presidential Documents*, February 15, 1982, p. 164.

6. "Reagan to the Nation's Governors: The Federal Aid Cupboard Is Bare," *National Journal*, November 28, 1981, p. 2110.

7. Quoted in Lester M. Salamon, "Nonprofit Organizations: A Lost Opportunity?" in John L. Palmer and Isabel V. Sawhill, eds., *The Reagan Record* (Washington: Urban Institute Press, 1984), p. 261.

8. Ronald Reagan, "Conservative Blueprint for the 1970s," reprinted in *Congressional Record,* October 1, 1975, p. 31184.

9. Ibid., p. 31185.

10. Robert Carleson, quoted in E. Clarke Ross, "Changing Policies and Program Trends in Publicly Financed Services to the Developmentally Disabled," *Word from Washington,* vol. 4 (September 1982), p.11.

11. Newt Gingrich, Speech to the Washington Research Symposium, November 11, 1994, reprinted in "New House Speaker Envisions Cooperation, Cuts, Hard Work," *Congressional Quarterly Weekly Report*, November 12, 1994, p. 3296.

12. Gingrich, Speech to the Washington Research Symposium, p. 3296.

13. Ibid.

14. Newt Gingrich, Address to the Nation, April 7, 1995, reprinted in *Washington Post*, April 8, 1995.

15. Ibid.

16. Newt Gingrich, Speech to the Republican National Committee, January 20, 1995, http://dolphin.gulf.net/Gingrich/1.20.95.I.

17. E. J. Dionne Jr., "Gingrich Plays It Safe," *Washington Post*, January 9, 1998.

18. Newt Gingrich, "Key Excerpts/Address to Cobb Chamber of Commerce," January 5, 1998, http://dolphin.gulf.net/Gingrich/J98.

19. Samuel H. Beer, "The Adoption of General Revenue Sharing: A Case Study in Public Sector Politics," *Public Policy,* vol. 24 (Spring 1976), pp. 127–96.

20. Paul E. Peterson, "The Politics of Deficits," in John Chubb and Paul E. Peterson, eds., *The New Direction in American Politics* (Brookings, 1985), pp. 365–97.

21. See Roger H. Davidson and Walter J. Oleszek, *Congress and Its Members*, 6th ed. (Washington: CQ Press, 1998), p. 261.

22. Lawrence D. Dodd and Bruce I. Oppenheimer, *Congress Reconsidered*, 6th ed. (Washington: CQ Press, 1997), p. 49.

23. Davidson and Oleszek, *Congress and Its Members*, p. 161.

24. David Cloud, "Speaker Wants His Platform to Rival the Presidency," *Congressional Quarterly Weekly Report,* February 4, 1995, p. 331.

25. Ibid., p. 332.

26. For a discussion of the meaning of devolution, see John Kincaid, "Devolution or Restoration in American Federalism?" paper prepared for the Colloquium on Devolution, Federal Reserve Bank of Boston, September 12, 1997.

27. U.S. Advisory Commission on Intergovernmental Relations, *Block Grants: A Comparative Analysis,* A-60 (Government Printing Office, 1977), p. 42.

28. For classic discussions of these issues, see Richard Musgrave, *The Theory of Public Finance* (McGraw-Hill, 1959); and Wallace Oates, *Fiscal Federalism* (Harcourt, Brace, Jovanovich, 1972). For more recent variations on this theory, see Paul E. Peterson, *The Price of Federalism* (Brookings, 1995); and Alice Rivlin, *Reviving the American Dream* (Brookings, 1992).

29. The principal exception to this pattern was the 1986 Committee on Federalism and National Purpose, cochaired by Senators Daniel Evans and Charles Robb. This committee developed a comprehensive plan for a "new division of labor," which included the nationalization of welfare and the potential devolution of hundreds of other programs. A bill to implement these recommendations was introduced in the Senate, but it never advanced. See U.S. Congress, Senate Subcommittee on Intergovernmental Relations, *Comprehensive Federalism Reform,* S. Hearing 99-906, 99 Cong. 2 sess., September 26, 1986.

30. Martha Derthick, "New Players: The Governors and Welfare Reform," *Brookings Review* (Spring 1996), p. 45.

31. See Thomas R. Dye, *American Federalism: Competition among Governments* (Lexington Books, 1990); and James M. Buchanan, "Federalism as an Ideal Political Order and an Objective for Constitutional Reform," *Publius,* vol. 25 (Spring 1995), pp. 19–27.

32. Richard E. Wagner, "A Competitive Federalism for the New Century," *Madison Review,* vol. 1 (Fall 1995), pp. 34–40.

33. John D. Donahue, *Disunited States: What's at Stake as Washington Fades and the States Take the Lead* (Basic Books, 1997), p. 7.

34. See Daniel Latouche, "State Building and Foreign Policy at the Subnational Level," in Ivo Duchacek, ed., *Perforated Sovereignties and International Relations: Trans-Sovereign Contacts of Subnational Governments* (Greenwood Press, 1988); and Jessica Matthews, "Power Shift," *Foreign Affairs,* vol. 76 (January/February, 1997), pp. 50–66.

35. For a study of regional government initiatives in Italy, see Robert Putnam, *Making Democracy Work* (Princeton, N.J.: Princeton University Press, 1993); in France, see John Newhouse, "Europe's Rising Regionalism," *Foreign Affairs,* vol. 76 (January/February 1997), pp. 67–84.

36. Richard Deeg, "Economic Globalization and the Shifting Boundaries of German Federalism," *Publius,* vol. 26 (Winter 1996), pp. 27–52.

37. Newhouse, "Europe's Rising Regionalism."

38. Warren Miller and J. Merrill Shanks, *The New American Voter* (Harvard University Press, 1996), chap. 7.

39. Gary C. Jacobson, *The Politics of Congressional Elections,* 4th ed. (Longman, 1997), p. 91.

40. See, for example, Paul Allen Beck, *Party Politics in America,* 8th ed. (Longman, 1997), p. 385.

41. Everett Carll Ladd, "1996 Vote: The 'No Majority' Realignment Continues," *Political Science Quarterly* 112 (Spring 1997), pp. 1–28.

42. Ibid., pp. 5–6.

43. Ibid., p. 25.

44. Ibid., pp. 6, 10.

45. Donahue, *Disunited States*, p. 36.

46. Ibid.

47. Quoted in Richard Leach, *American Federalism* (Norton, 1970), p. 117.

48. William H. Riker, *Federalism: Origin, Operation, Significance* (Little, Brown, and Co., 1964), p. 155.

49. Martin Shapiro, "The Supreme Court: From Warren to Burger," in Anthony King, ed., *The New American Political System* (Washington: American Enterprise Institute, 1978), pp. 179, 182.

50. See *South Dakota* v. *Dole* (1987) and *South Carolina* v. *Baker* (1988).

51. Samuel H. Beer, "The Modernization of American Federalism," *Publius,* vol. 3 (Fall 1973), pp. 50–95.

52. Conrad Weiler, "Foreign-Trade Agreements: A New Federal Partner?" *Publius*, vol. 24 (Summer 1994), p. 113.

53. Ibid., p. 133.

54. Paul Posner, "Unfunded Mandates Reform Act: 1996 and Beyond," *Publius,* vol. 27 (Spring 1997), p. 66.

55. Ben Wildavsky, "Pigging Out," *National Journal,* April 19, 1997, p. 754.

56. See Lloyd A. Free and Hadley Cantril, *The Political Beliefs of Americans: A Study of Public Opinion* (Rutgers University Press, 1967); and Tom W. Smith, "Public Support for Spending, 1983–1994," *The Public Perspective,* vol. 6 (April/May 1995), p. 2.

57. Free and Cantril, *Political Beliefs of Americans,* pp. 32, 36, 37.

58. CBS News/*New York Times,* February 22–24, 1996, cited in Ladd, "1996 Vote," p. 7.

59. For an analysis and illustration of this in the area of tax policy, see Timothy Conlan, Margaret T. Wrightson, and David R. Beam, *Taxing Choices: The Politics of Tax Reform* (Washington: Congressional Quarterly, 1990).

Index